HISTORICAL DICTIONARIES OF U.S. DIPLOMACY
Jon Woronoff, Series Editor

Historical Dictionary of Anglo–American Relations

Sylvia Ellis

Historical Dictionaries of U.S. Diplomacy, No. 10

The Scarecrow Press, Inc.
Lanham, Maryland • Toronto • Plymouth, UK
2009

SCARECROW PRESS, INC.

Published in the United States of America
by Scarecrow Press, Inc.
A wholly owned subsidiary of
The Rowman & Littlefield Publishing Group, Inc.
4501 Forbes Boulevard, Suite 200, Lanham, Maryland 20706
www.scarecrowpress.com

Estover Road
Plymouth PL6 7PY
United Kingdom

British Library Cataloguing in Publication Information Available

Library of Congress Cataloging-in-Publication Data
Ellis, Sylvia.
  Historical dictionary of Anglo-American relations / Sylvia Ellis.
    p. cm. — (Historical dictionaries of U.S. diplomacy ; no. 10)
  Includes bibliographical references.
  ISBN-13: 978-0-8108-5564-9 (cloth : alk. paper)
  ISBN-10: 0-8108-5564-X (cloth : alk. paper)
  ISBN-13: 978-0-8108-6297-5 (ebook)
  ISBN-10: 0-8108-6297-2 (ebook)
  1. United States–Foreign relations–Great Britain–Dictionaries. 2. Great
Britain–Foreign relations–United States–Dictionaries. I. Title.
  E183.8.G7E45 2009
  327.4107303–dc22   2008046336

To Anthony

Contents

Editor's Foreword

The "special relationship" existing between the United States and the United Kingdom (Great Britain) is exceptional in more ways than one. It is singular in the very positive sense that these two countries have managed to remain on sufficiently good terms for well over two centuries. Despite one having thrown off the colonial domination of the other and both having engaged in a nasty little war not so long after, they have maintained a relationship that has ranged from satisfactory to excellent. Certainly, the cooperation and support during two world wars and the Cold War was exceptional. Even now that Britain is drawn toward European partners, there is no doubt that it has stood by the United States more than could be expected . . . and sometimes even more than might have been deserved. The other side of this special relationship is that, despite the daunting switch from a twosome in which Britain was by far the stronger partner to a twosome in which it was an increasingly junior partner, the two countries know they can still count on one another. Moreover, this relationship remains fairly solid, buttressed not only on a common language and culture (although increasingly less so for the latter aspect) but also by their close cooperation on politics, defense, economics, trade, and many other fields.

The trajectory of this long relationship, including the many swings and roundabouts, is carefully and quite fairly described in this *Historical Dictionary of Anglo–American Relations*. The connections between the two countries are first charted over the years in an extensive chronology and presented more fully in the introduction. The dictionary section looks closely at the many details, with numerous entries on the more significant events and crises (from minor irritations to major wars) and the varied and sometimes quite impressive cast of characters, Americans and Britons and sometimes both. Other entries deal with the institutional framework and abiding issues. This passage through time and boundaries has generated numerous acronyms, which are included in a special list. Obviously, since there is so much history packed into this long period, it is important for readers to know where to look for further information. That is provided in a substantial and well-organized bibliography.

This new volume in the constantly growing series of Historical Dictionaries of U.S. Diplomacy has been written by an author who has experienced the two partners from both sides of the "pond." She was born and grew up in Britain, where she received most of her education, but then she obtained her master's from the University of Rhode Island and her doctorate from the University of Newcastle upon Tyne. Since then she has taught at the University of Sunderland and the University of Northumbria. Over the years, she has written articles, essays, and chapters as well as a book on a crucial and particularly trying period, *Britain, America, and the Vietnam War*. Having spent years explaining to her students and readers what separates the two countries and what holds them together, she has now embarked on a considerably more demanding task of showing how they have managed to hang together for so long. In what remains an insecure world, particularly in the field of diplomacy, the two countries will undoubtedly continue this special relationship in one way or another for many decades to come.

Jon Woronoff
Series Editor

Acknowledgments

In the course of writing this volume, I have incurred a number of debts. In particular, I would like to thank Jon Woronoff for his enduring patience and guidance, Peter Hutchings for his encouragement and understanding, and Lynn Dobbs and Cheryl Buckley for providing me with research time to work on this project. Thanks also go to my parents, sister, and brother-in-law for their willingness to help at short notice and always with enthusiasm. And finally, to my husband, Anthony, and my children, Cara, Aisling, and Harry, my thanks for their continuing love and support.

Acronyms and Abbreviations

ACUE	American Committee on a United Europe
AEF	American Expeditionary Force
ANF	Atlantic Nuclear Force
ANZUS	Australia–New Zealand–United States Alliance
BAAS	British Association for American Studies
BAFTA	British Academy of Film and Television Arts
BAP	British American Project
BAPG	British–American Parliamentary Group
BBC	British Broadcasting Corporation
BRIAM	British Advisory Mission
CAP	Common Agricultural Policy
CCS	Combined Chiefs of Staff
CENTO	Central Treaty Organization
CIA	Central Intelligence Agency
CND	Campaign for Nuclear Disarmament
CoCom	Coordinating Committee for Multilateral Export Controls
DEFCON	DEFense readiness CONdition
EC	European Community
ECSC	European Coal and Steel Community
EDC	European Defence Community
EEC	European Economic Community
ERP	European Recovery Program
ESU	English-Speaking Union
EU	European Union
FBI	Federal Bureau of Investigation
GATT	General Agreement on Tariffs and Trade
GCHQ	Government Communications Headquarters
HUAC	House Un-American Activities Committee
IFOR	Implementation Force

IMF	International Monetary Fund
INF	Intermediate-Range Nuclear Force
IRA	Irish Republican Army
ISAF	International Security Assistance Force
MAD	Mutually Assured Destruction
MDAP	Mutual Defense Assistance Program
MIT	Massachusetts Institute of Technology
MLF	Multilateral Force
MP	Member of Parliament
NATO	North Atlantic Treaty Organization
NMD	National Missile Defense
NSA	National Security Agency
NTA	New Transatlantic Agenda
NWP	National Woman's Party
OPEC	Organization of Petroleum Exporting Countries
PRC	People's Republic of China
RAF	Royal Air Force
SAS	Special Air Service
SDI	Strategic Defense Initiative
SEAC	South-East Asia Command
SEATO	South-East Asia Treaty Organization
SFOR	Stabilization Force
SHAEF	Supreme Headquarters of the Allied Expeditionary Force
START	Strategic Arms Limitation Talks
UDI	Unilateral Declaration of Independence
U.K.	United Kingdom
UN	United Nations
U.S.	United States
USAF	U.S. Air Force
USAFE	U.S. Air Force in Europe
VE-Day	Victory in Europe Day
VJ-Day	Victory in Japan Day
WEU	Western European Union
WMD	Weapon of Mass Destruction
WSPU	Women's Social and Political Union
WTO	World Trade Organization

Chronology

1585 England's first attempt to settle in North America by forming a colony on Roanoke Island.

1607 **14 May:** England establishes first permanent colony in America at Jamestown, Virginia.

1620 **21 December:** The *Mayflower* lands at Plymouth, Massachusetts.

1733 **17 May:** Great Britain passes the Molasses Act, taxing the import of non-British sugar.

1763 **10 February:** Treaty of Paris ends the Seven Years' War.

1764 **5 April:** Great Britain passes Sugar Act, reducing the level of taxation on the import of non-British sugar from the level of the 1733 Molasses Act.

1765 **22 March:** Parliament passes Stamp Act. **7–24 October:** Stamp Act Congress meets in New York City.

1767 **29 June:** Parliament passes Townshend Acts.

1770 **28 January:** Lord Frederick North becomes prime minister of Great Britain. **5 March:** Boston Massacre. **12 April:** Repeal of Townshend duties.

1773 **10 May:** Tea Act passed. **16 December:** Boston Tea Party.

1774 **20 May, 1 June, and 2 June:** Coercive Acts.

1775 **19 April:** Battles of Lexington Green and Concord mark the beginning of the American Revolutionary War. **17 June:** Battle of Bunker Hill.

1776 **4 July:** Declaration of Independence.

1777 **September–October:** Battle of Saratoga prompts French involvement in the American War of Independence from Great Britain.

1781 **19 October:** British surrender at Yorktown.

1783 **3 September:** Treaty of Versailles, end of the American War of Independence.

1789 **30 April:** George Washington becomes the first president of the United States.

1792 **13 October:** Construction of the White House (Executive Mansion) starts.

1793 **1 February:** Start of French Revolutionary Wars (1793–1802).

1794 **4 June:** U.S. Congress passes a Neutrality Act prohibiting Americans from fighting in the war between France and Great Britain. **19 November:** United States and Great Britain sign the Jay Treaty to conclude areas of contention not settled by 1783 Treaty of Paris.

1801 **4 March:** Thomas Jefferson becomes third president of the United States.

1803 Start of Napoleonic Wars.

1804 **December:** Napoleon crowns himself emperor.

1807 **2 March:** The United States bans participation in international slave trade. **25 March:** Great Britain bans participation in international slave trade. **22 June:** U.S. ship *Chesapeake* is fired upon by the British ship *Leopard*. **22 December:** Congress passes the Embargo Act.

1812 **18 June:** Maritime grievances cause the United States to declare war on Britain. **12 July:** American forces, led by American Brigadier General William Hull, invade Canada. **16 August:** British troops, under General Isaac Brock, force Hull to surrender at Detroit.

1814 **24 August:** British troops storm Capitol Hill in Washington, D.C. **25 August:** British troops set fire to the Executive Mansion in Washington, D.C. **24 December:** Treaty of Ghent officially concludes the 1812 War between the United States and Great Britain, although fighting continues until February 1815.

1815 **18 June:** End of Napoleonic Wars following Napoleon's defeat at Waterloo.

1823 **31 January:** British Anti-Slavery Society formed. **2 December:** Monroe Doctrine is stated publicly by the president.

1833 Great Britain abolishes slavery throughout the British Empire.

1837 **12 December:** Canadian authorities seize and burn the U.S. ship *Caroline* on the U.S. border at Niagara.

1838–1839 Aroostock War (bloodless border clash) between the United States and Canada during winter of 1838–1839.

1842 **9 August:** Webster–Ashburton Treaty between the United States and Great Britain signed to resolve the Northeast boundary dispute.

1845–1850 Irish potato famine results in massive emigration from Ireland to the United States.

1850 **19 April:** Clayton–Bulwer Treaty commits America and Great Britain to sharing the construction costs of a proposed Central American shipping canal.

1858 **17 March:** Fenian Brotherhood formed in the United States with the aim of overthrowing British rule in Ireland.

1860 **6 November:** Abraham Lincoln elected president of the United States.

1861 **12 April:** Start of American Civil War. **13 May:** Lord Palmerston declares British neutrality in relation to American Civil War. **8 November:** The *Trent* affair. **18 December:** Thirteenth Amendment to the U.S. Constitution signed by President Abraham Lincoln, abolishing slavery.

1865 **9 April:** American Civil War ends. **15 April:** President Abraham Lincoln assassinated.

1867 **29 March:** Canada is given self-governance as a dominion state with the passage of the British North America Act.

1871 **8 May:** The United States and Great Britain sign the treaty of Washington to settle outstanding issues between them following the American Civil War.

1893 International tribunal solves dispute between United States, Great Britain, and Canada over Bering Sea.

1895 November 1896: Venezuelan boundary dispute between British Guiana and Venezuela, threatens to break into war between Great Britain and the United States.

1898 25 April–10 December: Spanish–American War. **July:** Anglo–American League formed.

1899–1902 U.S.–Philippine War.

1899 11 October–31 May 1902: Anglo–Boer War.

1901 14 September: Theodore Roosevelt becomes president of the United States. **18 November:** The United States and the United Kingdom sign Hay–Pauncefote Treaty, stating that the Panama Canal should be open on equal terms to ships of all nations.

1902 26 March: Rhodes scholarships established. **11 July:** The Pilgrim Society established as a British–American society to promote goodwill.

1903 Great Britain and United States settle Alaskan frontier.

1904 Work begins on the Panama Canal.

1909 5 November: American chain store Woolworths opens its first English store in Liverpool.

1914 28 July: World War I begins after Austria–Hungary invades Serbia. **15 August:** Panama Canal opens to shipping.

1915 7 May: A German U-boat sinks the *Lusitania*, a British liner, killing 1,200 noncombatants.

1916 24–29 April: Failed Irish Republican uprising in Dublin. **1 July:** Battle of the Somme begins. **6 December:** David Lloyd-George becomes prime minister of Great Britain.

1917 17 January: Zimmerman telegram intercepted. **6 April:** The United States enters World War I as an "associate power." **25 October:** Bolshevik revolution in Russia. **2 November:** Balfour Declaration of British support for a Jewish state in Palestine.

1918   8 January: President Woodrow Wilson makes his Fourteen Points address to Congress. **4 July:** Evelyn Wrench launches the English-Speaking Union. **12–15 September:** U.S. troops fight in first solo offensive at St. Mihiel. **26 September–11 November:** American forces fight the Meuse–Argonne offensive, the biggest by the American Expeditionary Force, and final offensive of the war. **11 November:** Allied victory in World War I when Germany agrees to an armistice.

1919   18 January: Paris Peace Conference begins in Versailles to discuss a formal peace treaty after the end of the First World War. **28 June:** The Treaty of Versailles signed. **10 November:** Edward, Prince of Wales, later King Edward VIII, visits United States for the first time. **28 November:** American-born Lady Astor elected to British parliament.

1920   24 April: Palestine mandated as a British territory by the League of Nations at the San Remo Conference.

1921   12 November–6 February 1922: Washington Naval Conference. Britain, the United States, Japan, Italy, and France meet in Washington, D.C., to discuss limiting the size of each country's navy. **6 December:** Anglo–Irish Treaty grants Republic of Ireland its independence.

1922   27 October: Rhodesia becomes a self-governing British colony. **6 February:** Washington Naval Treaty signed.

1924   16 July–16 August: London Conference accepts U.S. General Charles Dawes's plan for German war reparations payments.

1928   27 August: Kellogg–Briand Pact signed in Paris.

1929   4–6 October: Ramsey McDonald becomes first British prime minister to visit Washington, D.C. **24 October** and **29 October:** U.S. stock market crashes known respectively as Black Thursday and Black Tuesday.

1931   18 September: Japan invades Manchuria.

1932   7 January: Stimson Doctrine issued.

1933   30 January: Adolf Hitler comes to power in Germany. **14 July:** Duke Ellington's first visit to Great Britain. **16 November:** President Franklin D. Roosevelt recognizes the Soviet Union.

1935 George Dangerfield's *The Strange Death of Liberal England* published. **2 October:** Italian dictator Benito Mussolini orders invasion of Ethiopia.

1936 **10 December:** King Edward VIII abdicates and takes the title "Duke of Windsor."

1937 **3 June:** Edward, Duke of Windsor (formerly King Edward VIII), marries Wallis Simpson.

1938 **29 September:** Munich Agreement. **17 November:** United States and Great Britain sign trade treaty.

1939 **1 September:** Germany invades Poland. **3 September:** Great Britain declares war on Germany.

1940 **3 September:** United States gives Britain 50 destroyers in exchange for bases in Newfoundland and West Indies.

1941 **6 January:** President Roosevelt announces his "Four Freedoms." **11 March:** United States introduces Lend-Lease Act. **9–12 August:** Atlantic Conference, meeting between Roosevelt and Churchill aboard USS *Augusta* and HMS *Prince of Wales* off the coast of Newfoundland. **14 August:** Atlantic Charter setting out postwar aims following Atlantic Conference. **7 December:** Japan attacks U.S. naval fleet based at Pearl Harbor, Hawaii. **8 December:** America declares war on Japan. **11 December:** Germany and Italy declare war on the United States. **22 December–14 January 1942:** Arcadia Conference between Churchill and Roosevelt in Washington, D.C. **25 December:** The governor of Hong Kong surrenders Hong Kong to Japanese.

1942 **1 January:** Declaration by the United Nations. **20 June:** Hyde Park meeting between Prime Minister Churchill and President Roosevelt.

1943 **14 January–24 January:** Casablanca Conference meeting between President Roosevelt, Prime Minister Churchill, and General Charles de Gaulle. **17 May:** BRUSA agreement explicitly acknowledging intelligence sharing between United States and Great Britain. **19 August:** Quebec Agreement on nuclear cooperation signed by Winston Churchill and Franklin D. Roosevelt in Quebec City, Canada. **28 November–1 December:** The first wartime conference between the leaders of the three Allied powers (Churchill, Roosevelt, and Stalin) takes place in Iraq. This became known as the Tehran Conference.

1944 6 June: D-Day landings, Allied troops land on the beaches of Normandy. **July:** Bretton Woods Agreement. **21 August–7 October:** Dunbarton Oaks Conference discusses proposed United Nations. **12–16 September:** Second Quebec Conference.

1945 4–11 February: Yalta Conference, the second wartime meeting between Churchill, Stalin, and Roosevelt. **12 April:** Harry S. Truman becomes president of the United States following the death in office of President Roosevelt. **25 April–26 June:** San Francisco Conference assembled to determine the final structure and form of the United Nations. **8 May:** Victory in Europe day (VE-Day). **11 May:** President Harry S. Truman cancels Lend-Lease to Britain. **16 July:** The United States detonates the first nuclear device at Alamogordo, New Mexico. **17 July–2 August:** Potsdam Conference. **6 August:** First nuclear bomb detonated over Hiroshima. **9 August:** Nuclear bomb detonated over Nagasaki. **14 August:** Japan surrenders. **15 August:** Victory in Japan day (VJ-Day). **12 September:** Hong Kong returned to British rule. **24 October:** United Nations officially comes into existence having been ratified by the major powers and a majority of signatories. **6 December:** Anglo–American loan agreement to replace Lend-Lease.

1946 5 March: Winston Churchill delivers his "iron curtain" speech at Westminster College in Fulton, Missouri. This is the first public use of the term "special relationship." **1 August:** The United States passes the McMahon Act, making it illegal for the United States to share nuclear research with other nations (repealed in 1958).

1947 UKUSA Agreement to share intelligence, signed in secret. **12 March:** Truman Doctrine. **5 June:** U.S. Secretary of State George C. Marshall outlines the European Recovery Program (known as the Marshall Plan) in a speech at Harvard University.

1948 American Committee on a United Europe (ACUE) established. **1 January:** General Agreement on Tariffs and Trade (GATT) signed. **17 March:** Brussels Treaty signed. **14 May:** Israel becomes an independent state. **24 June:** Russians blockade all land routes into Berlin. **26**

June: Anglo–American airlift of supplies of food and coal into Berlin. **18 June:** Great Britain declares a state of emergency in Malaya (which lasts until 1960). **28 June:** In response to the Berlin crisis, Prime Minister Clement Attlee invites the United States to station bombers on British soil. **22 September:** Fulbright Commission created.

1949   4 April: North Atlantic Treaty Organization established. **12 May:** End of Berlin blockade. **1 October:** After the communist victory in the Chinese civil war, People's Republic of China (PRC) proclaimed. **6 October:** Truman signs the Mutual Defense Assistance Program Act to strengthen NATO.

1950   6 January: Great Britain establishes relations with the communist People's Republic of China. **25 May:** Tripartite Declaration by France, United States, and Great Britain agreeing to control the sale of arms to Israel and the Arab states of the Middle East. **25 June:** Communist forces of North Korea invade South Korea, starting the Korean War. **25 June:** United Nations Security Council passes a resolution calling on the United States to direct UN military operations to drive North Korea from South Korea. **15 September:** American marines land at Inchon, Korea.

1951   April: Battle of Imjin River, Korea. **1 September:** Australia, New Zealand, and the United States sign ANZUS mutual defense treaty.

1952   18 February: Greece and Turkey join NATO. **27 May:** European Defence Community treaty signed by France, Italy, West Germany, the Netherlands, Belgium, and Luxembourg (the French Assembly later vetoes ratification in August 1954). **3 October:** British test their first atomic bomb successfully at Monte Bello. **5 November:** Dwight D. Eisenhower elected president of the United States.

1953   2 June: Coronation of Queen Elizabeth II. **27 July:** Korean War armistice. **4–8 December:** Bermuda Conference between Prime Minister Churchill and President Eisenhower secures American commitment to reinstate nuclear cooperation.

1954   26 April–21 July: Geneva Conference convened to discuss the formal ending of the Korean War and situation in Indochina. **9 September:** South-East Asia Treaty Organization set up in Manila. **23 October:** Western European Union created after modifying the 1948 Brussels Treaty, allowing the involvement of the Federal Republic of Germany and Italy in the collective defense pact of 1948.

1955 British Association for American Studies established. **4 February:** Middle East security agreement called Baghdad Pact signed by Great Britain, Iran, Turkey, Iraq, and Pakistan. **6 April:** Anthony Eden becomes prime minister of Great Britain. **9 May:** Federal Republic of Germany joins NATO. **14 May:** Warsaw Pact formed.

1956 Elvis Presley has first American chart success. **October–March 1957:** Suez Crisis. **7 November:** Eisenhower reelected president.

1957 Bill Haley and the Comets tour Great Britain. **5 January:** Eisenhower Doctrine announced (approved by Congress on 7 March 1957). **10 January:** Harold Macmillan becomes prime minister of Great Britain. **20–24 March:** Bermuda Conference between President Eisenhower and Prime Minister Macmillan. **25 March:** European Economic Community formed after the signing of the Treaty of Rome. **13 June:** Elvis Presley has first British number one hit.

1958 **February:** Campaign for Nuclear Disarmament founded. **3 July:** The United Kingdom and the United States sign a secret bilateral treaty allowing for nuclear cooperation.

1959 **31 August:** Prime Minister Macmillan and President Eisenhower make the first live broadcast from 10 Downing Street.

1960 **March:** During talks with President Eisenhower, Harold Macmillan agrees to let the U.S. Navy have a base for its Polaris nuclear submarines at Holy Loch in Scotland.

1961 **20 January:** John F. Kennedy becomes president of the United States. **3 March:** American ship *Proteus* arrives at Holy Loch. **27 March:** President Kennedy and Premier Andrei Gromyko agree on a plan for a three-part government in Laos. **3 May:** Ceasefire agreed in Laos. **13 August:** Berlin Wall erected.

1962 **7 February:** United States introduces a total economic embargo against Cuba. **4 July:** President Kennedy's "Declaration of Interdependence" speech. **18–29 October:** Cuban missile crisis. **November:** Skybolt crisis. **21 December:** Nassau Agreement.

1963 **5 August:** Great Britain, United States, and Soviet Union sign a Limited Nonproliferation Treaty in Moscow that outlaws nuclear testing in the atmosphere, outer space, and under water. **16 September:** Malaysian Federation established. **22 November:** President John F. Kennedy assassinated in Dallas, Texas. Vice President Lyndon Baines Johnson becomes president.

1964 **7 February:** The Beatles start their first U.S. tour. **4 March:** United Nations resolution introduces peacekeeping troops to Cyprus. **1 June:** The Rolling Stones start their first U.S. tour. **16 October:** Harold Wilson elected prime minister of Great Britain. **December:** Prime Minister Wilson proposes an Atlantic Nuclear Force.

1965 **23 March:** Labour government condemns American use of gas in Vietnam. **28 April:** United States' troops invade Dominican Republic. **11 November:** Unilateral Declaration of Independence by Ian Smith, Rhodesia's prime minister.

1966 **28 June:** Great Britain dissociates from American bombing of Hanoi and Haiphong.

1967 **5 June:** Start of the 1967 Arab–Israeli War, also called the Six-Day War.

1968 **16 January:** Great Britain announces its intention to withdraw all its military forces from the Far East (except Hong Kong) by 31 March 1971, referred to as East of Suez. **1 July:** Nuclear Nonproliferation Act signed.

1969 **20 January:** Richard Nixon becomes president of the United States.

1970 **19 June:** Edward Heath becomes prime minister of Great Britain.

1971 **15 August:** Bretton Woods system ends.

1973 **1 January:** United Kingdom joins the European Economic Community (EEC). **23 April:** Henry Kissinger, at the behest of President Nixon, declares that 1973 would be the "Year of Europe," signaling a change of direction in U.S. foreign policy. **6 October:** Start of the 1973 Arab–Israeli War, also referred to as the October War or Yom Kippur War.

1974 **20 July:** Turkey invades Cyprus. **9 August:** Gerald Ford becomes president of the United States following the resignation of President Richard Nixon after the Watergate affair.

1976 **March:** British pound falls against dollar, leading to IMF crisis.

1979 **January:** The United States establishes relations with the communist People's Government of China. **4 May:** Margaret Thatcher becomes the first woman prime minister of Great Britain. **24 December:** Soviet forces occupy Afghanistan. NATO agrees to deploy over 400 ground-launched cruise missiles in Europe.

1980 **18 April:** Rhodesia gains independence from Britain under the name of Zimbabwe; Robert Mugabe elected president. **14 July:** President Carter agrees with Prime Minister Thatcher to sell the U.S. Trident I nuclear missile to Great Britain. **4 November:** Ronald Reagan elected president of the United States.

1982 **2 April:** Argentina invades the Falkland Islands (Malvinas). **30 May:** Spain joins NATO. **14 July:** Argentinean forces on the Falkland Islands surrender.

1983 Gerry Adams elected president of Sinn Fein. **23 March:** President Reagan announces the Strategic Defense Initiative, commonly known as Star Wars. **25 October:** United States launches an invasion of Grenada.

1985 British American Project founded.

1986 **14 April:** United States uses British RAF bases to launch an air attack on Libya.

1987 **8 December:** Intermediate-Range Nuclear Force (INF) treaty.

1990 **6 July:** London Declaration. **2 August:** Iraq invades Kuwait. **22 November:** Transatlantic Declaration, an attempt to formalize relations between the United States and the European Union, is formulated. **22 November:** Margaret Thatcher resigns.

1991 **17 January:** Start of the Gulf War, codenamed "Operation Desert Storm." **28 February:** Liberation of Kuwait from Iraq. **24 October:** Bosnia-Herzegovina declares itself a sovereign nation. **28 November:** John Major becomes prime minister of Great Britain.

1992   20 December: President Bush and Prime Minister Major meet at Camp David to discuss cooperation on bringing about a peaceful settlement in the former Yugoslavia.

1995   1 January: World Trade Organization established. **30 November:** President William Jefferson Clinton visits Belfast. **3 December:** New Transatlantic Agenda signed at an EU–US summit in Madrid. **14 December:** Dayton Agreements signed in Paris to end conflict in Bosnia.

1996   12 March: America passes the Cuban Liberty and Democratic Solidarity Act, known as the Helms–Burton Act, tightening economic sanctions on Cuba.

1997   2 May: Tony Blair becomes prime minister of Great Britain. **30 June:** Britain's 90-year lease on Hong Kong expires. **11 December:** World leaders in Kyoto agree to the world's first treaty on climate change.

1998   10 April: Good Friday peace agreement sets up devolved governance of Northern Ireland.

1999   12 March: Czech Republic, Hungary, and Poland join NATO. **24 March:** NATO forces bomb Serbia in an attempt to force the withdrawal of Serbian troops from Kosovo. **10 June:** Milosevic agrees to withdraw Serbian troops from Kosovo. **11 June:** NATO ceases bombing Serbia.

2001   11 September: Terrorist attacks on World Trade Center and Pentagon. **7 October:** United States and Great Britain launch military invasion of Afghanistan.

2002   24 September: British government publishes the "September dossier" on Iraq and discusses it in the House of Commons. **10–11 October:** Congressional approval to use force in Iraq. **8 November:** UN Security Council Resolution 1441 passed, allowing for the reintroduction of weapons inspectors to Iraq.

2003   17 March: Robin Cook resigns as Leader of the House of Commons over Iraq. **20 March:** Operation Iraqi Freedom begins. **15 January:** Defence Secretary Geoff Hoon agrees to U.S. request to use RAF Fylingdales for U.S. national missile defense system. **18–21 Novem-**

ber: George W. Bush visits Great Britain for first state visit by a U.S. president.

2004   29 March: Bulgaria, Estonia, Latvia, Lithuania, Romania, Slovakia, and Slovenia join NATO.

2005   16 February: Kyoto Treaty comes into effect (U.S. Congress refused to ratify the treaty).

2006   15 March: U.S. Congress appoints Iraq Study Group. **27 July:** During the crisis in Lebanon, British Foreign Secretary Margaret Beckett makes an official protest against the American use of Prestwick Airport for transportation of bombs to Israel. **October:** British government calls for the closure of U.S. detention camp at Guantanamo Bay. **6 December:** Iraq Study Group final report released. **30 December:** Saddam Hussein executed. **31 December:** Great Britain makes final repayment on American loan to finance World War II debts.

2007   17 May: Final Bush–Blair press conference sees both leaders expressing admiration for the other. **27 June:** Tony Blair steps down as British prime minister to be succeeded by Gordon Brown. **29–30 July:** Gordon Brown meets President Bush at Camp David.

2008   20 March: Republican presidential candidate Senator John McCain meets Prime Minister Gordon Brown in London. **17 April:** Gordon Brown meets President Bush and presidential hopefuls Hillary Clinton, Barack Obama, and John McCain during visit to Washington, D.C. **26 July:** Democrat presidential candidate Senator Barack Obama meets Prime Minister Gordon Brown in London. **4 November:** Barack Obama elected first African American president of the United States.

Introduction

The bilateral relationship between Great Britain and the United States has always been important but complex. When Britain established its first permanent settlement in America at Jamestown in April 1607, it began 176 years of direct rule over the American colonies, during which time it exported its people, language, legal traditions, and a sense of shared history, thus ensuring a continuing rapport and affiliation with the American people that still endures into the 21st century. After American rebels rejected British rule and established the United States of America in the late 18th century, Anglo–American relations began to play a significant role in international history as the former mother country and the offspring nation became trading competitors, rival hegemonic powers, and, in the 20th century, military and political partners.

The following represents a brief overview of the major developments in Anglo–American relations from the American Revolution to the present day. Tracing that history, it is apparent that London and Washington have viewed one another differently at different times, depending largely on the power ratio between the two but also because the two nations' separate histories meant that often their worldviews, as well as national interests, diverged. The contours of the relationship have therefore changed over time, experiencing significant oscillations along the way, from periods of acrimony and war to times of shared values, mutual interdependence, and political unity. However, in more than two centuries of Anglo–American relations, two main themes emerge. Firstly, for much of the time, Anglo–American relations have been characterized by a remarkable degree of unity, friendship, and cooperation. The enduring kinship, common history, and cultural links between the peoples of the two nations fostered a sense of familiarity at the governmental and public levels. Moreover, a sense of shared values—particularly a sense of liberal democracy and, at times, Anglo–Saxon bonds—has meant mutual respect, if not always admiration. More often than not, British and American diplomats and politicians have negotiated and compromised to settle their differences. Faced with common enemies in the 20th century, an exceptional degree of Anglo–American political and military cooperation began in World War I, deepened during World War II, and endured into and after the Cold War. This closeness, particularly in terms of diplomacy and defense, led politicians, journalists, and scholars on both sides of the Atlantic to debate whether the relationship could be characterized as "special." Certainly, most scholars would argue that the post-1945 period saw not just the development of an Anglo–American relationship based on emotion and instinct but also an alliance with real structural and institutional links, especially in the nuclear and intelligence fields.

A second recurring theme in the history of Anglo–American relations has been disunity, rivalry, and competition. Bonds of shared language, tradition, and culture have not prevented mutual suspicions, distrust, and disagreements between Washington and London. At war with each other during the American Revolution and the War of 1812, the two countries have since managed to refrain from fighting one another but have nevertheless disagreed vehemently on several occasions over border clashes, maritime disputes, military strategy and tactics, and the wisdom of involvement in particular wars and conflicts. Great Britain's position in the 19th century as the leading world power—based on its large world empire, command of the seas, and early industrialization— meant that competition with the rapidly expanding and increasingly market-oriented United States was inevitable. At the turn of the 20th century, as America acquired overseas bases and territories, strengthened its economy, and enlarged its navy, strategic rivalry between the two also brought additional competition and wariness of each other's motives, modes of behavior, and differences of political culture. Disagreements were particularly noticeable in the 1920s and 1930s when naval rivalry, protectionism, and the United States' isolationist tendencies led to severe tensions between London and Washington. And, while often agreeing on political and military aims in public, in private there has been a tendency to disagree over the means of achieving them. Behind the public front of unity in World War II, the Cold War, and afterwards, Anglo–American relations have regularly been characterized by discord over military methods, diplomacy, and public rhetoric. Britain's economic weakness often meant, however, that London had little choice but to attempt to influence the United States through quiet diplomacy.

THE MOTHER COUNTRY AND THE COLONIES: FROM EARLY ENCOUNTERS TO WAR AND REVOLUTION

In 1497, the explorer John Cabot first established an English claim on land in America. Almost a century later, in 1585, Sir Walter Raleigh founded a colony at Roanoke Island, off the coast of present-day North Carolina, that ultimately failed to thrive. Britain's direct rule of the American colonies began in 1607 when 104 English settlers landed at Jamestown, Virginia, and established a permanent colony. This was followed in 1620 by the arrival of the *Mayflower*, bringing Puritans to Cape Cod in Massachusetts. The establishment of these early settlements marked the beginning of almost two centuries of British control. During these years, the American colonies—18 British ones by the time of the War of Independence, with over two and a half million inhabitants—remained bonded to Britain, partly because many of the immigrants retained links with their home country, but largely because, as the first settlers, they were able to establish communication based on the English language. The sense of kinship that developed between Britain and America was also based on a shared history and culture. Many of the new states modeled their legal and political systems, and lifestyles, on those they had experienced in Britain. Not surprisingly, most of the first American villages and towns were named after places the settlers had left behind, notably Boston and Plymouth. At the same time, however, the settlers adapted the British way of life to suit their surroundings and with the benefit of greater religious, economic, and political freedoms.

Still, despite a great deal of political autonomy, by the eve of the War of Independence, American identity was still largely related to a sense of British rule, however distant and noninvasive it was. And, for most of the time, British authority was exercised loosely. The American colonies were able to provide Britain with important goods, including tobacco and cotton, although it did not generate large sums for His Majesty's coffers. Only after the end of the Seven Years' War in 1763 did the British Crown turn its attention to the American colonies. Success against the French resulted in Britain's dominance in the Americas and the doubling of its empire worldwide, but it had been a costly affair, with the British national debt doubling during the course of the war. Consequently, the British needed to help offset the costs by increasing revenue from the American colonies through the imposition of taxation. The road to the American Revolution was thus traveled as King George III's governments introduced a series of unpalatable acts on the colonies aimed at ensuring they paid their way.

The theme of disunity became particularly apparent during this period. Misunderstandings between Britain and America became common. While it is now clear that the king and his ministers did not necessarily want to move the colonies away from self-government, and were often enforcing existing legislation rather than introducing new laws, the perception in America was somewhat different as fears of autocratic rule and cries of "no taxation without representation" became prevalent. The origins of the War of Independence therefore lay in the questioning of political authority in the American colonies: Were Americans British subjects with equal rights or were they imperial subjects? By 1775, 13 British colonies were controlled by rebel colonists, war with the Loyalists began, and in 1776 the United States of America declared its independence from Britain. America's victory at Yorktown in 1781 and the subsequent settlement outlined in the Treaty of Versailles of 1783 meant that, as the United States emerged out of the chaos of war, the history of Anglo–American relations, as a relationship between two separate powers, began. Initially, the new nation was focused on establishing its own form of government; on 17 September 1787 the U.S. Constitution was adopted by the Constitutional Convention in Philadelphia, and on 30 April 1789 George Washington became the first elected U.S. president. Britain and America still had some outstanding territorial, maritime, and financial issues to deal with, however, and when Britain became embroiled in the French Revolutionary Wars (1793–1802) these became more pressing. Despite French support for the American colonists during their own war with the British, Washington remained neutral during the conflict, recognizing it was in no position to fight against Britain again, not wanting to disturb its transatlantic commercial ties, and still dealing with establishing the United States as a new nation. In November 1794, by signing the Treaty of Amity, Commerce, and Navigation, commonly known as the Jay Treaty, the government of William Pitt the Younger, and especially the British negotiator, Lord Grenville, agreed to withdraw its remaining troops from forts in America's Northwest Territory and, in essence, recognized the United States as a sovereign state. Anglo–American relations then experienced a 10-year period of relative harmony.

ANGLO–AMERICAN RELATIONS IN THE 19TH CENTURY

The 19th century saw the United States continue to develop as a nation free from external British control, while Britain had to adjust to dealing with a new and increasingly powerful nation across the Atlantic. Not surprisingly, given the years of conflict with Britain, many Americans still held largely negative views of their former rulers, associating the British with aristocracy and tyranny, although even Thomas Jefferson had acknowledged the "ties of our common kindred" in the Declaration of Independence. Due to U.S. military and economic weakness and Britain's ability to quickly reestablish control of the seas, the first American presidents recognized the need to establish reasonable relations with Britain and therefore conducted a cautious foreign policy. Although the United States did not sway from George Washington's advice to avoid permanent alliances, it had little choice but to engage with Britain. American farmers relied on British markets for their produce, particularly cotton and tobacco, and the new nation depended on imported British manufactured goods. Consequently, the United States' key priority was freedom of trade.

The Napoleonic Wars between Britain and France (1803–1815) threatened this freedom as both sides tried to prevent the other from trading with America. Fearing for its very existence, Britain was prepared to sacrifice the recent improvement in relations with the United States in its efforts to defeat Napoleon. Displaying arrogance, ineptitude, and highhandedness, the British continually violated U.S. neutrality and sovereignty rights by impressing American seaman into the British navy and by issuing Orders in Council that led to the seizure American ships. When British sailors attacked and boarded an American ship, the USS *Chesapeake*, on 22 June 1807, President Jefferson finally responded firmly to this provocation by persuading Congress to pass the Embargo Act of December 1807 that prohibited trade with Britain. By 1812, as British interference with American shipping continued, a younger generation of congressmen began to press for war with Britain to defend U.S. national honor. The resulting War of 1812, known to many in America as the "Second War of Independence," encouraged anti-British sentiment in the nation. Two of America's most potent nationalist symbols emerged from the war. Although the Executive Mansion in Washington, D.C., had been named the White House in 1811, a myth developed that it got that name after British troops set fire to it (then occupied by President James Madison) and it was painted white afterwards to cover the scorch marks from the fire. And it was during the 1812–1814 conflict that the United States also got its national anthem—"The Star-Spangled Banner"—composed by Francis Scott Key after the British invaded Washington, D.C., in August 1814. Still, the war was a huge risk for the new nation, especially as it attempted an invasion of Canada (British North America). The war did not have the same significance for the British as it did for the Americans; they were more concerned with the military war against Napoleon. Consequently, the Canadians fought to defend their territory against American attack but were only supported by British troops when the war in Europe came to an end. The war ended with the signing of the Treaty of Ghent in December 1814 with neither side achieving anything of note. The issue of impressments was no longer relevant as Napoleon had been defeated; the British now had a surplus of sailors and the United States agreed to return all Canadian land back to the British. By signing the treaty, Britain and America agreed to return to the status quo *ante bellum*.

Despite feeling that Britain was still the country most likely to do the United States harm, Washington understood that a balance had to be sought between American assertions of independence and the need to maintain important trading links with Britain. Canada remained the subject of several disputes between Washington and London, including the *Caroline* affair (1837–1842) and the bloodless border clashes of the Aroostock War of 1838, but by the middle of the century, an Anglo–American accommodation was beginning to be achieved as territorial issues were resolved. The Northeast boundary dispute was settled by the Webster–Ashburton Treaty of 1842 when U.S. Secretary of State Daniel Webster worked with British Foreign Secretary Lord Ashburton to establish the border between the United States and Canada, and in 1850 the Clayton–Bulwer Treaty attempted to deal with Anglo–American rivalry in Central America by establishing joint control of what later became known as the Panama Canal.

The improvement in Anglo–American relations was halted by events that occurred during the American Civil War. Northerners felt Britain acted out of pure economic self-interest in deciding to adopt a neutral position on the war and were infuriated by Britain's regular violation of its naval blockade. During the *Trent* affair of November 1861—when the U.S. Navy seized a British ship transporting Confederate diplomats to Britain—Britain and the United States came close to another war. Outraged that a U.S. ship had interdicted a British one on the high seas (and seemingly unaware that they had behaved similarly prior to the War of 1812), 11,000 British troops were sent to Canada as Britain prepared for war. Recognizing that the United States faced the threat of an invasion by the British from Canada into Maine, and understanding the difficulty of fighting a two-front war, the administration of Abraham Lincoln engaged in intense diplomacy to prevent such a catastrophe. Lincoln was correct in fearing that the British might be persuaded to intervene on the Confederate side. British attitudes to the American Civil War varied but many amongst the British elite were pleased to see that U.S.-style democracy, with its weak central government, had led to discord and some relished the thought of the nation splitting into rival powers, believing the British Empire could capitalize on the situation. However, Prime Minister Lord Palmerston's decision to declare neutrality was based largely on the calculation that Britain relied on the South for supplies of cotton for its textile mills and on the North for the supply of grain. By the middle of the war, sentiment in Britain had shifted to the Northern cause, largely due to a dislike of the South's practice of slavery. Nevertheless, relations remained strained between the British government and the Union leadership because the Confederacy had been supplied with British-built merchant vessels that were converted for wartime purposes after they left the dockyards. These commerce raiders, including the *Alabama* and the *Shenandoah*, were successful in sinking over 150 Northern ships and the United States demanded a huge amount of financial compensation from the British. The so-called *Alabama* claims were finally resolved by international arbitration under the Treaty of Washington of 1871, when Britain was ordered to pay $15.5 million to the United States for the loss of shipping and additional Anglo–American territorial and fishing rights disputes were also dealt with.

In the aftermath of the Civil War, as the United States dealt with Reconstruction in the South and the growth of big business in the North, relations with Britain began to improve gradually. The two peoples had begun to appreciate each other's cultures much more. In the first decades of the United States' existence, the British had been intrigued to see how the new nation, experimenting in new forms of democracy, would develop; although Britain recognized that the United States shared a commitment to liberal values such as individual liberty and private property rights, there was a feeling that its democracy went too far. Prevailing perceptions of the United States and its national character were often gained from curious British travelers to the United States, including British businessmen and women and novelists such as Charles Dickens and Frances Trollope. Until the late 19th century, British opinions on American identity were often negative, noting a range of failings from individual idiosyncrasies, such as a perceived lack of table manners, to a wider-held abhorrence of slavery and its racial legacy, a dislike of displays of excessive materialism, and contrasts between American innocence compared to British experience in worldly affairs. Such views began to be challenged as social and cultural links between the two peoples grew in the second half of the 19th century as more Britons migrated to the United States; transatlantic connections in the business world and between reform and religious movements, such as the antislavery groups, women's rights campaigners, and the Quakers, led to exchanges of ideas, finance, and people. By the late 19th century, cultural ties among the Anglo–American elites were also strengthened by the "marriage market" that saw British aristocrats marrying American heiresses, such as Nancy Astor and Jennie Churchill, in what was characterized in the popular press as "money-for-title" arrangements.

In the last decades of the 19th century, the United States had begun to grow in confidence as continental America was settled and its economic power increased markedly with mass immigration, urbanization, and industrialization. At the same time, Anglophobic opinion declined in strength in the late 19th century, partly due to the thinking of opinion shapers such as Josiah Strong, the Protestant minister who argued in *Our Country* (1885) that the "Anglo–Saxon" race had a responsibility to "uplift and civilize" the world, thus providing an intellectual framework for an improvement in Anglo–American diplomatic relations. America's overseas expansionism in the late 19th century and early

20th century—acquiring territories and protectorates in Cuba, Haiti, Nicaragua, Hawaii, the Philippines, Puerto Rico, Guam, and Samoa— also led U.S. foreign-policy makers and businesspeople to not only widen the concept of "manifest destiny" but also to view the British Empire in a new, slightly less condemnatory manner. By the 1890s, Britain had begun to question its policy of "splendid isolation." Recognizing that its industrial preeminence was now being challenged by the United States and faced with an external threat from the growing German empire, London began to feel that its fellow Anglo–Saxons across the Atlantic might prove useful allies. By the late 19th century a "great rapprochement" developed between Britain and America that was encouraged by President Theodore Roosevelt in the early 20th century and supported by the formation of the Anglo–American League, the Pilgrims Society, and Rhodes scholarships. Britain acquiesced in American imperialism and supported the United States during the Spanish–American War of 1898, after which British poet Rudyard Kipling urged the Americans to take up the "White Man's Burden." Relations became more peaceful between London and Washington and cooperation increased, especially during the Alaskan boundary dispute, the Venezuelan boundary dispute (1895–1899), and the Anglo–Boer War (1899–1902).

It is noticeable that during this period, British policymakers began to inject sentiment into their analysis and discussion of relations with the United States, often describing Americans as "friends." Equally remarkable, given the obvious economic and political rivalry between the two nations, Washington reciprocated London's affectionate feelings. By 1901, Winston Churchill—along with many other important intellectuals, businessmen, politicians, and clergymen on both sides of the Atlantic—had begun to recognize that an Anglo–American war would be entirely wrong, indeed unthinkable, in the 20th century.

ANGLO–AMERICAN RELATIONS
FROM WORLD WAR I TO WORLD WAR II

The relative diplomatic harmony between Britain and America in the early 20th century suited both nations. However, Britain now recognized its supremacy in the world was being challenged by two major rivals: Germany in Europe and the United States in the Western hemisphere, both with growing navies, expanding empires, and economic strength. At this stage, Washington was not yet desirous of an interventionist presence in the world; Britain, which was comfortable with U.S. liberalism, proved correct in thinking that Germany, led by Prussian aristocrats with militaristic intent, was a more immediate threat.

With the outbreak of World War I in July 1914, Britain was fighting to maintain its great power status; although it had allies in Europe through the Triple Entente, as the war of attrition in the trenches of northern France and Belgium dragged on into 1915, the Liberal prime minister, Herbert Asquith, began to press the administration of Woodrow Wilson to become involved militarily. President Wilson had made it clear from the beginning of the war that this was a European conflict and had declared that the United States must remain "neutral in fact as well as name." Several factors impeded strict neutrality on America's part. With 8 million German Americans and 4.5 million Irish Americans, the United States had a significant proportion of its 105 million population who did not care for a British victory. However, pro-British sentiment was even stronger, not least on Wall Street and among significant political figures, including former president Theodore Roosevelt and Wilson's close adviser, Colonel Edward House. By 1915 American neutrality also favored the Allies because, although the United States continued to trade with all belligerent nations, Britain benefited the most from this due to its dominance on the high seas. Britain was also tied to the United States financially as the country began to receive American loans in October 1915 from the House of Morgan to fund the war. It was the German use of U-boat submarine warfare and Britain's blockade of Germany that finally dragged the United States into World War I as merchant vessels faced attack or seizure and American commercial interests were badly affected. Prompted by the public knowledge of the Zimmerman telegram, at Wilson's request, the U.S. Congress declared war on the German empire on 6 April 1917, joining the Allied nations as an "associate power" rather than signing a treaty of alliance. Washington was willing to cooperate with London but wanted to retain the right to sign a peace treaty on its own terms. This decision reflected Wilson's internationalist principles and his understanding that the United States had differing war aims. Whereas Britain was concerned with its own security and that of its empire, the United

States focused on the concept of making the world "safe for democracy" and reforming international politics.

As far as the British were concerned, particularly Prime Minister David Lloyd-George, American forces were slow to mobilize for war. General John Pershing, the commander of the American Expeditionary Force (AEF) and its 1st Division did not arrive in France until June 1917 and by December only 175,000 troops had arrived. Pershing and Wilson were adamant that American forces should be an independent fighting force that was well trained and not rushed into battle. Consequently, very few U.S. troops fought in the land war until July 1918, although they did go on to play a major role in the St. Mihiel offensive launched on 12 September and the Meuse–Argonne offensive that began later that month. Despite the United States' "associate" status, there was a significant degree of Anglo–American military cooperation during the war. Washington accepted the grand strategy of the allies that focused on the Western Front, and as it became clear that American troops were essential to the land campaign, the American and Royal navies cooperated in transporting approximately two million servicemen safely to the Continent. Washington retained some independence, however. It insisted on guarding against intensified U-boat activity off the coast of America in the early months of U.S. involvement, and later Wilson pushed for a more aggressive naval offensive in European waters. The influx of U.S. materiel and 1.2 million American servicemen tipped the balance in the Allies' favor and Germany agreed to an armistice on 11 November 1918.

The switch in Anglo–American fortunes was cemented by the end of World War I. Not only did Britain suffer large numbers of war casualties—almost 900,000 dead—the financial cost of the war had also been great, with costs estimated at $35 billion. Britain also lost its position as the world's leading overseas investor, instead ending the war facing enormous interest payments on wartime loans. Despite America's late entry to the war, it also suffered almost 120,000 war dead but its financial burden was lower, $22 billion. More importantly, America moved from being a debtor nation before the war to being a net creditor nation after it. In the 1920s and 1930s, as both nations struggled to come to terms with their new positions in the world order, diplomatic relations between the two deteriorated markedly. In particular, these years saw growing naval and financial rivalry as Britain and the United States battled for world supremacy. Although the British Empire still retained the largest navy at the end of World War I, it was soon being challenged by the United States as both nations embarked on massive shipbuilding programs. The administration of Warren G. Harding organized the Washington Naval Conference that began in November 1921 and aimed to halt the naval race between Japan, the United States, and Great Britain. The Liberal government of David Lloyd-George was forced to accept naval parity with the United States in the Five-Power Treaty that was signed in 1922 in an acknowledgment that the United States' superior economic strength would ultimately allow it to win any arms race. The American negotiator at the Washington conference, Secretary of State Charles Evans Hughes, was willing to accept a degree of U.S. naval disarmament as long as it stemmed the power of Japan in the Pacific and because he was well aware of the isolationist sentiment within Congress and among the American public.

Most importantly in the 1920s, Anglo–American tensions grew over the repayment of war debts to America. By the end of the war, Britain owed $4.3 billion to American financial institutions that expected to be paid back as soon as possible. London, in turn, was owed war reparations from the Germans under the terms of the Treaty of Versailles (1919), but Germany, despite the Dawes Plan of 1924, was not in a position to pay them. This financial impasse led to much anger and resentment on both sides of the Atlantic, with the United States suspecting Britain of perfidy and the British feeling the United States should have more patience considering the "blood" cost it had incurred in fighting World War I. In the end, Britain repaid $2.2 billion to the United States and reneged on the remaining debt, leaving many Americans with a lesson learned, especially when, in the 1930s, the country entered its worst depression. Britain's lapse into protectionism, ending its commitment to free trade and introducing imperial preference, led to still further bitterness in Washington. To add to Anglo–American woes, the 1930s saw the rise of totalitarianism in Europe and Asia and neither country proved up for the fight. Having refused to enter Woodrow Wilson's League of Nations, America took a noninterventionist stance; Britain chose appeasement. The administration of Franklin D. Roosevelt believed Britain was still motivated primarily by a desire to strengthen its empire and was disturbed by British appeasement policy, not least when it led to British acceptance of Italy's gains in East Africa after the Second Italo–Abyssinia War in 1936. Britain, in turn, continued to view U.S. concerns about its foreign policy as further evidence of America's brashness and naiveté in world affairs and did not appreciate Washington's belief in its own moral authority on such questions. Instead, Prime Minister Neville Chamberlain felt the British were experienced peacemakers who did not need lessons in diplomacy. And yet, despite the distrust and suspicions, relations began to improve with the Anglo–American Trade Agreement of 1938, and it was understood in both London and Washington that eventually Britain and America might need to establish a friendship and an alliance in order to deal with the threat to democracy and national security posed by fascist Germany and militaristic Japan.

An Anglo–American concord seemed unlikely in the short term. The American public's perception that it had been sucked into World War I because of U.S. financial and commercial interests was reinforced with the findings of the Nye Committee, a Senate investigation into the munitions industry that reported in February 1936. The report showed that the Allies had been loaned over $2.3 billion between 1915 and America's entry into the war in April 1917, whereas Germany had only been loaned $27 million. In an attempt to avoid a similar experience, a series of Neutrality Acts were passed in the 1930s, although after Britain declared war on Germany on 3 September 1939, President Roosevelt recognized that it was impossible to stay "neutral in thought." This was an acknowledgment that public opinion polls showed a majority of Americans favored the Allies, were willing to aid Britain and France, but remained convinced that the United States should stay out of the war. During the so-called phony war of late 1939 and early 1940, Washington attempted to maintain its distance from events in Europe, and London understood that strong, organized isolationist forces explained America's position. The noninterventionist sentiment in the United States began to weaken with Adolf Hitler's invasion of Finland, Belgium, and the Netherlands in the spring of 1940 and with reporter Ed Murrow's emotional radio broadcasts describing the London "blitz" between September 1940 and May 1941. Fearing for Britain's survival, the new British prime minister, Winston Churchill, also began to press more forcefully for help from the United States, and Roosevelt agreed that the United States should become the "arsenal of democracy" and provide Britain with sufficient military and financial aid to win the war.

Help came in the shape of the destroyers-for-bases deal in August 1940 and Lend-Lease in March 1941. And, although not involved militarily in the war, Roosevelt became increasingly concerned to shape the postwar settlement, first by outlining the "Four Freedoms" that humans were entitled to and then by meeting Churchill at Placentia Bay in August 1941 to agree to the Atlantic Charter.

Despite continuing pressure from London, it was the Japanese attack on Pearl Harbor on 7 December 1941 that ended isolationist sentiment, triggered U.S. entry into World War II, and led the Atlantic Alliance to take shape. Faced with common enemies and having a unity of purpose, Britain and America worked together in an unprecedented manner. At the Arcadia Conference of late December 1941 and early January 1942, Roosevelt and Churchill agreed to establish an Anglo–American alliance, embarked on a "Germany first" policy, and created the Combined Chiefs of Staff with its headquarters in Washington (allowing for joint military command during the Second World War). This was the beginning of a series of unparalleled developments in the bilateral relationship. Shared responsibility was also established for the military planning of Operation Overlord, the D-Day landings in Normandy, under the leadership of General Dwight D. Eisenhower, who had control of the Supreme Headquarters of the Allied Expeditionary Force (SHAEF). The extent of Anglo–American military cooperation proved not only unmatched but, more importantly, successful. The United States sent almost 12 million service personnel overseas to fight the Allied cause (and lost 292,000 in combat). The first U.S. troops arrived in Britain on 24 January 1942, American pilots joined the Royal Air Force in air raids by July 1942, and Anglo–American naval (and intelligence) cooperation secured victory against German U-boats in the battle for the Atlantic that took place in 1942 and 1943. British and American forces fought together in North Africa and in the invasion of Sicily before the invasion of France on 6 June 1944, and after D-Day pressed on together to liberate Europe (with French, Canadian, and Russian forces). This level of defense cooperation was enhanced by personal relationships at the highest levels, notably the close one between Churchill and Roosevelt but also the friendship between the U.S. Army Chief of Staff General George C. Marshall and Field Marshal Sir John Dill, head of the British military mission.

The extraordinary degree of wartime collaboration did not prevent differences between Washington and London over military strategy, operations on the battlefield, and wider political issues. Often the differences centered on how far British military plans were connected to imperial concerns, with tensions apparent over Britain's preference for a Mediterranean campaign before an invasion of France, and disagreements between U.S. General "Vinegar Joe" Stilwell and his British superior, Lord Louis Mountbatten, commander of the South-East Asia Command (SEAC) over the decision that British and Commonwealth ground forces should retake Burma, a British colony, from the Japanese. And, as the war progressed and the United States grew in confidence, Britain's declining power and status became clear, so that by the time of the Yalta and Potsdam conferences in April and July of 1945, Roosevelt and his successor Harry S. Truman began to cut Churchill out of some discussions with the Soviet leadership. Regardless of such late war Anglo–American tensions, when the world war ended on 15 August 1945, after the United States dropped atomic bombs on Hiroshima and Nagasaki to end the war in the Pacific, the foundations of the postwar "special relationship" had been laid. The United States had accepted the need for it to have a wider worldview, had worked with the British and its other allies to create the United Nations in September 1945, had established its own military bases in Great Britain, and had negotiated an intelligence-sharing agreement; and the two partners had participated in joint research on the development of the atomic bomb via the Quebec Agreement of 1943. Moreover, the institutional and bureaucratic contacts between London and Washington had increased markedly. The number of British diplomats and ministry officials in Washington rose from a 1939 level of fewer than 20 to over 9,000 by the end of the war.

THE "SPECIAL RELATIONSHIP" AND THE COLD WAR

By the end of World War II, Britain's status as a "great power" had been reduced greatly by a lengthy and costly war. The human costs had been great, with over 250,000 casualties; many of Britain's cities had faced physical destruction from continuous aerial bombing; and the financial costs had been severe, with Britain losing a quarter of its prewar value.

The war also saw the process of decolonization increase rapidly, and by 1947 Britain had left the Indian subcontinent and by 1948 had ceded its mandate in Palestine. In contrast to a war-ravished and weakened Britain, America was now a confident economic and military superpower, and the dominant power in the Anglo–American relationship. It was imperative for Britain's future influence on the world stage to be able to maintain a close working relationship with the United States.

In Britain and America, the desire to continue the Atlantic alliance in the postwar era had an economic imperative. Prior to the war's end, London and Washington had worked together to try to prevent a return to the protectionism of the 1920s and 1930s and ensure a more stable world economic order by establishing an international exchange rate system pegged to the value of gold in the Bretton Woods Agreement of 1944. But with the war's end, the administration of Harry S. Truman acted swiftly to end its program of Lend-Lease to the Soviet Union and Great Britain, leaving London to contemplate its sterling balance problem and Britain's reconstruction without sufficient funds to do so. From September to December 1945, Britain's key economist, John Maynard Keynes, negotiated in Washington over an Anglo–American loan. By agreeing to a low-interest loan of $3.75 billion, U.S. Secretary of the Treasury Fred Vinson recognized it would help secure British involvement in the Bretton Woods system (including the International Monetary Fund [IMF] and the World Bank) that had become operational in 1946. The United States proved crucial to British economic recovery by providing the Anglo–American loan and by providing Marshall aid in 1948. In later years, America also provided support for the pound sterling on several occasions, particularly before it was devalued by Prime Minister Harold Wilson in 1967 and during the IMF crisis of 1976. Economic cooperation was also noticeable in 1948 when the United States and Great Britain were both founding members of the General Agreement on Tariffs and Trade (GATT), later the World Trade Organization (WTO), which was set up to promote free trade and reduce protectionist measures amongst its membership.

The most pressing factor urging the continuance of a strong Anglo–American relationship was the emergence of the Cold War. Despite the United States' nuclear superiority, very quickly it became apparent that Washington was faced with an ideological and strategic battle with its former ally, the communist Soviet Union. Former prime minister Winston Churchill made it clear in his Fulton, Missouri, speech in March 1946 that both Britain and America would not only benefit from the continuance of the wartime cooperation but that a "special" relationship was a necessity in order to combat the threat to the Western world from communism. The cash-strapped postwar Labour government, led by Prime Minister Clement Attlee, could no longer afford to provide economic and military assistance to Greece and Turkey and encouraged the United States to take on this financial burden, as these countries were facing communist insurrections. The resultant Truman Doctrine issued by the president to Congress on 12 March 1947 formalized the policy of containment of communism.

In the zero-sum atmosphere of the Cold War, Washington decided that Britain would be its key ally. The rationale behind this decision was clear: Britain was a stable democracy; it was well placed to act as a leader in Europe, and certainly act as a bridge between America and the other European allies; it had important strengths overseas, including a significant military capability; and it had its Commonwealth links. The continued defense cooperation between the two nations remained the most striking example of real, practical cooperation. The willingness of Great Britain to allow a foreign power, however friendly, to retain and grow military bases on its soil was a staggering development. Significantly, the two nations also demonstrated their willingness to work together to deal with the communist threat during the Berlin blockade crisis in 1948 when they operated a joint airlift. During the crisis in Berlin, British Foreign Secretary Ernest Bevin's decision to invite the United States to station B-29 bombers, capable of carrying nuclear weapons, at RAF air bases was another acknowledgment of how much London felt it needed a U.S. military commitment to safeguard the security of Europe and in September 1954 Britain became a crucial "forward-base" for possible strikes against the Soviet Union with the arrival of the first U.S. nuclear weapons in Britain. Berlin also pushed Bevin and U.S. Secretary of State Dean Acheson to work together closely to complete the formation of the military alliance, the North Atlantic Treaty Organization (NATO) on 4 April 1949. The United States was now involved in an "entangling alliance."

In the first decade of the Cold War, Anglo–American defense collaboration did not extend to cooperation in the nuclear field. In August 1946 the U.S. Congress had prevented the sharing of nuclear secrets with the passage of the McMahon Act. By the time the act had been repealed in 1958, Britain had developed its own atomic and hydrogen bombs. Anglo–American nuclear cooperation resumed with the passage of the U.S.–U.K. Mutual Defense Agreement, under which the two parties worked together to aid each other's nuclear planning and development processes, and embarked on joint nuclear testing. In effect, Britain's independent nuclear deterrent was increasingly dependent on American assistance as they came to rely on sharing of technology, missiles, information, and materiel. During a meeting with Prime Minister Harold Macmillan in Bermuda in 1957, President Eisenhower agreed to station American Thor missiles in Britain as Britain struggled to deliver its own Blue Streak missiles. This dependence on U.S. missiles meant Britain had to negotiate to gain U.S. Polaris and Trident missiles in the 1960s and 1970s. Although nuclear cooperation became another concrete dimension of the "special relationship," Britain's close alliance with the United States was partly justified by the feeling that it could provide a moderating influence on Washington in an era of nuclear proliferation—indeed, it might be able to restrain the U.S. colossus—and thus debates continued over the degree of British involvement in nuclear decision making and military planning. As concerns about nuclear proliferation grew in the aftermath of the Cuban missile crisis of October 1962, a global treaty on nuclear arms limitation was negotiated in 1963. During the negotiations between President John F. Kennedy, Premier Nikita Khrushchev of the Soviet Union, and Prime Minister Macmillan, there was some degree of Anglo–American discord. Although Washington and London were keen to see an East–West agreement on the issue, Macmillan had a stronger preference than Kennedy for a comprehensive test ban treaty (banning testing underground in addition to the ban on atmospheric and above-ground testing that was agreed) and played an important role in ensuring the final Limited Nuclear Test Ban Treaty was agreed to by all parties. Britain and America also worked together during the negotiations with the Soviet Union on the Nuclear Nonproliferation Treaty of 1968, which recognized existing nuclear powers but prevented nonnuclear powers from acquiring the weapons. Despite an Anglo–American commitment to nuclear disarmament, successive postwar British governments felt that the Anglo–American nuclear deterrence safeguarded British national interests, namely its physical security.

The need for a continuing, strong Anglo–American alliance was accepted by most of the British and American public, principally because of the perceived threat from the Soviets but also because cultural ties and emotional bonds had grown during World War II and continued into the postwar decades. The two peoples had shared the wartime experience; there had been an American "occupation" of Britain by approximately three million GIs who passed through Britain during 1942 and 1945, with up to 70,000 British war brides and 14,000 children returning to the United States after the war. Other forms of cultural interaction continued to grow and often proved reciprocal as mutual imitation thrived. Not only did cinema and literature continue to influence perceptions of each other's national character, but the United States increased its export of American music to Great Britain, notably blues music and rock 'n' roll music in the 1950s, with Elvis Presley proving a huge phenomenon among British youth. American popular music lovers were, in turn, enamored by the British "invasion" in the 1960s, when the Beatles and Rolling Stones, among others, found success in the United States. And from the 1950s onward, British and American television audiences watched television programs from the other side of the Atlantic and networks copied popular formats for their respective populations. And yet during the postwar period, Anglophobic tendencies still existed within America. The U.S. Congress, concerned by spiraling defense budgets, felt that Britain and other European powers should take more responsibility for their own defense and related costs. Anti-Americanism also ebbed and waned in Great Britain. Opposition to American foreign policy, particularly in relation to the stationing of American nuclear missiles on British soil (leading to accusations that Britain had become the 51st state) and the war in Vietnam, saw groups like the Campaign for Nuclear Disarmament (CND) flourish in the 1950s and 1960s.

When North Korea invaded South Korea in June 1950, the "special relationship" faced its first major challenge during the Cold War. Just five years after the end of World War II, Britain demonstrated its credentials as a loyal ally and committed cold warrior by sending 63,000 troops to join America's 480,000 troops to repel the North Koreans. This was the second-largest troop commitment in the UN-backed allied force, and Britain's involvement allowed Prime Minister Clement Attlee to portray the British government as a voice of reason when, in a press conference, Truman refused to rule out General Douglas MacArthur being able to use nuclear weapons in the military campaign. Attlee famously flew to Washington in December 1950 to discuss the president's comments, and although the two leaders never really discussed the issue, Attlee returned to London assured that Truman was in full control and the prime minister was able to portray himself as a moral influence on the White House.

While Britain proved a staunch, anticommunist ally, and the two demonstrated public unity and cooperation during the Korean War, London and Washington had differing views on how to deal with the communist threat. In general terms, over the course of the Cold War, Britain took a more pragmatic, accommodationist approach than the United States, who preferred to take a harder line with what they perceived as monolithic communism. Disagreements emerged over how best to deal with China after it turned communist in 1949. Britain recognized the reality of its existence and extended diplomatic recognition to the People's Republic of China (PRC) in 1950, while the United States maintained its recognition of the Republic of China government based in Taiwan, did not allow the PRC to take China's seat at the United Nations until October 1971, and took until 1979 to officially recognize the PRC. Similarly, Britain preferred to continue to trade with Cuba after the Castro regime aligned itself with the Soviet Union in the early 1960s, despite pressure from the White House and U.S. Congress to join their trade embargo.

And, of course, the Cold War period saw other serious breaches in Anglo–American unity. The most important and most public rift came during the Suez crisis of 1956. When Britain, along with France and Israel, launched a military attack against Egypt after it nationalized the Suez Canal, the administration of Dwight D. Eisenhower forced an end to the invasion and a cease-fire through diplomatic and financial means. Britain's inability to sustain a military venture without U.S. support proved humiliating to the government of Anthony Eden and marked the decline of Britain's military power by reminding London that Washington now called the shots. Such an open display of disagreement was mostly avoided in future years, although when Secretary of Defense Robert McNamara announced the cancellation of the Skybolt missile in 1962, another high-profile rift resulted. Having been promised the ballistic missile, Macmillan appeared to outnegotiate President John F.

Kennedy at the Nassau Conference in December 1962 when it was agreed that Britain would receive the Polaris intercontinental missile instead of Skybolt. Anglo–American political discord was also apparent in the 1960s when the limits of U.S. power were demonstrated during the Vietnam War. In December 1964 the administration of Lyndon B. Johnson was unable to persuade the government of Harold Wilson to send troops to the conflict—partly because Britain was overstretched militarily and partly because many within the Labour Party did not agree with the war—and yet, publicly, Britain went on to provide diplomatic support for the American war. Behind the scenes, the British government attempted to assert its views over the military methods used in Vietnam (and were condemnatory in private of the American use of gas in March 1965) and attempted to act as an "honest broker" in peace talks.

During the period of the pro-European government of Edward Heath, Anglo–American relations lost some of their vitality, and again saw a degree of discord during the 1973 Arab–Israeli War, when Britain refused to allow the United States to use its base in Cyprus during American operations to aid Israel. And despite their concerns about the risk of a nuclear conflict between the two superpowers, Britain was concerned that during the Strategic Arms Limitation Talks (SALT) of the 1970s the United States might do a deal with the Soviets over their heads, and leave Britain vulnerable to Soviet attack. As a result, the administration of President Jimmy Carter was willing to gain British approval of the SALT treaty by agreeing in 1979 to station cruise missiles on British soil. Even during the love-fest years of Prime Minister Margaret Thatcher and President Ronald Reagan, when the two took a hard line on Soviet communism and Thatcher was willing to court unpopularity at home by allowing American planes to launch an attack on Libya in 1986 from British bases, there were disagreements between Washington and London. The United States' national interests led them to ponder the wisdom of supporting the British attempt to recapture the Falklands Islands from its Latin American ally, Argentina, in 1982, and Thatcher condemned U.S. military action in Grenada in October 1983. Thatcher was also concerned by Reagan's apparent desire to try to eliminate nuclear weapons via talks with Soviet leader Mikhail Gorbachev at Reykjavik in 1986. In the aftermath of the talks, Thatcher flew to Washington and gained affirmation that Britain's Trident nuclear fleet would be modernized. Despite disagreements over the Strategic Defense Initiative (SDI), the United States and Soviet Union negotiated the Intermediate-Range Nuclear Forces (INF) Treaty of 1987 that included an American commitment to withdraw such weapons from European soil. America's cruise missiles were subsequently withdrawn from British bases, such as Greenham Common, by 1992, and in June 2008 it was reported that the last U.S. nuclear weapons had been withdrawn from RAF Lakenheath in Suffolk, ending a 50-year nuclear presence in Britain.

Despite a number of serious disagreements during the Cold War era, both Britain and American were keen to see the Anglo–American relationship remain a strong one. Britain rarely challenged the United States in public, instead providing rhetorical support for most of its foreign policy. And, importantly, as a fellow anticommunist nation, Britain was prepared to maintain an overseas military presence in key parts of the world, especially before its withdrawal of troops from East of Suez in the early 1970s. Even after that time, Britain still remained an important Cold War ally for the United States because of its willingness to station American weapons and troops on its soil, and the two countries continued to maintain crucial intelligence links. For Britain, the relationship had even more significance. Postwar governments believed in the nuclear deterrent, to varying degrees, and were keen to shelter under the U.S. nuclear umbrella. And as a declining world power, Britain took comfort in appearing to have power and significance through its relationship with the United States. The complicating factor on many occasions was Britain's relationship with Europe. For its own economic benefit, Britain applied for entry into the European Economic Community (EEC) in the 1960s. General Charles de Gaulle's rejection of the application in January 1963 and November 1967, in part because he felt Britain would act as a Trojan horse for the United States, reminded the Macmillan and Wilson governments that having a foot in both the American and European camps was always going to be a difficult game to play. With Britain's eventual entry into the EEC in 1973, with the exception of Edward Heath, who was openly pro-European, successive postwar British leaders have attempted to maintain a special relationship with America, while hoping to take a more decisive role in Europe. In general, the United States encouraged Britain to move closer to Europe not only because in Washington's eyes it would help secure a stable Europe, with one of its key allies at its center, but also because as Dean Acheson had famously remarked in 1962, Britain had lost an empire and not yet found a role.

THE POST–COLD WAR RELATIONSHIP

As the "special relationship" was formed during a period when there was a clear enemy and the common objective of containing communism, the end of the Cold War presented Anglo–American relations with a new challenge. British foreign-policy makers feared there would be a less-interventionist and more-isolationist trend in U.S. foreign policy, and worried that Washington would no longer value its relationship with London to the same extent. The utility of the institutions and alliance frameworks that bound Britain and the United States together during World War II and the Cold War was now questioned. While Britain still hoped to remain loyal to the United States, it also hoped for deeper integration within Europe; across the Atlantic, the United States had also developed "special relationships" with other countries as well, including Israel and Mexico. Britain's currency in Washington appeared less valuable in the immediate post–Cold War years, despite the political and military cooperation shown between the administration of George H. W. Bush and the government of John Major during the Persian Gulf War of 1991, and was at a low point during the years of the first administration of Bill Clinton. In particular, Downing Street began to realize that Washington was willing to risk offending British sensibilities by tackling the impasse in Northern Ireland. The Anglo–American relationship also appeared disunited over the crisis in Bosnia that began in 1992, when Major and his foreign secretary, Douglas Hurd, made great efforts to persuade President Clinton and Secretary of State Warren Christopher to join Britain in sending ground troops to support UN peacekeeping operations to defend Muslim "safe havens." By August 1995 the United States had agreed to NATO-led air strikes against Bosnian Serbs and after the Dayton Peace Accords of November 1995 joined British and French forces in safeguarding the settlement. Similarly, despite a much warmer working relationship between President Clinton and Prime Minister Tony Blair, the United States resisted British calls to contribute ground troops during the humanitarian crisis in Kosovo in 1999, instead agreeing to NATO bombing of Serbia and introducing American forces to the subsequent international peacekeeping operation.

The Anglo–American alliance was revitalized after the al-Qaeda terrorist attacks in New York and Washington on 11 September 2001. The sense of having "friends" in a hostile world became important again. Prime Minister Tony Blair immediately offered British sympathy and pledged to support the United States in facing "the fight for freedom." And, as when working with Clinton, Blair developed a close relationship with President George W. Bush, with an obvious personal chemistry between them. Indeed, many would argue that the Bush–Blair tandem probably marked a recent high point in Anglo–American relations, one that is unlikely to be achieved again. This personal dimension to the Anglo–American relationship added a sense of moral crusade to the "war on terror." Although coming from different political horizons (Blair the left, Bush the right), the two were both highly moralistic in matters of foreign relations and took strong stands, often stronger than their fellow citizens approved of. Blair realized Britain's weight was insufficient to pursue a policy of its own, emphasized its value as a bridge between the United States and Europe, and was willing to second Bush as appropriate. Britain agreed to let the United States use the Fylingdales early warning station in North Yorkshire in the development of its National Missile Defense (NMD) system in 2003; and British and American forces took the lead in the invasion of Afghanistan in October 2001 and of Iraq in March 2003, and in the subsequent military operations in those countries. As in past endeavors, however, the public front of unity masked some serious disagreements between London and Washington. Most importantly, Blair attempted to influence Bush by recommending Britain and America gain international approval, through the United Nations, of their planned invasion of Iraq. And, in both Afghanistan and Iraq, Britain expressed its unease at the noncombatant casualties caused by high-level bombing campaigns. Moreover, given the unpopularity of the invasion of Iraq in Britain, the debate over the reasons behind the Anglo–American invasion of Iraq—suspected weapons of mass destruction (WMDs) or regime change—highlighted a long-standing belief that the United States takes British support for granted.

Reflecting well-established custom and practice, the post–Cold War period has witnessed London still willing to disagree with the United States over important issues while remaining committed to the principle of a strong Anglo–American alliance. Blair was willing to voice British concerns about the American use of Guantanamo Bay to detain suspected Middle East terrorists without trial and disagreed with Bush over international action on climate change. And when Blair was replaced by Gordon Brown, it became clear that Britain might be even less forthcoming. Indicating that Brown would follow a policy of engagement rather than coercion—and following the pragmatic, nonconfrontational approach that had led to the release of 15 British sailors and marines captured by Iranians off the coast of Iraq in March 2007—less was heard from Britain on the need to block nuclear developments in Iran. Britain was also not among those gladly twisting the dragon's tail over Tibet during the Olympics in Beijing or baiting the bear after Russia invaded Georgia in August 2008. While the Bush White House supported pro-Western Georgia's efforts to suppress the attempted breakaway of the state of South Ossetia, publicly criticized Vladimir Putin's Russia over its recognition of the state of South Ossetia and subsequent military intervention, and sent U.S. warships to the Black Sea (ostensibly for relief purposes), the European Union (EU), including Britain, concentrated on brokering a cease-fire. And as an Atlanticist who stresses mutual rights and responsibilities, in addition to mutual interests, Brown appears less concerned with personal loyalty to the incumbent of the White House and more focused on his government's need to cope with serious problems, political and economic, and even the rising danger of Labour being replaced by the Conservatives. It is unlikely, however, that David Cameron, should he come to power, would take a more aggressive stance as a relative newcomer to world politics.

Just as there might be changes in personnel in Britain, which would inevitably alter its foreign policy and allow for the possibility of a reassessment of Anglo–American relations, there will undoubtedly be changes in the United States as George W. Bush is replaced by Barack Obama. Obama is unlikely to be as pushy or aggressive as Bush, who will leave office with strong opposition to the war in Iraq and general dissatisfaction with his foreign policy more broadly, not only among Democrats but also from some Republicans. Perhaps recognizing that

Brown was not convinced that in recent years Britain had had sufficient influence or payback for its loyalty to the United States, during a visit to 10 Downing Street in May 2008, Obama spoke of the need to "recalibrate" the "special relationship" with Britain, arguing that London and Washington should be "full partners." In addition, the new president will face a challenging international environment. Rather than being obsessed by the "war on terror," the new president faces global economic problems as well as two rapidly emerging powers, not quite superpowers yet, but certainly dangerous rivals if not suitably addressed, namely a resurgent Russia and the People's Republic of China, who Britain and America would like to see operating within the established international system. As other powers challenge America's global dominance, Washington may have to exercise leadership at a time when liberal democracy is increasingly questioned as the only way forward for emergent nations.

Thus, Anglo–American relations must be inserted in the broader context. While American power has continued rising over recent decades, Britain's power base has kept on shrinking. London could endorse policies adopted in Washington, but it could not do much more and it could certainly not impose its own even within the European Union, whose foreign policy machinery it was increasingly absorbed into. So, as an ally, Britain was of shrinking significance. However, it could still play an important role as a friend, even as "best buddy." The most serious drawback to much of recent American policy has been that it was concocted in Washington, often without too much concern as to what others thought of it, and on occasion the American president even looked like the bully. Calling its opponents enemies, let alone part of an axis of evil, did not help matters. Yet, as Afghanistan and Iraq showed, even the United States could not always go it alone even against rather second- and even third-rate opponents, while the "war on terror" depended much more on cooperation than power. Thus, Britain could again, as it had under Blair, provide coaching on how to get along with other countries and present policies that seem less one-sided and aggressive. More simply, it could pass along the knowledge that except for rather special cases, international relations is not about good versus bad (let alone evil) but seeking mutually agreeable solutions to concrete problems and only resorting to force, threats, or bullying when all else fails. It is apparent that in fighting the war on terrorism, Britain would like to take the moral high ground by taking a criminal justice or civil libertarian approach. Anglo–American relations may therefore face a period of readjustment as Britain continues to attempt to educate the White House on the benefits of its approach to counterterrorism over the United States' quick-fix, military approach that leaves the West open to castigation for the use of preemptive strikes, extraordinary renditions, and the use of torture.

In the 21st century, while the power disparity between Britain and the United States remains enormous, the bilateral relationship between the United States and Great Britain remains grounded in strong emotional ties of language, culture, trade, and history, and continues to have tangible links in the fields of defense and intelligence. Central to British foreign policy and still of great significance to Washington, the Anglo–American relationship remains a fascinating and key dynamic in international politics.

The Dictionary

– A –

ABOLITIONISTS. A transatlantic network of abolitionists was established as early as the 1780s. Recognizing that the slave trade was international in scope, abolitionists in the United States and Great Britain understood that it was essential to collaborate with each other. In 1807, both nations banned their citizens from participation in the international slave trade. The British Anti-Slavery Society, formed in 1823, turned its attention to the abolition of slavery throughout the British Empire, which it achieved with the passage of the 1833 West Indian Emancipation Act. American abolitionist William Lloyd Garrison of the American Anti-Slavery Society was inspired by abolitionists in the British Anti-Slavery Society, particularly George Thompson, and the organization modeled its activities on similar lines. Understanding the need to mobilize public opinion, Garrison and fellow abolitionist and slave Frederick Douglass embarked on international tours that included Britain, partly to raise funds for their campaigns. Garrison visited Britain in 1833 and 1846 to help in the British antislavery campaign and received great encouragement for his activities in the United States, including his writings in *The Liberator*. He received great acclaim in Britain when he visited in 1867 and 1877, commenting on the **American Civil War**, President **Abraham Lincoln**, and the 13th Amendment to the Constitution that abolished slavery in 1865.

Douglass arrived in Liverpool in August 1845 and spent 18 months traveling around Britain and Ireland, raising the profile of the antislavery movement by delivering hundreds of lectures and enjoying liberties he was not accorded in his home country. His visit also provided him with sufficient personal funds to buy his own freedom on his return home, largely as a result of a donation from a wealthy supporter, Miss Ellen Richardson from Newcastle upon Tyne. He also collected enough money to fund an independent, abolitionist, African American newspaper, the *North Star*, which he founded in 1847.

ACHESON, DEAN (1893–1971). Dean Acheson was American undersecretary of state between 1945 and 1947 and secretary of state between 1949 and 1953. On 21 February 1947, Britain informed the United States that it could no longer afford to provide financial aid to **Greece** and Turkey and urged the administration of **Harry S. Truman** to take over financial responsibility in order to prevent a communist victory in Greece. Acheson was instrumental in persuading the U.S. Congress of the need for immediate American support when he warned them that a success for the communists in Greece would lead to the spread of the "infection" throughout Europe and Africa, like "apples in a barrel infected by one rotten one." On 12 March 1947, the president announced what became known as the **Truman Doctrine**, and persuaded Congress to appropriate funds of $400 million in aid to Greece and Turkey. Acheson was also considered a friend to the British because he had been the original instigator behind the European Recovery Program (**Marshall Plan**) after the end of **World War II** and because he had worked closely with **Ernest Bevin**, British foreign secretary, on the formation of the **North Atlantic Treaty Organization** (NATO). Acheson was later impressed by Britain's military commitment during the **Korean War** (1950–1953). However, in 1962, Acheson appeared to chastise the British for their closeness to the United States when he described Britain in the following terms: "Great Britain has lost an Empire and has not yet found a role. The attempt to play a separate power role— that is, a role apart from Europe, a role based on a '**special relationship**' with the United States, a role based on being the head of a 'Commonwealth' which has no political structure, or unity, or strength and enjoys a fragile and precarious economic relationship— that role is about to be played out." Despite President **John F. Kennedy**'s attempts to distance himself from Acheson's words, they were poorly received in British political circles, partly because he had touched a nerve but also because the government of **Harold Macmillan** suspected it reflected a weakening of the Anglo–American relationship.

ADAMS, CHARLES FRANCIS, SR. (1807–1886). As minister to England between 1861 and 1868, Charles F. Adams was awarded the lesser title of minister rather than ambassador due to a dispute with fellow Massachusetts congressman Charles Summer, also head of the Foreign Relations Committee. Adams was instrumental in maintaining British neutrality during the **American Civil War**. Working with the British minister in Washington, **Lord Lyons**, Adams helped to contain the fallout from incidents such as the *Trent* **affair**, which had threatened war between Britain and the United States.

ADAMS, GERRY (1948–). Gerry Adams is an Irish Republican politician in Northern Ireland who was elected president of Sinn Fein in 1983 and elected as member of Parliament (MP) from West Belfast in the same year. Adams refused to take his seat in Westminster because of the compulsory oath of allegiance to the British queen. Under a ban imposed by Prime Minister **Margaret Thatcher** in 1988, Adams's voice could not be broadcast by the media and his words were commonly read by an actor while his image appeared on screen. The reason for the ban, which applied to all Irish Republican organizations, was to "deny terrorists the oxygen of publicity." The ban received much criticism by organizations advocating freedom of speech and was lifted by Prime Minister **John Major** in 1994. Adams became a central figure in the Northern **Ireland** peace process in the 1990s. In February 1994, President **Bill Clinton** granted Gerry Adams a visa to visit the United States to attend fund-raising events at Irish American societies. Clinton's decision was a reversal of a 20-year U.S. policy of denying his entry and was made against the strenuous objections of the British government, who argued that Adams would take the opportunity to promote the Irish Republican Army (IRA) with Irish Americans. President Clinton denied that he was being "soft on terrorism," instead arguing that by engaging Irish Republicans in debate they could be persuaded to leave violence behind. After the IRA declared a cease-fire in August 1994, President Clinton visited Belfast in November 1995, shaking Adams's hand when they met on the Falls Road. On five occasions Clinton also invited Adams to visit the White House on St. Patrick's Day. Clinton's successor, President **George W. Bush**, continued the policy of speaking directly with Adams over the decommissioning of arms and power-sharing agreements in Northern Ireland, but in the wake of the **September 11** attacks and Sinn Fein's opposition to the war in **Iraq**, the Bush White House preferred telephone conversations rather than face-to-face meetings.

AFGHANISTAN (1979). In December 1979, Soviet forces occupied Afghanistan after nationalist and religious unrest erupted in the country, threatening anarchy in a state bordering the communist superpower. This action was condemned by most Western nations and the border states of India and Pakistan. The United States, under the administration of **Jimmy Carter**, led a call for a boycott of the 1980 Olympic Games due to be held in Moscow. The government of **Margaret Thatcher** in Britain joined the call for a boycott but was defied by the British Olympic Association, which voted to send British competitors to the games.

AFGHANISTAN, INVASION OF (2001). In the wake of the terrorist attacks on **September 11, 2001**, the United States and Great Britain launched a military invasion of Afghanistan on 7 October 2001, beginning with an aerial bombing campaign. Codenamed Operation Enduring Freedom, the invasion marked the beginning of President **George W. Bush**'s "war on terror" and aimed to target Osama bin Laden, the instigator of the 9/11 attacks, his terrorist network al-Qaeda, and the fundamentalist Taliban government in Afghanistan, which was suspected of supporting al-Qaeda and providing the group with a safe haven. Prime Minister **Tony Blair** did not hesitate in offering British military support for the invasion. After the initial stage of the invasion, American and British forces fought alongside forces from Afghanistan's Northern Alliance and received moral and practical support from other coalition nations, including Australia, Bahrain, **Canada**, Denmark, France, Germany, Italy, Japan, Jordan, the Netherlands, New Zealand, Norway, Portugal, Romania, and **Russia**. The joint invasion of Afghanistan also marked a new closeness in the relationship between Blair and Bush.

The war succeeded in removing the Taliban from power but Taliban insurgency continued to thwart efforts to establish a new democratic government. In December 2001, the **United Nations** authorized an International Security Assistance Force (ISAF), led by the **North Atlantic Treaty Organization** (NATO), to assist the Afghan government in its efforts to control and reconstruct the country. In October 2006, ISAF took over command of international military forces in eastern Afghanistan from the U.S.-led coalition. In 2007, the United States had 26,000 troops in Afghanistan—the highest of the war—and Great Britain still had approximately 7,000 troops there. In August 2007, the first **friendly fire incident** in Afghanistan marred Anglo–American cooperation in Afghanistan when three British soldiers were killed while on patrol in the Helmand province after a U.S. F-15 bombed the convoy.

ALABAMA **CLAIMS.** The *Alabama* claims were a major source of tension between Great Britain and the United States in the aftermath of the **American Civil War**. During the war, the British had built warships (disguised as merchant ships in order to get around Britain's official neutrality), including the *Alabama*, for the Confederate forces. These cruisers inflicted great damage on the U.S. merchant marine, sinking around 150 Northern ships. When the war was over, the United States claimed compensation from the British for violating its neutrality, for the loss of its ships, and also for prolonging the war by enabling the Confederates to undertake commerce raiding. Although some initial estimates of the costs incurred to the United States were as high as $2 billion, the government of William Gladstone eventually agreed to pay $15.5 million in damages in 1872. The settlement of the *Alabama* claims came after the establishment of an international tribunal in Geneva, Switzerland.

ALASKAN BOUNDARY DISPUTE. In the 19th century, the boundary between **Canada** (a British dominion) and the Alaskan panhandle was poorly defined and a serious dispute over the matter started when gold was discovered in 1896 along the Klondike River. In the early 1900s, Great Britain chose to back the United States rather than Canada on this issue after it was referred to international arbitration. Settlement of this dispute was seen as a positive development in Anglo–American relations and reflective of the "**great rapprochement**" between the two nations. *See also* BERING SEA DISPUTE.

ALBRIGHT, MADELEINE (1937–). Madeleine Albright served as the first woman U.S. secretary of state from 1997 to 2001, thus becoming the highest ranking woman in the history of the U.S. government at that time. Albright had earlier served as U.S. ambassador to the **United Nations**, 1993–1997. During her time as secretary of state in the second administration of **William Clinton**, Anglo–American relations improved noticeably. Although Albright spent time in Britain during **World War II**, she did not appear to have any special affection for the country but did appear to share the ethical worldview of the British foreign secretary, **Robin Cook**. Their mutual abhorrence of ethnic apartheid was a factor in the more proactive policy of the United States and Great Britain toward **Bosnia** and **Kosovo**. On 30 June 1997 Albright also announced that she would, along with Cook, boycott the Chinese ceremony to mark the transfer of **Hong Kong** to Chinese sovereignty.

AMERICAN BASES IN BRITAIN. The United States has maintained a number of military bases in Great Britain since **World War II**. Because of the secrecy surrounding the issue, the exact number of bases has been difficult to determine and has changed over time. In the mid-1980s—with the **Cold War** still ongoing—it was estimated that there could be as many as 135 American military bases in Britain; most of these were facilities that were used by the U.S. armed forces but 25 were major operational bases or military headquarters. There are currently 12 active U.S. Air Force in Europe (USAFE) bases in Great Britain.

The establishment of the major bases began during **World War II** and grew with the **Berlin blockade** crisis in 1948 when **Ernest Bevin**, British foreign secretary, asked the administration of **Harry S. Truman** to send B-29 bomber groups to Britain. **James Forrestal**, U.S. secretary of defense, had been planning for a permanent air force base in Britain and the Royal Air Force (RAF) had begun preparing some of its bases for a U.S. bomber presence. Bevin's request was encouraged by Washington and the decision to invite the United States to station the bombers in Britain was made in secret on 28 June 1948 by Prime Minister **Clement Attlee** and a small group of ministers, including Bevin, Herbert Morrison, A. V. Alexander, and the chiefs of staff. These planes could carry atomic bombs and reach Moscow from Britain. In July 1948, the National Security Council agreed to send 60 bombers to three RAF stations in East Anglia, and the first American Air Strategic Command on British soil was established at RAF Lakenheath. The agreement was formalized later in 1949. Although Bevin was pleased with this decision—as it ensured an American commitment to the defense of Europe—this act was extremely controversial, not least because the British government did not report the matter to Parliament. U.S. Air Force bases were established at Mildenhall, **Greenham Common**, Upper Heyford, Brize Norton, and Fairford in 1950, and the B-29 bombers were then fitted to carry nuclear weapons. As Britain became a base for a U.S. nuclear attack on the Soviet Union, it placed itself in the frontline of any future nuclear war. One of the major points of controversy was the issue of a British government veto on the use of American nuclear weapons from British bases.

In addition to air force bases, the United States also maintains communications and intelligence bases in the United Kingdom, including NSA Menwith Hill. The American presence has been the focus of protests by groups such as the **Campaign for Nuclear Disarmament** (CND), and the secrecy surrounding the bases is currently challenged by the Campaign for the Accountability of American Bases. *See also* ATOMIC BOMB; COLD WAR.

AMERICAN CIVIL WAR (1861–1865). After decades of tension between the largely antislavery Northern states and the proslavery Southern states, war broke out on 12 April 1861 between the Union forces of the United States of America, led by President **Abraham Lincoln**, and the Confederate forces, led by President Jefferson Davis of the secessionist Southern states. The Civil War lasted four years, ending on 9 April 1865 with the surrender of the Confederate army. At the beginning of the war, it was clear that the Union had a military advantage over the Confederacy due to its industrial base, its strength in numbers, and the ability of its navy to blockade the South in order to stifle its economy. The position taken by external powers was, therefore, of real importance. During the American Civil War, Great Britain adopted a position of neutrality. Declared officially by the government of Lord Palmerston on 13 May 1861, British neutrality was a disappointment to both sides in the conflict.

Confederate leaders assumed that Southern cotton was of such importance to the British economy that this would ensure London's support; many Southerners began to embargo shipments of cotton to Europe in the hope of prompting British or French intervention in the war. Although British cotton mills and the textile industry, particularly in Lancashire, imported 80 percent of their cotton from the American South, "cotton diplomacy" as it became known, proved to be less of a consideration due to a bumper crop in 1860 that ensured European warehouses had a good supply of cotton. Later in the war, as Northern blockades of Southern ports became effective, British manufacturers turned to other sources for the crop, including Egypt and India. Nevertheless, by early 1862 the blockade of Southern ports by the Northern navy led to a "cotton famine" as the supply of raw cotton dried up and, waiting for cotton prices to rise still further, wealthy merchants refused to release the warehoused stock of cotton. Mills in and around Manchester, England, began to close and textile workers lost their jobs and were forced to ask for poor law relief. Despite this, many of the workers pledged their support to the Union cause during a famous meeting at the Free Trade Hall in December 1863, and Lincoln acknowledged this personally in January 1864. In other ways, the impact of the American Civil War on the British economy proved positive. Noticeably, British arms manufacturers received a boost as they produced armaments and ships for the conflict and Britain's North American colonies provided agricultural produce and manufactured goods to the Union. The Confederacy nevertheless put pressure on the British government, particularly in 1861 and 1862, to recognize them diplomatically and to consider intervention in the war. The prime minister, British Foreign Secretary Lord John Russell, and Chancellor of the Exchequer William Gladstone were sympathetic to the Confederate case and would have had no objection to the growing power of the United States being curtailed. However, they were well aware that official recognition of the Confederacy would lead to war with the Union as President Lincoln had threatened that any foreign intervention would bring war with the United States. Northerners were equally dismayed at British neutrality. Although the moral issues surrounding slavery had not been highlighted by the Union as the reason for war, its leaders expected Britain—as a country that had abolished slavery throughout its empire by 1833—to have some sympathy for its cause. In late 1861, the *Trent* **affair**—in which the British ship *Trent* was seized by the USS

San Jacinto in international waters—threatened to bring Britain into the conflict on the side of the Confederacy, but the emergency was diffused by the diplomatic efforts of **Charles F. Adams**, minister to England, and **Lord Lyons**, British envoy in Washington.

Relations between Britain and the United States remained strained and, fearing that the Union might invade **Canada**, Britain sent 11,000 troops to protect its North American colony. The war thus increased London's concerns over maintaining Canada's security in the long term and fueled the move toward independence in 1867. As the war went on, the North's effective diplomacy reminded the British government of its abhorrence of slavery, and British public opinion began to support the North. British behavior during the war was nevertheless perceived as helping the South, particularly the use of British dockyards to build Confederate ships. The fallout from this issue dragged on until 1872 when a tribunal in Geneva ruled that Britain should pay damages of $15.5 million to the United States. The Confederate government also made efforts to purchase an entire fleet of warships from the British that had originally been sold to China and, as they were reliant on British goods such as arms and armament, were supplied via the Bahamas and Bermuda in an attempt to evade the U.S. naval blockade. Despite not entering the war, an estimated 50,000 British troops fought in the war on both sides, although most fought for the Confederacy. *See also* ABOLITION; *ALABAMA* CLAIMS; BRITISH NORTH AMERICA ACT; *SHENANDOAH*.

AMERICAN COMMITTEE ON A UNITED EUROPE (ACUE). The American Committee on a United Europe was established in 1948 by leading figures in the U.S. intelligence community to encourage political integration in Europe in order to fight the communist threat in Europe. Great Britain, in particular, was seen as an obstacle to the achievement of such unity. Based in New York, the ACUE's first chairman was General William J. Donovan, former head of the wartime Office of Strategic Services, and its vice-chairman was Allen Dulles, director of the Central Intelligence Agency (CIA). Although a private organization with private donors, much of its funding came from the CIA. In its attempts to persuade European public opinion of the desirability of a united Europe, the ACUE funded the European Movement, partly at the behest of former prime minister and leader of the Conservative Party **Winston Churchill**, who traveled to New York in March 1949 to appeal for financial support. It is estimated the ACUE donated up to $4 million to the European Movement in the early 1950s, although its members were unaware of the source of this funding. The ACUE was defunct by 1960, three years after the signing of the Treaty of Rome that established the **European Economic Community** (EEC).

AMERICAN DECLARATION OF INDEPENDENCE (1776). The founding document of the United States of America in which the 13 colonies—Connecticut, Delaware, Georgia, Maryland, Massachusetts, New Hampshire, New Jersey, New York, North Carolina, Pennsylvania, Rhode Island, South Carolina, and Virginia—declared their independence from Great Britain at the Second Continental Congress in Philadelphia. The Declaration was drafted by **Thomas Jefferson** between 11 and 26 June 1776 and was adopted on 4 July 1776. *See also* WAR OF INDEPENDENCE.

AMERICAN STUDIES. American studies developed as an academic discipline after 1945. The term "American studies" is taken to embrace the history, government and politics, economics, sociology, geography, literature, and culture of the United States. The British Association for American Studies (BAAS) was founded in 1955 by a group of British university lecturers. BAAS aims to promote and encourage the study of the United States within universities, colleges, and schools in the United Kingdom and has played an important part in the growth and popularity of American studies in Great Britain as an academic discipline through conferences, publications, and advocacy.

ANGLO–AMERICAN LEAGUE. In July 1898, a group of **Anglo–Saxonists** from Great Britain and America met in London and founded the Anglo–American League. Organized with the purpose of securing "cordial and constant cooperation" and stressing the blood ties between the two nations, it was chaired by British Liberal MP James Bryce and had members in major cities in the United States and Great Britain. The league appears to have hosted large annual banquets of leading American and British elites in order to foster improved Anglo–American relations.

ANGLO–AMERICAN LOAN AGREEMENT (1945). In the aftermath of **World War II**, Great Britain faced the mammoth task of reconstruction, needed money to import food to feed a nation weary of wartime rationing, and faced a £5 billion balance of payments deficit. At the end of the war, the United States announced it was ending its **Lend-Lease** system that had provided Britain with financial and military aid during the war. Consequently Britain had little choice but to negotiate a loan from the United States to help revitalize the struggling British economy. In the autumn of 1945, British economist **John Maynard Keynes** was sent to Washington to head the British negotiating team and faced William Clayton of the State Department and Fred Vinson of the Treasury Department. Initially, the British hoped for an American gift, or a part loan, but the United States was in a position to dictate the terms. Discussions lasted three months until an agreement was reached on 6 December 1945 that the United States would lend Britain $3.75 billion. The loan terms were advantageous for the British at a fixed rate of 2 percent to be repaid over a 50-year period. At the time, however, many in British circles felt this was harsh treatment considering the sacrifices made during the war and in contrast to the easier credit that Lend-Lease represented. There were heated discussions in the British Parliament where the Conservative Party in the House of Commons (by then Her Majesty's Opposition) took a clearly anti-American stance. The last payment on the loan was made on 31 December 2006.

ANGLO–AMERICAN TRADE AGREEMENT (1938). On 17 November 1938, the United States and Great Britain signed a **trade** treaty that demonstrated closer economic cooperation between the two countries and an increased commitment to the liberalization of trade. Prior to the agreement, the United States was concerned about British discrimination against American goods, particularly as Britain was its most valuable trading partner. During the 1930s, Britain's trade within its empire was increasing and Washington, particularly Secretary of State **Cordell Hull**, came to see Britain's system of **imperial preference** (lower tariffs for those within the empire) as a major contributor to the dire situation of American farmers. In addition, Hull believed that economic nationalism was at the forefront of world instability and consequently argued for the lowering of tariffs and trade barriers. The agreement saw Britain make concessions on many American agricultural products, including the removal of duties on wheat, lard, and some fruit juices and the reduction of duties on many others. In return, the United States reduced its tariffs on high-grade cotton, wool, pottery, glassware, and leather products. The agreement was seen as a major step forward in boosting trade between the two countries.

ANGLO–BOER WAR (1899–1902). At the height of **Anglo–Saxonism**—the concept of racial superiority that allowed Great Britain and the United States to justify their empires—both nations were faced with colonial revolt. For the United States, this resulted in the Philippine–American War; for Britain, it was the South African War or the Anglo–Boer War. Leaders on both sides of the Atlantic felt it necessary to intervene to expand their empires and argued that the territories they eventually secured were incapable of statehood. To protect its gold and diamond mining interests in South Africa and to secure the southern end of its British African empire, Britain went to war with the Boer (Dutch) republics of the Transvaal and Orange Free State led by Paul Kruger. The Boers feared the mass influx of British and other foreign prospectors who poured into the Transvaal after the discovery of gold in the area in 1886. The population of Johannesburg had reached more than 100,000 by 1896 but included only a small percentage of white Boer citizens. Refusing the new arrivals any voting rights and placing high tax burdens on the speculators, the Boers tried to prevent British encroachment on their territory. In December 1895, more than 500 British adventurers attempted to seize control of the Boer republics by force and, although the unofficial coup failed, it served to convince the Boers that the British were determined to annex their territory into the British Empire. In October 1899, after the Boers and the British government refused to negotiate further over full equality for British citizens in the Transvaal, war broke out. Despite being outnumbered by the British forces by nearly five to one, the Boers, who were determined to remain independent, were not defeated until May 1902.

The U.S. government, led by President William McKinley, remained neutral on the Anglo–Boer war, although it did issue many pro-British statements. The "yellow press," including the newspapers of William Randolph Hearst, supported the British. There were, however, dissenting voices in the United States. Public opinion in the United States, and in most of Europe, was largely pro-Boer and anti-British, especially as reports of British brutality in their suppression of the Boers were published in the newspapers. Indeed, some Americans volunteered to fight with the Boers against the British. As a result, for the last time, Britain held Americans as prisoners of war. Discussions over their imprisonment led to diplomatic tension between London and Washington and the issue was not resolved until October 1902 when British Foreign Secretary Lord Lansdowne let U.S. Secretary of State **John Hay** know that the Americans would be repatriated.

ANGLOPHILE. Anglophile is a term used to describe non-English people who admire all things English. The term has also been used as a term of abuse, describing those people who are unduly sycophantic toward the British. In the United States, Anglophilia has usually outweighed **Anglophobia**, especially on the East Coast and among those of British descent, including the White, Anglo–Saxon, Protestant (WASP) elements who dominated the political life of the United States in the 19th and 20th centuries.

ANGLOPHOBE. Anglophobe is a term used to describe people who dislike or fear all things English. The first known use of the word "Anglophobia" came in a letter from **Thomas Jefferson** to James Madison in May 1793 and its origins lay in the antipathy felt by many Americans for monarchies and aristocracies, and for King **George III** and **Lord North** in particular. Other factors undoubtedly contributed to the growth of Anglophobia in the United States, including a dislike of British imperialism and economic power and the influence of British manners and culture. Anglophobia reached its height during the **Venezuelan boundary dispute** of 1895 but was also a feature of the years between the two world wars, when American isolationists were suspicious of British attempts to engage the United States in European politics. Certain ethnic groups in the United States have been more prone to Anglophobia, noticeably Irish Americans and German Americans, but at certain times most political groups have engaged in a certain degree of Anglophobia. Anglophobia declined during and after **World War II** as the United States developed a closer allied relationship with Great Britain. *See also* ANTI-AMERICANISM IN BRITAIN; WORLD WAR I.

ANGLO–SAXONISM. By the late 19th century, the United States and Great Britain were becoming geopolitical rivals. The rapid industrialization of the United States in the latter half of the 19th century had led more and more Americans to engage in foreign activities. America's foreign **trade** and overseas investment increased markedly in these years and the nation's prosperity became increasingly dependent on foreign markets. At the same time, prominent elites and intellectuals on both sides of the Atlantic, including American philosopher John Fiske and Congregational clergyman Josiah Strong, promoted and popularized the racial theory of "Anglo–Saxonism." Tapping into the American belief in their "manifest destiny" and Social Darwinist theories of "the survival of the fittest," Anglo–Saxonists believed the English-speaking peoples were racially superior and it was the "**white man's burden**" to uplift and civilize other ethnic groups. In the United States, this was partly in response to the fear surrounding a mass influx of immigrants from southern and eastern Europe and Asia, who were neither English speaking nor Protestants. Between 1870 and 1900, almost 12 million immigrants arrived in the United States, many of them from outside of western Europe. The threat to the dominant white Anglo–Saxon Protestant (WASP) supremacy led many upper- and middle-class Americans to draw closer to their cousins in Britain in an attempt to preserve Anglo–Saxon supremacy not only in the United States but also around the world. Anglo–Saxonism was used to legitimate calls to limit immigration into the United States and justified the Anglo–American drive for empire in the late 19th and early 20th century. It also provides a partial explanation for the "**great rapprochement**" between the United States and Great Britain at the end of the 19th century. Elites on both sides of the Atlantic formed groups to foster the Anglo–Saxon alliance, including the **Anglo–American League** (1898) and the **Pilgrims Society** (1902). *See also* SPANISH–AMERICAN WAR; THEODORE ROOSVELT.

ANGLOSPHERE. Anglosphere is a contemporary term used to describe the English-speaking nations dominated by the United States in the cultural, economic, and political sphere.

ANNENBERG, WALTER (1908–2002). An American media tycoon and philanthropist, Walter Annenberg was U.S. ambassador to Great Britain during the presidency of **Richard Nixon** (1969–1974). He helped smooth relations between Nixon and British Conservative Prime Minister **Edward Heath**, who placed less value on the Anglo–American relationship than his predecessors. In 1974, as Nixon was facing impeachment over the Watergate scandal, Annenberg helped shelve a proposed presidential visit to London after the government of **Harold Wilson** indicated it might prove embarrassing to the queen. He was made a Knights Commander of the Order of the British Empire (KBE) and is credited with introducing **Ronald Reagan** to **Margaret Thatcher**.

ANTI-AMERICANISM IN BRITAIN. Anti-American sentiment has been present in Great Britain since the settlement of the United States. It is characterized by an opposition to U.S. values, culture, and policies. Over the centuries, anti-Americanism in Britain has peaked over specific incidents but has also been connected to a fear of the pervasive influence of American culture on British life, a culture viewed as morally bankrupt and overly commercialized. In the post-1945 period, the focus of much of British anti-Americanism has been U.S. foreign policy, noticeably over the stationing of U.S. forces and bases on British soil, and over the **Vietnam War** and the **Iraq War**. *See also* AMERICAN BASES IN BRITAIN.

ANZUS. This mutual defense treaty was signed in September 1951 by Australia, New Zealand, and the United States and recognized that the United States was the dominant Pacific power. The formation of ANZUS was a response to the fall of **China** to communism in 1949, the outbreak of the **Korean War** in 1950, and the United States' lenient peace treaty with the Japanese (after **World War II**) in order to use Japan as a regional force against communism. Cautious about the rise of Japan, and despite **United Nations** membership, Australia and New Zealand desired a powerful ally that was capable of taking over Britain's role as protector. For the United States the treaty formalized the role they had played during and since World War II and was part of a series of alliances aimed at containing communism. The British government was concerned at being left out of a pact that involved its major ally and involving two countries with whom it had traditionally close relations, and was relieved to be involved in the **South-East Asia Treaty Organization** (SEATO) of 1954. *See also* COLD WAR.

APPEASEMENT. In the 1930s, Great Britain and the United States were slow to react to world events. The rise of expansionist and dictatorial powers in Europe and Asia was watched carefully in London and Washington, but neither country was willing to intervene when Japan invaded Manchuria in 1931, when Adolf Hitler came to power in Germany in 1933, when he rearmed and outlined his plans for an Aryan empire, or when Italian dictator Benito Mussolini invaded Ethiopia in 1935. Britain and the United States were dealing with severe economic depressions in the 1930s that had led to high levels of unemployment, and in the aftermath of **World War I** congressional politics in the United States were firmly isolationist, and the nation was militarily unprepared for overseas action. In relation to events in Europe, the Conservative government in Britain followed a policy of appeasement. In an attempt to avoid another world war, the government headed by Prime Minister **Neville Chamberlain** (1937–1940) attempted to appease Nazi Germany by making concessions and agreeing to deal with its grievances, most of which stemmed from the **Treaty of Versailles** signed after the end of **World War I**. Chamberlain allowed Germany to annex the German-populated Sudetenland area of Czechoslovakia in the **Munich Agreement** of 1938. This did not prevent Germany from invading Poland in 1939 and the subsequent British declaration of war against Germany in September 1939. Appeasement was duly discredited in both Britain and America.

ARAB–ISRAELI WAR (1967). In the months prior to the Arab–Israeli War of June 1967—also known as the Six-Day War—both Great Britain and the United States had supported Israel through regular, secret arms shipments. On 2 June 1967, British Prime Minister Harold Wilson met with President Lyndon Johnson in Washington and discussed ways to avoid the impending war, looking in particular at ways in which the Egyptians might be forced to open the Straits of Tiran, which they had closed on 22 May, to Israeli shipping. When Israel launched a preemptive attack against Egypt, Syria, and Jordan on 5 June 1967 and took land from all three, the United States and Great Britain sided with Israel. The United States put its Sixth Fleet on alert to defend Israel if it became necessary and the Wilson government was noticeably more cooperative than the government of Edward Heath during the Yom Kippur War in 1973, agreeing to allow the Israelis to transport arms and military vehicles from Britain through Royal Air Force (RAF) airfields. *See also* ARAB–ISRAELI WAR (1973).

ARAB–ISRAELI WAR (1973). On 6 October 1973, on the Jewish holiday known as Yom Kippur (thus the war is often referred to as the October War or Yom Kippur War), Egypt and Syria led a military assault on Israel in an attempt to avenge their defeat in the **Arab–Israeli War of 1967**. Great Britain and America clashed in their response to the crisis. The United States feared an imminent defeat for Israel—a key ally in the Middle East—and began to organize an airlift of supplies to aid them. Britain, along with its European partners, preferred to take an "even-handed" approach and not side with either Israel or the Arab states, partly due to the recognition that 80 percent of Europe's oil imports came from the Middle East and a consequent desire not to antagonize the Arab-dominated Organization of Petroleum Exporting Countries (OPEC). Washington had hoped to use **North Atlantic Treaty Organization** bases in its airlift operation but only Portugal and the Netherlands agreed. Believing the crisis was out of the NATO region, Britain refused, in private, to allow the United States to use its bases. Within weeks Israeli had achieved a military advantage and the prospect of a major military disaster for Egypt prompted the **Soviet Union** into considering intervention in the war.

The prospect of a superpower conflict led the United States to move its military forces to a state of alert, DEFCON III, on 24 October; although the United States informed the British of this action before its other European allies, this did little to reduce Anglo–American tensions. Much to Washington's annoyance, the government of **Edward Heath** refused to use its influence to convince the rest of Europe of the wisdom of American action and in Britain the decision to go to DEFCON III renewed anxiety in London about **American bases in Britain** and the lack of consultation with the British before putting nuclear forces on alert. American frustration with the British over the Arab–Israeli War (that ended in a cease-fire on 26 October) led to a temporary stop in intelligence sharing with the British. In the longer term, disagreements over the crisis left the United States, particularly **Henry Kissinger**, asking questions about reciprocity within NATO and Britain feeling indignant at being used in superpower politics without full consultation.

ARCADIA CONFERENCE (1941–1942). Just two weeks after the Japanese attack on **Pearl Harbor**, Prime Minister **Winston Churchill** and President **Franklin D. Roosevelt** held their second wartime meeting in Washington, D.C. (codenamed ARCADIA). On hearing the news of Pearl Harbor, Churchill began arranging to visit Washington to ensure his voice was heard in the debate over the immediate focus of the U.S. war effort. The prime minister was well aware that many in Washington, including the American navy, were urging Roosevelt to concentrate U.S. forces on the war in the Pacific, while leaving the battle of the Atlantic to the British. Meeting over Christmas (22 December 1941 to 14 January 1942), the two leaders and their staff agreed that the priority should be to defeat Germany first and postpone a full-scale war in the Pacific. Once a "Germany first" strategy had been adopted, approval was given for the invasion of North Africa. During the three weeks of the conference, and at the suggestion of General **George C. Marshall**, the U.S. Army's chief of staff, British and American military leaders agreed to establish a Combined Chiefs of Staff (CCS) to jointly plan war strategy. The Arcadia Conference marked a new closeness in Anglo–American relations, not least between Roosevelt and Churchill, whose personal relationship became increasingly warm during the lengthy and intense discussions in Washington. Roosevelt dispatched the first American GIs to the British Isles in the weeks following Arcadia.

ARGENTINA. *See* FALKLANDS ISLANDS.

AROOSTOCK WAR. The Aroostock War was a bloodless border clash between the United States and **Canada** (then part of the British Empire) in the winter of 1838–1839. The **Treaty of Paris** (1783) had failed to determine the exact boundaries between the district of Maine and the British colony of New Brunswick in Canada, and in the winter of 1838 lumberjacks from both sides of the disputed area clashed as the British attempted to build a road in the area. The militias of Maine and New Brunswick were called out and the U.S. Congress authorized the mobilization of 50,000 troops and appropriated $10 million to the conflict. Despite this, no shots were fired as General Winfield Scott was sent by the United States to persuade the New Brunswick representatives that full-scale war could break out. Both sides participated in a commission, whose findings provided the basis of the 1842 **Webster–Ashburton Treaty** that resolved the affair. This dispute is often referred to as the Northern boundary dispute or the Pork and Beans War.

ASTOR, VISCOUNTESS NANCY (1879–1964). Born in Danville, Virginia, divorcée Nancy Witcher Langhorne moved to England in 1905 and married her second husband, a fellow American expatriate Waldorf Astor, 2nd Viscount Astor. Lady Nancy Astor was one of many American women from wealthy families who found titled husbands in England during this time. At the turn of the 20th century, the Astors were attuned to the thinking of fellow **Anglo–Saxonists** in advocating an alliance of English-speaking peoples and an expansion of the British Empire. She served as the first female member of Parliament in the House of Commons, representing the constituency of Plymouth Sutton (vacated after her husband became the 2nd Lord Astor and became a member of the House of Lords). Elected on 29 November 1919, Lady Astor served in Parliament until 1945. Although she had an undistinguished career as an MP, she was well known in Anglo–American circles, not least because of her witty exchanges with **Winston Churchill**, who did not appreciate having a female in Parliament.

ATLANTIC CHARTER (1941). Issued on 14 August 1941, the Atlantic Charter was a declaration signed by Prime Minister **Winston Churchill** and President **Franklin D. Roosevelt** and publicized after their secret meeting at Placentia Bay, Newfoundland. The United States had not yet entered **World War II** but was keen to ensure the British did not make secret peace agreements. Churchill agreed to sign the charter hoping to encourage U.S. entry to the war and welcoming a public show of common interests between Great Britain and the United States. The Atlantic Charter was an agreed-upon set of principles that would shape the peace settlement and included a commitment to the freedom of the seas, self-determination, free government, liberal and Open Door economic policies, and the creation of a permanent security system. Churchill chose to view the principle of self-determination to be concerned with enemy-occupied countries and not relating to the peoples of the British Empire. Roosevelt, on the other hand, made it clear to Churchill that world peace could only be achieved through the end of British colonialism. Considering the desperate situation Britain faced during the war, Churchill was not in a position to argue and signed the charter reluctantly. Historians have considered the Atlantic Charter a "smokescreen" for the war planning that Churchill and Roosevelt engaged in during the **Atlantic Conference**, at a time when the United States was still officially neutral and American public opinion was still against a U.S. declaration of war against Germany. The Atlantic Charter served as forerunner to the Declaration of the **United Nations** on 1 January 1942. By its demonstration of Anglo–American unity against totalitarianism, the declaration of the Atlantic Charter served to boost British morale during one of the most difficult phases of the war. News of the charter also encouraged nationalists around the globe in their struggle for independence.

ATLANTIC CONFERENCE (1941). Between 9 and 12 August 1941, Prime Minister **Winston Churchill** and President **Franklin D. Roosevelt** and their staffs met on board the USS *Augusta* and HMS *Prince of Wales* at Ship Harbor, Placentia Bay, off the coast of Newfoundland. Considered the first summit meeting of **World War II**, this was also the first personal meeting between Churchill and Roosevelt in over 20 years. Although the United States was not yet a belligerent in the Second World War, the secret summit meeting was arranged so that Roosevelt and Churchill could discuss the general strategy to be adopted in the war against the Axis powers, especially given that Germany had attacked the Soviet Union on 30 June. During the conference, Roosevelt agreed to increase aid to England through the **Lend-Lease** program, military staff discussed strategy, and the two leaders declared the **Atlantic Charter**. The Atlantic Conference laid the foundations for the wartime alliance and the two leaders—the "Big Two"—agreed to meet on a regular basis.

ATLANTIC NUCLEAR FORCE (ANF). In December 1964, Prime Minister **Harold Wilson** proposed an Atlantic Nuclear Force as an alternative to the **Multilateral Force** (MLF), an American proposal for a nuclear surface fleet manned by crews of mixed nationality. The MLF had been formulated in order to deal with German interest in joining the nuclear club and U.S. hostility to a European independent deterrent. Wilson and his defense secretary, **Denis Healey**, worked on an alternative that might satisfy American objectives: an ANF. This proposal envisaged British and U.S. nuclear submarines, as well as mixed-manned land-based Minuteman missiles in the United States and V-bomber squadrons, incorporated into a new command structure of participants under the umbrella of the existing **North Atlantic Treaty Organization**. For the British, ANF avoided the increased costs of establishing a new surface fleet. Within a year, plans for an ANF were shelved. During a meeting in December 1964, Wilson persuaded President **Lyndon Johnson** to consider ANF as a viable alternative to the MLF, although both schemes were shelved shortly afterward.

ATOMIC BOMB. Development of the atomic bomb was initially a secret collaborative venture between the United States and Great Britain. In 1940, two refugee physicists at Birmingham University discovered that it was possible to use nuclear fission to develop a new powerful weapon of war. Believing it might be available in time for use in **World War II**, in September 1941 British Prime **Winston Churchill** agreed that the weapon should be developed as soon as possible. At the same time, American scientists were also working on nuclear fission and President **Franklin D. Roosevelt** asked Churchill to consider a joint Anglo–American effort. As the United States had not yet entered the war, Churchill declined but agreed that scientists in both countries should share their knowledge. At their **Hyde Park meeting** in December 1941, Churchill and Roosevelt agreed that Britain and America should be "equal partners" in nuclear research. By mid-1942, it had become apparent to the British that the U.S. nuclear project—the **Manhattan Project**—had pulled ahead of the British one (codenamed the Tube Alloys project) and Churchill asked Roosevelt to consider full cooperation between the two. General Leslie Groves, director of the Manhattan Project, could not see any advantage in this for the Americans, and for many months the British received little information from the Manhattan scientists.

The situation changed during a meeting between Churchill and Roosevelt in 1943 when the two leaders signed the **Quebec Agreement**. The nuclear partnership was resumed on an equal basis and it was agreed that it should continue after the end of World War II. Britain had to confirm that it did not intend to use the research to develop nuclear energy for commercial purposes and, due to British financial constraints and the war in Europe, the United States agreed to develop the bomb, eventually spending over $2 billion to do so. After Quebec, British scientists were based at the American research laboratories at Los Alamos, New Mexico. The first nuclear device was detonated at Alamogordo in the New Mexico desert on 16 July 1945 and the first uranium bomb, codenamed "Little Boy," was dropped on Hiroshima on 6 August 1945, killing at least 90,000 Japanese civilians. A second bomb was dropped three days later on Nagasaki, and Japan surrendered on 14 August 1945. Britain was consulted over the decision to drop the bomb but only after the decision was taken. With the end of the war, the United States ended nuclear cooperation with the British, formalized by Congress through the passage of the **McMahon Act** in August 1946. This decision was perceived as a betrayal by the British government, leading them to develop their own atomic bomb, successfully tested at Monte Bello on 3 October 1952.

ATTLEE, CLEMENT R. (1883–1967). Clement Attlee was British Labour prime minister between 1945 and 1951, and was then leader of the Opposition until 1955. Attlee replaced **Winston Churchill** at the **Potsdam Conference** when the Labour government won the general election on 26 July 1945. The Labour government had been elected on a program that included state control of the country's resources, the construction of a welfare state, and the nationalization of major industries, and while all of these commitments placed a financial burden on British's troubled economy, Clement Attlee was determined that Great Britain should not lose its status as a leading world power. He publicly declared his belief that the United States saw things in black and white, while the British saw matters in shades of gray. This view—that the United States needed the wise counsel of the British—guided much of his government's foreign policy. He was quickly faced with harsh realities when the United States ended **Lend-Lease** abruptly after the end of the war in Europe and he was forced to send **Lord Keynes** to Washington to negotiate a loan to enable Britain to survive and reconstruct. Despite the closeness of the wartime alliance, Attlee also found that President **Harry S. Truman** and the U.S. Congress no longer wanted to share nuclear secrets with the British. He visited Washington in November 1945, meeting with Truman and Secretary of State James F. Byrnes. To ensure Britain's security and prestige on the world stage, the Labour prime minister approved the research and development of Britain's own **atomic bomb**.

It was clear by early 1947 that the relationship between Britain and the United States was increasingly being tested. In that year, there were noticeable tensions between Attlee and Truman when the president encouraged more Jewish immigration to **Palestine**. Attlee also had little choice but to inform Truman that Britain could no longer afford to fund the anticommunist battle in **Greece** and Turkey, forcing the president to outline the **Truman Doctrine** and ask Congress to appropriate funds for the United States to take over. The **Marshall Plan** aid that began to arrive in Britain in 1948 helped heal a breach that had developed between Britain and America in the early postwar years, although Attlee was suspicious that the Truman administration was pushing an integrationist agenda in Europe. He was, however, enthusiastic about cooperating with the United States on the formation of the **North Atlantic Treaty Organization** (NATO). The **Korean War** saw another occasion to work with the United States, and Attlee was keen to do so. When Truman appeared to suggest that the United States might use nuclear weapons in Korea, Attlee was urged by members of Parliament to fly to Washington to discuss the matter with the president. At this meeting Attlee gained reassurance that the United States was not considering using atomic weapons in Korea and would consult with Britain before doing so. Attlee's concern was linked to a key difference between himself and Truman over policy toward communist **China**. Unlike President Truman, Attlee took an accommodationist approach toward the People's Republic of China and was willing to admit the new government to the **United Nations**. *See also* ANGLO–AMERICAN LOAN AGREEMENT; McMAHON ACT.

– B –

BAGHDAD PACT (1955). In 1955, Great Britain, **Iran**, **Iraq**, Pakistan, and Turkey signed a Middle East security agreement known as the Baghdad Pact. Aimed at defending the Middle East from invasion by the **Soviet Union**, it became known as the Central Treaty Organization (CENTO) after 1959. The United States became an associate member in 1959. *See also* COLD WAR.

BAKER III, JAMES A. (1930–). James Baker served as U.S. secretary of the treasury between 1985 and 1988 and was secretary of state from 1989 to 1992 under President **George H. W. Bush**. As secretary of state, Baker helped to organize coalition forces during the **Gulf War** of 1991. It was believed that Baker was suspicious of the close personal relationship British Prime Minister **Margaret Thatcher** enjoyed with President **Ronald Reagan** and viewed her as an outdated cold warrior and anti-German, and initially wanted to mark the Bush administration as being different from its predecessor by creating distance between the "Iron Lady" and President Bush. Much to British unease, Baker was instrumental in Washington's attempts to manage and accelerate European integration and led negotiations that resulted in the **Transatlantic Declaration** of November 1990. The Iraqi invasion of Kuwait in August 1990 and Thatcher's decisive support of President Bush's hard-line response led Baker to appreciate the benefits of a strong Anglo–American relationship, especially as he worked with the British to gain a **United Nations** resolution to take military action in the Gulf. In 2006, Baker cochaired the Iraq Study Group. *See also* BAKER–HAMILTON COMMISSION; GULF WAR (1991); IRAQ WAR.

BAKER–HAMILTON COMMISSION (2006). In March 2006, former secretary of state **James A. Baker** and former Democratic Representative Lee Hamilton were appointed by the U.S. Congress to cochair the **Iraq** Study Group, a bipartisan group of Americans whose function was to conduct an independent investigation into the situation regarding the **Iraq War** and to offer policy recommendations. The Baker–Hamilton Commission collected information on Iraq from a variety of sources, including the British. The commission spoke with the British ambassador to the United States, **Sir David Manning**. It issued a final report on 6 December 2006 arguing that U.S. policy in Iraq was not working and recommending the United States should not increase its military commitment there but instead increase its diplomatic efforts in the region.

BALFOUR, ARTHUR J. (1848–1930). Arthur Balfour served as British prime minister between 1902 and 1905. As British secretary of state for foreign affairs he made the first official visit to the United States by a member of the British cabinet in April 1914. The visit marked an improvement in Anglo–American relations. Balfour also informed Washington about the **Zimmerman telegram** and was a British representative at the **Paris Peace Conference** in 1919 and at the **League of Nations** in 1920. He is best remembered for the Balfour Declaration of 2 November 1917 in which he declared British support for a Jewish state in **Palestine**, although with the proviso that the rights of non-Jewish communities be respected.

BARINGS BANK (1763–1995). Established in 1763 by John Baring and Francis Baring, Barings Bank was Britain's oldest merchant bank until its collapse in 1995. In 1803, the bank helped finance the $11.25 million Louisiana Purchase for the United States, despite Britain being at war with the French. Known as the Baring Brothers and Company after 1806, the bank developed global financial interests and continued to invest in the United States as a developing debtor nation, particularly in the years 1837–1861. *See also* TRADE.

BEATLES, THE. The Beatles were part of the so-called Second British Invasion of America that took place between 1964 and 1966, when several British pop groups traveled to the United States and achieved popular success. The Beatles paved the way for the **Rolling Stones**, the Kinks, the Animals, the Dave Clark Five, Herman's Hermits, and Freddy and the Dreamers. Making their musical breakthrough in 1962, the Beatles were comprised of four men from Liverpool—John Lennon, Paul McCartney, George Harrison, and Ringo Starr—who changed the face of popular music. Influenced by American music, including Elvis Presley, in their early years, the Beatles represented a new kind of music that was characterized by self-penned songs and upbeat melodies, and a new kind of performer with a new look and manner, particularly their mop-top hair and charismatic personalities. Having achieved chart success in Britain with "Love Me Do" (1962), "Please Please Me" (1962), "From Me to You" (1963), and "She Loves You" (1963), the Beatles set out to conquer America. The Beatles arrived in New York City for their first visit to the United States on 7 February 1964 to adoring crowds. Two days later they appeared live on the *Ed Sullivan Show*, achieving an audience of 73 million Americans. On 11 February they played at the Coliseum, Washington, D.C., and were received at the British Embassy. On 12 February they became the first rock 'n' roll band to play at Carnegie Hall, New York. They also traveled to Miami to appear on the *Ed Sullivan Show* there, and while relaxing there for a few days, met Mohammad Ali. The following year the Beatles toured the United States, bringing "Beatlemania" to venues across the nation. They were the first to play a major outdoor stadium, Shea Stadium in New York, achieving an attendance of 55,000. The hysteria in the stadium—fans were screaming and crying—meant the Beatles could not hear themselves sing. Their success in the American charts was unparalleled. Their first number-one single in the United States was "I Want to Hold Your Hand," and during the week of 4 April 1964 the Beatles occupied the top five slots of the U.S. Billboard single charts, with "Can't Buy Me Love" at number one. Quickly they were charged with corrupting the youth of America. On 4 March 1966, John Lennon was interviewed by journalist Maureen Cleave of the London *Evening Standard* and was asked about his thoughts on God and Christianity. His response, including the statement that the Beatles "were more popular than Jesus now," was taken out of context and appeared in an American teen magazine, *Datebook*, on 1 July 1966. The public response, particularly in the Southern Bible Belt, was extreme, with Beatles albums and photos burned in public; the band members received hate mail and death threats. On 12 August, before embarking on the American leg of the Beatles' world tour, John Lennon apologized for his comments on Christianity, but this failed to ease the controversy. On 29 August 1966, the Beatles gave their last live performance at Candlestick Park in San Francisco. As the direction of their music changed, the Beatles stopped playing live and concentrated on recording. On 10 April 1970, they disbanded. John

Lennon and Paul McCartney went on to have successful solo careers in Britain and the United States, and all four Beatles married American women. Lennon lived in the United States after he married Yoko Ono and the two campaigned against the **Vietnam War**. After Lennon's assassination by Mark Chapman in New York City on 8 December 1980, the Strawberry Fields memorial was erected in Central Park.

BECKETT, MARGARET (1943–). Margaret Beckett was appointed the first woman British foreign secretary in 2006 by Prime Minister **Tony Blair**. In July 2006, she was criticized by many within her own party and by the public in Great Britain for failing to call for an immediate cease-fire in hostilities between Israel and Hezbollah forces in the Lebanon in 2006, although she did protest to **Condoleezza Rice** about the United States' use of Prestwick Airport in Scotland for the transportation of American bombs to Israel. In October 2006, she called for the closure of the U.S. detention camp at **Guantanamo Bay** on the grounds that the continued detention of suspected terrorists without fair trial was an abuse of human rights and could be counterproductive in terms of winning the war on terror. She left office in June 2007 when Prime Minister **Gordon Brown** came to power and appointed **David Miliband** as her successor.

BERING SEA DISPUTE (1893). In 1893, an international tribunal solved a dispute between the United States and Great Britain and **Canada** over the status of the Bering Sea. In 1867, the United States acquired Alaska from Russia and its territorial boundary ran through the Bering Sea, located at the northern part of the Pacific Ocean. Disagreement over the waters emerged when the United States found that British and Canadian trawlers were killing seals that were swimming through the sea on their way to islands that were part of the Alaskan territory. This activity threatened the business interests of the U.S. Alaska Commercial Company that had monopoly rights on the killing of seals for fur and was subject to limits on the numbers that could be killed. Claiming that it had authority over all the Bering Sea waters and that it had an obligation to protect the future of the seal, the United States began to seize British and Canadian vessels in 1886. The British and Canadian governments disputed the U.S. claim and in 1893 international arbitration resolved that the United States did not have full control of the Bering Sea and awarded damages to the owners of the seized ships. The tribunal also attempted to place restrictions on the level of seal culling. *See also* ALASKAN BOUNDARY DISPUTE.

BERLIN BLOCKADE (1948–1949). In 1945, as the **Cold War** in Europe intensified, Germany was divided into four zones (Russian, American, British, and French) and the capital, Berlin, was occupied by all four powers. Although the four occupying powers were supposed to draw up a peace treaty, establish a new democratic government in Germany, and then withdraw, by 1948 it was clear that there was much disagreement on the country's future. By 1948, Great Britain and the United States had persuaded France that Germany needed to be self-sufficient and began to prepare for a new state in West Germany. The **Soviet Union** was not ready to move forward with the creation of a new German state, as it had concerns about its own security; in June 1948, when the Western powers introduced a new currency in their zones and began to receive **Marshall aid** to rebuild, the Russians responded on 24 June by imposing a blockade on all land routes into Berlin. Initially uncertain how to respond, Washington even considered forcing a way into Berlin with tanks or an armored train. British Foreign Secretary **Ernest Bevin** instead proposed an Anglo–American airlift of supplies of food and coal from West Germany into Berlin.

The airlift began on 26 June and, although the blockade was lifted on 12 May 1949, lasted until 6 October 1949, during which time an estimated two million tons of supplies were dropped into Berlin, nearly 8,000 tons per day. The Berlin blockade had three major consequences for Anglo–American relations. Firstly, as the first major incident in the Cold War, it demonstrated the unity of purpose of the British and Americans in relation to containing the Soviet Union. Secondly, the blockade made it all the more urgent to speed up talks about an Atlantic security pact, and the **North Atlantic Treaty Organization** (NATO) was formed on 4 April 1949. And lastly, the crisis highlighted America's lack of military preparedness in Europe; in June 1948, Bevin responded positively to American requests to allow their bombers to use British bases, and on 18 July 60, U.S. planes (B-

29 bombers) arrived in Britain to much publicity. *See also* AMERI-CAN BASES IN BRITAIN; BERLIN CRISIS.

BERLIN CRISIS (1958–1962). In late 1958, Berlin became the source of another crisis in superpower relations. Since the end of **World War II**, the city of Berlin, located in East Germany, had been divided into four sectors with West Berlin being controlled by the United States, Great Britain, and France, and East Berlin by the **Soviet Union**. By the mid-1950s, the Western sectors were vanguards of the capitalist system, and discontent in East Berlin about living conditions had resulted in strikes, rioting, and refugees fleeing to the West. By 1958, Premier Nikita Khrushchev of the Soviet Union was determined that Berlin should become integrated into East Germany and in November, as a first step, he issued an ultimatum to the West that if the Berlin problem was not resolved within six months, including the withdrawal of occupation forces in Berlin, then the Soviet Union would make a separate deal with the government of East Germany. The United States, led by President **Dwight D. Eisenhower**, was opposed to Khrushchev's ultimate aim and refused the deadline on talks. Fearing an escalation of tensions over Berlin, Prime Minister **Harold Macmillan** flew to Moscow in February 1959 to have talks with Khrushchev on the matter, taking up an earlier invitation to visit the Soviet Union. Eisenhower was concerned that Macmillan might make too many concessions to Khrushchev in his attempt to avoid increased confrontation between the two superpowers. In any event, Macmillan was able to get Khrushchev's agreement that the deadline would be dropped if a summit meeting between America, Russia, Britain, and France could be arranged.

After Khrushchev met with Eisenhower at Camp David in 1959, the Russian premier agreed to drop the ultimatum in exchange for a summit meeting in Paris in May 1960. The shooting down of an American U-2 spy plane over Russia and the refusal by the Eisenhower administration to apologize for its reconnaissance activity in Soviet air space meant that the meeting dissolved before any formal sessions could take place. Macmillan remained loyal to Eisenhower over the matter but was privately dismayed that the United States refused to come up with a reasonable explanation for its behavior and felt that the Paris summit had been a lost opportunity to resolve the issue of Berlin.

The crisis over Berlin reemerged in 1961 during the presidency of **John F. Kennedy**, when Khrushchev remained intransigent on this issue during their meeting in Vienna in June. Macmillan remained committed to a negotiated solution to the problem but Kennedy felt that a buildup of conventional weapons on the European continent would serve as a message to Khrushchev on Berlin. Anglo–American disagreement over Berlin was ended by the East German erection of the Berlin Wall in August 1961, when all movement between the Berlin zones was ended. London and Washington protested against the wall and the Americans moved forces into West Berlin to show their determination to maintain their military presence there. Kennedy continued to express his support for West Germany when he visited West Berlin on 26 June 1963, where he delivered his "Ich bin ein [I am a] Berliner" speech. *See also* BERLIN BLOCKADE.

BERMUDA CONFERENCE (1953). When Republican **Dwight D. Eisenhower** became president in January 1953, British Prime Minister **Winston Churchill** and his foreign secretary, **Anthony Eden**, hoped that relations between Great Britain and America might become closer after a sometimes tense and distant relationship with President **Harry S. Truman** and Secretary of State **Dean Acheson**. In particular, Britain hoped that after the successful explosion of its own **atomic bomb** in October 1952, the new president, who was known to have some sympathy for the British sense of betrayal over the 1946 **McMahon Act**, might be prepared to reinstitute Anglo–American nuclear cooperation. Churchill went to meet with Eisenhower in Bermuda in December 1953 and reminded him of the **Hyde Park meeting** of 1941 in which it was agreed that Britain and America would be equal partners in nuclear research. The major outcome of the conference was that Eisenhower promised to ask Congress to allow greater nuclear collaboration between Britain and America. In February 1954, the president duly asked Congress to amend the McMahon Act, which it did.

BERMUDA CONFERENCE (1957). In the aftermath of the **Suez crisis**, Anglo–American relations faced their first test at the Bermuda Conference in March 1957. President **Dwight D. Eisenhower** invited the new British Prime Minister **Harold Macmillan** to meet with him in the British territory in Bermuda. The decision to meet in Bermuda rather than Washington, D.C., was an obvious face-saving attempt by the president to prevent Macmillan from looking like he was coming begging. The meeting helped to restore the working relationship between top-level officials and present a united Anglo–American front in public. Eisenhower agreed to station 60 U.S. **Thor** intermediate-range missiles in Britain until the planned Anglo–American **Blue Streak** missile was ready. Both governments felt they had made real benefits from the deal. Britain had a nuclear deterrent earlier than expected and the United States had missiles that could reach the Soviet Union.

BEVIN, ERNEST (1881–1951). A vehement anticommunist, internationalist, and supporter of the United States and the "**special relationship**," Ernest Bevin was British foreign secretary between 1945 and 1951. As a leading member of the Labour government elected to office on 26 July 1945, Bevin saw it as his responsibility to educate Washington about the dangers posed by the Soviet Union and other communist forces around the world. He played a key part in the advent of the **Marshall Plan** and the decision to develop British nuclear weapons after the **McMahon Act** of 1946 ended Anglo–American nuclear cooperation. He is reported to have said to opponents of a British atomic weapon, "We've got to have this thing over here, whatever it costs. We've got to have a bloody Union Jack on top of it." Bevin encouraged the United States to take a less confrontational approach to the **Berlin blockade** crisis in 1948, encouraging an Anglo–American airlift. In March 1948, Bevin informed U.S. Secretary of State **George C. Marshall** of a plan to form a union of Western European countries to coordinate matters of European security and defense. As the key architect behind the **Brussels Treaty** of March 1948, Bevin helped pave the way for a U.S.-led military coalition and the formation of the **North Atlantic Treaty Organization** (NATO) in April 1949. It was of great personal—as well as political—importance to Bevin, who had long wanted to tie the United States to the defense of Europe. He is also known for advocating a role for Britain as a socialist "third force" in world politics, supported by covert propaganda supplied by the Foreign Office's Information Research Department, although by 1950 this mission had been abandoned as the government of **Clement Attlee** moved openly toward supporting a U.S.-led anticommunist Western alliance. *See also* COLD WAR.

BILLIÈRE, GENERAL SIR PETER (1934–). Army General Sir Peter de la Billière played an important role in the Persian **Gulf War** of 1991. He was commander in chief of the British forces during the war and established close working relations with the commander of the coalition forces, U.S. General **Norman Schwarzkopf**.

BLAIR HOUSE. The official state guesthouse of the president of the United States since 1942, used by British dignitaries when visiting Washington, D.C., including **Winston Churchill**, **Queen Elizabeth II**, **Margaret Thatcher**, and **Tony Blair**.

BLAIR, TONY (1953–). The Labour Party's longest serving British prime minister and the only Labour MP to serve three consecutive terms in 10 **Downing Street**. Tony Blair was elected prime minister on 1 May 1997, was reelected in 2001 and 2005, and resigned from office on 27 June 2007. During his 10 years as British leader, Blair placed Anglo–American relations at the forefront of his foreign policy. Blair, and many of his closest aides and advisers within the Labour Party, admired the Clinton Democrats and very quickly forged a close personal and working relationship with President **William J. Clinton** (1993–2000). Blair met with Clinton in London in November 1995 and the two leaders developed a friendship and mutual respect based on shared liberal and generational values, and similar backgrounds in the law. But their relationship was aided by agreement on important issues; noticeably, both leaders believed in fiscal responsibility as well as social justice. Blair and Clinton worked together successfully on Northern Ireland. Unlike his predecessor, **John Major**, Blair welcomed U.S. involvement in the peace process, and collaboration between London, Dublin, and Washington helped in the negotiations that resulted in the 1998 Good Friday agreement. Blair was also willing to cooperate with the United States over a weapons inspection crisis in **Iraq** in February 1998 and to sanction British participation in air assaults on Iraq in December of that year.

Differences arose between Blair and Washington over the potential impact of the **Helms–Burton Act** on British businesses, and Blair was alarmed on occasions by unilateral action taken by President Clinton, including the U.S. bombing of suspected terrorist sites in Sudan and **Afghanistan** in 1998. The only major disagreement between Blair and Clinton came during the **Kosovo** crisis of 1999. Blair believed that the policies of Serbian leader Slobodan Milosevic were so barbaric that the world must respond, even if events in Kosovo did not pose an external threat. Blair believed intervention by the **North Atlantic Treaty Organization** was the morally correct thing to do and he was supported in this by his foreign secretary, **Robin Cook**, who posited the idea of an ethical foreign policy. When Blair believed a land invasion might be necessary, in addition to a bombing campaign against Serbia, and that U.S. troops would be needed, he found strong opposition to the idea from President Clinton.

Despite coming from different political backgrounds, Blair also formed a strong working alliance with Clinton's successor, **George W. Bush**, most notably over the **invasion of Afghanistan** in 2002 and the **Iraq War** in 2003. Blair appeared to develop a clear sense of foreign policy mission in the aftermath of the **September 11** attacks on the World Trade Center. Within hours of the terrorist attacks Blair made a speech pledging to stand "shoulder to shoulder" with the United States in the fight against terrorism. Fearing Bush might take rash military action in response to 9/11, Blair was keen to attempt to influence the president's thinking and was relieved that he was the first foreign leader President Bush phoned on his arrival back in Washington and to find that the focus was on al-Qaeda bases in Afghanistan. Bush also invited Blair to attend his address to a joint session of Congress. Seated in the "heroes gallery," Bush thanked Blair for coming to Washington to show unity with the Americans and referred to him as a "friend." Blair's attempts at influencing the Bush administration proved limited, especially in regard to the need for international support for the invasion of Iraq.

Blair's apparent unswerving support and closeness to President Bush post-9/11 led many in Britain to label him Bush's "poodle," especially after the U.S. president was overheard greeting him at the G8 summit in September 2006 with "Yo, Blair." Criticism of Blair increased in Britain once it became clear after the invasion of Iraq that there were no stockpiles of weapons of mass destruction. This was compounded by the death under suspicious circumstances of Dr.

David Kelly, a government scientist who was the source for the BBC journalists who claimed Blair had knowingly exaggerated the threat from Iraq in its published intelligence dossier of September 2002. Although the Hutton Inquiry was established to investigate the death of Dr. Kelly and reported in January 2004 that the British government had not altered intelligence reports for its own purposes, criticism of the Blair government's actions in relation to Iraq continued and there were calls for his resignation. Instead, Blair announced a government inquiry into the intelligence on Iraq and in July 2004 the Butler Report published its findings that included a criticism of "unsubstantiated" intelligence claims in the September 2002 dossier. Blair and Bush retained their public admiration for one another until the prime minister resigned office on 27 June 2007. *See also* IRELAND.

BLIX, HANS (1928–). Former Swedish minister for foreign affairs and later head of the International Atomic Energy Agency, Dr. Hans Blix served as executive chairman of the United Nations' Monitoring, Verification, and Inspection Commission between January 2000 and June 2003. In this role, he came into conflict with the **George W. Bush** administration and the British Labour government, led by **Tony Blair**, over the disarmament of Iraqi weapons of mass destruction (WMDs). In the months before U.S. and allied forces invaded **Iraq** in March 2003, Blix and his team of inspectors visited Iraq and carried out over 400 unannounced inspections at 300 sites. He reported on 13 February 2003 that no stockpiles or evidence of WMDs had been found but argued that Iraq should provide unconditional cooperation in the disarmament process. In February 2003, prior to the invasion of Iraq, Blix argued that Bush and Blair had exaggerated the threat posed by Iraqi weapons in order to help justify their actions, and urged that the inspectors be given more time to continue their search for weapons of mass destruction. After leaving his post as chief weapons inspector, Blix continued to criticize Bush and Blair for a lack of "critical thinking" on Iraq, claiming they had failed to question the sources of intelligence. Blix also claimed that his offices had been bugged by American intelligence agencies. *See also* IRAQ WAR.

BLUE STREAK. In the 1950s, Britain lagged behind the **Cold War** superpowers in nuclear missile development and launch delivery systems. The Blue Streak project was an attempt to develop a medium-range nuclear missile system of its own, capable of reaching the **Soviet Union**. The development of Blue Streak proved somewhat difficult. Firstly, it proved necessary to use American technology for its rocket engine and its guidance system. Secondly, it became clear that even if developed it would not provide an adequate deterrence against a Soviet preemptive strike as it was liquid-fueled and could not be launched quickly enough. For these reasons it was canceled in February 1960 before further money was wasted on research and development costs. Instead, Britain turned to the Anglo–American **Skybolt** missile.

BOLTON, JOHN ROBERT (1948–). A prominent neoconservative, John Bolton became U.S. undersecretary of state for arms control in the administration of **George W. Bush** on 11 May 2001. In this role, he played an important part in the discussions within the Bush administration over Saddam Hussein and weapons of mass destruction (WMDs) in 2002 and early 2003. As a result, he was party to discussions with the British over the invasion of **Iraq**. On 7 March 2005, he was nominated by President Bush as U.S. ambassador to the **United Nations**. *See also* IRAQ WAR.

BOSNIA. Anglo–American relations reached a low point during the years between 1993 and 1995, largely as a result of a disagreement over the best response to the crisis in Bosnia. The end of the Cold War in Europe led to the revival of ethnic tensions and eruption of ethnic wars in the former Yugoslavia, and the crisis over Bosnia suggested strong Anglo–American relations might not survive in the post–Cold War world. In October 1991, Bosnia-Herzegovina declared itself a sovereign nation and in February 1992 held a referendum on independence. Shortly afterward fighting broke out between the Bosnian Serbs, Bosnian Croats, and Bosnian Muslims, resulting in approximately 250,000 deaths. Serbia, led by Slobodan Milosevic, began armed attacks on Bosnia in support of the Bosnian Serbs and the country saw attempts at "ethnic cleansing." The situation in Bosnia resulted in disagreements between the administration of **William Clinton** and the government of **John Major** over the most appropriate response to events. Former secretary of state **Cyrus**

Vance and former British foreign secretary **Lord Owen** attempted a peace initiative in August 1992 but the United States refused to be drawn into the conflict, despite the passage of **United Nations** resolutions authorizing the use of all measures to ensure that food and medical supplies reached Bosnia.

In the post–Cold War world, the United States was not prepared to act as the world's policeman and encouraged its European allies to take the lead in solving regional problems. After President Clinton's election, the United States was urged by its European allies to introduce ground troops to help prevent a humanitarian tragedy. Secretary of State **Warren Christopher** presented an alternative plan to the Europeans that included lifting the arms embargo against the Muslims in Bosnia. British Foreign Secretary **Douglas Hurd** argued that this would merely provide a "level killing field" and continued to press the United States to consider sending in troops for peacekeeping purposes. In July 1995, Serbian forces began attacking the six UN-designated Muslim safe havens, taking control of two of them— Zepa and Srebrenica—and resulting in mass atrocities. This led Britain on 23 July to send 1,200 forces to relieve the Serb-controlled capital city, Sarajevo. Forces from the Devon and Dorset regiment, along with the Royal Artillery, joined 500 French Legionnaires and 180 Dutch soldiers. By the end of August, the United States agreed to participate in NATO-led air strikes against the Bosnian Serbs with the British and 13 other nations. By December 1995, the warring Serb, Croat, and Muslim forces agreed to begin negotiations. During a summit meeting at Dayton, Ohio, led by Warren Christopher, an agreement was reached that ended the conflict in Bosnia. The Dayton Peace Accords were reached on 21 November 1995 and formally signed in Paris the following month. The political divisions that were agreed to at Dayton were monitored for the first year by a NATO-led Implementation Force (IFOR) that included British, American, and French peacekeepers and subsequently another multinational Stabilization Force (SFOR) until 1998.

BOSTON MASSACRE (1770). On 5 March 1770, British troops, led by Captain Thomas Preston, fired upon a crowd in Boston that was throwing snowballs at them. The details of how the incident escalated and who gave the order to fire were disputed. Five Bostonians were killed as a result of the incident and they are considered the first casualties for the cause that resulted in the American Revolution. The incident appears to have been sparked partly because of the heavy presence of Royal troops who had been stationed in the city since 1768 after rioting followed the seizure of the American ship *Liberty* for **trade** violations. The soldiers involved in the Boston Massacre were put on trial and defended by John Adams, who feared lower-class violence was not the best way to fight British policies. Two of the soldiers were found guilty of manslaughter and seven were found not guilty. The massacre was depicted in an engraving by Paul Revere, and although not entirely accurate in its depiction of the event, this fueled resentment against the British that ultimately resulted in the **War of Independence**.

BOSTON TEA PARTY (1773). The Boston Tea Party was a significant incident in the breakdown in relations between the American colonies and the British Crown as American rebels began to question British rule. Despite the repeal of the **Townshend Duties** in 1770, American colonists continued to boycott many British goods, including tea; in 1773 the British Parliament passed the Tea Act in an effort to aid the failing East India Company, which faced bankruptcy partly due to its poor sales of tea in the colonies. The act, passed on 10 May 1773, allowed the giant trading company to export tea directly to the American colonies and not pay import taxes, while the colonists remained liable for them, thus undercutting the American tea merchants who were smuggling to avoid such duties and reigniting the debate about "no taxation without representation." On 16 December 1773, a group of American patriots, including members of the Sons of Liberty, disguised themselves as Mohawk Indians, boarded three ships in Boston Harbor, and destroyed chests of tea by throwing them into the sea. The incident cost the East India Company approximately £10,000 and led the British Parliament to pass the Intolerable Acts (also known as the **Coercive Acts**) in 1774, interpreted by the American colonists as threatening their political freedoms still further. *See also* WAR OF INDEPENDENCE.

BREMER, L. PAUL (1941–). A former diplomat and ambassador, Paul Bremer was appointed by President **George W. Bush** in May

2003 as director of reconstruction and humanitarian assistance, and headed the Coalition Provision Authority, a transitional government in **Iraq** after its liberation from Saddam Hussein in April 2003. Bremer worked with British envoy, **Sir Jeremy Greenstock**, in trying to organize Iraq's civil administration until control was handed over to the new Iraqi government in late June 2004. *See also* IRAQ WAR.

BRETTON WOODS AGREEMENT. In July 1944, delegates of the 44 Allied nations met at the **United Nations** Monetary and Financial Conference held in the Mount Washington hotel in the town of Bretton Woods, New Hampshire, with the aim of regulating the world's monetary and financial order after the end of **World War II**. For two years prior to the conference, the treasuries of Great Britain and the United States had been working on rival plans to find solutions to the financial chaos that characterized the interwar years. **John Maynard Keynes**'s plan was eventually superseded by the plan of Harry Dexter White of the U.S. Treasury, although both plans had areas in common. The result of the Bretton Woods Conference was a series of signed agreements that set up the International Monetary Fund and the International Bank for Reconstruction and Development. These bodies became operational in 1946 and the Bretton Woods agreement established an exchange rate system pegged to the value of gold. The Bretton Woods system was ended on 15 August 1971 when President **Richard Nixon** ended the convertibility of the U.S. dollar to gold.

BRITISH AMERICAN PROJECT (BAP). Founded in 1985, at the suggestion of former Labour candidate Nick Butler, as the British American Project for the Successor Generation, later shortened to British American Project (BAP), BAP's aim is to strengthen the "special relationship" by fostering "transatlantic friendships and professional contacts" during an annual four-day conference—to which no press are invited—at alternate American and British venues. New members of the BAP must be between 28 and 40 years old and are nominated by existing members.

BRITISH–AMERICAN PARLIAMENTARY GROUP (BAPG). The British–American Parliamentary Group was established to promote friendship and understanding between members of the U.S.

Congress and the British Parliament. The exact date of formation of the group is unknown but it is believed to have been in either 1937 or 1941. Since the 1940s, there have been annual conferences of the BAPG and numerous visits of British members of the group to the United States, especially to Washington, D.C., and U.S. politicians and VIPs have been invited to Great Britain, usually to Westminster. Funded by the British Treasury, and recently also by member subscription in its efforts to encourage better relations between parliamentarians on both sides of the Atlantic, British MPs have observed courses undertaken by new members of the U.S. Congress, have been invited to attend the annual conventions during presidential election years, and special delegations have visited New York and Washington to discuss topics such as health, defense, the environment, and **trade**.

BRITISH NORTH AMERICA ACT (1867). In the aftermath of the **American Civil War**, and after requests by the provinces of **Canada**, New Brunswick, and Nova Scotia, Britain granted dominion status to Canada in 1867. Under the act, it was envisaged that Canada would adopt a constitution similar to that of Great Britain.

BROWN BROTHERS. In the mid-19th century, the House of Brown became the leading Anglo–American merchant bank, succeeding its competitor, the **Baring Brothers**. The banking empire had its origins in Alexander Brown, a linen merchant from Ireland, who immigrated with his family to Baltimore, Maryland, in 1800 and quickly established himself as a leading import–export dealer in the city. In 1810, Alexander's eldest son, William Brown, established Brown, Shipley & Co. in Liverpool, England, primarily importing raw cotton from the United States but quickly becoming a general merchant and dealer in foreign exchange. By 1832, the firm was in control of one sixth of the trade between Great Britain and the United States. In 1818, Alexander's sons, John and George, established Brown Brothers in Philadelphia. Brown Brothers & Co. became investment bankers, extending credit for American imports from England as well as helping to finance American railroads, and becoming a key financier of Anglo–American trade throughout the 19th century. *See also* TRADE.

BROWN, GORDON (1951–). A Scottish member of Parliament, Gordon Brown served as chancellor of the exchequer between 1997 and 2007 in the Labour governments led by **Tony Blair**. During this time, he became a regular visitor to the United States, often taking vacations in Cape Cod, and remained pro-American on a personal as well as political level. In 2003, he supported the allied invasion of **Iraq**. He became prime minister on 27 June 2007 when Blair resigned from office. Brown attempted to put some distance between himself and **George W. Bush** during his early months in 10 **Downing Street** by downplaying the role of personal relationships and emphasizing shared values and links between Great Britain and America. He continued to defend the invasion of Iraq, although emphasizing the lessons to be learned from it. He indicated in November 2007 that he still believed the United States to be Britain's most important ally and was prepared to take strong action against **Iran**. In his first year in office, Brown made two visits to the United States, first in July 2007 and second in April 2008 when he met President Bush and presidential hopefuls John McCain, Hilary Clinton, and Barack Obama. *See also* IRAQ WAR.

BRUCE, DAVID K. E. (1898–1977). David Bruce served as American ambassador to Great Britain (1961–1969) during the administrations of **John F. Kennedy** and **Lyndon B. Johnson**. Bruce was an experienced and well-respected diplomat who helped ease some of the tensions in the personal relationship between President Johnson and Prime Minister **Harold Wilson** in the mid-1960s when Anglo–American relations suffered due to tensions over the **Vietnam War** and Britain's world role. *See also* EAST OF SUEZ.

BRUSA AGREEMENT (1943). During **World War II**, Britain and America began sharing intelligence information through a series of secret, informal understandings. An acknowledgment of intelligence sharing was made explicit under the Britain–United States agreement that was signed on 17 May 1943.

BRUSSELS TREATY (1948). Signed by Great Britain, France, and the Benelux countries (Belgium, the Netherlands, and Luxembourg) in Brussels on 17 March 1948, the Treaty on Economic, Social and

Cultural Collaboration and Collective Self-Defence was a collective defense agreement aimed at defending one another against any attack in Europe, but particularly from a resurgent Germany or the **Soviet Union**. The Brussels Treaty led to the creation of the Western European Defence Organisation in September 1948 and the **North Atlantic Treaty Organization** (NATO) in April 1949. The British foreign secretary, **Ernest Bevin**, initiated the Brussels Treaty with the aim of showing the United States that Western European nations could work together and thus encourage a commitment by Washington to the defense of Europe. The treaty was valid for 50 years and in May 1955 was modified to create the Western European Union (WEU) and extended to include West Germany and Italy. *See also* COLD WAR.

BRYSON, BILL (1951–). Born in Des Moines, Iowa, Bill Bryson is a best-selling author, famous for his amusing travel books—such as *The Lost Continent: Travels in Small-Town America* (1989) and *Notes from a Small Island* (1995)—that describe British and American culture in the late 20th century. Popular in both countries, Bryson has been influential in relating the idiosyncrasies of the respective cultures. Bryson has lived in England since 1977 with his English wife and was appointed chancellor of Durham University in 2005.

BUNKER HILL, BATTLE OF (1775). The battle of Bunker Hill—misnamed because it took place on nearby Breed's Hill—took place on 17 June 1765 and was a famous British victory in Boston during the American Revolutionary War. British troops at the Boston garrison fought the American Continental Army and drove them from the Charlestown peninsula. Although the British forces were successful, it was at the cost of many lives and casualties, and the American stand against the greater number of British forces encouraged greater unity among the rebels. As a result of the battle of Bunker Hill, King **George III** finally declared the colonies to be in rebellion. *See also* WAR OF INDEPENDENCE.

BUSH, GEORGE HERBERT WALKER (1924–). Republican politician George H. W. Bush was a member of Congress for Texas (1967–1971) before serving as director of the Central Intelligence Agency (1976–1977). He became American vice president under

Ronald Reagan between 1981 and 1989 and was elected 41st president of the United States in November 1998, serving in the White House for one term between 1989 and 1993. During his period as president, relations with the British were conducted within Bush's plans for a "new world order" after the end of the Cold War. Bush took steps to distance himself from the cozy relationship that had existed between his predecessor, Ronald Reagan, and the British prime minister, **Margaret Thatcher**. London feared that the "**special relationship**" was being challenged by Washington's increasingly close relationship with the newly united Germany as part of its attempt to establish strong relations with the **European community**. The invasion of Kuwait by **Iraq** in August 1990 revitalized Anglo–American relations when Thatcher immediately pledged to help the United States and joined the **United Nations'** coalition force to liberate the country. Thatcher's successor, **John Major**, became prime minister shortly before Operation Desert Storm began and the successful Anglo–American military cooperation during the **Gulf War** helped to establish a strong personal relationship between Bush and Major. The Bush administration had a disagreement with the Major government at the end of the Gulf War over its decision to declare the end of the military mission after just four days of ground troop activity, when the British would have preferred the campaign to continue on to Baghdad.

Aside from events in the Persian Gulf, the Bush administration concentrated much of its attention on dealing with the collapsing **Soviet Union** and the envisaged "peace dividend." It encouraged Britain and France to accept the integration of a united Germany into the **North Atlantic Treaty Organization** and the European Community, and encouraged European leaders to take greater responsibility for their own regional affairs. George Bush worked with Major over Anglo–American policy regarding the disintegration of Yugoslavia. Meeting at **Camp David** on 20 December 1992, the two leaders issued a statement agreeing to work together to ensure a peaceful settlement of the former Yugoslavia and to prevent the spread of fighting to Kosovo and Macedonia. By this stage, Britain had already committed 2,000 troops to the former Yugoslavia to help in the humanitarian effort and, despite the unified statement, Bush believed that the Balkans was an area that the Europeans should deal with. *See also* BOSNIA.

BUSH, GEORGE W. (1946–). Son of President **George H. W. Bush** and former governor of Texas, George W. Bush became president after the disputed 2000 election campaign against Democratic candidate Al Gore, and was reelected in 2004. During his time in the White House, Bush developed a close working relationship with British Prime Minister **Tony Blair**, and the two leaders forged a steadfast Anglo–American alliance in the war on terror. Coming after Blair's friendly relationship with Bush's Democratic predecessor, **Bill Clinton**, and given the two leaders' politics, the bond between Bush and Blair was somewhat surprising. Bush later described his relationship with Blair as "forged in battle." With the terrorist attacks against the United States on **September 11, 2001**, the bonds between Great Britain and the United States strengthened noticeably. Both leaders shared religious convictions that underscored their belief in interventionism on the world scene.

Bush was able to count on British military support in the war against the Taliban and al-Qaeda in **Afghanistan** in 2002 and also found the British firm partners in the invasion of **Iraq** that began in March 2003, despite most of their European counterparts openly opposing British and American intervention. The British ambassador to the United States, Sir **Christopher Meyer**, later published his memoirs stating that just days after 9/11 Bush discussed with Tony Blair his belief that Saddam Hussein had to be removed from power in Iraq. It is believed that Blair helped to persuade Bush in September 2002 of the need to secure support from the **United Nations** for military action in Iraq, and in November 2002 Resolution 1441 gave Iraq a final chance to abide by previous resolutions requiring disarmament of its weapons of mass destruction. Bush did not feel an additional UN mandate was necessary before going to war but supported Blair's attempt to gain an additional resolution in January 2003, as he understood the prime minister's domestic difficulties on this matter. Bush found that the British disagreed openly on the issue of the environment, particularly over U.S. failure to ratify the **Kyoto Treaty**, and also protested at the detention of suspected terrorists at **Guantanamo Bay** without trial. Bush was invited to Great Britain for the first state visit by a U.S. president on 18–21 November 2003. He visited London and Sedgefield in County Durham, the constituency home of Tony Blair. The decision to accord Bush this honor was controversial due to the president's personal unpopularity in Great Britain, focused largely on opposition to the **Iraq War**.

– C –

CALLAGHAN, JAMES (1912–2005). Before becoming British Labour prime minister in 1976, James Callaghan had served as chancellor of the exchequer (1964–1967), home secretary (1967–1970), and foreign secretary (1974–1976) in the **Harold Wilson** governments. After the coolness of the Nixon–Heath years, Callaghan placed the Atlantic alliance back at the center of British foreign policy and was able to establish a cordial relationship with President **Gerald Ford** and an extremely good one with President **Jimmy Carter**. At home, the Callaghan government faced serious economic difficulties and, after the pound sterling began to struggle against the U.S. dollar, it was forced to appeal to the United States for help in June 1976 during the **IMF crisis**. He prepared for the replacement of **Polaris** by the **Trident missile**. Callaghan found the Carter administration cooperative over the implementation of economic sanctions against **Rhodesia**. Carter visited Britain in 1977 and Callaghan visited Carter in Washington in March 1978.

CAMP DAVID. Camp David (a U.S. Navy support facility) is located in Frederick County, Maryland, and is the mountain retreat of the president, set up by President **Franklin D. Roosevelt**. It has often been used as a site for summit meetings between the heads of state of the American and British governments; Prime Minister **Winston Churchill** was the first foreign leader to visit in May 1943.

CAMPAIGN FOR NUCLEAR DISARMAMENT (CND). Founded in February 1958 in opposition to the British government's nuclear policy and advocating unilateral nuclear disarmament, the Campaign for Nuclear Disarmament is a mass political protest movement. Founding members included Bertrand Russell, J. B. Priestley, Michael Foot, Fenner Brockway, Peggy Duff, A. J. P. Taylor, E. P. Thompson, Canon John Collins, Dora Russell, and Victor Gollanz. The symbol of CND quickly became a universal symbol for peace protest. During Easter 1958, supporters marched from London to Aldermaston, gaining much attention in the process. The stationing of U.S. cruise and Pershing missiles in Europe led to the revitalization of the movement in the early 1980s. *See also* GREENHAM COMMON.

CANADA. From the 18th century to the late 19th century, Canada proved an area of contention between Britain and the United States. Canada was known as British North America when it was a British colony and on numerous occasions was the focus of disharmony between Great Britain and the United States, particularly over boundary disputes and raids launched by anti-British rebels. Canada was granted dominion status in 1867, allowing the country to rule itself within the British Empire and later British Commonwealth. *See also* AROOSTOCK WAR; BRITISH NORTH AMERICA ACT; *CAROLINE* AFFAIR; FENIAN BROTHERHOOD.

CARNEGIE, ANDREW (1835–1919). Born in Dunfermline, Scotland, Andrew Carnegie immigrated to the United States with his family in 1848 and became one of the leading industrialists and philanthropists of the Gilded Age. After working in the railroad industry and investing wisely, he moved on to concentrate on the iron and steel industry in Pittsburgh. By 1892, he had formed the Carnegie Steel Company and in 1901 this became part of U.S. Steel. Carnegie made his fortune in steel partly because he was a pioneer of the vertical integration of raw materials but also because of his knowledge of the needs of the railroad industry. Throughout his life, Carnegie remained a British loyalist and advocate of a coalition of English-speaking peoples. He caused controversy in Britain through his writings. In 1886, he published *Triumphant Democracy*, which promoted the republican system of government over one based on monarchy, and in 1889 he published his *Gospel of Wealth* article in which he advocated philanthropy as the best way to use accumulated wealth. He was also critical of empire-building and became a member of the American Anti-Imperialist League, formed in response to the Spanish–American War of 1898. In 1910, he founded the Carnegie Endowment for International Peace. He returned to Britain on a regular basis, in the process observing advances brought by the Industrial Revolution, notably the Bessemer steel converter, and started using such innovations in his businesses. In 1881, he went on a tour of Britain, returning to Dunfermline to fund a library, a swimming pool, and a science laboratory. In 1899, he also donated a substantial sum to help found the University of Birmingham in the English Midlands.

CAROLINE **AFFAIR (1837).** The *Caroline* affair involved a rebellion by a small group of malcontents in an attempt to free **Canada** from British rule that led to serious tension between the British and American governments. The rebels included French Canadians and British Canadians who demanded democratic institutions along the lines of the United States. Led by William Lyon MacKenzie, a Canadian revolutionary, the rebels set up headquarters on Navy Island near Niagara Falls and began looting raids in Canada, aided by the supplies of men, food, and weapons brought in by Americans sympathetic to the cause on the U.S.S. *Caroline*. On 12 December 1837, Canadian militia crossed the Niagara River, seized and burned the *Caroline*, killing an American in the process. Despite American outrage about the violation of U.S. territory, including some calls for a U.S. invasion of Canada, President Martin Van Buren remained calm, punished some of the U.S. insurrectionists, and issued a formal protest to the British government in London. The crisis did not develop, although its repercussions lingered on into the 1840s as those involved faced legal action.

CARRINGTON, LORD PETER (1919–). Lord Carrington was British foreign secretary when Argentina invaded the **Falkland Islands** on 2 April 1982. On receiving intelligence that the Argentinean fleet was bound for the Falklands in late March 1982, Lord Carrington attempted to prevent a conflict over the Falklands by asking the United States to intervene. Although U.S. Secretary of State **Alexander Haig** agreed to try to resolve the conflict, Carrington expressed his indignation to the Americans when they described both Britain and Argentina as "good friends." The United States was unable to prevent the invasion of the Falklands and the following day Carrington resigned as foreign secretary to be replaced by Sir **Francis Pym**. Carrington took full responsibility for the British failure to foresee the invasion, something he described as a "British humiliation," and acknowledged his role in the failure of diplomatic negotiations. Carrington later served as the secretary-general of **North Atlantic Treaty Organization** (1984–1988).

CARTER, JAMES EARL "JIMMY" (1924–). During the presidency of Democrat Jimmy Carter (1977–1981), Anglo–American relations continued in importance on both sides of the Atlantic, although more so in Great Britain than the United States. Carter's relationship with British Labour Prime Minister **James Callaghan** was a warm one. The Labour government was less interested in the **European Economic Community** (EEC) than the government of **Edward Heath** and was keen to maintain a strong relationship with America. Carter visited England in the spring of 1977 and was taken by Callaghan to visit Newcastle and Durham in northeast England, where the president had distant family roots. While in the region he visited Washington Old Hall, the ancestral home of the first president, **George Washington**.

Carter tried to help in finding a solution to the **Rhodesia** question, continuing the U.S. policy of economic sanctions and working with Britain in applying diplomatic pressure to ensure democratic elections. The nuclear **special relationship** was revitalized during the Carter presidency when Callaghan negotiated, and **Margaret Thatcher** later concluded, a deal to secure the **Trident** system. There was some discord between Britain and America during the Carter years. When the Carter White House condemned the Soviet invasion of **Afghanistan** in 1979, Prime Minister Thatcher supported him. However, Britain did not go along with the U.S. request to boycott the 1980 Olympic Games in Moscow.

CASABLANCA CONFERENCE (1943). By 1943, the Anglo–American alliance, forged during **World War II**, was becoming divided over wartime strategy. Both Washington and Moscow were becoming increasingly suspicious of Prime Minister **Winston Churchill**'s strategy for defeating Germany's Adolf Hitler, which appeared to be concerned with securing the British Empire after the war. The British planned to use success in North Africa—Anglo–American forces had landed in French North Africa in November 1942—to launch a military assault against Italy and weaken the Axis before a final assault on Hitler and Germany. President **Franklin D. Roosevelt** suspected that the motive behind this strategy was to secure the Suez Canal and maintain British influence in the Middle East. Between 14 and 24 January 1943, President Roosevelt met with Prime Minister Churchill and leader of the Free French, General Charles de Gaulle, at Casablanca, Morocco, to discuss plans for Europe after the victories in North Africa. The Americans arrived in Casablanca divided among themselves over future strategy and were persuaded by the British of the need for a Mediterranean campaign rather than an invasion of northern Europe. Churchill and Roosevelt also decided on a policy of "unconditional surrender" in order to secure postwar peace.

CASH AND CARRY (1939). At the onset of **World War II**, President **Franklin D. Roosevelt** forced through Congress an amendment to the 1935 and 1937 **Neutrality Acts**—which forbade the sale of arms, ammunition, and weapons to belligerent nations—that allowed nations to buy war goods on a "cash-and-carry" basis. This allowed Great Britain and France to collect goods in their own ships once they were paid for. Temporarily this aided the Allied war cause, although very quickly Britain ordered more goods than it could pay for, leading Roosevelt to pursue further revisions to the Neutrality Acts. *See also* LEND-LEASE.

CHAMBERLAIN, NEVILLE (1869–1940). As British Conservative prime minister from 1937–1940, and earlier as chancellor of the exchequer, Neville Chamberlain had an uneasy relationship with the administration of **Franklin D. Roosevelt**. His less-than-positive attitude toward the United States appears to have developed during the early 1930s when he was chancellor under the National government led by **Ramsay MacDonald**. During this period, the British economy was in depression and the pound sterling was devalued in 1931. Britain defaulted on war debts to the United States and became increasingly protectionist, raising **trade** tariffs and implementing a system of **imperial preference**. As prime minister, Chamberlain presided over the **Anglo–American Trade Agreement** in 1938, which was seen as a concession to Washington's complaints about imperial preference. He is best known, however, for following a policy of **appeasement** in relation to Nazi Germany that culminated in the **Munich Agreement**. Chamberlain had a cordial but cool relationship with President Roosevelt, refusing his attempt to establish a peace conference in 1938.

CHAPLIN, CHARLIE (1889–1977). An iconic figure in Hollywood history, Charlie Chaplin was born in London, England, but spent much of his working life in the United States. Chaplin had a difficult, poverty-stricken childhood but found solace in performing on stage in music halls. Chaplin began working in America in 1910 and starred in his first comedy film, *Making a Living*, in 1914. His career as a comedic actor in silent movies flourished and he became known for his character "The Tramp." He went on to make numerous successful films, including *The Kid* (1921), *Gold Rush* (1925), *Modern Times* (1935), and *the Great Dictator* (1940), and scripted, directed, and produced many of them. During the McCarthy era of the late 1940s and early 1950s, Chaplin came under the scrutiny of the Federal Bureau of Investigation because his films were considered procommunist. His personal lifestyle was also questioned by conservative forces in the United States, notably his short-lived marriages and many affairs with Hollywood actresses and very young women. Although he had been a U.S. resident for 40 years, when Chaplin visited England in 1952, his reentry visa was revoked. He did not return to America until 1972 when he was awarded an Honorary Oscar. Chaplin was made a Knight Commander of the British Empire in 1975, having been considered for it in 1956 but not receiving it because the Conservative government, led by Anthony Eden, feared it might disturb Anglo–American relations.

CHENEY, RICHARD "DICK" (1941–). Dick Cheney worked as an adviser to President **Gerald Ford** and ran his 1974 presidential election campaign. When Ford was defeated, Cheney sought political office and was elected Republican congressmen for Wyoming in 1978. He later worked in the administration of **Ronald Reagan** and also served in the administration of **George H. W. Bush** as defense secretary. On 20 January 2001 he became vice president to President **George W. Bush**. During the lead-up to the **Iraq War**, Cheney was unsympathetic toward Prime Minister **Tony Blair**'s attempt to assemble an international coalition through the **United Nations** and was prepared to invade **Iraq** without the British if necessary.

CHEQUERS. Chequers has been the official country residence of British prime ministers since 1921. Located in Buckingham (40 miles from London), it has often been used by prime ministers on weekends and during holidays. Many U.S. presidents and secretaries of state have stayed at Chequers as guests of the British, including **Dwight D. Eisenhower** in 1959, **Richard Nixon** in 1970, **George Shultz** in 1972, and **George W. Bush** in 2001.

CHESAPEAKE **AFFAIR (1807).** During the **Napoleonic Wars**, Great Britain antagonized the United States by impressing sailors into the Royal Navy. Many of these British sailors had deserted the Royal Navy for better pay and conditions available on American merchant ships. Some had even become American citizens, and for this reason their capture and impressment back into the Royal Navy was perceived as a slight against American sovereignty. It is estimated that between 1803 and 1812 approximately 6,000 Americans were impressed. This festering problem in Anglo–American relations came to a head on 22 June 1807 when a British warship, the HMS *Leopard*, attacked an American navy frigate, the USS *Chesapeake*, in waters near Norfolk, Virginia. After refusing to be boarded, the *Leopard* opened fire, damaged the ship severely, killed three Americans, and injured many others. Four "deserters" were captured on the ship by the British, and one deserter was later hanged. As this was the first time the Royal Navy had boarded an American government ship and seized four sailors, three of whom were now American citizens, the *Chesapeake* incident led to public outrage in the United States. President **Thomas Jefferson** remarked that the incident provoked anger and unity in the United States similar to that experienced at Lexington in 1775 and led him to ask Congress to pass the **Embargo Act**.

CHINA. By the end of the 19th century, both Great Britain and America agreed on an **Open Door policy** toward China. On 6 February 1922 the two nations signed a treaty in Washington, along with Belgium, China, France, Italy, Japan, the Netherlands, and Portugal, to safeguard its main principles of stabilizing conditions in the Far East, encouraging trading and commercial relations on an equal basis for all nations, and to safeguard the rights of China. Despite this treaty, London and Washington stood back and watched as Japan attempted to strengthen its sphere of interest in China by invading Manchuria in 1932. Although U.S. Secretary of State **Henry Stimson** had wanted to withhold diplomatic recognition of Japan's conquests—the Stimson Doctrine—Britain's foreign secretary, Sir John Simon, had refused because Britain had extensive commercial and diplomatic ties with both Japan and China.

Since 1927 the Chinese Nationalist government of Chiang Kai-shek had been in conflict with the Communist Party of China led by Mao Zedong. After 1941, when China declared war on Japan after **Pearl Harbor**, the U.S. government aided the Chinese in their fight and continued to help Chiang's nationalist government when civil war broke out again at the end of **World War II**. The administration of **Harry S. Truman** continued to support the Nationalist government when it was forced to flee from the mainland to the island of Taiwan after the communist victory in October 1949. When the People's Republic of China (PRC) was proclaimed on 1 October 1949, the British government responded cautiously and pragmatically. Hoping for a normalization in relations, the government of **Clement Attlee** established diplomatic relations with the PRC on 6 January 1950. The decision to recognize Mao's government was not only a continuation of British policy to recognize de facto governments but, in regard to China, was predicated on the need to maintain good relations with the new regime because of the British colony of **Hong Kong** and because of economic interests in the country. In the grip of McCarthyism at home, the United States' reaction contrasted sharply with Britain's swift recognition of the PRC. The United States chose to recognize the defeated Nationalist forces—the government of the Democratic Republic of China—on Taiwan. Consequently, China became a major irritant in Anglo–American relations for much of the **Cold War**.

U.S. concerns about the new communist state were increased by Mao's signing of a treaty of friendship with the **Soviet Union** in February 1950. With the outbreak of the **Korean War** later that year, London and Washington were temporarily united on their policy on the Far East, and with the intervention of Chinese forces in the war, fought a land war in Asia together. Britain still took a more cautious approach in their dealings with China, often disagreeing with U.S. unilateral actions during the war, not least of which was Truman's suggestion that he was considering the use of atomic weapons. Anglo–American policy also differed over the entry of the People's Republic of China into the **United Nations**. The United States worked actively to prevent such an occurrence, while British diplomats viewed it as a fait accompli. Britain also relaxed **trade** controls—introduced by the Western nations under the Coordinating Committee for Multilateral Export Control (CoCom)—with the People's Republic much sooner than the United States, expanding its trade with China in 1957. Britain was perturbed by President **Richard Nixon**'s visit to China in February 1972, believing London should have been consulted beforehand due to its colony of Hong Kong. The United States finally established diplomatic relations with the PRC on 1 January 1979.

CHRISTOPHER, WARREN (1925–). A professional lawyer, Warren Christopher served as deputy secretary of the state (1977–1981) in the administration of **Jimmy Carter** and was secretary of state (1993–1997) in the first term of the administration of **William Clinton**. As secretary of state, Christopher attempted to realign U.S. foreign policy, suggesting it had been too Eurocentric in the past. As part of this plan, and without consulting Britain, he advocated changing the composition of the **United Nations** permanent Security Council, suggesting Japan and Germany should become members. The government of **John Major** felt this was somewhat insensitive to the long-standing friendship with Britain. The dispute between the British government and the Clinton administration over **Bosnia** was also fueled by Christopher, who stressed the need for a multilateral approach, played down the humanitarian angle, and stressed U.S. strategic interests. Christopher's plan for Bosnia included the lifting of an arms embargo against the Muslims but no introduction of American ground troops. However, despite several trips to Europe, he failed to persuade British and European leaders of the wisdom of the American position. He later led the negotiations to end the war in Bosnia that took place in Dayton, Ohio.

CHURCHILL, SIR WINSTON (1874–1965). British prime minister between 1940–1945 and 1951–1955, Winston Churchill's iconic status in world history, and in the history of Anglo–American relations, was established during **World War II**. Churchill was half-American by birth as his mother, **Jennie Jerome**, later Lady Randolph Churchill, was from New York and the daughter of the millionaire proprietor of the *New York Times*, Leonard Jerome. Churchill was proud of his American heritage. From October 1911 to May 1915, he served as First Lord of the Admiralty and helped ready the British naval fleet for war. After a period out of high office, during which he was a critic of **appeasement**, Churchill returned to the same position at the beginning of **World War II**. As prime minister of the British wartime coalition government (1940–1945), Churchill established a close working relationship with President **Franklin D. Roosevelt**, which he wrote about in his memoirs of the war. During the war and afterward, Churchill spoke and wrote about the Anglo–American relationship with an emphasis on the cultural ties between the two nations, reflecting his view that an alliance of the English-speaking peoples was a natural force for good in the world. With the publication of the actual correspondence between the two leaders, however, it became clear that although the personal relationship was a good one, there were still areas of disagreements, including over British policy toward **Greece** in 1944 and over civil aviation.

Despite U.S. neutrality in the early stages of the war, Churchill was able to persuade Roosevelt to provide Britain and its allies with food, munitions, and other vital supplies through **Cash and Carry** in 1939 and **Lend-Lease** in 1941. While providing great inspiration to the British in their fight against Nazi Germany, Churchill continued to try to encourage the United States to enter the war. Meeting for the first time at Placentia Bay in August 1941, Roosevelt and Churchill signed the **Atlantic Charter**, declaring their common principles for a peaceful world. They went on to meet on another eight occasions. Churchill's enthusiasm for transatlantic air travel facilitated his regular meetings with the American president and in effect began modern summit diplomacy. Toward the end of the war Churchill was aware that Roosevelt (and his successor **Harry S. Truman**) was moving closer to Joseph Stalin in the Big Three summits (**Tehran**, **Yalta**, **Potsdam**). In his attempts to persuade President Truman and the American public to be alert to the dangers of Soviet communism, he delivered one of his most famous speeches on 5 March 1946 at Westminster College in **Fulton, Missouri**. With Truman on the same platform, Churchill warned that "From Stettin in the Baltic to Trieste in the Adriatic, an iron curtain has descended across the Continent." In order to deal with this threat, Churchill called for an alliance of the English-speaking peoples, speaking of "a **special relationship** between the British Commonwealth and the United States." As a keen historian, he stressed the theme of Anglo–American unity in one of his most important books, *A History of the English-Speaking Peoples*, published in four volumes between 1956 and 1958.

During his second period as prime minister (1951–1955), Churchill focused his attention on the threat posed by the **Soviet Union** and was able to establish a cordial relationship with presidents Harry S. Truman and **Dwight D. Eisenhower**. The Truman–Churchill period was dominated by the **Korean War**. Churchill was able to establish a closer personal relationship with Eisenhower when he came into office in January 1953. He had met Eisenhower in 1941 when visiting the White House and worked with him as supreme commander of Allied forces in Europe. Eisenhower, who had some sympathy with British claims that they had been treated unfairly at the end of World War II when the United States ended nuclear cooperation, agreed at a meeting with Churchill in **Bermuda** to ask Congress to allow some exchange of information. As with Roosevelt, Churchill established a regular private correspondence with Eisenhower. Churchill's relationship with Eisenhower was somewhat strained as it became apparent to the prime minister that the president regarded Britain as just one of many important allies around the world. One of Churchill's main aims during this period was to try to get the United States more involved in the Middle East, as he hoped to reduce the number of British forces stationed there. In December 1954, the Anglo–Egyptian Treaty agreed to withdraw British forces from Egypt within two years. By the time he left office, Washington had decided to take on a greater and more independent role in the Middle East. Churchill found Eisenhower willing to listen to his concerns about Soviet influence in **Iran** and approved the overthrow of Mohammed Mossadeg in August 1953 by Central Intelligence Agency and MI6 action.

In 1963, under the presidency of **John F. Kennedy**, Churchill was given the unique distinction of being named an honorary citizen of the United States by the U.S. Congress. He remains a symbol of Anglo–American cooperation and has been admired by many U.S. presidents. *See also* MCMAHON ACT; NEW LOOK DEFENSE STRATEGY.

CLAYTON–BULWER TREATY (1850). By 1850, Great Britain and the United States had considered the feasibility of building a ship canal through Central America to link the Atlantic and Pacific oceans to reduce shipping costs. Although neither country wanted to undertake such a massive building project at the time, the treaty committed Great Britain and the United States to joint construction and control of any canal built in the future. This treaty was negotiated by the U.S. secretary of state, John M. Clayton, and the British representative, Sir Henry Bulwer, and also included a provision that neither country would colonize Central America. The treaty proved to be very unpopular in the United States, despite Senate ratification, and by the turn of the century the United States wanted the treaty terminated. After the **Spanish–American War** and with the acquisition of other overseas territories, the U.S. government recognized the military advantages that a canal would bring to its navy. U.S. President William McKinley sent Secretary of State John Hay to London to discuss a revised agreement, and in 1901 the **Hay–Pauncefote Treaty** was signed, providing Washington with the legal authority to build a canal by itself and the British with an agreement that its ships be charged the same tolls as American ships.

CLINTON, WILLIAM JEFFERSON "BILL" (1946–). Bill Clinton was the Democratic president between 1993 and 2001 and presided over the United States in the post–Cold War decade. Despite studying at University College, Oxford, on a Rhodes scholarship in the late 1960s, and appointing 20 other **Rhodes scholars** to positions within his administration, Bill Clinton was not known as an **Anglophile** on his arrival in the White House.

Having developed a close relationship with President **George H. W. Bush**, during the 1992 presidential election campaign, British Prime Minister **John Major** had sent the Conservative campaign director, Sir John Lacy, and his deputy, Mark Fulbrook, to the United States to offer the Bush campaign advice on how to defeat Clinton. In addition, British Home Office files were scrutinized to assess whether Clinton had attempted to renounce his U.S. citizenship while at Oxford and thus avoid the **Vietnam War**. No evidence of this was found but documents were released outlining Clinton's anti–Vietnam War protests at Oxford. Clinton's success in the 1992 presidential election meant that the new president was forced to work with a British prime minister who had actively tried to help his opponents.

Despite this unwelcome interference in U.S. politics, the Clinton administration invited Major to the **White House** as the first European leader to meet the new president. Clinton's attitude to the "**special relationship**" was revealed in the lead-up to the visit in February 1993, when he laughed at having to be reminded by his advisers to use the term during the discussion. Although Clinton did claim that the Anglo–American relationship was "special" to him personally, the media reported the visit negatively. The president made further efforts to improve relations with Great Britain by paying special attention to Major when he visited America in 1994. Major was invited to stay overnight at the White House, an honor last extended to **Winston Churchill** in 1942. The visit by Major had been upgraded partly in an attempt to ease Anglo–American tensions that had emerged over the president's decision to grant Sinn Fein leader **Gerry Adams** a visa to visit the United States in 1994. Diplomatic relations between the Clinton administration and Britain were put under more strain over disagreements on how to deal with the crisis in **Bosnia** between 1993 and 1995.

Relations improved with the election of Labour Prime Minister **Tony Blair** in May 1997. Clinton and Blair established a close friendship and strong working relationship based partly on a shared center–left political philosophy and both were lawyers, Oxford educated, and from the same generation. President Clinton's continued involvement on the issue of Northern **Ireland** was welcomed by the new Labour government, particularly the dispatch of former U.S. senator **George Mitchell** to help facilitate peace talks, and contributed to the Good Friday agreement in 1998. Although initially reluctant, Clinton agreed to U.S. intervention in **Kosovo** in 1998, partly as a result of pressure to do so by Blair. After leaving the White House, Clinton received an honorary doctorate from Oxford University in June 1994. He continued to meet privately with Tony Blair, who sought the former president's guidance and public intervention on the United Nations resolutions that led up to the **Iraq War** that began in 2003. *See also* SEITZ, RAYMOND.

CODY, SAMUEL FRANKLIN (1867–1913). An American by birth, Samuel Franklin Cody, made his name by bringing his Wild West show to the music halls in Britain. Cody toured Britain in the 1890s, entertaining the crowds with his cowboy and Wild West show. When British interest in the Wild West declined, Cody turned his talents to aviation. He patented several kites, built gliders, and became a pioneer of manned flight. In 1907, Cody began working with the British army at Aldershot, who helped him to fund the development of his airplane, British Army Aeroplane No. 1. On 16 October 1908, Cody flew this plane on what was deemed the first officially recorded powered flight in the British Isles. Cody continued to the push the boundaries of manned flight until his death in a plane crash in 1913.

COERCIVE ACTS, THE (1774). Passed in response to the **Boston Tea Party**, the Coercive Acts as they became known in England (properly known as the Restraining Acts) were four parliamentary acts drafted by **Lord North**, with the encouragement of King **George III**, with the aim of dealing harshly with the colony of Massachusetts to prevent further insurrection by the other American colonies. The most notorious of the acts was the Boston Port Act, passed on 1 June 1774, which closed Boston harbor until the destroyed tea was paid for. The other acts were the Administration of Justice Act and the Massachusetts Government Act passed on 20 May 1774 and the Quartering Act passed on 2 June 1774, which permitted British soldiers to be billeted in occupied buildings throughout the American colonies. Known as the "Intolerable Acts" in America, Lord North's measures further antagonized American colonists and led to the First Continental Congress. *See also* WAR OF INDEPENDENCE.

COLD WAR, THE. Between 1945 and 1991, the United States and the **Soviet Union** were locked in an ideological and strategic battle that was named the Cold War by one of President **Harry S. Truman**'s advisers, Bernard Baruch. Tensions between Washington and Moscow had their origins in the Russian Revolution of 1917 but implacable hostility between the archcommunist and archcapitalist nations began in earnest at the end of World War II when the United States and the Soviet Union emerged as superpowers. After working together to defeat Germany and Japan, the United States and the Soviet Union became antagonistic toward each other as they became increasingly suspicious of the other's motives: the United States disliked communism and feared Soviet expansionism in Eastern Europe and the

Middle East, and the Soviets desired a secure western border (a buffer zone against external attack) and were threatened by the U.S. refusal to share its nuclear secrets. Disagreements at the **Potsdam Conference** in July 1945, the dropping of the **atomic bombs** on Japan in August 1945, and the abrupt ending of **Lend-Lease** by the Americans fueled mistrust between the two nations. By 1947, the Cold War was being declared by the United States in the **Truman Doctrine**, America and its allies were committed to George Kennan's policy of containing communism. With the formation of the **North Atlantic Treaty Organization** (NATO) in 1949 and the subsequent formation of the Soviet-led Warsaw Pact, the Cold War became militarized. The Cold War witnessed a nuclear arms race, and in the zero-sum atmosphere of the times, the rest of the world was forced to take sides. At the end of World War II, the British Labour government, led by Prime Minister **Clement Attlee**, pressed the Truman administration to take the Soviet threat seriously, and the ensuing Cold War proved instrumental in cementing the wartime Anglo–American alliance. As one of the few remaining powers with a worldwide presence, the United States was keen to have British support during the Cold War. This was forthcoming, mainly because of the common enemy but also because a weakened Great Britain felt a "**special relationship**" with the United States, which would allow it continuing influence on the world stage. Britain encouraged the United States to establish military bases on British soil, established stronger intelligence links with the United States through the **UKUSA Agreement** of 1947, and played an important role in the **Berlin blockade** and the formation of NATO. Britain, as a member of NATO, also was able to shelter under the U.S. nuclear umbrella. Although the Anglo–American alliance remained strong throughout the Cold War and witnessed military cooperation during the **Korean War**, Washington and London often disagreed over the best way to deal with the communist nations, with Britain willing to **trade** with the Soviet Union and **Cuba** and also being willing to admit communist **China** into the **United Nations**. The most alarming Cold War crisis, the **Cuban missile crisis**, saw the special relationship in action as the Americans informed the British in advance of the impending crisis and the British supported the American position. There is some evidence that the United States may have accepted and acted upon some advice from the

British government during the crisis. In contrast, Anglo–American disagreements were also seen during the Cold War. During the **Vietnam War**, the British supported U.S. action but refused to send troops. *See also* AMERICAN BASES IN BRITAIN.

CONCORD, BATTLE OF (1775). The battles of Lexington Green and Concord marked the beginning of the American Revolutionary War. In an attempt to confiscate arms and munitions held by American patriots in Concord, Massachusetts, and after failing to capture John Hancock and Samuel Adams in Lexington, British forces led by Major Pitcairn marched toward the village but met and fought a group of Minutemen on the way. After much fighting, the British were forced to retreat. The colonists suffered 49 killed and 39 wounded but the British suffered more, losing 73, having 174 wounded, and their reputation damaged. The colonists, however, realized the British were vulnerable to unconventional warfare, including sniper attacks. *See also* WAR OF INDEPENDENCE.

COOK, ROBIN (1946–2005). When Robin Cook became foreign secretary (1997–2001) in the Labour government headed by Prime Minister **Tony Blair**, he pledged Great Britain would follow an ethical foreign policy. This ethical aspect of British foreign policy played a fundamental part in the decision making surrounding British intervention in **Kosovo** and Sierra Leone on humanitarian grounds. Cook famously resigned as leader of the House of Commons (2001–2003) on 17 March 2003 over British military action in **Iraq**, giving a personal statement to the House explaining his decision was based on his inability to support a war "without international agreement or domestic support" and explaining his doubts about the existence of weapons of mass destruction in Iraq. The statement received a standing ovation in the House. *See also* IRAQ WAR.

COOKE, ALISTAIR (1908–2004). Print, television, and radio journalist, Alistair Cooke became a specialist on Anglo–American relations. Born in England, Cooke became a U.S. citizen in 1941. Cooke worked as the London correspondent for NBC from 1936–1937 before serving as *The Guardian*'s United Nations' correspondent between 1945 and 1948, and then becoming their American correspondent until 1972. Cooke played a key role in interpreting America for Britons for over 58 years. He was best known in Great Britain for his weekly BBC radio address, *Letter from America*, that began in 1947, in which he presented life in the United States for the rest of the world. In 1972, he presented and wrote a BBC documentary series entitled *Alistair Cooke's America* that was broadcast in Britain and America and received a British Academy of Film and Television Arts (BAFTA) award and a Golden Globe award in the United States. Its success also led Cooke to be invited to take part in American bicentennial celebrations in 1976 by addressing the joint Houses of Congress. In America, Cooke was probably better known as the host of *Masterpiece Theatre*, broadcast on the PBS network from 1971–1992.

COWARD, NOEL (1899–1973). A well-known and successful British playwright, songwriter, actor, and director, Noel Coward appeared to typify the British aristocrat, dressed in a silk dressing gown, speaking in a clipped British accent, and demonstrating a keen wit. However, Coward was born in Teddington, Middlesex, to ordinary middle-class parents. He quickly developed a love of music and a talent for acting, making his first stage appearance in 1910. Coward made his first trip to the United States in 1921 and soon proved popular with American theatergoers. In 1929, he starred in a Broadway production of his romantic musical *Bitter Sweet*. By the 1930s, he was a successful playwright, with hits such as *Private Lives* and *Blithe Spirit* helping him to establish his domination of British theater. It is alleged that in 1940, Coward acted as an intelligence agent for the British Secret Service when he went to California to report back on American opinion on the war. He also entertained the troops on the battlefields during **World War II**. In 1943, he wrote, starred in, and codirected (with David Lean) the patriotic war film *In Which We Serve* (1943). The film received a special Academy Award. He went on to receive critical acclaim for writing the screenplay for the film *Brief Encounter* (1945). After the war, Coward spent more time in the United States, appearing on popular television shows such as *Together with Music* with Mary Martin. Knighted in 1970, Coward died in Jamaica in March 1973.

CREOLE **AFFAIR.** The 1840s saw a number of commercial disputes between the United States and Great Britain. One major incident occurred in 1841, when 130 Virginia slaves mutinied on the ship *Creole*, killing one crewmember in the process. Sailing on to the Bahamas, the slaves received asylum from British officials, despite demands by the U.S. government for their return. The British decision reflected the British government's ongoing fight against the slave **trade** and the affair, coming shortly after the *Caroline* **affair**, further increased Anglo–American tensions. *See also* ABOLITIONISTS.

CUBA. When Cuba became allied with the **Soviet Union** after the 1959 revolution that saw Fidel Castro come to power, the British and American governments took differing positions on how to proceed. The **John F. Kennedy** administration, under pressure from factions in Congress that demanded firm action in response to having a communist power 90 miles off the coast of Florida, introduced a total economic embargo against Cuba in February 1962. Despite pressure from Washington, the British government refused to engage in economic sanctions against the Cuban government, feeling they would have little effect. This belief was based partly on Britain's own attempt to use sanctions to gain concessions in the Middle East, which had failed against the Iranian nationalist leader, Mohammad Mossadeq, and Egyptian leader, Gamal Abdul Nasser. Britain also relied heavily on overseas **trade** and British shipowners were strongly opposed to the idea of trade sanctions. On 16 October 1959, the United States urged Britain not to go through with their plan to sell jet fighters to Cuba. Although Britain agreed not to supply arms to Cuba, British shipping continued to trade with the Castro government and the issue remained a contentious one. When Prime Minister **Alec Douglas-Home** visited Washington in February 1964, he led the press to believe that he had acted firmly in response to American criticism about British trade with Cuba, particularly the sale of Leyland buses. President **Lyndon Johnson** was livid at the imputation that he had allowed an allied leader of diminishing international significance to speak to him in such a manner, and apparently, Johnson never spoke to Douglas-Home again.

Although the U.S. trade embargo has continued, successive British governments have preferred a policy of "constructive engagement" in order to encourage democratic tendencies to flourish. Although not openly challenging the United States on Cuba, the government of **Tony Blair** disagreed with the judgment of the administration of **George W. Bush** that Cuba was a "rogue" nation that sponsors terrorism and was mildly critical of the detention of suspected terrorists at the U.S. naval base at **Guantanamo Bay**. *See also* CUBAN MISSILE CRISIS.

CUBAN MISSILE CRISIS (1962). The crisis over Soviet missiles stationed on Cuban soil, which brought the world to the brink of nuclear war in October 1962, revealed the strengths and weaknesses of the so-called **special relationship**. It is now recognized that Prime Minister **Harold Macmillan** was kept informed of the crisis by President **John F. Kennedy**, to the extent that some scholars have described Macmillan and British Ambassador **David Ormsby-Gore** as de facto members of the executive committee of senior military, diplomatic, and political advisors established by the president to handle events in **Cuba**. There is little doubt that the British had advance warning of the missile crisis, although the timing is in dispute. It is likely that the British were initially told of the photographic evidence of the presence of the missiles on Cuba via Major-General Sir Kenneth Strong of British Intelligence on 16 October. Strong, who happened to be in Washington that day, was told the news by Ray Cline, the Central Intelligence Agency deputy director of intelligence, who earlier that day had briefed President Kennedy on the matter. Macmillan was told of the impending crisis the next day, four days before the news broke. At first, the prime minister felt that a decisive military response was preferable, but once invasion had been ruled out, shifted his position to warning of possible adverse opinion in Europe to a crisis based on the proximity of enemy nuclear weapons (Europeans had been living with this threat for many years) and favoring a diplomatic settlement, suggesting the Americans trade their **Thor** missiles stationed in Britain for the Soviet missiles in Cuba.

Although Kennedy does not appear to have given this proposal any serious consideration, he did stay in communication by letter, telephone, cable, and through diplomatic exchanges with Macmillan and

Ormsby-Gore throughout the 10-day crisis, and Kennedy did listen to the advice of the British ambassador and reduced the line of the naval quarantine to 500 miles, overruling Secretary of Defense **Robert McNamara**, who advocated an 800-mile range. Despite some behind-the-scenes disagreements over the best way to handle the crisis, the British presented a united front with the U.S. government, arguing for the removal of the Soviet missiles in Cuba without deals. American nuclear forces stationed in Britain were on high alert, as was Britain's Royal Air Force and the dual-key-controlled Thor missiles. The resolution of the crisis, involving a private deal with Nikita Khrushchev to remove Jupiter missiles stationed in Turkey, meant that the extent of British influence on American decision making did not face the ultimate test as a nuclear confrontation was avoided.

CYPRUS. A British colony since 1878, Cyprus was granted its independence on 16 August 1960 after several years of armed struggle, although Great Britain would not allow its incorporation within **Greece**. In December 1963, Turkish Cypriots and Greek Cypriots began fighting over disagreements surrounding the Cypriot constitution; when it appeared that Turkish Cypriots were suffering the greater number of casualties, the United States feared Turkey would invade. Moreover, Washington was convinced that the Cypriot leader, Archbishop Makarios, had the potential to be the "Castro of the Mediterranean." Britain and the United States wanted to prevent two important **North Atlantic Treaty Organization** (NATO) allies from fighting one another. Instead, in 1964 President **Lyndon Johnson** sent his undersecretary of state, George Ball, on a mission to try to persuade all parties of the merits of partition and the introduction of a neutral NATO peacekeeping force. Makarios refused this suggestion and the issue was referred to the **United Nations** Security Council, which issued a resolution on 4 March 1964 that introduced a UN peacekeeping force that is still in place today.

In October 1973, Prime Minister **Edward Heath** refused to allow U.S. planes to use a British base on Cyprus for airlifting supplies to Israel during the **Arab–Israeli War**. The following year, Cyprus reemerged as a major issue in Anglo–American relations. In July 1974, inspired by the military regime in Athens, the Greek Cypriot military overthrew the Makarios government and declared the unification of Cyprus with Greece. The government of **Harold Wilson** in Britain hoped the United States would help defuse the crisis and prevent Turkish intervention but on 20 July 1974 Turkey invaded Cyprus. London called for an Anglo–American military intervention but the administration of **Richard Nixon** was facing the last stages of the Watergate crisis and the American secretary of state, **Henry Kissinger**, refused to cooperate, instead declaring U.S. neutrality on this issue. Prime Minister Wilson and Foreign Secretary **James Callaghan** felt Washington's inaction had encouraged Turkish intervention. On 30 July 1974, the prime ministers of Great Britain, Greece, and Turkey signed a peace agreement to provide for a ceasefire and eventually allowing for the division of Cyprus into Greek and Turkish sectors.

– D –

D-DAY LANDINGS (1944). The D-Day landings in Normandy, France, began the Allied invasion of Europe (codenamed Operation Overlord) during **World War II** and marked a decisive act in the war in Europe. The D-Day landings also came to symbolize Anglo–American wartime unity and cooperation. The Allied troops landed on the beaches of Normandy on 6 June 1944 with armored vehicles, guns, and other equipment. U.S. forces took the western beaches codenamed Utah and Omaha, British forces took the eastern beaches named Gold and Sword, and British and Canadian forces took another eastern beach named Juno. Allied forces suffered many casualties, with the losses suffered by the American forces on Omaha beach being the worst with 3,000 casualties. Although the troops fought against German forces for a month in Normandy, the landings enabled the Allied forces, under Supreme Allied Commander General **Dwight D. Eisenhower**, to march across Europe, reaching Germany by 12 September. The D-Day landings continue to hold a place in the public imagination of Britain and America, not only because of the feature movie *Saving Private Ryan* (1999) and the television series *Band of Brothers* (2001) but also because the spirit and sacrifice of the wartime generation has been commemorated in subsequent ceremonies.

DALTON, HUGH (1887–1962). British chancellor of the exchequer (1945–1947) in the government of **Clement Attlee**, Hugh Dalton was faced with handling the British economy in the aftermath of **World War II**. Britain's balance-of-payments problems were exacerbated by attempts to maintain a worldwide presence. Dalton was disappointed by the **Anglo–American loan agreement** finalized in December 1946 and negotiated by **John Maynard Keynes**, and presided over the tightening of rationing in Britain when the loan failed to produce significant results.

DANGERFIELD, GEORGE (1904–1986). A prominent Anglo–American historian and journalist, George Dangerfield is best known for his book *The Strange Death of Liberal England* (1935). Born in Newbury, Berkshire, and educated at Oxford University, Dangerfield moved to the United States in 1930 and became a U.S. citizen in 1943. He was editor of *Vanity Fair* magazine between 1933 and 1935. During **World War II**, he served in the U.S. Army in Europe. In 1953, he won the Pulitzer Prize and the Bancroft Prize for his book on Jacksonian and Jeffersonian democracy, *The Era of Good Feelings*. He lectured at the University of California from 1968–1972.

DAWES PLAN (1924). In April 1924, Charles Dawes and Reginald McKenna, American and British bankers, chaired respective committees of experts (including representatives from Belgium, Britain, France, Italy, and the United States) to recommend revisions to the 1919 **Treaty of Versailles**. The Dawes Plan, as it became known, was agreed to in August 1924 and attempted to ensure that Germany paid its wartime reparations by reducing the amount. In addition, the plan led to a loan (half-funded by the United States, a quarter by Britain) to support the German central bank, and the Dawes Plan temporarily aided Germany in its efforts to stabilize its economy and increased international confidence in European finance.

DESTROYERS-FOR-BASES DEAL. In August 1940, President **Franklin D. Roosevelt** agreed to exchange 50 old **World War I** American destroyers for Britain providing 99-year leases on British territories in the West Indies and **Canada** (Antigua, Bermuda, British

Guiana, Jamaica, Newfoundland, St. Lucia, Trinidad) where the United States could establish military bases. Prime Minister **Winston Churchill** had requested the destroyers to help the British repel a German invasion of England and to provide military escorts for merchant vessels bringing essential war material to Great Britain. Roosevelt struck a hard bargain with Churchill because U.S. neutrality legislation prevented him from selling or giving warships to a military power. Roosevelt's use of his executive power was widely criticized at home and fears were raised about a growing American empire. In Britain, concern was expressed about selling parts of its empire.

DICKENS, CHARLES (1812–1870). Charles Dickens was the preeminent British novelist of the Victorian age. Experiencing popular as well as critical success on both sides of the Atlantic for novels such as *Oliver Twist* (1838), *A Tale of Two Cities* (1859), *David Copperfield* (1850), *Hard Times* (1854), and *A Christmas Carol* (1843), Dickens traveled to the United States on two separate occasions. On 3 January 1842 he sailed from Liverpool to arrive in Boston on 22 January to be mobbed by adoring crowds, an experience that was repeated wherever he went in the United States. Expecting to admire all things American, Dickens came away disappointed to find that his privacy was invaded during the visit, and he found little sympathy for his attempts to persuade Americans to agree to international copyright protection. On returning to England, Dickens published his experiences and observations of the United States in *American Notes* (1842), particularly his abhorrence of slavery and his criticism of political bosses in the cities. Some of Dickens's perceptions of American failings eventually appeared in the serialized novel *Martin Chuzzlewit* (1843–1844). Dickens's second and much more positive visit to the United States came in 1867 when he embarked on a major, profitable reading tour.

DIEGO GARCIA. In 1965, the British government led by Prime Minister **Harold Wilson** negotiated with Mauritius over the colony's independence. During these negotiations, Wilson made it clear that Mauritius would gain its independence in 1968 but without the Chagos Islands, which would be retained by Britain. The Chagos Islands became part of Great Britain's Indian Ocean Territory in 1965 but Wilson had already made a deal with the administration of **Lyndon Johnson** that they would lease the largest of the islands, Diego Garcia, to the United States for use as a military base. Located in the middle of the Indian Ocean, Diego Garcia was and is of great strategic significance, and the United States has made great use of the island as an air and naval base, and as a refueling location. There are now approximately 2,000 U.S. military personnel stationed there. The island's status as a "stationary aircraft carrier" has meant that American B-52 and Stealth bombers have taken off from Diego Garcia on route to bombing raids in several conflicts, including the **Gulf War** of 1991, **Afghanistan**, and the **Iraq War**.

The most controversial aspect of the leasing of the British territory to the United States was the treatment of the island's inhabitants. Since the late 18th century, Diego Garcia had been populated by the Ilois, Chagos Islanders descended from African slaves and Indian plantation workers. As the U.S. administration did not want a "population problem" on the island they were going to lease, by 1970 the British government had relocated the native population of between 1,200 and 2,000 Ilois to Mauritius without choice or compensation. This colonial act has been challenged in the British courts but to date the Chagos Islanders have been unsuccessful in their attempts to be allowed home and have not received any compensation.

DITCHLEY FOUNDATION. Based at Ditchley House in Oxfordshire, England, the Ditchley Foundation was founded in 1958 by Sir David Wills with the aim of promoting Anglo–American understanding. Although its aims have been widened in recent years, it has continued to host regular conferences on transatlantic issues, and its attendees have been senior academics, politicians, business leaders, members of the armed forces, and the media. Its director has usually been a former ambassador.

DOUGLAS-HOME, SIR ALEC (1903–1995). Alec Douglas-Home became prime minister in October 1963 after the resignation of **Harold Macmillan**. A Conservative politician since 1931, and the first peer to become prime minister since Lord Salisbury in 1885, Douglas-Home was perceived as aloof and aristocratic and was defeated by Labour MP **Harold Wilson** in the October 1964 general election. Prior to becoming prime minister, he had acted for three years as British foreign secretary and had, along with Prime Minister Macmillan, considered calling for an international conference to solve the **Cuban missile crisis**. During his yearlong tenure in 10 **Downing Street**, Douglas-Home struggled to develop a close relationship with the United States. His relationship with President **John F. Kennedy** did not have time to develop due to the assassination in Dallas, and his first visit to Washington in 1964 to meet President **Lyndon Johnson** proved problematic. Johnson was reported to be furious after Douglas-Home suggested during his visit that he had responded strongly to U.S. criticism of British sales of Leyland buses to **Cuba**. As foreign secretary and prime minister, Douglas-Home opposed the American plan for a **multilateral force** (MLF) but worked with the United States on **Cyprus**. As British foreign secretary in the government of **Edward Heath** (1970–1974), Douglas-Home was surprised when he was not informed by **Henry Kissinger** of U.S. plans to make 1973 the "**Year of Europe**" and to negotiate a "new **Atlantic Charter**."

DOWNING STREET, NO. 10. Since 1730, No. 10 Downing Street in Whitehall, London, has been the workplace of the British prime minister. It also became the home of the prime minister and his or her family. As well as being the political office of the prime minister and witnessing regular cabinet discussion and important meetings, including visits from several U.S. presidents, it has also been the site of public protest and external attack. Downing Street suffered bomb damage during **World War II** and in 1991 the Irish Republican Army attempted to mortar bomb the building.

DULLES, JOHN FOSTER (1888–1959). A former lawyer, legal adviser at the Paris Peace Conference in 1919, and U.S. adviser at the San Francisco Conference in 1945, John Foster Dulles was President **Dwight D. Eisenhower**'s secretary of state between 1953 and 1959. A stern figure and vehemently anticommunist, Dulles was willing to confront communism and even began to speak of "liberation" and plans to "roll back" the iron curtain. Dulles believed firmly in dealing with the Soviet threat by promising "massive retaliation" and in

1956 articulated the policy of "brinkmanship." In Great Britain, Prime Minister **Winston Churchill** and **Anthony Eden**, the foreign secretary, were alarmed by this attitude to communism, which differed from their view that communism should be controlled and moderated. Dulles and Eden had a poor relationship. Dulles was annoyed over Britain's position on Vietnam at the 1954 **Geneva Conference** and his relationship with Eden never recovered. Dulles strongly opposed the Anglo-French invasion of Egypt in 1956 and was blamed by the British for helping to cause the **Suez crisis**, and certainly there was some confusion surrounding the American position. Dulles had abruptly withdrawn from an Anglo–American loan to build the Aswan dam and the Egyptian president, Colonel Gamal Abdul Nasser, subsequently turned to the Soviets for financial support.

DUMBARTON OAKS CONFERENCE. Between August and October 1944, representatives of **China**, Great Britain, the **Soviet Union**, and the United States met at Dumbarton Oaks, near Washington, D.C., to discuss the form that the proposed **United Nations** would take.

– E –

EAST OF SUEZ DECISION (1967). On 16 January 1968, the Labour government headed by Prime Minister **Harold Wilson** announced its plans to withdraw all forces from the Far East (except **Hong Kong**) by 31 March 1971 and would withdraw all forces from the Persian Gulf by the same date. This decision was recognition by the British that they could no longer afford a worldwide military role and was made to ensure the success of the devaluation of the pound of November 1967. The announcement to withdraw East of Suez was made as part of a statement on sizeable budget cuts in government spending on 16 January 1968 and was endorsed by the cabinet and Parliament. The military cuts resulted in a reduction of 75,000 military personnel and 80,000 civilians. Great Britain also cancelled its order for 50 U.S. F-111 long-range reconnaissance aircraft. The East of Suez decision proved a damaging blow to the "**special relationship**," especially as the United States was still fighting the **Vietnam War**, and the administration of **Lyndon Johnson**, particularly Secretary of

State **Dean Rusk**, had made extensive efforts to try to persuade the British against such a plan. President Johnson even made a last-minute personal appeal direct to Wilson, claiming the decision was tantamount to a British withdrawal from world affairs.

EDEN, SIR ANTHONY (1897–1977). Anthony Eden became British Conservative prime minister in 1955 after the retirement of **Winston Churchill**, having served as British foreign secretary on three occasions. During his first period as foreign secretary (1935–1938), he worked under Prime Minister **Ramsay MacDonald** until 1937 and then under Prime Minister **Neville Chamberlain**. He resigned from office after disagreeing with Chamberlain over his **appeasement** policies. He served his second term as foreign secretary (1940–1945) under Winston Churchill, and became a regular visitor to the United States dealing with Anglo–American cooperation during **World War II** and attending the wartime conferences, including **Potsdam**, until the election of the Labour government on 26 July 1945. During his third term as foreign secretary (1951–1955) under the peacetime Churchill government, Eden had a poor relationship with U.S. Secretary of State **John Foster Dulles**, whom he disliked. Relations were made worse by disagreements between the two at the 1954 Geneva Conference and over the **European Defence Community** (EDC).

By the time Eden became prime minister in April 1955, he was a skilled and experienced diplomat. By this stage, he had lost faith in the "**special relationship**" with the United States as a means of dealing with British security. This partly explains the defining feature of his premiership—the **Suez crisis**. After the Suez Canal was nationalized by Gamul Abdul Nasser, Eden did not appreciate the sensitivity of the timing of British and French attempts to regain control of the canal. Having waited so long to become prime minister, he was to stay in office less than two years, resigning in January 1957 in the aftermath of the Suez debacle on the grounds of ill health. When Eden fell ill in the United States, while spending Christmas with Averell Harriman, Prime Minister **James Callaghan** sent the Royal Air Force to bring him home to die in England in January 1977.

EDWARD VIII (1894–1972). King of the United Kingdom on the death of his father, George V, on 20 January 1936 until his abdication on 11 December 1936, Edward VIII is most commonly remembered for his relationship with American divorcée **Wallis Simpson**. As Edward, Prince of Wales, he had become a well-known celebrity figure on both sides of the Atlantic as a young, much-traveled, fashionable, and sociable royal. He made an official visit to the United States for the first time in 1919 when he traveled to New York after a tour of **Canada** and met with financiers on Wall Street and with President **Woodrow Wilson**. On 7 April 1920, he made an unofficial stopover in San Diego, California, on his way back from Australia. By the time of his social visit to New York in 1924, the prince of Wales's visit was announced as the arrival of the "most eligible bachelor." An unattached 29-year-old at the time of the visit, the prince embraced American culture, enjoying jazz, clothes shopping, and socializing with New York's elites. He made a visit to the United States in 1941, five years after he had abdicated the British throne, in order to marry Wallis Simpson. *See also* SIMPSON, WALLIS.

EGYPT. *See* SUEZ CRISIS.

EISENHOWER DOCTRINE (1957). On 5 January 1957, two months after the **Suez crisis** demonstrated the impotency of British and French power in the Middle East, President **Dwight D. Eisenhower** proclaimed U.S. aid or military support for any state in the region that felt threatened by aggressive communism. Congress approved the doctrine on 7 March 1957. Despite the presence of the Sixth Fleet of the U.S. Navy in the Mediterranean, the limitations of this doctrine soon became apparent and it was only put into practice twice during the Eisenhower years. The first occasion was in April 1957 when support was provided to King Hussein in Jordan, along with British intervention, and in July 1958 when 10,000 U.S. marines were sent into to Beirut in the Lebanon to help with the Iraqi-backed Muslim insurgency. The Eisenhower Doctrine marked an increased level of activity in the Middle East by the United States.

EISENHOWER, DWIGHT D. (1890–1969). Before becoming Republican president (1953–1961), General Dwight D. Eisenhower served in **World War II** as supreme Allied commander in Northern Europe 1944–1945 and Supreme Allied Commander in Europe

(SACEUR) 1950–1952. His military experience in Europe, with his headquarters in **Grosvenor Square**, London, meant that he was well known by the British political and military establishment. On entering the White House he developed an easy working relationship with Prime Minister **Winston Churchill** but it was clear that in the postwar world he regarded Great Britain as one of a number of important allies. This new attitude was confirmed by President Eisenhower at the **Bermuda Conference** in December 1953, and by the **New Look defense strategy**, which placed greater emphasis on alliance systems such as the **North Atlantic Treaty Organization** and the **Baghdad Pact**. Eisenhower worked with the British in concluding the **Korean War** but found British and American interests diverging in Southeast Asia. At the 1954 **Geneva Conference** it became apparent that France was going to suffer a military defeat against nationalist forces at Dien Bien Phu in **Vietnam** and was likely to withdraw from Indochina as a result. Eisenhower wrote to Churchill on 4 April 1954 suggesting a joint military effort to prevent a French defeat but he refused. Both nations subsequently joined the **South-East Asia Treaty Organization** (SEATO). Eisenhower also found that Britain and America still had differing attitudes on how to deal with **China**.

It was the Middle East that proved the area of greatest Anglo–American cooperation and dissent during the Eisenhower presidency. In **Iran**, Eisenhower agreed with British fears that the Mohammad Mossadeq regime was communist-inspired and in 1954 British and American intelligence worked together to overthrow it. Anglo–American relations faced its biggest postwar crisis in the summer and autumn of 1956 when the United States forced the withdrawal of British and French troops from Egypt after their attempt to secure access to the Suez Canal. In Britain, Eisenhower was charged with devaluing the **special relationship**, but after the **Suez crisis** and his own reelection in November 1956, Eisenhower worked toward reestablishing a strong Anglo–American relationship. The Eisenhower administration soon recognized that its bilateral relationship with Britain brought benefits, not least in terms of their joint and leading involvement in NATO. Meeting with the new British Prime Minister **Harold Macmillan** at the **Bermuda Conference** in March 1957, Eisenhower agreed to provide the British with 60 **Thor missiles** as a stopgap until the development of the British **Blue Streak** missile. In his final year in the White House, Eisenhower secured British agreement that the **Holy Loch Naval Base** in Scotland could be used by the U.S. Navy to house nuclear submarines. And, in October 1957, after bilateral talks in Washington, Eisenhower and Macmillan issued a "Declaration of Common Purpose" that envisaged close collaboration in facing the communist threat.

ELIZABETH II, QUEEN (1926–). Reigning over the British since 1952, Queen Elizabeth II has contributed to a sense of Anglo–American friendship through her leadership that has emphasized and reinforced the strong and enduring links between the two countries. She first visited the country in 1951 as a princess and has made five official visits to the United States since becoming the British monarch. In October 1957, she visited President **Dwight D. Eisenhower** and hosted a dinner for him in Washington as queen of **Canada**. On the same visit she addressed the **United Nations** General Assembly. Her next visit came as part of the 1976 bicentennial celebrations, when she arrived in New York on board the royal yacht *Britannia* and attend a state dinner at the **White House** on 7 July 1976 hosted by President **Gerald Ford**. In March 1983, Queen Elizabeth II visited **Ronald Reagan** on the West Coast of America. In May 1991, after the Persian **Gulf War**, she visited President **George H. W. Bush** and became the first British monarch to address a joint session of the U.S. Congress. As part of a state visit to the United States in May 2007, the queen contributed to the 400th anniversary of the founding of **Jamestown**, Virginia, by visiting the site of the settlement, addressing the Virginia State Assembly, as well as attending a state banquet at the White House, hosted by President **George W. Bush**.

Queen Elizabeth has also played host to several U.S. presidents at Chequers, Windsor Castle, and Buckingham Palace: President **Dwight D. Eisenhower** visited London in 1959; **John F. Kennedy** in June 1961; **Richard Nixon** in February 1969 and October 1970; Ronald Reagan in June 1982, June 1984, and June 1988; George H. W. Bush in May 1989; **Bill Clinton** in June 1994, November 1995, and December 2000; and George W. Bush in July 2001 and November 2003.

ELLINGTON, EDWARD KENNEDY "DUKE" (1899–1974). In the summer of 1933, African American jazz pianist and orchestra leader

Duke Ellington made his first visit to Europe, spending six weeks in Great Britain. In addition to receiving critical acclaim, Ellington also played at a private event for royal guests, where Edward, Prince of Wales (later Edward VIII) played drums with him. Ellington remained a popular jazz musician in Britain. *See also* JAZZ.

EMBARGO ACT (1807). The Embargo Act was passed by the U.S. Congress in an attempt to ensure American neutrality during the **Napoleonic** wars. The United States had profited as its vessels upheld their freedom to **trade** with the French and the British in goods that were not war materials. After many years of American ships being seized and boarded by both belligerents, President **Thomas Jefferson** responded by trying to highlight how important it was to both France and Britain not to restrict neutral trade. The Embargo Act confined American ships to port, except those engaging in coastal trade, and banned British ships from entering American waters. The act backfired on Jefferson, as the economic sanctions hit the United States harder than Great Britain. *See also CHESAPEAKE AFFAIR.*

ENGLISH-SPEAKING UNION. Formed by British journalist Evelyn Wrench and launched on 4 July 1918, the English-Speaking Union is an educational charity with branches throughout Great Britain and the world. Established at the end of **World War I** and based at Dartmouth House in London, the aim of the union was to encourage international understanding by promoting closer ties between English-speaking peoples. Its first chairman was Sir **Winston Churchill**. Since its foundation, the union has become best known for its educational exchange programs and its debating and public speaking competitions. In the United States, British **war brides** were helped to settle in their new country by clubs organized by the English-Speaking Union.

EUROPEAN DEFENCE COMMUNITY (EDC). In the post–World War II period, Europe attempted to form a supranational army with common institutions, including a rearmed Germany. Prime Minister **Winston Churchill** had suggested the idea but it was formally proposed by French Prime Minister Rene Pleven in October 1950 and a treaty to establish the European Defence Community was signed on

27 May 1952 by six countries about to enter the forerunner to the European Economic Community, the European Coal and Steel Community—France, Italy, West Germany, the Netherlands, Belgium, and Luxembourg. Great Britain declared its support for the EDC but did not sign the treaty due to its overseas commitments. Despite being proposed by the French, the vexing question of German rearmament led the French Assembly to veto ratification of the treaty in August 1954.

EUROPEAN ECONOMIC COMMUNITY (EEC)/ECONOMIC COMMUNITY (EC)/EUROPEAN UNION (EU). In the aftermath of World War II, the United States supported efforts to create a strong and stable Europe. The **American Committee for a United Europe** (ACUE) encouraged British public opinion to be more pro-European in outlook by financing the **European Movement**, which worked for the political and economic integration of Europe. The administration of **Harry S. Truman** implemented the **European Recovery Program** (ERP) to aid the reconstruction of war-torn Europe, organized the **North Atlantic Treaty Organization** (NATO), and established diplomatic relations with the European Coal and Steel Community (ECSC) on 11 August 1952. The European Economic Community was formed on 25 March 1957 after the signing of the Treaty of Rome by its six original members: France, West Germany, Italy, Belgium, the Netherlands, and Luxembourg. The EEC was known as "the Common Market" and was founded as an economic association to promote free **trade**, abolish trade and tariff barriers, establish the free movement of capital and labor among member nations, and to follow joint financial and social policies. The ultimate agreed aim of the EEC was to create a single economic market in Europe. However, some supporters of the EEC hoped for a supranational organization that would include political and military union. This prospect made the British suspicious of entry into the union but by the late 1950s they were persuaded by the economic success of the EEC to apply for membership. At first, the United States protested the Treaty of Rome, arguing that it violated the **General Agreement on Tariffs and Trade** (GATT), but by the time of the administration of **John F. Kennedy**, the United States had decided it must try to increase its trade with the EEC. In addition, the British received much encouragement from the United States to join the EEC not only because of their desire to see a strong, integrated Europe as a bulwark against Soviet communism but also because by the 1960s the United States was hoping that Great Britain could help modify the EEC's increasingly protectionist policies, especially the Common Agricultural Policy (CAP). Moreover, Washington believed that an EEC with Britain as a member would be much more outward looking.

The first British application for full membership of the EEC came under the government of **Harold Macmillan** on 31 July 1961, and the second under the government of **Harold Wilson** on 10 May 1967. Both these applications were vetoed by the French under President Charles de Gaulle, who feared Britain would act as a "Trojan horse" for the Commonwealth nations and the United States. The United Kingdom finally became a member of the EEC on 1 January 1973 after Prime Minister **Edward Heath** negotiated British entry.

After joining the EEC, known officially as the European Community after July 1967, British governments struggled to reconcile their foreign policy objective of closer European ties and a continuing strong political relationship with the United States. This became an increasing problem as the European Community began to move toward increased political as well as economic cooperation. In 1987, the Treaty of Rome was revised in the Single European Act and cooperation between the United States and the European Community became formalized in 1990 in the **Transatlantic Declaration** and was built on in 1995 with the signing of the **New Transatlantic Agenda**, when common action was agreed on a variety of economic, environmental, and security issues. The European Union was created after the Treaty of Maastricht was signed on 7 February 1992 and came into force in November 1993. The EU soon established a single market for European goods, services, and people, and in 1999 a European currency—the euro—came into circulation within 11 member states. The EU also began to increase its foreign policy role under the Common Foreign and Security Policy (CFSP). Increasingly, Britain has worked with the EU to address foreign and defense policy problems, notably in humanitarian aid and in joint action on peacemaking and peacekeeping initiatives in the Balkans, Africa, and in relation to the Russian invasion of Georgia in August 2008. The U.S.–EU economic relationship remains the most important trading relationship in the world. With 27 members, the European Union's trade in goods and services with the United States amounted to over $600 billion annually in 2007.

On 30 April 2007, further steps toward the harmonization of trade between the EU and the United States were taken with the founding of the Transatlantic Economic Council.

EUROPEAN MOVEMENT, THE. Established on 25 October 1948, the European Movement was founded as an extragovernmental group to promote the economic and political integration of democratic Western Europe as a buffer against Soviet communism. Founded by former British prime minister **Winston Churchill** and Conservative politician **Duncan Sandys**, the European Movement played an active role throughout Europe in supporting and coordinating efforts in achieving a united Europe. In its early years, the European Movement was supported financially by the **American Committee on a United Europe** (ACUE). Still in existence, the European Movement continues to promote the merits of membership in the **European Union**.

EUROPEAN RECOVERY PROGRAM. *See* MARSHALL PLAN.

– F –

FALKLANDS WAR (1982). Between April and June 1982, Britain engaged in an undeclared war with Argentina in order to regain control of the Falklands Islands (the Malvinas) and liberate the 1,800 British settlers after General Leopoldo Galtieri ordered the invasion of the islands on 2 April. The Falklands Islands in the southern Atlantic Ocean had been under British rule since 1833 but Argentina had long protested British occupation of the islands and laid claim to the territory on the grounds of proximity, pointing out the United Kingdom was 8,000 miles away. For Prime Minister **Margaret Thatcher**, Britain had no choice but to resort to a military conflict as it was a question of external invasion and the self-determination of the islanders. At the time there was speculation that Britain did not want to lose the Falklands as there might be oil deposits in the seas of the south Atlantic, although this has remained speculation. At the outset of the conflict, and much to Margaret Thatcher's anger, the United States adopted a public role as a neutral mediator. Secretary of State **Alexander Haig** engaged in shuttle diplomacy in an attempt to prevent war, partly because the United States had treaty obligations to both sides in the dispute. Most advisers in the administration of **Ronald Reagan**, including Haig and Assistant Secretary of State for Political Affairs Lawrence Eagleburger, argued that failure to support the British could undermine the **North Atlantic Treaty Organization**. But despite Argentina being led by a military junta, Washington also viewed Argentina as a staunch anticommunist ally and a fellow member of the Rio Pact (the Inter-American Treaty of Reciprocal Assistance); some, including the U.S. ambassador to the **United Nations**, **Jeanne Kirkpatrick**, feared that support for Britain might scupper U.S. plans in Latin America.

While the United States was still considering its best response, the Thatcher government in London assembled a military task force that included 30 warships, supporting ships, and the *Queen Elizabeth II* liner (which was requisitioned to transport troops to the conflict). Once it was clear that Thatcher's government was determined to retake the islands and that Haig's attempts at mediation had failed, Washington's loyalty to Great Britain superseded any damage that might be done to American interests in Latin America and by the end of April the United States formally ended its neutrality. By the beginning of May, Washington agreed to supply all the military resources it could, although Secretary of Defense **Caspar Weinberger** had already begun to supply Great Britain with military intelligence and supplies, and had authorized British use of the U.S. airbase on Ascension Island, halfway between Britain and the Falklands. American support proved crucial to the British effort and its forces in recapturing Port Stanley on 13 July, and Argentina surrendered the following day. British forces suffered 255 killed and lost six ships and Argentina lost 746 personnel, almost half of these during the sinking of their cruiser *General Belgrano* by torpedo attack. General Galtieri and his military government lost power, largely as a result of the Falklands War, and Argentina became a democratic country in 1983. Margaret Thatcher's popularity was boosted by the war and played a part in her electoral victory in 1983.

FENIAN BROTHERHOOD. Formed in the United States in 1858, the Fenian Brotherhood aimed to overthrow British rule in **Ireland**. Becoming active after the **American Civil War** and prepared to take up arms to achieve their goal, the Fenians launched several raids into British North America (**Canada**) in an attempt to force their case. The most famous raid took place from 1–3 June 1866 on the Niagara border when the Fenians managed to defeat a small Canadian militia at the battle of Ridgeway. Fenian activity died down after 1871 but the Americans' failure to deal with the secret society antagonized the British and contributed to strained Anglo–American relations in the aftermath of the American Civil War.

"FLEXIBLE RESPONSE" STRATEGY. Robert McNamara, U.S. secretary of defense, moved the Kennedy administration away from the "**massive retaliation**" strategy by introducing "flexible response" in 1961. During the 1960 presidential election campaign, **John F. Kennedy** criticized President **Dwight D. Eisenhower** for allowing the United States to fall behind the **Soviet Union** in terms of conventional forces and missile technology, referring to it as the "missile gap." On entering the White House, Kennedy was informed by the Central Intelligence Agency (CIA) that there was no gap but began a military buildup based on the strategy of flexible response: the ability to make the most appropriate kind of war, from guerrilla warfare to full-scale nuclear war. For the British, "flexible response" might include a tactical nuclear warfare contained to the European continent and for this reason its centrality in the Kennedy foreign policy caused alarm.

FORD, GERALD (1913–2006). A Republican politician, Gerald Ford was the 38th president of the United States who had been vice president until **Richard Nixon**'s resignation in August 1974. President until January 1977, Ford lost the 1976 presidential election to **Jimmy Carter**, and therefore had the distinction of not having been elected to national office, despite being vice president and president. Ford established a good working relationship with prime ministers **Harold Wilson** and **James Callaghan**, despite disagreements during the 1976 sterling crisis. During Ford's time in office, the United States celebrated its bicentennial, and as part of the commemoration **Queen**

Elizabeth II and Prince Philip arrived in the country aboard the royal yacht *Britannia* to embark on a state visit. The president hosted a state dinner at the **White House** for the queen and Prince Philip on 7 July 1976 and, as a great admirer of the Anglo–American cultural relationship, paid tribute to the role played by British custom, fortitude, law, and government in the history and culture of the United States. *See also* IMF CRISIS.

FORRESTAL, JAMES (1892–1949). Appointed as secretary of the navy toward the end of **World War II**, James Forrestal oversaw the integration of the American armed forces that was dictated under the 1947 National Security Act. He went on to become the American secretary of defense (1947–1949) until he was asked to resign by President **Harry S. Truman**. Forrestal committed suicide shortly afterward. During his time as secretary of defense, he negotiated with his counterpart in Great Britain, **Ernest Bevin**, over the introduction of B-29 bombers to Britain during the **Berlin crisis** of 1948. *See also* AMERICAN BASES IN BRITAIN.

FOUR FREEDOMS. Prior to U.S. entry into **World War II**, in his State of the Union address on 6 January 1941, President **Franklin D. Roosevelt** outlined what he believed were the four freedoms that all humans should enjoy as a basis for world peace and security. The four freedoms—freedom of speech and expression, freedom to worship, freedom from want, and freedom from fear—reflected Roosevelt's internationalist perspective on U.S. foreign policy.

FOUR POLICEMEN. During planning for the **United Nations** organization of collective security, President **Franklin D. Roosevelt** and the U.S. State Department were determined not to repeat the mistakes of the **League of Nations**, and decided that the Great Powers— **China**, Great Britain, the **Soviet Union**, and the United States— should have more power within the United Nations and, recognizing the regional and global power of these nations, referred to them as the "four policemen" of the world.

FOURTEEN POINTS. On seizing power in Russia and gaining possession of the tsar's papers, the Bolsheviks published secret treaties that confirmed that the Allied powers in **World War I** intended to carve up Europe on the defeat of Germany and the Central Powers, with Great Britain expected to be the main beneficiary of the defeat of the Turkish Empire. On 8 January 1918 President **Woodrow Wilson** made his Fourteen Points address to Congress outlining his plan for a lasting peace after the end of World War I that would help shape the Old World in the image of the New World. He did not consult his major allies in Europe over the Fourteen Points, and the first five points appeared to be a direct challenge to British power as they called for (1) an end to secret diplomacy and secret treaties, instead of "open covenants of peace, openly arrived at," (2) freedom of navigation upon the seas, (3) the removal of **trade** barriers, (4) arms reduction and disarmament, and (5) the referral of colonial disputes to international arbitration. Points 5–13 dealt with specific territorial disputes among the European powers. Point 14 called for "a general association of nations . . . formed on the basis of covenants designed to create mutual guarantees of the political independence and territorial integrity of the States, large and small equally." This last point resulted in plans to create a **League of Nations**.

When the fighting ended in October 1914 Wilson insisted the Fourteen Points should provide the basis of the peace settlement and negotiated an armistice with Germany independently. Great Britain refused to accept point 2, which struck at Britain's naval power, and other European powers disputed several of the Fourteen Points. While Wilson was away in Europe attending the **Paris Peace Conference** in early 1919, the mood of the U.S. Congress had changed. In the midterm election of November 1918, the Republicans had achieved a majority in both houses of Congress, and opposition to the **Versailles Treaty** had grown, particularly in relation to Wilson's cherished League of Nations. To many in Congress, the Versailles Peace Treaty violated **George Washington**'s guidance that the United States should avoid "entangling alliances" and compromised the **Monroe Doctrine**. Despite making minor compromises and appealing directly to the U.S. public—traveling over 8,000 miles by train across America to deliver over 40 speeches on the issue—Wilson was unable to convince Congress and was unable to gain the approval of the treaty by the necessary two-thirds of the U.S. Senate.

FRANKS, SIR OLIVER (1905–1992). Sir Oliver Franks was the British ambassador to Washington between 1948 and 1952. Franks developed a close working relationship with U.S. Secretary of State **Dean Acheson** and in the process helped improve and cement Great Britain's relationship with the United States. Acheson and Franks met weekly to discuss world events, and the ambassador encouraged the government of **Clement Attlee** to commit ground troops to the **Korean War** because he believed this was the price that needed to be paid in order to ensure the continuation of the "**special relationship**" and for support in Europe.

FREEMAN, JOHN (1915–). Former British Labour MP John Freeman served as British ambassador to the United States during the first administration of **Richard Nixon** from 1969–1971. During his time in Washington, Freeman established a warm working relationship with presidential adviser **Henry Kissinger** through lengthy, in-depth, off-the-record discussions. This relationship helped smooth over some of the difficulties evident in Anglo–American relations during these years.

FRENCH REVOLUTIONARY WAR (1793–1802). In 1794, the U.S. Congress passed a Neutrality Act that prohibited Americans from fighting in the war between France and Great Britain (1793–1802). It also prevented the navies of belligerents in the war from using American ports. Until the agreement reached under the **Jay Treaty** in November 1794, relations between the U.S. and Great Britain worsened when the British seized American cargo ships that carried nonwar goods. *See also* NAPOLEONIC WARS.

FRIENDLY FIRE INCIDENTS. So-called friendly fire incidents, or "blue-on-blue" incidents as the British military term them, involve allied forces firing on one another instead of the enemy. There have been several incidents of this kind involving British and American forces, most notably in the **Gulf War** of 1991, during the campaign in **Afghanistan**, and the **Iraq War**. In some British circles, friendly fire incidents have become synonymous with American military incompetence, and on several occasions American attacks on British forces have caused tensions in the Anglo–American defense and political relationship.

FUCHS, KLAUS (1911–1988). A Germany nuclear physicist who fled to Great Britain from Nazi Germany in the 1930s, Klaus Fuchs worked with British scientists on the **atomic bomb** project and was later convicted of supplying atomic secrets to the **Soviet Union**. He was arrested on 2 February 1950 as a communist spy, convicted, and served nine years in prison. Fuchs's arrest damaged prospects for renewed Anglo–American nuclear cooperation in the aftermath of the **McMahon Act**.

FULBRIGHT, WILLIAM J. (1905–1995). A member of the U.S. Senate representing Arkansas (1945–1974) and chairman of the Senate Foreign Relations Committee (1959–1974), William Fulbright introduced legislation that established the Fulbright Program with the aim of promoting peace and understanding through educational exchanges. Fulbright was a **Rhodes scholar** who had studied at Oxford University and as part of the Fulbright Program, the U.S.–U.K. Fulbright Commission was created in 1948. This included the U.S. Educational Advisory Service to provide information and advice to students considering studying in the United States, and the U.S.–U.K. Fulbright Scholarship Program.

FULTON, MISSOURI, SPEECH. On 5 March 1946, former British prime minister **Winston Churchill** delivered a speech at Westminster College in Fulton, Missouri (the hometown of President **Harry S. Truman**). Although on a private visit to the United States, it is clear that Churchill intended to alert the Truman administration and the American public to the dangers of the Soviet threat in Europe. Churchill warned that "From Stettin in the Baltic to Trieste in the Adriatic, an iron curtain has descended across the Continent." Urging Western resolve in the face of the threat from the **Soviet Union**, he said he was "convinced that there is nothing they admire so much as strength." With Truman sitting on the stage, Churchill argued for the need of an Anglo–American partnership to resist the challenge. This speech was welcomed by President Truman (in private) as it coincided with a hardening of his attitude to the Soviet Union that came with the 22 February 1946 "Long Telegram" from the American chargé d'affaires in Moscow, **George Kennan**, which warned the president of the Kremlin's "neurotic view of world affairs" and argued that short-term understanding with the Soviets was impossible.

However, the speech shocked the American people and Truman was forced to dissociate from it in public. The adverse public reaction to the speech appeared to indicate that the United States was not yet ready for a close alliance with Great Britain but did contribute to the beginning of the **Cold War**.

FYLINGDALES RADAR INSTALLATION. As part of Anglo–American defense cooperation, Britain agreed to the stationing of an American early warning station at RAF Fylingdales in Yorkshire. Completed in 1962, the radar base's main function during the **Cold War** was to detect incoming ballistic missiles, but as part of the wider "**special relationship**," intelligence data collected by Fylingdales has been shared with the United States. It is has been the site of anti-American and **Campaign for Nuclear Disarmament** (CND) protests, including after 2003 when Britain agreed to let the United States use the base for its proposed **National Missile Defense** (NMD) system.

– G –

GALLATIN, ALBERT (1761–1849). Albert Gallatin was U.S. secretary of the treasury and a diplomat who negotiated the **Treaty of Ghent** in 1814 and was later appointed minister to Britain (1826–1827).

GENERAL AGREEMENT ON TARIFFS AND TRADE (GATT). In an attempt to avoid a recurrence of the economic woes witnessed during the interwar period, on 10 April 1947 representatives from 23 nations met in Geneva, Switzerland, to discuss how to achieve a world trading system that was free and open. Signed on 1 January 1948 by 21 nations, including Great Britain and the United States, GATT was an international treaty that encouraged free **trade** between member states by regulating, reducing, and eliminating tariff duties. Although Britain and the United States had been the key promoters of GATT, there were significant disagreements over certain aspects of the treaty. Washington insisted that Article I of the treaty was the most-favored nation clause that aimed at nondiscrimination in trade, and in the process aimed to prevent discrimination against U.S. products by the British system of **imperial preference**. Although largely successful in its aims of reducing protectionism—due to periodic negotiations such as the Kennedy round of talks during the 1960s and the Tokyo round of the 1970s—certain areas of world trade, notably agriculture, have been more difficult to liberalize and in recent years preferential bilateral and regional trade agreements have threatened the multinational emphasis of GATT. GATT was succeeded by the World Trade Organization (WTO) in 1995, and currently has 153 members.

GENEVA CONFERENCE (1954). The first major gathering of the world's leaders since the **Potsdam Conference** in 1945, this conference was convened to discuss the formal ending of the **Korean War** (1950–1953) and France's colonial struggle in Indochina (**Vietnam**, Laos, and Cambodia). The major participants throughout the conference were France, Great Britain, the People's Republic of **China**, the **Soviet Union**, and the United States, but were joined by other countries concerned with the issues being discussed. Prior to the conference, it was clear that London and Washington had differing hopes and expectations for the conference, especially in relation to Southeast Asia. U.S. secretary of state **John Foster Dulles** had little confidence that the conference would produce sufficient compromise from the communists in attendance, and had already begun to organize a regional pact—the **South-East Asia Treaty Organization** (SEATO)—while British foreign secretary **Anthony Eden** favored accommodation with the communists and proper negotiations and was reluctant to preempt them by agreeing in advance to the organization of SEATO.

The conference opened on 27 April 1954 and ended almost three months later on July 21. Britain, along with the Soviet Union, was appointed cochair of the Geneva Conference. Although the conference began by discussing the holding of all-Korean elections and the withdrawal of all foreign forces, it ended without an agreement on the matter. On Indochina, the conference was forced into more decisive action due to the defeat of the French at Dien Bien Phu on 7 May 1954. The United States had considered helping the French militarily at Dien Bien Phu but President **Dwight D. Eisenhower** had wanted

British involvement, which was not forthcoming. The conference agreed to the Geneva Accords and, on 21 July, it adopted a final declaration that brought about an end to the war in Indochina and temporarily divided Vietnam at the 17th parallel pending elections two years later to decide the fate of the nation. Although Britain signed the declaration, the United States did not and prepared to defend Western interests in the region through the establishment of SEATO in September 1954.

GEORGE III, KING (1738–1820). Hanoverian monarch, King George III, sat on the British throne between 1760 and 1820 and it was under his rule that Britain lost the American colonies. As a ruler George III believed he should take a personal role in government, notably in appointing his ministers, and took a hard line in relation to the American colonies, disfavoring any concessions to the rebels who viewed him as a tyrant. He had gained this reputation due to the increasing numbers of taxes collected from the American colonies without consultation, levied largely in an attempt to pay for the high costs of the Seven Years' War. He proclaimed the colonies to be in open rebellion on 23 August 1775, although fighting had been ongoing since April 1775. George III ignored the Olive Branch petition issued by the Continental Congress on 5 July 1775, which was a direct appeal to the king to try to resolve the problems. *See also* WAR OF INDEPENDENCE.

GHENT, TREATY OF (1814). The Treaty of Ghent was signed on 24 December 1814 after four months of talks in Ghent, Belgium, to end the **War of 1812** between the United States and Great Britain that had begun in 1812. The treaty was ratified by the U.S. Senate on 16 February 1815 but failed to deal with many of the issues that had led the two countries to war, including the issue of neutral rights, impressments, fisheries, and boundaries.

GRANT, CARY (1904–1986). Born Archibald Leach in Bristol, England, Cary Grant became one of Hollywood's most celebrated and successful actors. Although British born, Grant settled in the United States and became famous for his work in screwball comedies such as *Bringing Up Baby* (1938) with Katharine Hepburn and *His Girl*

Friday (1940) with Rosalind Russell. Grant later went on to make a series of thrillers and was one of **Alfred Hitchcock**'s favored actors, working with him on *Suspicion* (1941), *Notorious* (1946), *To Catch a Thief* (1955), and *North by Northwest* (1959). During **World War II**, Grant stayed in Hollywood to promote the British cause and in 1942 he became an American citizen.

GREAT AWAKENING. Between the 1730s and 1750s, the British colonies in America experienced a period of fervent religious activity. A series of intermittent evangelical revivals, the "Great Awakening" was characterized by attacks on rationality in religion, authoritarian religion, a belief in personal conversion and salvation, and religious piety. The revivals were encouraged by the English preacher **George Whitefield**, who traveled around the United States beginning in 1738 on a mission to convert the people to spiritual equality and the power of the Holy Spirit in revivals. The Great Awakening led more Americans to break away from established churches and establish new denominations.

GREAT RAPPROCHEMENT. The term "great rapprochement" has been used by Anglo–American scholars to describe the growing cordiality in relations between Great Britain and the United States that emerged in the late 19th century. Although for much of the 19th century it appeared that the two countries would be rivals, or even enemies as they became great power competitors, by late in the century Anglo–American relations improved noticeably, described as peace "breaking out." After the successful resolution of the **Venezuelan boundary dispute**, it was clear that both Britain and America wanted to avoid future confrontations that might lead to war between the two countries. In January 1897, a treaty was signed that agreed to submit major disputes to arbitration, although it failed to be ratified in the U.S. Senate.

The two countries recognized that as leading democratic nations they had objectives in common, noticeably in relation to the rise of the autocratic empires of Russia, Japan, and Germany. As German–British rivalry intensified—over empire and arms—and as the United States rose to world-power status, so London became keener on friendship with Washington. Much of this improvement appears to have come through the rise of **Anglo–Saxonism** and the recognition of mutual bonds of language, race, history, and culture. British author and poet **Rudyard Kipling** encouraged Americans to take up the "**white man's burden**" of empire. **Trade** and investment ties between the two countries also fed the rapprochement. By 1914, more than 140 U.S. companies operated in Great Britain. Anglo–American elites also established societies such as the **Pilgrims Society** and the **English-Speaking Union** to help secure closer relations between Britain and America. A key manifestation of better relations came in 1898 during the **Spanish–American War** when the British were largely supportive of the United States and in 1901 were cooperative over the Panama Canal. *See also* HAY–PAUNCEFORTE TREATY.

GREECE. In October 1944, Prime Minister **Winston Churchill** met with Soviet leader Joseph Stalin to discuss the influence each nation would have in southeast Europe. The "percentages agreement" that was reached divided control 90/10 in Britain's favor. Although the **Soviet Union** did not interfere in events in Greece, the country faced communist insurgency and was embroiled in civil war from 1944 onward. On 21 February 1947, the British government led by **Clement Attlee** informed the administration of **Harry S. Truman** that it could no longer afford to aid Greece in its civil war, stressed its importance (along with Turkey) in the emerging **Cold War**, and expressed the hope that the United States would take over the assistance. The British government, still in financial and economic difficulty since **World War II**, had spent millions of pounds in Greece trying to prevent a communist victory. It is now clear that the British foreign secretary, **Ernest Bevin**, had serious doubts over the likelihood of the anticommunist regime in Greece succeeding in the civil war. The Truman administration had been expecting Britain to make this decision but was surprised by its suddenness. Although there was some debate among congressman about helping Britain yet again, **Dean Acheson**, undersecretary of state, was able to effectively warn that a communist victory in Greece would lead to further "infection," like "apples in a barrel infected by one rotten one," with France and Italy the next affected. In order to persuade Congress and the American public of the necessity of fighting the battle of containment of communist, Truman addressed a joint session of Congress on 12 March

1947, issuing what became known as the **Truman Doctrine**. Congress approved an extra appropriation of $400 million in aid for Greece and Turkey, and Britain handed power in the area over to the United States.

GREENHAM COMMON. In 1983, Greenham Common Royal Air Force Base in Berkshire was the site of the first American cruise missiles on British soil. In response to the **Soviet Union**'s deployment of the medium-range SS-20 nuclear missile in the mid-1970s, in December 1979 the **North Atlantic Treaty Organization** (NATO) agreed to deploy over 400 ground-launched cruise missiles in Europe to counter the perceived threat to Europe from the SS-20s. As part of this agreement, it was announced in June 1980 that 96 missiles would be based at Greenham Common and it would become a maximum security base that would include nuclear shelters. This decision was the subject of protest by the **Campaign for Nuclear Disarmament** (CND) but it was peaceful protest by women's groups that made the headlines. After failing to engage the military in a debate over the wisdom of siting cruise missiles at the base, the women set up camp on the perimeter of the base. Living in tents and caravans in primitive conditions, many of these women lived at the base for a number of years. The Women's Peace Camp activists used nonviolent direct action, including fence cutting and human blockades, in an attempt to disrupt the activities of the U.S. Air Force. Some of the women were arrested, charged, and imprisoned for their activities but still returned to the camp. The cruise missiles were removed from Greenham Common after the Intermediate-Range Nuclear Force (INF) Treaty of 1987. The "Greenham women" attracted publicity to their cause and remained at the base until it was closed in 2000.

GREENSTOCK, SIR JEREMY (1944–). In the prelude to the **Iraq War**, Sir Jeremy Greenstock played a crucial part in the unfolding events in his capacity as British ambassador to the **United Nations** (1998–2003). In September 2002, at a meeting at **Camp David**, Prime Minister **Tony Blair** persuaded President **George W. Bush** that before planning an invasion of **Iraq** he should go back to the United Nations to gain a resolution on suspected Iraqi weapons of mass destruction. Greenstock helped draft UN Security Council

Resolution 1441 and secure its passage on 8 November 2002. Resolution 1441, accusing Iraq of violating cease-fire agreements and previous resolutions on disarmament, allowed for the reintroduction of inspectors, led by Dr. **Hans Blix**, but was unclear on what would happen if Iraq did not comply. Some countries on the Security Council were adamant that there was no "trigger" for war contained in the resolution, which the United States felt there was. When in February 2003 Blair pressed for further diplomacy and a second resolution on Iraq, largely to appease his critics at home who were not convinced of the need for war, Greenstock was less successful, partly because Washington was not fully behind the endeavor but largely because Germany, France, and Russia felt further time should be given to the arms inspectors. After the invasion and capture of Baghdad on 9 April 2003, Greenstock was appointed the first British envoy to Iraq, working with U.S. envoy **Paul Bremer** on the establishment of a transition government. He later criticized Blair for losing focus and not ensuring security in Iraq after its liberation from Saddam Hussein. Greenstock's memoirs, entitled *Costs of War: Iraq and the Paradox of Power*, were due for publication in 2006 but faced heavy censorship from the Foreign Office and were delayed.

GRENADA. On 25 October 1983, the United States launched a surprise invasion of the small Caribbean island of Grenada ostensibly in an effort to secure the safety of 1,000 American students—and avoid another **Iran**-style hostage crisis—in the aftermath of a bloody coup d'état. Grenada had achieved independence from Great Britain in February 1974 but was a British Commonwealth country that still had **Queen Elizabeth II** as its head of state. But, despite last-minute efforts by Prime Minister **Margaret Thatcher** to persuade President **Ronald Reagan** not to sanction an invasion, the Americans pressed ahead. The Reagan administration had long had serious concerns about the strength of communist forces in the Caribbean, and since the left-wing New Jewel Movement seized power in March 1979, led by Maurice Bishop, the United States had noted with alarm the alliance between Grenada, **Cuba**, and the **Soviet Union**. Specifically, Cuban aid had allowed the Grenadians to begin work on a new and larger airport. Although the airport was meant to promote tourism on the island, the United States suspected it might have a military purpose.

When Bishop was toppled, and subsequently executed, by a more extreme Marxist leader, Prime Minister Bernard Coard, on 19 October 1983, the United States was asked by some of Grenada's neighbors to intervene. Also fearing for the safety of its medical students on the island, the United States agreed to intervene, supplying over 7,000 troops alongside a small number of troops from the islands of Antigua, Jamaica, Saint Lucia, Barbados, Bermuda, and Dominica. Fighting lasted only a few days and resulted in 19 U.S. fatalities. By December 1983, U.S. forces had left the island after an advisory council had been named that would administer the country until free and fair general elections could be held in December 1984. British Prime Minister Thatcher condemned the Americans for the invasion. Considering American support for Britain in the **Falklands War** during the previous year, Thatcher's response to Grenada was considered disappointing in U.S. political circles. In Britain, where the invasion was unpopular, it was felt a diplomatic solution to the crisis could have been found and Mrs. Thatcher's inability to influence Reagan on Grenada illustrated the limits of their personal relationship. Disagreements over the crisis led to short-term diplomatic tensions between Britain and America.

GRENVILLE, GEORGE (1712–1770). Serving as British Whig prime minister for just two years (1763–1765), George Grenville had a major impact on the history of Anglo–American relations due to his attempts to pay off the British national debt. To help raise tax revenue he decided to enforce the Navigation Acts and introduced the **Sugar Act** in 1764 and the **Stamp Act** in 1765. All these actions were aimed at the American colonies and were instrumental in aggravating American grievances against the mother country that ultimately led to the **War of Independence.**

GROSVENOR SQUARE. Since 1785, when John Adams became the first U.S. minister to Great Britain and lived at a house on Grosvenor Square in Mayfair, London, it has been the site of the U.S. diplomatic presence in Britain. During **World War II**, the United States occupied two sides of the square as General **Dwight D. Eisenhower**'s headquarters were housed there and consequently the British public began to refer to it as "Little America." Since 1960, the U.S. Embassy has been housed in a large modern building (133,300 sq. ft) that occupies the west side of the square. In 1968, Grosvenor Square was the focus of British anti–**Vietnam War** protests. The square is also the site of several statues and memorials commemorating key figures in the history of Anglo–American relations, including President **Franklin D. Roosevelt**, President **Dwight D. Eisenhower**, and the **September 11** memorial garden. Since 9/11 and the **Iraq War**, upgraded security measures led to the installation of security barriers around the U.S. Embassy building, which has since acquired the nickname "Little **Iraq**."

GUANTANAMO BAY. Following the military invasion by the United States and Great Britain of **Afghanistan** in late 2001, the U.S. government established a prison and interrogation center at the U.S. naval base in Guantanamo Bay, Cuba, to deal with those captured during the "war on terror." The U.S. detention facility led to tensions between the administration of **George Bush** and the government of **Tony Blair** and was the subject of protest by human rights groups around the world. Gitmo, or Camp X-Ray as it was known, has been used to detain suspected al-Qaeda and Taliban terrorists who are described as "enemy combatants" by the U.S. government. Critics around the world have alleged that the prisoners have been ill treated and argued these detentions, mostly without trials, are illegal and that the detainees should be treated as prisoners of war and treated accordingly under the Geneva Conventions. While never directly criticizing Guantanamo, Prime Minister Blair described the camp as an "anomaly" that must be addressed eventually and pressed for the release of Britons. *See also* BECKETT, MARGARET.

GULF WAR (1991). When Saddam Hussein's Iraqi forces invaded Kuwait on 2 August 1990, British Prime Minister **Margaret Thatcher** was in the United States and she immediately urged President **George H. W. Bush** to resist this breach of international law and assured him of British military support. Bush's own resolve on the matter led to Anglo–American diplomatic cooperation in the **United Nations** where a mandate for military action was sought. Despite this unity there were disagreements between Thatcher and U.S. Secretary of State **James Baker** over whether a UN resolution was needed for military action. Thatcher felt that Kuwait could respond militarily (with its allies) under the right to self-defense enshrined in Article 51 of the UN Charter.

The United Nations immediately condemned the invasion and on 29 November passed Resolution 678 giving **Iraq** a deadline of 15 January 1991 for withdrawal. Great Britain became part of the 33-nation coalition force assembled by the United States, eventually sending the largest European military contingent of 43,000 troops to fight in the conflict (and members of the Special Air Service [SAS] to engage in crucial reconnaissance operations), which began in earnest on 17 January with a massive strategic bombing campaign (codenamed Operation Desert Storm) that focused on targets in Baghdad and involved British Royal Air Force aircraft. The British government, now led by Prime Minister **John Major**, secured approval to take military action against Iraq during a House of Commons debate on 15 January, on a vote of 534 to 57. Political support for military action against Iraq had been less convincing in the United States. The air campaign was followed by a ground assault beginning on 24 February and lasting four days. By 28 February, Kuwait had been retaken and President Bush ended the war.

As the United States sent over 500,000 troops to the region, it was clear that the war was being directed by the Americans, but Anglo–American military cooperation was aided by the close working relationship between U.S. Commander General **Norman Schwarzkopf** and British Commander General Sir **Peter de la Billière**. It was clear, however, that military operating practice often differed, with the most notable difference being the wearing of Arab headdress by some British soldiers. Tensions between the U.S. and British military did develop over a **friendly fire incident** in which nine British soldiers from the Royal Regiment of Fusiliers were killed and 12 seriously injured when an American A10 Tankbuster aircraft targeted them believing they were Iraqi troops.

The decision to call a cease-fire to the war just four days into the ground war, and after the liberation of Kuwait, was made by the United States without consultation with its allies and raised some debate over whether the coalition forces should have pressed on to Baghdad to overthrow the regime of Saddam Hussein. Without a UN mandate to do so, and recognizing that the wartime coalition, involving several Arab nations, was unlikely to hold together in such circumstances, the United States was instead persuaded to implement a plan suggested by Major to establish "safe havens" for Iraqi Kurds in the north of the country. The successful achievement of the UN objective to liberate Kuwait and the military cooperation between British and American forces appeared to revitalize Anglo–American relations in the post–Cold War period.

– H –

HAIG, ALEXANDER MEIGS (1924–). American secretary of state (1981–1982) under President **Ronald Reagan**, Alexander Haig is best remembered for his attempt to play honest broker during the **Falklands** crisis. He engaged in shuttle diplomacy in order to demonstrate the United States' desire to prevent a war between two of its allies, Great Britain and Argentina. He famously characterized the American reaction to the crisis as "a Gilbert and Sullivan battle over a sheep pasture between a choleric old John Bull and a comic dictator in a gaudy uniform." Although sympathetic to Britain, Haig, responding partly to pro-Latin American diplomats within his State Department, felt Argentina should gain something from the crisis, and proposed that Argentina leave the islands but be allowed to have representation on the Falkland Islands councils. He traveled 33,000 miles in 12 days in search of a settlement to the crisis, visiting London (8 April) and Buenos Aires (12 April, 19 April) following the Argentine invasion and while the British navy was sailing to the Falkland Islands.

HAIG, FIELD MARSHAL SIR DOUGLAS (1861–1928). Commander-in-chief of the British Expeditionary (BEF) in **World War I** from December 1915, Haig was in charge during the battle of the Somme and criticized by many for his tactics. Haig was annoyed with the delay in the U.S. Army entry into the fighting on the Western Front, complaining to General **John Pershing**—commander of the American Expeditionary Forces (AEF)—that the Americans did not realize the urgency of the situation.

HALEY, BILL (1825–1981). Bill Haley and the Comets introduced the British public to American rock 'n' roll. In December 1954, Haley's version of "Shake, Rattle, and Roll" became the first rock 'n' roll single to enter the British music charts. Although it reached number four in the British charts, it was the re-release of "Rock Around the Clock" in October 1955, after its use in the film *Blackboard Jungle*, which made Haley synonymous with rock 'n' roll when it reached number one, bringing it to mass attention. In 1956, Haley's film *Rock Around the Clock* arrived in Britain and he had several more chart hits in Britain, including "See You Later Alligator" and "Rip It Up." In 1957, Haley was the first rock 'n' roll star to tour in Britain. Despite being mobbed by adoring crowds on his arrival in Britain, he was quickly overshadowed by the younger and better-looking **Elvis Presley**.

HALIFAX, LORD (1881–1959). Nicknamed "the Holy Fox" by **Winston Churchill** because of his churchgoing nature and political guile, Edward Wood, 3rd Viscount Halifax, was a Tory aristocrat who has gone down in history as one of the key architects of British **appeasement** in the 1930s. Halifax served as viceroy of India (1926–1931), foreign secretary (1938–1940), and British ambassador to the United States (January 1941–May 1946). Viewed as pro-German, unlike Foreign Secretary **Anthony Eden**, **Neville Chamberlain** sent Lord Halifax to meet with Adolf Hitler and German propaganda minister Joseph Goebbels in November 1937. Halifax expressed admiration of the Nazi regime, acknowledging its domestic achievements and firm handling of communists, and called it a "bulwark against bolshevism." By the time of the **Munich Agreement** of 1938, Halifax had begun to demand the destruction of Nazism. Although he stayed on as foreign secretary when **Winston Churchill** became prime minister in May 1940, the two men did not like each other and Churchill sent Halifax off to Washington as British ambassador. In this capacity, Halifax oversaw the strengthening of the Anglo–American wartime alliance. In an attempt to encourage America away from its isolationist tendencies, he traveled around the United States explaining Britain's perilous situation, despite often being received by hostile crowds. Halifax was heavily involved in the negotiation over the **Anglo–American loan agreement** in 1945 and was a British delegate at the **San Francisco Conference**.

HARLECH, LORD (1918–1985). David Ormsby-Gore, 5th Baron Harlech, served as a Conservative Party MP from 1950 until 1961 when he became British ambassador in Washington, serving in the post until 1965. Ormsby-Gore is credited with having a close, friendly relationship with President **John F. Kennedy**. The two had met in London during the 1930s when JFK was living there while his father, **Joseph P. Kennedy**, served as U.S. ambassador to Great Britain, and the two were distantly related. It is believed that on becoming president, Kennedy asked that Ormsby-Gore serve as British ambassador and it is clear that once in post Ormsby-Gore acted as a trusted confidant and adviser to the president, visiting the **White House** often. Ormsby-Gore played an important role in the **Cuban missile crisis**, consulting on several occasions and suggesting to Kennedy that the line of the naval quarantine be reduced from 800 miles to 500 miles in order to provide the Soviets with more time to consider their position.

HAY, JOHN (1838–1905). Believing that U.S. foreign policy should be predicated on friendly relations with England, John Hay was important in helping to establish a rapprochement between Britain and America. In his position as secretary of state (1898–1905), the Republican politician was often criticized in his own country as a Yankee **Anglophile**. He is remembered for describing the **Spanish–American War** of 1898 as a "splendid little war." His key importance in relation to Britain was his negotiation of the **Hay–Pauncefote Treaty** in 1901 and his **Open Door** notes in 1899.

HAY–PAUNCEFOTE TREATY (1901). This treaty was an important indicator of the improvement in Anglo–American relations that was described as the "**great rapprochement**" and superseded the **Clayton–Bulwer Agreement** of 1850. In the hope of establishing closer relations with the United States, Britain stepped aside from the Panama Canal project. The treaty, negotiated in November 1901 by U.S. Secretary of State **John Hay** and British ambassador to Washington Lord Julian Pauncefote, stated that the Panama Canal, to be constructed by the United States beginning in 1908 and linking the Atlantic and Pacific oceans, should be open on equal terms to the ships of all nations.

HEALEY, DENIS (1917–). Denis Healey served as British secretary of state for defense from 1964–1970 and as chancellor of the exchequer between 1974–1979. He was also Opposition spokesman for foreign affairs between 1980 and 1987, and narrowly missed out on becoming Labour leader in 1980. In his youth, Healey had been a member of the Communist Party but by the time he became a Labour MP in 1952 he was firmly pro-American and remained so throughout his political career. When Healey became defense secretary he had the advantage of already having established relationships with **Dean Rusk**, secretary of state, and presidential adviser Walt Rostow, whom he had met at Oxford University. As secretary of defense, Healey made severe defense cuts, including the cancellation of the TSR-2 aircraft, and was instrumental in the decision in 1967 to remove British troops **East of Suez**. As chancellor of the exchequer, Healey presided over the negotiations that took place between the British and American governments during the **IMF crisis** of 1976. Healey famously turned back from Heathrow Airport on his way to Washington in order to visit the Labour Party conference in Blackpool to brief its delegates on the IMF loan and was booed as he took to the podium.

HEATH, EDWARD (1916–2005). Edward Heath served as British leader of the Conservative party between 1965 and 1975 and prime minister between 1970 and 1974. On a personal level, Heath was not instinctively pro-American and viewed the "**special relationship**" as a possible obstacle to his aim of securing British entry into the **European Economic Community** (EEC). He reassured French President George Pompidou that Britain would not be a "Trojan horse," representing the United States in Europe. Consequently Heath asked Washington not to proffer special status on him, preferring instead to be treated like any other European leader. Heath did not intend to alter the fundamentals of the "special relationship" such as the nuclear or intelligence relationship but sought to reexamine it in light of Britain's closer relations with Europe. Heath negotiated the British entry into the EEC in January 1973.

The greatest crisis faced by London and Washington during the Heath years came over the October 1973 **Arab–Israeli War**. The Heath government feared that the United States might take military action in the Middle East to secure access to oil supplies and might ask to use the **Diego Garcia** base in the process. Heath was furious when the United States declared a full-scale nuclear alert on October 25 — in response to Soviet naval activity in the eastern Mediterranean — without informing him, only learning about it on the news. The British prime minister did not feel the alert was necessary. During the crisis, **Henry Kissinger** prevented President **Richard Nixon** from speaking to Heath because the president appeared too drunk to talk.

HELMS–BURTON ACT. In 1996, President **Bill Clinton** signed the Cuban Liberty and Democratic Solidarity (Libertad) Act. Known as the Helms–Burton Act, after Republican Senator Jessie Helms and Republican Representative Dan Burton who sponsored it, the act tightened the economic blockade against **Cuba** by extending it to cover foreign firms trading with the Castro government. Prime Minister **Tony Blair**, along with the European Union, **Canada**, and Mexico, made complaints to the Clinton administration objecting to the act's extraterritorial provisions and fearing that British businesses trading with Cuba might face restrictive penalties. Britain agreed with U.S. calls for democratic reform in Cuba and condemned breaches of human rights under the Castro government, but by 1997 the United Kingdom's exports to Cuba totaled £15 million and it imported even more. The Blair government opposed the U.S. **trade** embargo against Cuba and sent a strongly worded diplomatic note to the United States when it was extended under the Helms–Burton Act. British law was amended to help protect British companies who fell under the provisions of Helms–Burton.

HENDERSON, SIR NICHOLAS (1919–). As British ambassador to the United States, 1979–1982, Sir Nicholas Henderson helped to secure U.S. support for Great Britain during the **Falklands War**.

HEREN, LOUIS (1919–1995). One of Great Britain's most famous journalists, Louis Heren worked for the *Times* from 1933 to 1981. During this time, he became an important commentator on American affairs for the British public. In 1961, he became chief Washington correspondent for the *Times* and became the paper's deputy editor in 1970. While stationed in Washington, he spent time covering the civil rights movement in the American South, reported on the assassination of President **John F. Kennedy** on 22 November 1963, and later established close links with President **Lyndon B. Johnson** that allowed him insights into the **Vietnam War**. He wrote two books on American politics, *The New American Commonwealth* (1968), which covered the Kennedy years, and *No Hail, No Farewell* (1970), which spanned the Johnson years.

HITCHCOCK, ALFRED (1899–1980). Anglo–American film director Alfred Hitchcock began his film career in silent movies in his native Great Britain and went on to become one of the most important film directors and producers of the 20th century. Born in London in 1899, in the 1920s and 1930s Hitchcock established a successful career in British movies by making films characterized by suspense and fear, including *The Man Who Knew Too Much* (1934), *The 39 Steps* (1935), and *The Lady Vanishes* (1938). In 1939, Hitchcock moved to Hollywood to work with David O. Selznick but was committed to furthering the British cause in **World War II** by improving representations of British characters in Hollywood films. His first film with Selznick, *Rebecca*, earned an Academy Award for Best Picture. By 1946, Hitchcock had begun to produce his own films, many of which received critical acclaim, notably *Notorious* (1946) and *Rope* (1948), but his own production company, Transatlantic Pictures, proved short lived. Despite living in the United States, many of his films were based in Britain. In the 1950s, Hitchcock made several thrillers that were popular successes featuring actress Grace Kelly— *Dial M for Murder* (1954), *Rear Window* (1954), and *To Catch a Thief* (1955). He went on to make several more suspense films that were viewed as some of his best works, including *Vertigo* (1959), *North by Northwest* (1959), *Psycho* (1960), and *The Birds* (1963). Hitchcock became an American citizen in 1956, although maintaining his British citizenship at the same time, thus allowing him to receive a knighthood in 1980. *See also* GRANT, CARY.

HOLY LOCH NAVAL BASE. In March 1960, during a meeting with President **Dwight D. Eisenhower**, Prime Minister **Harold Macmillan** agreed to let the U.S. Navy have a base for its **Polaris** nuclear submarines at Holy Loch in Scotland. Macmillan agreed to this reluctantly after reaching an understanding with Eisenhower that Britain would be allowed to purchase Polaris nuclear missiles from the United States in the future. The decision to site the nuclear base on the west coast of Scotland, close to the densely populated city of Glasgow, proved unpopular with much of the Scottish population and antinuclear protesters, who feared that the move meant it would be a key target for Soviet attack. The base was closed in 1992. *See also* COLD WAR.

HONG KONG. In the postwar period, the status and future of Great Britain's colony in Hong Kong played a part in U.S. strategic interests in the Far East. As a result, Hong Kong became an issue in Anglo–American relations. Hong Kong was an important colony to the British economically and was symbolic of their world role. During **World War II**, the surrender of Hong Kong to Japanese forces in December 1941 meant the recapture of the colony became crucial to the maintenance of Britain's empire. This was achieved by August 1945 after the United States defeated Japan in Asia. With the coming of the **Cold War**, and especially after the communist victory in **China** in 1949, Hong Kong took on a new importance to Washington and London. Britain now faced defending Hong Kong from a strong Chinese government and, unlike the United States, adopted a moderate stance in dealing with Mao Zedong's China in order to prevent retaliation that might threaten their control of the lucrative colony. The Labour government of **Clement Attlee** therefore argued that it agreed with the containment policy by preventing Chinese aggression toward Hong Kong through its conciliatory approach to Beijing. Washington understood that the colony was important to the British and therefore important to Anglo–American relations, and by the early 1950s, with the closure of its embassies in China, the United States had begun to base its intelligence gathering operations in Hong Kong. Continuing numbers of Vietnamese refugees entering Hong Kong in the 1980s and early 1990s led to some Anglo–American tension over their fate. Britain's 90-year lease on Hong Kong expired on 30 June 1997.

HOON, GEOFF (1953–). Appointed secretary of defense by Prime Minister **Tony Blair** in 1999, Geoff Hoon oversaw British military operations in Sierra Leone in 2000, **Afghanistan** in 2001, and **Iraq**

in 2003, and engaged in a defense review that resulted in plans to make major changes to British armed forces. In the months preceding the war in Iraq, Hoon liaised with his counterpart in the United States, **Donald Rumsfeld**, over military planning and postwar strategy. In February 2003, Hoon telephoned Rumsfeld to warn that Blair might not be able to get House of Commons backing for the war in Iraq without a second **United Nations**' resolution authorizing war. Controversially, in an interview with David Frost on the BBC on 2 February 2003, Hoon said that nuclear weapons might be used in Iraq in conditions of extreme national self-defense. Hoon disagreed with Rumsfeld over the decision to dismiss the Iraqi Army and police force before reconstruction and later argued that other fatal errors were made in Iraq, partly because the U.S. administration, particularly Vice President **Dick Cheney**, was not willing to listen to British arguments. Recognizing that British forces were fighting simultaneous conflicts in Afghanistan and Iraq, Hoon extended his government white paper on defense by publishing "Delivering Security in a Changing World: Future Capabilities" on 21 July 2004 that announced troop reductions, restructuring and reorganization, and a strengthening of British "special forces."

HOPE, BOB (1903–2003). One of America's most cherished comedians, Bob Hope was born in Eltham, London, England, in 1903 before immigrating with his family to Cleveland, Ohio, in 1908. He later quipped that he left England when "I found out I couldn't be king." As one of many immigrants working in vaudeville in the 1920s, Hope quickly established a reputation as a talented singer, dancer, and fast-talking comedic actor and by 1933 was starring in the successful theater musical *Roberta*. He then turned his talents to radio and film. In 1938, he starred in *The Big Broadcast* and gained a theme song, "Thanks for the Memory." The same year he began a 10-year stint on the radio series *The Pepsodent Show* on NBC. His movie career went from strength to strength, notably with Bing Crosby and Dorothy Lamour in *The Road to Singapore* (1940) and the subsequent six "Road" movies. One of Britain and America's favorite entertainers, throughout his life Hope retained his connection with England, not only by entertaining American troops stationed there during World War II but also by regular visits to the country. He raised money to save a theater close to where he was born in Eltham, now named the Bob Hope Theatre, and also organized golf tournaments in Britain.

HOPKINS, HARRY L. (1890–1946). A close friend and advisor to President **Franklin D. Roosevelt**, Harry Hopkins played a crucial role in ensuring the solidity of the Anglo–American relationship that developed during **World War II**. Known as one of the main architects of the New Deal of the 1930s, Roosevelt asked Hopkins to act as an unofficial diplomat during the war, focusing in particular on Great Britain and the **Soviet Union**. As a result, Hopkins was sent on a number of missions to London and acted as a mediator between Roosevelt and British Prime Minister **Winston Churchill**. During Hopkins's first mission in January 1941, when he met Churchill for the first time and stayed at 10 **Downing Street** for six weeks, from 9 January to 10 February, Hopkins sent numerous cables to Roosevelt listing British armament needs and established a strong working relationship with Churchill. Visiting Britain during the German blitz, Hopkins observed the war-ravaged country and advised Roosevelt that contrary to the opinion of the former American ambassador **Joseph P. Kennedy**, Britain still had the will to fight on and was worth supporting. Hopkins's reports were therefore essential in explaining Roosevelt's decision to provide war materials to Great Britain under the **Lend-Lease** program. Hopkins also visited London in July 1941 before continuing on to Moscow to discuss the role of the Soviet Union in the war and the extension of Lend-Lease aid to the Soviets. In August 1941, he again acted as go-between during the meeting of Roosevelt and Churchill at the **Atlantic Conference**. By 1942, Hopkins's skills as an intermediary were needed when sharp disagreements emerged between Roosevelt and Churchill over the future of the British Empire, particularly over Churchill's refusal to allow India's independence. In 2004, there were reports in the press that Hopkins was rumored to have been a Soviet spy.

HOUSE, EDWARD M. (1858–1938). "Colonel" Edward House was one of President **Woodrow Wilson**'s most trusted advisers and became the major figure in U.S. relations with Britain during **World War I**. Drawing on his personal links with key members of Prime

Minister Herbert Henry Asquith's Liberal government, he was influential in smoothing over the dispute with Great Britain over the **Panama Canal**. In 1913, he was sent on an unofficial visit to meet with Sir Edward Grey, British foreign secretary, and the following spring was sent on a mission to Europe to attempt to prevent world war. After the outbreak of war and while the United States remained neutral, House was dispatched to Europe on three occasions to attempt to negotiate an end to the war. With the U.S. entry into the war in 1917, House spent much time in England and worked closely with Asquith, **Arthur Balfour**, **David Lloyd-George**, and Edward Grey. House was part of the U.S. delegation at the **Paris Peace Conference** in 1919 and carried on negotiations for the United States when Wilson returned home in February 1919.

HOWARD, ESME (1863–1939). Esme Howard served as a British delegate at the **Paris Peace Conference** of 1919 and later became British ambassador to the United States (1924–1930). While serving in Washington he announced that the British Embassy would become "dry" after local residents had criticized the abuse of diplomatic immunity that had allowed the importation of intoxicants despite prohibition.

HULL, CORDELL (1871–1955). Longest-serving U.S. secretary of state (1933–1944), Cordell Hull was instrumental in formulating the **Anglo–American Trade Agreement** of 1938. Hull masterminded a series of reciprocal **trade** treaties that were aimed at encouraging the liberalization of world trade in an attempt to boost the U.S. economy and reduce the potential for world conflict. Britain's system of **imperial preference** was the target of Hull's fierce criticism, calling such economic discrimination an evil. Once Britain was embroiled in **World War II**, Hull supported President **Franklin D. Roosevelt** in his bid to provide military support to the British in order to keep the United States out of the war. As a well-known internationalist, Hull also worked with the British on the creation of a collective organization that eventually became the **United Nations** in 1945 and for which he received the Nobel Peace Prize.

HURD, DOUGLAS (1930–). A former diplomat, Douglas Hurd became British foreign secretary in 1989 in the Conservative government led by **Margaret Thatcher**. He continued to serve under Thatcher's successor, **John Major**, until 1995. Hurd worked hard at establishing a close relationship with President **George H. W. Bush** and oversaw the British response to the Iraqi invasion of Kuwait in August 1990 and the subsequent British role in the **Gulf War** of 1991, including the involvement of over 45,000 British troops. Hurd's only real disagreement with the Bush administration over the conduct of the Gulf War came when the United States declared ground operations at an end after just four days and refused to allow allied forces to encircle Iraqi forces, press on to Baghdad, and oust Saddam Hussein. Believing the military mission was complete and wanting to prevent further casualties, Washington took the decision without consultation with the British, and Hurd considered arguing the point with the American leadership. Relations between the Major government and the administration of **William Clinton** were so strained that Hurd later recalled that in late 1994 Anglo–American relations were at their lowest point since **Suez**. The major clash came over European and American responses to events in **Bosnia**. Hurd refused to be persuaded of the wisdom of President Clinton's plan in 1995 to lift the arms embargo against Bosnian Muslims, arguing that this would only provide a "level killing field." Hurd wanted to take a much harder line against Serbian aggression in Bosnia and urged the Clinton administration to join the **United Nations**' peacekeeping operation that was attempting to provide safe havens for the Muslims.

HYDE PARK MEETING (1942). Prime Minister **Winston Churchill** met with President **Franklin D. Roosevelt** at his home in Hyde Park, New York, on 19 and 20 June 1942 to discuss the latest developments in **World War II**. During this third meeting of the "Big Two," the two leaders reaffirmed their commitment to a "Europe first" strategy. It was also at this meeting that the two agreed to share "as equal partners" the research needed to develop an **atomic bomb**.

– I –

IMF CRISIS (1976). In March 1976, the British pound began to slide against the U.S. dollar and by June the British government appealed to the United States for help. The administration of **Gerald Ford** helped to arrange a standby credit of $5.3 billion with central banks, with the Americans putting up £2 billion. This arrangement came with the proviso that the loan would come with a six-month time limit, after which it must be repaid in full. Although this time-limit was resented by the British government, the loan was accepted. However, tense negotiations ensued; by September 1976, the pound was still in trouble as industrial action at British Leyland and a threatened seaman's strike further unnerved international markets, and the British government was forced to consider applying to the International Monetary Fund (IMF) for a bailout. It was clear that the IMF would demand concessions, notably heavy cuts in public expenditure, and the British considered making severe defense cuts, including scrapping **Polaris**, in order to avoid going to the IMF for help. Many within the Ford administration feared such action as it threatened the stability of the **North Atlantic Treaty Organization**, not least because it would leave France as the only European power with a nuclear capability, and an economic crisis in Britain might lead the country in a leftward, protectionist direction and harm the **European Economic Community** (EEC).

Nevertheless, key members of the Ford administration, including U.S. Treasury Secretary William Simon, were not sympathetic to the British plight, having lost patience with recurrent sterling crises, and had no intention of underwriting the Labour government's spending plans, instead believing the British government must address its financial and economic malaise. Despite appealing directly to President Ford, Prime Minister **James Callaghan** was forced to accept the IMF's deflationary terms in exchange for a loan of £2.3 billion. When Callaghan announced the cuts in public expenditure to the House of Commons required under the IMF loan agreement, he received an extremely hostile response from Labour members of Parliament who believed international capital was bullying the left-wing government. *See also* HEALEY, DENIS.

IMPERIAL PREFERENCE. During the Great Depression of the 1930s, Great Britain implemented a policy of imperial preference in an attempt to ease the country's economic difficulties. At the Imperial Economic Conference in Ottawa in 1932, it was agreed to build up **trade** within the British Empire by implementing lower tariffs on imports from member-nations. The policy was viewed as protectionist by the United States and was heavily criticized as a form of protectionism that increased the likelihood of war. The trade barriers against goods from non-empire countries meant that the percentage of imports into Britain from the United States was much lower than that from the empire. *See also* ANGLO–AMERICAN TRADE AGREEMENT; CHAMBERLAIN, NEVILLE; GENERAL AGREEMENT ON TARIFFS AND TRADE; HULL, CORDELL; TRADE.

IRAN. Iran became an Anglo–American concern with the coming of the **Cold War**. After **World War II**, it was clear that the United States and the **Soviet Union** needed greater access to Middle East oil and Britain's traditional dominance in the region was challenged. The United States was instrumental in ensuring that Iran did not succumb to Soviet penetration in 1946. In addition to increasing superpower interest in the region, in Iran the British-dominated Anglo–Iranian Oil Company (renamed British Petroleum in 1954) was also seen by many Iranians as a symbol of imperial exploitation. After negotiations with the British failed to gain greater oil royalties, nationalist forces headed by Prime Minister Mohammed Mossadeq threatened to nationalize the oil industry in Iran in the early Cold War years and eventually did so in May 1951. The initial British response, led by Foreign Secretary Herbert Morrison, to the nationalization of a major company and key revenue earner was to consider an armed attack on Iran to recover Anglo–Iranian property, including the Abadan oil refinery. The administration of **Harry S. Truman** opposed such a plan, believing the British government had invited nationalization by not modernizing its oil policy by involving Iranians more closely in its operations and engaging in greater profit-sharing with them. Britain abandoned its plan for a military recovery of its assets but attempted to gain concessions form the Iranians by seeking legal redress, withdrawing British oil personnel from Iran, and urging other major companies not to buy Iranian oil. As a result, and with oil production halted, the Iranian economy began to falter, leading Washington to fear that Mossadeq might turn to communism.

When the administration of **Dwight D. Eisenhower** came into office in January 1953, the British found a more receptive audience for their concerns about Mossadeq, and the president and his secretary of state, **John Foster Dulles**, were persuaded of the need for a non-communist leadership in Iran. Not wanting to use military force overtly, the U.S. and British intelligence forces cooperated in identifying Iranian opposition forces and planned to overthrow Mossadeq. In its first major "covert operation," Operation Ajax, the Central Intelligence Agency (CIA) , led by Kim Roosevelt (**Teddy Roosevelt**'s grandson and **Franklin D. Roosevelt**'s cousin) and working with MI6, helped Iranian military forces to overthrow Mossadeq in August 1953. In the aftermath, although Britain's control of oil in Iran had ended, the government secured the Anglo–Iranian Oil Company a 40 percent share of the country's oil and the U.S. companies gained another 40 percent. As a result, the United States now had a major interest in Middle Eastern affairs and in the fate of their new ally, the shah of Iran.

IRAQ. Britain's interest in Iraq has longer historical roots than those of the United States, which developed in the period after **World War II**. A part of the Ottoman Empire in the 19th century, Iraq (Mesopotamia) was taken from the Ottoman Turks during **World War I** by invading Britons. At the **Paris Peace Conference** of 1919, Iraq was made a British mandate under Article 22 of the **League of Nations** Covenant. Arab nationalist unrest meant that British rule was relatively brief and Iraq entered the League of Nations as an independent nation in 1932. The Anglo–Iraqi Treaty of 1930 tied Iraq to Britain in a 25-year military alliance, and the oil fields in Iraq meant that Britain retained interest in the country's future. Oil strikes in Kirkuk in October 1927 meant that Iraq began to export crude oil by 1934 and constructed pipelines to the Mediterranean coast. Indeed, until 1961, Britain dominated the Iraq Petroleum Company, but by 1971 it had been nationalized by the Iraqi government. U.S. interest in Iraq increased after World War II when it became reliant on Middle Eastern oil supplies, was keen to prevent Soviet domination of the region, and became increasingly alarmed by Arab nationalism. Although the leading foreign oil power in the Middle East by the mid-1950s, initially the United States refused to join Britain, **Iran**, and Iraq in the **Baghdad Pact** formed in 1955. With the issue of the **Eisenhower Doctrine** in January 1957, the United States indicated its deepening commitment to the Middle East and on 14 July 1958, when the pro-Western regime was overthrown in Iraq, the United States intervened in Lebanon.

By 1979 the Baath Socialist Party led by Saddam Hussein ruled Iraq. Both Britain and the United States backed Iraq during the Iran–Iraq War (1980–1988), providing crucial intelligence, arms, and equipment to Saddam's regime. When Saddam Hussein invaded Kuwait in August 1990, President **George H. W. Bush** worked with Prime Minister **Margaret Thatcher** on organizing a **United Nations** response. When Iraqi forces failed to leave Kuwait, British and American forces worked with other allied nations to secure its liberation. Despite **friendly fire incidents**, the **Gulf War** helped to improve Anglo–American relations, not least in demonstrating the ability of British and American military and intelligence forces to work effectively together. In the aftermath of the war, under a UN Security Council resolution of 6 April 1991, British and American aircraft continued to police a no-fly zone in order to protect the Kurdish people from possible chemical attack by the Saddam Hussein regime. In the lead-up to the **Iraq War** that began in March 2003, attacks against Iraqi targets in the no-fly zone increased.

IRAQ WAR (2003–). As part of the cease-fire agreements after the **Gulf War** of 1991, the **United Nations** adopted Security Council Resolution 687 on 3 April that year, requiring **Iraq** to destroy its chemical, biological, and nuclear weapons, commonly known as weapons of mass destruction (WMDs). By 2002, the United States and many of its key allies, including **Tony Blair**'s Labour government in Great Britain, believed Iraq had failed to comply with this resolution and had instead actively developed its WMD program. Despite denials from the Iraqi regime and a failure by UN arms inspectors, led by **Hans Blix**, to find evidence of stockpiles of such weapons, President **George W. Bush** began to plan for an invasion of Iraq, by this stage believing it was a necessary requirement of the "war on terror" that he had initiated in the aftermath of the **September 11** attacks. In a series of meetings in 2002 and early 2003, Prime Minister Blair and President Bush discussed future policy on Iraq. During a meeting in April 2002 between Blair and Bush at the president's ranch in Crawford, Texas, it became clear to the British prime minister that the U.S. administration was determined to force Saddam Hussein from power. Blair was adamant that rather than emphasizing regime change, in Britain he would have to emphasize the dangers posed by Iraqi weapons of mass destruction. On 10 and 11 October 2002, President Bush was boosted by a joint resolution passed by Congress giving him authority to use force if necessary in dealing with threats posed by Iraq (House Joint Resolution 114).

The Bush White House and the Blair government used intelligence sources in their attempts to persuade their respective public and encountered similar problems regarding its reliability. On 24 September 2002, Blair announced to the House of Commons that the intelligence service had evidence that Iraq had chemical and biological weapons and that these could be ready to use in 45 minutes. The British government published a dossier on WMDs providing further detail but the debate about the necessity for a military intervention continued in Great Britain. In order to help secure the backing of the House of Commons and the British public, Blair insisted on securing a UN resolution for military action in Iraq. Britain's ambassador to the United Nations, **Jeremy Greenstock**, helped secure the passage of the U.S.–U.K. sponsored UN Security Council Resolution 1441 on 8 November 2002, which offered Iraq a final opportunity to comply with previous UN resolutions on disarmament. During negotiations, it was made clear that there was no automatic trigger to war contained in Resolution 1441, and in Britain it was believed that an additional UN resolution would be required before military action against Iraq could be undertaken. When the UN weapons inspectors reported on 13 February 2003 that no WMDs had been found in Iraq, Britain and the United States proposed an additional resolution to mandate the invasion of Iraq. When it became clear that the UN was unlikely to pass another resolution—Germany, Russia, and France were strongly opposed to a military attack—the Bush administration, backed by the British government, began to prepare for war.

On 17 March 2003, the diplomatic process on Iraq ended and the arms inspectors were evacuated. The following day, in a televised address, President Bush gave Saddam Hussein two days to leave Iraq or face war. On the same day, a debate was held in the British Parliament on a government motion endorsing military action in Iraq, which was then passed 412 to 149. Unlike the previous allied action during the **Gulf War** of 1991, the United States only managed to secure a large-scale military commitment from Great Britain. Although the Bush administration had assembled a "coalition of the willing" that involved over 30 nations, only Poland and Australia were willing to send combat forces to join the Anglo–American invasion force.

The invasion of Iraq—Operation Iraqi Freedom—led by General Tommy Franks, began in the early hours of 20 March 2003 (shortly after the 48-hour deadline had passed) when U.S. aircraft bombed Baghdad, leading to an invasion from the south by coalition forces, including British marines who invaded the Faw peninsula. Washington committed 250,000 troops to the war in Iraq and took charge of occupying central and northern Iraq, including Baghdad, while Britain sent 46,000, taking responsibility for securing Basra in the South. By 9 April 2003, U.S.-led coalition forces had taken control of Baghdad and by 1 May 2003 President Bush felt confident enough to announce that major operations had ended in Iraq. **Paul Bremer** was appointed U.S. envoy to Iraq and worked with British envoy Jeremy Greenstock in establishing a transitional government in Iraq. In the aftermath of the occupation of Iraq, a multinational force was approved on 16 October 2003 by the United Nations Security Council to support the reconstruction. Saddam Hussein was captured in Iraq in December 2003, was brought to trial, found guilty of crimes against humanity, and executed on 30 December 2006. Blair did not believe in the death penalty but kept quiet on the issue. Chancellor of the Exchequer **Gordon Brown** spoke out against the filmed scene of the execution and abuse directed at Saddam.

On 6 December 2006, the Iraq Study Group reported a bleak picture of the situation in Iraq. As a result of increasing attacks against U.S. and Iraqi government forces, including suicide bombings and vehicle attacks, and because of growing domestic criticism of U.S. involvement in Iraq, in February 2007 the Bush administration adopted a new military strategy in Iraq, known as "the surge," which involved the introduction of an extra 30,000 troops in and around Baghdad to step up security. On 21 February 2007, the British government announced that it would cut its troop numbers in Iraq but would remain in Iraq into 2008. After five years of war, 134 British soldiers had been killed in action in Iraq (173 deaths in total), and the United States had suffered 4,000 dead.

From the beginning of its plans for invasion, the Bush administration and Blair government faced significant opposition to actions in Iraq. Not all the British cabinet agreed with Blair's assessment of the threat posed by Iraq or the need for immediate military action. Foreign Secretary **Robin Cook** and Secretary of State for International Development Claire Short resigned shortly after the beginning of military action in Iraq, acknowledging their disagreement with the Labour government's decision to go to war without a second UN resolution. Protests against the invasion of Iraq took place throughout the world, including mass marches and student walkouts throughout Britain in early 2003.

In July 2004, the Butler Report criticized the Blair government for leading the public to believe that the intelligence on Iraq's WMDs was much "firmer and fuller" than was actually the case. The same month, the Senate Intelligence Committee reported that the United States and its allies went to war in Iraq on the basis of "flawed" intelligence from the Central Intelligence Agency (CIA) and other agencies. *See also* BAKER–HAMILTON COMMISSION.

IRELAND. Since the mid-19th century, Ireland has been a recurrent issue in Anglo–American relations. Ireland was part of the British Empire until it was granted its independence under the Anglo–Irish Treaty of 1921. Irish immigration to the United States had begun in the late 18th century but increased markedly from 1846 as the potato famine took hold in Ireland, resulting in mass starvation and disease. In less than a decade, over two million emigrated from Ireland to the United States, most settling in the largest cities. Irish Americans formed the **Fenian Brotherhood** in 1858 to fight for an end to British rule in Ireland. Anglo–American tension during the **American Civil War** was exacerbated by Fenian activity as they sought to press their case by engaging in border raids into British North America (**Canada**). Although Britain felt the Americans were unhelpful in dealing with the Fenians, tension over this issue decreased after the **Treaty of Washington** of 1871.

The increasing numbers of Irish Americans in the United States by the late 19th century meant that they were able to become an effective pressure group and a political force within the Democratic Party, Catholic Church, and labor unions. The same period also saw a growth in Irish American societies with political aims, such as the Ancient Order of Hibernians and the American Protective Association. By the turn of the 20th century, British and American foreign policymakers were well aware that Irish nationalists on both sides of the Atlantic, frustrated at the continuing battle for home rule in Ireland, were working together to put increasing pressure on their respective governments to find a solution to the "Irish problem."

When **World War I** broke out in Europe, President **Woodrow Wilson** understood that Irish Americans within the Democratic Party were wholly opposed to American intervention on the side of Britain, especially after the brutal suppression of the Easter rising in Dublin by the British in 1916. With American entry into the war, Irish Americans were reassured by President Wilson's commitment to his **Fourteen Points**, and particularly by his reference to the "self-determination" of peoples, which they took to mean an American commitment to independence in Ireland. Although Wilson had given a vague commitment to press the British on the Irish question—and despite constant Irish American lobbying to put Ireland on the agenda at the **Paris Peace Conference**—he did not want to risk antagonizing Prime Minister **David Lloyd-George** on the matter, and the **Versailles Treaty** made no reference to it. As a result, Irish Americans made great efforts to ensure Congress did not ratify the treaty.

In 1921 the Anglo–Irish Treaty was signed granting independence to Ireland and leading to the formation of the Irish Free State the following year. Independence had only been granted to 26 counties in Ireland, with the six predominantly Protestant counties in the north remaining part of the United Kingdom. For Irish Americans, the struggle to end partition of Ireland became their major focus but for the White House it was not worth jeopardizing Anglo–American relations by interfering in a domestic concern for the British. The emergence of "the troubles" in Northern Ireland in the late 1960s brought some tension between Washington and London as it was believed in British circles that Irish American groups, including Noraid, had begun financing the armed struggle in the province, but it was only after the end of the Cold War that the administration of **William Clinton** was able to actively intervene on the issue. President Clinton caused great controversy by granting the Sinn Fein leader, **Gerry Adams**, a visa to visit the United States in 1994. Clinton believed it might encourage an Irish Republican Army (IRA) cease-fire but in Britain, the Conservative government led by Prime Minister **John Major** was outraged, not least because his party had a close allegiance to the unionist politicians. After the IRA declared a cease-fire in August 1994, the United States remained engaged in the peace process, with President Clinton traveling to Belfast to encourage further engagement by all concerned. An international commission on the decommissioning of arms was established and led by Senator **George Mitchell**. Further progress was made after the Labour government was elected to power in May 1997 and the new prime minister, **Tony Blair**, welcomed American involvement on Northern Ireland. Dublin, Washington, and London worked together on the issue and the Good Friday peace agreement—allowing for devolved government for Northern Ireland—was reached on 10 April 1998.

– J –

JAMES, HENRY (1843–1916). A prolific and celebrated writer, Henry James became a major figure in transatlantic literature. Born in New York City to wealthy parents, he spent much of his time in England as a child and an adult. His most famous works were the classic novels *The American* (1877) and *The Portrait of a Lady* (1881), but he also published his travel writings in *The Nation* and other periodicals, including his observations of the English from his travels around the country. In 1876, he immigrated to England and took British citizenship in 1915, partly because he objected to American neutrality in the early years of World War I.

JAMESTOWN. In 1607, English settlers arrived in Jamestown, Virginia, establishing the first permanent English colony in America. After crossing the Atlantic Ocean in three ships—the *Susan Constant*, *Discovery*, and *Godspeed*—on 24 May 1607, 104 men and boys, sponsored by the Virginia Company of London, arrived in Jamestown hoping to make money trading local resources, including minerals. In the early years, the settlers faced harsh conditions in the swampy, mosquito-ridden area on the James River, particularly poor quality drinking water and encounters with local Native Americans from the

Powhatan tribe. Consequently, by 1611 most of the first settlers had died from heat, infections, dysentery, and Indian attack. The colony endured, however, as women and indentured servants arrived and the settlers began to grow and **trade** in tobacco and wheat. The settling of Jamestown marked the start of British rule that lasted 176 years. In May 2007, **Queen Elizabeth II** visited the site of the settlement as part of the 400th anniversary of the founding of Jamestown.

JAY TREATY (1794–1795). In 1794, President **George Washington** sent Supreme Court Chief Justice John Jay to England to resolve maritime, territorial, and financial issues that dated back to the American **War of Independence** and not settled by the 1783 **Treaty of Versailles**. By then engaged in the **Napoleonic Wars**, the British had since November 1793 seized over 250 American ships sailing from the West Indies bound for France and had confiscated their cargoes of sugar as wartime contraband. The treaty, signed by Jay and Lord Grenville for the British on 19 November 1794, provided for the withdrawal of British garrisons from six forts in the American Northwest, agreed to establish a commission to resolve outstanding boundary disputes in the northwest and northeast, and agreed to arbitration of American commercial claims arising from the seizure of American ships. Although ratified by the U.S. Senate, the treaty was seen as pro-British by many American critics, especially as it required the United States to compensate British creditors for all prewar debts owed by its citizens and acknowledged Britain's right to board neutral ships and remove French property.

JAZZ. An all-American form of music, jazz emerged in the early 20th century in the African American communities of the South but became popular with a broader audience in big cities such as Chicago and New Orleans. Characterized by improvisation and syncopation, jazz was an American art form that was adopted by the British in the 1920s. Jazz arrived in Great Britain in 1919, when the all-white Original Dixieland Jazz Band arrived to play and record in London and the all-black Southern Syncopated Orchestra toured Britain. Arriving in Britain just after the end of World War I, jazz appealed to young people who listened to it on 10-inch, 78-rpm phonograph discs. Because of its association with speakeasies and underground clubs, its encouragement of free-form dancing, and its sexual and racial connotations, jazz was seen as risqué music. Its popularity with British youth, combined with the arrival of American films, prompted fears of Americanization in Britain and was often spoken of as a "jazz invasion." Although the British establishment viewed jazz as immoral when it first arrived and banned jazz bands from touring, by 1926 the Royal Albert Hall in London was hosting a Charleston ball, and a magazine, the *Melody Maker*, was actively promoting American jazz in Britain. Edward, Prince of Wales (later **Edward VIII**), also helped make it fashionable by playing jazz with **Duke Ellington** in 1933. Over the decades, jazz took on many forms in Britain, often emulating American jazz but appealing to a range of British peoples. Swing bands remained popular throughout the 1930s and early 1940s. In 1944, American jazz musician Glenn Miller played with the U.S. Army Air Force Band in wartime England, performing across the country entertaining the troops and boosting wartime morale with such numbers as "Chattanooga Choo-Choo" and "In the Mood." In the 1940s and 1950s, traditional jazz, or "trad jazz" as it became known, was popular with a predominantly white working-class audience. Trad jazz was an imitation of black American jazz (also known as the New Orleans revival) and saw Louis Armstrong and Jelly Roll Morton become popular artists on the scene. Skiffle music—blending blues, jazz, and folk and emphasizing the guitar, bass, and washboard—also came out of the trad-jazz scene and saw vocalist and guitarist Lonnie Donegan achieve cult status among British youth looking for their own culture. Donegan popularized skiffle—and in the process influenced many of the famous musicians of the 1960s, including members of the **Beatles** and the Who—through his speeded-up version of Led Belly's "Rock Island Line" released in 1954. In the 1980s, another British jazz movement emerged led by saxophonist Courtney Pine, the all-black Jazz Warriors fused jazz with contemporary British drum and bass music as well as hip-hop. Jazz has remained popular on the British club scene, helped by the notoriety of Ronnie Scott's jazz club, which did much to popularize jazz in Britain.

JEFFERSON, THOMAS (1743–1826). Thomas Jefferson was the third president of the United States (1801–1809) and principal author of the **American Declaration of Independence**. He is also reputed to have been the first to use the term "**Anglophobia**" in May 1793 in a letter written during his time as the first secretary of state to his friend James Madison. As one of the Founding Fathers, Jefferson played an influential part in the American Revolution; as a leading republican, his negative views on the British system of government never diminished. Jefferson's own Anglophobia was most apparent during the period of the **French Revolutionary Wars** (1793–1802) and the **Napoleonic Wars** (1804–1815) when he supported the French Revolution and later disagreed with President **George Washington**'s apparent pro-British stance when Britain and France went to war in 1793. In particular, Jefferson attacked Britain's violation of U.S. neutrality during the wars, especially the impressment of sailors seized from American ships, including the *Chesapeake*, and British interference with American **trade** through the naval blockade of American ports in 1805. Attempts at diplomacy with the British were carried out by James Madison and William Pinkney, but relations between Britain and the United States deteriorated still further when the British said that any American ships sailing to Europe had to stop in England to receive permission. President Jefferson then introduced the **Embargo Act** into Congress that prevented any ships sailing into or out of the United States. This act was considered a failure for Jefferson as it further enflamed tensions with the British and damaged American trade more than it hurt the British. *See also* WAR OF INDEPENDENCE.

JEROME, JENNIE (1854–1921). Famous for being a beautiful socialite and the mother of British Prime Minister **Winston Churchill**, Jennie Jerome was the daughter of wealthy American businessman and financier Leonard Jerome. As an American heiress, born in New York, Jenny Jerome traveled to England and as a 19-year-old debutante, met Lord Randolph Churchill, and within three days they were married. Although some English peers married wealthy American heiresses for financial reasons, and some rich American heiresses married to gain English titles, Churchill and Jerome appear to have married for love. Either way, the marriage lasted until Churchill's death in 1895. Their son, Winston, who was instrumental in establishing the Anglo–American "**special relationship**," would often emphasize his mother's origin.

JOHNSON, LYNDON BAINES (1908–1973). Texan Democrat and vice president, Lyndon Baines Johnson became 36th president of the United States after the assassination of President **John F. Kennedy** in Dallas, Texas, on 22 November 1963. Johnson believed strongly in the value of the Anglo–American relationship and spoke extremely highly of **Winston Churchill** and his role in **World War II**. Unlike his East Coast, urbane predecessor, he did not have especially strong links with Great Britain. His relationship with British Prime Minister **Alec Douglas-Home** was not strong. Douglas-Home annoyed Johnson by coming to Washington in February 1964 and making a public statement that indicated he had dealt strongly with American criticism of British sales of buses to **Cuba**. Johnson's relationship with Douglas-Home's successor, Labour Prime Minister **Harold Wilson**, elected in October 1964, was also mixed. Although Wilson was keen to establish a close Anglo–American relationship, based on regular meetings with President Johnson, this was unlikely to occur after the new British prime minister refused to contribute troops to the American effort in Vietnam during their first summit meeting at the White House in December 1964. Johnson, whose presidency became dominated by the **Vietnam War**, became increasingly frustrated by Wilson's requests to visit Washington and his attempts to broker peace in Vietnam.

Johnson was able to work effectively with Britain on other foreign policy issues. In December 1964, he agreed to consider Wilson's suggestion of an **Atlantic Nuclear Force** (ANF) instead of a **multilateral force** (MLF). Despite reservations about the lack of British military support in Vietnam and also feeling uneasy about the Wilson government's domestic spending on social programs, Johnson agreed that the United States should support the ailing pound sterling. Britain and the United States also cooperated in their response to the 1967 **Arab–Israeli War**. The Anglo–American relationship came under further strain in 1967 when it became clear that the British government was planning to withdraw its military forces from **East of Suez**. Johnson hoped to persuade the British to maintain a worldwide military commitment, but failed, and on 16 January 1968 the Wilson government announced its plans to withdraw all forces from the Far East (except **Hong Kong**) on 31 March 1971 and to withdraw all forces from the Persian Gulf by the same date.

– K –

KELLOGG–BRIAND PACT. Named after U.S. Secretary of State Frank B. Kellogg and French Foreign Minister Aristide Briand, this multilateral pact was signed in Paris on 27 August 1928 by the representatives of Australia, **Canada**, Germany, Great Britain, India, the Irish Free State, Italy, New Zealand, South Africa, and the United States. Signatory states renounced war as an instrument of national policy and, although the pact did not prevent the outbreak of **World War II**, the premise that aggressive war should be considered a breach of international law was later built upon by the **United Nations** Charter.

KENNEDY, JOHN F. (1917–1963). When John F. Kennedy became president of the United States in January 1961, he faced a healthy Anglo–American relationship that had recovered much ground since the low point of **Suez**. An Irish American Democrat, Kennedy nevertheless had **Anglophile** tendencies. He had spent a lengthy period in Britain during the tenure of his father, **Joseph Kennedy**, at the Court of St. James, and had written his undergraduate thesis on British **appeasement** during the **Munich crisis** of 1938, which was published as a book, *While England Slept*, in 1940 and became a bestseller. As a Massachusetts congressman, Kennedy also visited London on a private visit in early June 1951, meeting with **Queen Elizabeth II** and Prime Minister **Harold Macmillan**. Kennedy was well prepared for dealing with Anglo–American relations when he entered the White House. Kennedy was able to establish a very close relationship with Macmillan despite the 23-year age gap, partly facilitated by the efforts of British Ambassador David Ormsby-Gore and American Ambassador **David Bruce**. Kennedy's first year in office saw some disagreement between London and Washington over **Berlin** and **Laos**, when Macmillan felt the Kennedy administration needed to be restrained from taking confrontational action. Relations improved after Kennedy's summit meeting with Premier Nikita Khrushchev of the **Soviet Union** in Vienna in June 1961, when the president was confronted by Moscow's intransigence. Kennedy met with Macmillan a few days later at 10 **Downing Street**, where he was able to have an informal and friendly discussion about the meeting.

Kennedy's relations with Great Britain were part of his "grand design" for the United States and Europe, outlined in his "Declaration of Interdependence" speech on 4 July 1962. He expressed his desire for "a true partnership" for Europe and the United States, although Britain was disappointed to find that in reality Kennedy intended the United States to control the Western alliance. While the British felt interdependence should mean a pooling of efforts and resources, the Kennedy administration was interested in "burden sharing" and U.S. leadership. The limits of interdependence were exposed when the United States cancelled the **Skybolt** missile, and Anglo–American relations were strained when Kennedy met with Macmillan at Nassau in December 1962. During the **Cuban missile crisis** in October 1962, Kennedy rang Macmillan regularly to keep him informed of developments and gain reassurance from the experienced British politician. Kennedy received encouragement from the British over the subsequent **Nuclear Test Ban Treaty** that was signed in the aftermath of the missile crisis in August 1963.

When Kennedy was assassinated in Dallas, Texas, on 22 November 1963, the British public mourned his loss and at his funeral Britain was represented by the Duke of Edinburgh, Prime Minister Sir **Alec Douglas-Home**, and leader of the Opposition, **Harold Wilson**. In May 1965, a British memorial to JFK was dedicated at Runnymede, Surrey (the site of the Magna Carta), with Jacqueline Kennedy in attendance. The memorial, a stone tablet with JFK's famous inaugural speech inscribed on it, was placed on a one-acre site donated to the United States of America by the British people. *See also* HARLECH, LORD; NASSAU AGREEMENT.

KENNEDY, JOSEPH PATRICK (1888–1969). Irish American businessman and father of President **John F. Kennedy**, Joseph Kennedy served as British ambassador to Great Britain between 1938 and 1940. A Bostonian of Irish extraction, Kennedy lobbied President **Franklin D. Roosevelt** to be sent to the Court of St. James. Arriving in London as **appeasement** was proving ineffective at halting Adolf Hitler's advance through Europe, Joe Kennedy witnessed the drift to war. After Britain declared war on Germany in September 1939, Kennedy remained noninterventionist and in May 1940, as Germany began bombing Britain, did not support **Winston Churchill**'s pleas for further American military equipment. He was encouraged to resign from his office after offending his host country, and his own, when he declared democracy finished in Britain during the battle of Britain in November 1940.

KEYNES, JOHN MAYNARD (1883–1946). British economist John Maynard Keynes played a key role as adviser to the treasury (1940–1946) in negotiations surrounding the establishment of the **Bretton Woods** system and later in negotiating the **Anglo–American loan agreement** of 1945.

KIPLING, RUDYARD (1865–1936). In February 1899, British author and poet Rudyard Kipling wrote a poem entitled "The **White Man's Burden**: The United States and the Philippine Islands" that was published in *McClure's* magazine in the United States. The poem was received by U.S. imperialists as a call to "empire" as it was written in the aftermath of the **Spanish–American War** of 1898 when the United States annexed the Philippines, and its publication coincided with the beginning of the U.S.–Philippine War (1899–1903). The controversial poem appeared to encourage **Anglo–Saxonism** and its notions of racial superiority, prevalent in Britain and the United States during that time.

KIRKPATRICK, JEANNE (1926–2006). Jeanne Kirkpatrick was the first woman to serve as the U.S. ambassador to the **United Nations** and was a member of President **Ronald Reagan**'s cabinet and National Security Council. During the **Falklands** crisis in 1982, Kirkpatrick's pro-Argentine views led to clashes not only with the British but also with Secretary of State **Alexander Haig**. Kirkpatrick had studied Argentina for her doctorate, and in relation to the Falklands believed it best to avoid alienating Argentina, a potential U.S. ally in the anticommunist struggle in Latin America. Kirkpatrick had dined with the Argentines on the evening of the invasion. Famously, in June 1982 during a vote in the UN Security Council on a resolution calling for an immediate cease–fire in the Falklands, Kirkpatrick cast a U.S. veto, only to announce minutes later that she had been instructed to abstain. Kirkpatrick blamed this confusion on a delay in communication but many believed it indicated a split in the Reagan administration between Kirkpatrick and the pro-British Haig.

KISSINGER, HENRY (1923–). Serving as special assistant for national security affairs (1969–1973) and as secretary of state (1973–1977) under President **Richard M. Nixon** and his successor President **Gerald Ford**, Henry Kissinger contributed to a cooling of Anglo–American relations. In 1973, Kissinger formulated the "**Year of Europe**," a policy initiative that only served to confuse and annoy the British government led by Prime Minister **Edward Heath**. Kissinger was annoyed in return when Heath refused to allow the United States to use its base in Cyprus to airlift supplies to Israel during the 1973 **Arab–Israeli War**. In 1974, Kissinger refused British requests to intervene to help stop the intercommunal fighting in **Cyprus**. Relations between Britain and the United States remained cordial, partly due to the warm relationship that developed between Kissinger and the British ambassador in Washington, **John Freeman**, to whom he confided his anxieties about the Nixon administration. In 1976, with British support, Kissinger intervened in **Rhodesia**, introducing a six-step plan to ensure black majority rule in the country.

KOREAN WAR (1950–1953). In the early hours of 25 June 1950, the communist forces of North Korea crossed the 38th parallel to invade South Korea with the aim of destroying its regime and reunifying the country. In that moment, the **Cold War** extended from Europe to Asia. The United States quickly organized an allied military response through the **United Nations**, assembling a 16-nation coalition force, with the aim of repelling the North Koreans to north of the 38th parallel. Under pressure from Washington, and agreeing with the American view that the **Soviet Union** was behind the invasion, the British cabinet agreed to send British troops to Korea, eventually sending over 63,000 personnel. On 15 September 1950, U.S. and South Korean marines landed at Inchon, led by General Douglas MacArthur. The North Koreans were soon pushed northward, reaching the Yalu River—the border between Korea and **China**—on 24 October 1950. This move beyond the 38th parallel led the British government to encourage Washington to change the aim of operation to the reunification of Korea and the British organized UN endorsement of MacArthur's actions.

On 30 November 1950, in response to the Chinese intervention in the war and in an unguarded moment during a press conference,

President **Harry S. Truman** admitted that the United States had considered the use of nuclear weapons in Korea and acknowledged the choice of targets would be a military matter and thus a decision for General MacArthur. The British government was so alarmed by these comments that Prime Minister **Clement Attlee** flew to Washington immediately. As Great Britain had recently permitted the stationing of B-29 bombers at U.S. Air Force bases in Britain, Truman's remarks had again raised the issue of consultation on the use of the bomb. Although Truman managed to allay Attlee's fears over an imminent use of the bomb, the remarks had resulted in increasing **anti-Americanism in Britain**, and Attlee was only able to get the White House to promise to keep its allies informed over any potential use of the bomb.

In reaching the Yalu River, MacArthur prompted Chinese intervention in the war and by January 1951 the North Koreans had retaken Seoul, the capital city of South Korea. Although UN forces managed to retake some ground, by 8 July 1951 peace talks had begun. A cease-fire agreement was signed on 27 July 1953 by representatives of the UN, China, and North Korea. Although relatively small in numbers, in comparison to American forces, the British 29th Infantry Brigade faced Chinese attack at the Battle of Imjin River, 22–25 April 1951, suffering many casualties. The United States suffered 36,934 deaths in Korea, while the British death toll was 1,109. *See also* FRANKS, SIR OLIVER.

KOSOVO (1998). In 1998, Prime Minister **Tony Blair** put great pressure on President **Bill Clinton** to use U.S. military force to help end Serbian aggression against **Kosovo**. World attention had been drawn to the "ethnic cleansing" of Albanians in the Kosovo region of Serbia (former Yugoslavia) by Serbian government and paramilitary forces. In addition to the thousands murdered, hundred of thousands of refugees fled the province. Blair took a hard line against the Serbian president, Slobodan Milosevic. Taking the moral high ground, Blair spoke of Milosevic's barbaric acts in Kosovo and appealed to other Western nations to join a crusade to save the Muslim victims of aggression. President Clinton was willing to allow U.S. forces to contribute to a **North Atlantic Treaty Organization** bombing campaign against Serbia but only reluctantly. Sensitive to American public opinion over U.S. casualties, Clinton resisted pressure from Tony Blair to commit ground troops to Kosovo. Between 24 March and 11 June 1999, NATO forces bombed Serbia, changing the nature of NATO strategy in the process (shifting from a defensive role to an offensive one), and on 10 June 1999 Milosevic agreed to withdraw his troops, allowing international peacekeepers to enter the province. Clinton sent U.S. troops to contribute to this peacekeeping force, which included British, French, and other NATO forces.

KUBRICK, STANLEY (1928–1999). Disillusioned by the lack of independence for filmmakers in Hollywood, American-born director and producer Stanley Kubrick moved to England in 1962. Known in the United States as the director of the blockbuster *Spartacus* (1960), Kubrick felt he would have more artistic freedom working in Britain. His most famous works include *Dr. Strangelove* (1964), *2001: A Space Odyssey* (1968), *A Clockwork Orange* (1971), *The Shining* (1980), and *Full Metal Jacket* (1987). He remained in England until his death, and rarely appeared in public.

KYOTO PROTOCOL. The Kyoto Protocol to the **United Nations** Framework Convention on Climate Change was the first international agreement on global warming and was negotiated by world leaders in Kyoto, Japan, in December 1997. The treaty—which went into effect on 16 February 2005 and expires in 2012—was designed to reduce greenhouse gas emissions, setting targets for each of the treaty's signatories. While Great Britain endorsed the treaty and began to plan for a 60 percent reduction in its carbon dioxide emissions by 2050, the United States did not ratify the treaty. President **William J. Clinton** signed the treaty but the U.S. Senate refused to ratify it. Clinton's successor in the White House, President **George W. Bush**, maintained a steadfast objection to it, arguing until recently that the evidence for man-made global warming was not convincing, that the U.S. economy would be damaged by it, and that the treaty was flawed because **China** (the second-largest emitter of greenhouse gases) was not required to reduce its emissions. The Labour government came under pressure from MPs and environmental groups to urge the United States to ratify the Kyoto Protocol. Prime Minister **Tony Blair** acknowledged that he "agreed to differ" with Bush on climate change.

– L –

LAOS. By 1961, Laos was a "hot spot" in the **Cold War** and viewed in Washington as the key to maintaining a noncommunist Indochina (Laos, Cambodia, **Vietnam**). A crisis arose in the former French colony after the civil war between the U.S.-backed royal Lao government and communist insurgents, the Pathet Lao, supported by North Vietnamese communists, threatened to end with the communists taking control of Laos. Prior to a meeting between Russian leader Andrei Gromyko and President **John F. Kennedy** at the **White House**, the British prime minister, **Harold Macmillan**, flew to Key West, Florida, to discuss a British cease-fire proposal. Macmillan suggested, and Kennedy agreed, to press Gromyko for a three-nation control commission in Laos and a 14-nation international conference, leading to a coalition government that would include members of the Pathet Lao. The Kennedy administration also had a military contingency plan in place should a cease-fire not be possible. Macmillan was willing to consider a British troop commitment to a U.S.-organized military intervention in Laos aimed at defeating the communist Pathet Lao. Kennedy rejected the military plan, instead favoring a negotiated settlement, and during his meeting with Gromyko on 27 March 1961 gained an agreement for a three-part government that include pro-communist, pro-American, and neutral groups. A cease-fire was agreed to on 3 May 1961. This policy of neutrality was agreed to in 1962 at a Geneva Conference that issued a Declaration on the Neutrality of Laos.

LAUREL AND HARDY. Stan Laurel (1890–1965) and Oliver Hardy (1892–1957) established the most famous Anglo–American comedy partnership in feature film history. Laurel was born in Ulverston, Cumbria, England, and Hardy was born in Harlem, Georgia. After establishing himself within British music hall theater as an actor and director, Laurel immigrated to the United States in 1912. He worked with Hardy for the first time in 1917 when they starred in a short silent film, *The Lucky Dog*. It was not until 1927 that Laurel and Hardy worked together as a comedy duo playing "Stan" and "Ollie" for the first time in *The Second Hundred Years*. They quickly became famous for their verbal humor as well as slapstick comedy. The phys-

ical and intellectual contrast between the two comedy partners—
"Stan" was shorter, thinner, and dim, while "Ollie" was taller, fatter,
and the ideas man—worked ideally, with their onscreen friendship
characterized by failed ventures but enduring loyalty. They made 106
films together between 1927 and 1950 and among their most popular
films were *Sons of the Desert* (1933), *Way Out West* (1937), *Block-
Heads* (1938), and *A Chump at Oxford* (1939).

LEAGUE OF NATIONS. The League of Nations was first proposed
as Point 14 in President **Woodrow Wilson**'s **Fourteen Points** address to the U.S. Congress on 8 January 1918 in which he outlined
the conditions of peace once the fighting in **World War I** had ended.
The league became an integral part of the **Versailles Treaty** negotiated at the **Paris Peace Conference** in 1919. Although Wilson was
able to convince the European nations of the need for an international
organization aimed at maintaining world peace by promoting cooperation between all nations, the U.S. Congress refused to ratify the
treaty; consequently, the United States' noninvolvement in the league
weakened the organization from its beginning. Great Britain was an
original member of the league with a permanent seat on the council
and was frustrated by the United States' refusal to take its seat on the
council, along with the other great powers, and Prime Minister **David
Lloyd-George** noted that "America had been offered the leadership
of the world, but the Senate had tossed the sceptre into the sea."

LEIGH, VIVIEN (1913–1967). Academy Award–winning British actress, Vivien Leigh is most famous for securing the part of American
Southern heroine Scarlett O'Hara in the film version of *Gone with the
Wind* (1939). She was also known as a successful stage actress and
later played another Southern character, Blanche DuBois, in *A Street-
car Named Desire* in a London production of the play and in the Hollywood film version (1951). Married to British Shakespearian actor
Laurence Olivier, Leigh received two Oscars for her American roles
and was the first Englishwoman to win an Academy Award, for her
performance in *Gone with the Wind.*

LEND-LEASE (1941). Building on the **destroyers-for-bases deal** and
Cash and Carry, the Lend-Lease Act of March 1941 allowed the

United States to provide war goods to the Allied nations without breaching its official position of neutrality. The Lend-Lease program allowed President **Franklin D. Roosevelt** to "sell, transfer title to, exchange, lease, lend, or otherwise dispose of, to any such government [whose defense the president deems vital to the defense of the United States] any defense article." Lend-Lease was arranged largely as a result of pressure from British Prime Minister **Winston Churchill** who wrote to Roosevelt explaining the dire state of the British economy and the British government's inability to pay for much-needed war materials. The program was of symbolic as well as material importance as Lend-Lease aid was only extended to Allied nations and indicated the United States' increasing involvement in wartime events and its gradual abandonment of neutrality. Lend-Lease proved extremely important in the months before U.S. entry into **World War II** and was also significant after December 1941 when much of Britain's aircraft, ships, munitions, vehicles, and food were provided for through Lend-Lease. In total, more than $50 billion of aid was distributed to Great Britain and the Allies during World War II under Lend-Lease. The program strengthened Anglo–American relations, especially as Roosevelt described the decision to implement Lend-Lease to the American people as "helping to put out the fire in your neighbor's house before your own house caught fire and burned down." Lend-Lease was cancelled by President **Harry S. Truman** on 11 May 1945 after the end of the war in Europe. The abrupt ending of Lend-Lease left Britain devastated economically. *See also* NEUTRALITY ACTS.

LEXINGTON GREEN, BATTLE OF (1775). The battle of Lexington Green was the military skirmish that started the American **War of Independence** in Concord, Massachusetts, on 19 April 1775. The colony of Massachusetts had been the scene of colonial unrest for several years, and after **Lord North** introduced the **Coercive Acts** in 1774 to punish the colony for the **Boston Tea Party**, the colony began preparations for war against the mother country, including the collection of arms and munitions, and the training of local militias, including the Minutemen. In an attempt to deal with the growing threat, the governor of Massachusetts, General Thomas Cage, sent an expeditionary force from Boston to confiscate weapons stored in the village of Concord and to arrest two major patriot leaders, John Hancock and Samuel Adams, in the village of Lexington. The patriot forces in the colony had sufficient intelligence sources to hear of the departure, by boat, of the British troops, and three messengers—Paul Revere, William Dawes, and Samuel Prescott—rode on horseback to alert villages. At dawn on 19 April 1775 British forces led by Major John Pitcairn faced approximately 70 Lexington Minutemen on the village green; when they refused to disperse, shots were fired leaving eight Minutemen dead. Having failed to find Hancock and Adams, the British forces moved on to the village of Concord, where further fighting broke out. *See also* CONCORD, BATTLE OF.

LIBYA, BOMBING OF (1986). When the United States bombed Libya on 14 April 1986 they used British Royal Air Force bases to refuel and launch over 40 U.S. Air Force F-111 fighter jets on route to the attack. The United States had decided to launch a strike against General Muammar el-Qaddafi's regime, after claiming they had evidence that linked Libya to acts of international terrorism, including the murder by a Palestinian terrorist of 16 passengers at Rome and Vienna airports; the bombing of a TWA plane en route from Rome to Athens, killing four Americans; and the bombing of a West German nightclub, La Belle, in which one American was killed and dozens were injured. The decision by the government of **Margaret Thatcher** to allow the U.S. Air Force to use British bases to launch the attack caused great controversy in Great Britain and according to opinion polls over two thirds of the British public condemned her actions. Although Thatcher had previously spoken out against retaliatory strikes in response to terrorism—and indeed a British policeman, Yvonne Fletcher, had been killed by shots from the Libyan Embassy in London in April 1984—she reasoned in public that the use of the F-111s stationed on British soil was essential to the success of the mission due to their greater accuracy. President **Ronald Reagan**'s desire for political support from a European ally—France and Spain had denied the United States the use of their airspace—was also part of Thatcher's thinking, and given her condemnation of the U.S. invasion of **Grenada**, her positive response on Libya repaid her debt to the Reagan administration over its support for Britain during the **Falklands War**. *See also* AMERICAN BASES IN BRITAIN.

LINCOLN, ABRAHAM (1809–1865). Abraham Lincoln was elected president in 1860 shortly before the outbreak of **American Civil War** in 1861. Consequently, his foreign policy toward Britain focused on preventing its intervention in the war on the side of the Confederacy. The diplomacy of his ambassador to Great Britain, **Charles Adams**, proved important in preventing serious incidents escalating into war, particularly the *Trent* **affair**. Lincoln's policies toward Britain proved successful, and when Lincoln was assassinated on 15 April 1865, Queen Victoria sent a letter of condolence to Mary Todd Lincoln.

LLOYD-GEORGE, DAVID (1916–1922). Before becoming prime minister in December 1916, Liberal MP David Lloyd-George had served as minister of munitions in 1915 and then minister of war in 1916 in the wartime coalition government. Serving in 10 **Downing Street** until 1922, Lloyd-George presided over the end of **World War I** and was Great Britain's representative at the **Paris Peace Conference** in 1919. David Lloyd-George's relationship with President **Woodrow Wilson** during the war gradually deteriorated as the two leaders became increasingly more suspicious of each other's motives. Lloyd-George was considered an aggressive war-maker and was dismissive of Wilson's attempt to discuss the postwar world and his plan for a **League of Nations** while the conflict was still ongoing. During the war itself, the two leaders disagreed over military strategy, with each pursuing his nation's interests, and Lloyd-George requesting additional U.S. troops. After the war, Lloyd-George played a mediation role at the **Paris Peace Conference** as he attempted to forge a way forward between the idealism of Wilson's **Fourteen Points** and the vengefulness of the French delegates. Although agreeing with most of Wilson's Fourteen Points in private, Lloyd-George often sided with French Prime Minister George Clemenceau because he knew that, like the French, the British electorate wanted Germany to suffer a harsher peace settlement. Lloyd-George also became increasingly annoyed at Wilson's constant focus on the **League of Nations** but continued to support it. Lloyd-George remained a popular figure in the United States. When he went on a tour of North America in 1923, hundreds of thousands turned out to hear him speak.

LLOYD, SELWYN (1904–1978). Selwyn Lloyd served as British foreign secretary on two separate occasions. During 1951–1954, he was foreign secretary under Prime Minister **Winston Churchill**. His second period as foreign secretary, from 1955–1960, was dominated by the **Suez crisis** and its aftermath. In the weeks before the crisis, Lloyd sought a meeting with President **Dwight D. Eisenhower**. After Great Britain was forced to withdraw from Egypt because of a lack of U.S. support, on 17 November, Secretary of State **John Foster Dulles** confused Lloyd by asking why the British did not "go through with it and get Nasser down."

LONDON DECLARATION (1990). As the **Soviet Union** disintegrated, President **George H. W. Bush** met with Premier Mikhail Gorbachev in Washington and the meeting resulted in the Strategic Arms Reduction Talks (START) treaty and a treaty on conventional forces in Europe. As the North Atlantic Alliance looked forward to a post–Cold War world, the **North Atlantic Treaty Organization** Council of Heads of State and Government met in London and on 6 July issued a Declaration on a Transformed North Atlantic Alliance. In a switch from its previous policy, NATO stressed a no-first-strike policy, and developed policies to encourage closer relations with the countries of Central and Eastern Europe.

LOTHIAN, LORD (1882–1940). Philip Kerr, 11th Marquess of Lothian, became known as an advocate of improving Anglo–American relations. Lord Lothian's earlier diplomatic career was spent serving in the South African government but he became private secretary to **David Lloyd-George** in 1916. He was influential during the **Paris Peace Conference** in 1919 and in the interwar years became a leading proponent of **appeasement**. However, he eventually came to believe Adolf Hitler was evil and not be trusted, was appointed British ambassador to the United States in 1939, and remained in the position until his death in 1940. Lord Lothian played an important part in establishing the wartime Anglo–American alliance by winning the trust and support of American politicians in the White House and Congress. Lothian helped to convince President **Franklin D. Roosevelt** to agree to the **destroyers-for-bases deal** in 1939 and the

Lend-Lease program of aid for the British in January 1941 and helped improve impressions of the British Embassy in Washington.

LUSITANIA. On 7 May 1915, without warning, a German U-boat submarine sank the British Cunard liner *Lusitania* off the coast of Ireland, killing 1,200 noncombatants, including 128 Americans. The Germans had declared unrestricted submarine warfare in response to a British blockade of Germany during **World War II** and had placed advertisements in newspapers warning Americans not to travel on the *Lusitania*, charging the liner with carrying munitions and other contraband. The United States, officially neutral in relation to the European war, asserted the right to travel unharmed. After the sinking of the *Lusitania*, U.S. popular opinion became more sympathetic to the British and President **Woodrow Wilson** warned that another German attack on merchant ships and liners that affected U.S. citizens would lead to war between the two nations.

LYONS, LORD (1817–1887). Richard Bickerton Pernell Lyons served as British envoy extraordinary and minister plenipotentiary in Washington, D.C., from December 1858 to February 1865, sending regular dispatches back to London during the **American Civil War** (1861–1865) and helping to prevent a conflict between the United States and Great Britain, mostly notably in relation to the *Trent* **affair** and the *Alabama* **claims**.

– M –

MACDONALD, RAMSAY (1866–1937). A Scottish MP, Ramsay MacDonald became the first Labour prime minister in January 1924. Taking an active interest in foreign affairs, he acted as both foreign secretary and prime minister during his first period in office from January to November 1924. During this time, he focused his attention on dealing with what he viewed as the shortcomings of the **Versailles Treaty** and organizing the London Reparations Conference, a gathering of representatives of the Allied governments. Taking place between 16 July and 16 August 1924, the conference saw the former allies adopt the **Dawes Plan**. During his second period in 10 **Downing**

Street, when he was prime minister of a National government (1929–1931), he was the first British prime minister to visit Washington in October 1929. His visit to meet with President Herbert Hoover was extremely successful and included a ticker-tape parade in New York and an address to the U.S. Senate. In January the following year, an agreement on naval arms control was reached during another conference in London. As unemployment increased in Britain, after the stock market crash of October 1929 and the subsequent economic crisis, its budget deficit began to threaten sterling. MacDonald was forced to ask **J. P. Morgan** for assistance. The help came with strings attached, and the British government had to make cuts in its unemployment benefits. MacDonald served as prime minister in the second National government between 1931 and 1935, when he was criticized by **Winston Churchill** for failing to stand up to Adolf Hitler.

MACMILLAN, HAROLD (1894–1986). Becoming Conservative prime minister in January 1957, just two months after the **Suez crisis**, former foreign secretary (1955) and chancellor of the exchequer (1955–1957) Harold Macmillan was determined to restore the Anglo–American relationship as soon as possible. An experienced, gentlemanly politician, Macmillan had an American-born mother and was well disposed toward the United States. He had the advantage of having worked with **Dwight D. Eisenhower** as a political adviser during the North African campaign in **World War II**. Keen to regain American confidence, Macmillan's first chance to improve relations came at the **Bermuda Conference** in March 1957 when he was able to persuade Eisenhower to provide **Thor missiles** to Great Britain. Macmillan also attempted to play the role of middleman between Moscow and Washington, noticeably when he flew to Moscow in February 1959 to have discussions with Nikita Khrushchev over the **Berlin crisis**, becoming the first Western leader to visit the **Soviet Union** since World War II. As well as wanting to strengthen Britain's Atlantic link, Macmillan also made efforts toward a British entry into the **European Economic Community**, encouraged by the United States. Macmillan and Eisenhower made history by making the first live television broadcast from 10 **Downing Street** on 31 August 1959, discussing their views on the communist threat and global poverty.

Despite the age difference between the two leaders, Macmillan was also able to establish a friendly working relationship with President **John F. Kennedy** after the Democratic president came to power in January 1961. Despite this, Macmillan found that the Kennedy administration was only interested in minimal consultation when it came to some major issues. Since 1957, Macmillan had been encouraging the United States and the Soviet Union to consider a **nuclear test ban treaty**. He pressed this issue with Kennedy as a better method of dealing with Khrushchev rather than taking any hawkish action on Berlin or **Laos**. A treaty was signed in 1963 in the aftermath of the **Cuban missile crisis**. During the crisis of October 1962, Kennedy discussed events in Cuba with Macmillan on the telephone and through diplomatic channels, and the British prime minister expressed real concern about possible Soviet action in Berlin in response to the situation. Macmillan recalled the week of the crisis as the most stressful of his life and admitted to not sleeping for most of it. His first real conflict with the Kennedy administration came, however, over the cancellation of the U.S. **Skybolt** missile, which had been promised to the British by President Eisenhower. Macmillan met with Kennedy at **Nassau** in December 1962 and negotiated successfully over the maintenance of Britain's status as an independent nuclear power, with the president agreeing to allow the British to purchase the **Polaris missile** instead.

MAJOR, JOHN (1943–). John Major became British Conservative prime minister after the resignation of **Margaret Thatcher** in November 1990. He had served previously as the chancellor of the exchequer from 1989 to 1990. Relatively inexperienced in foreign affairs, Major came into the office in the middle of the **Gulf War** crisis. He worked well with President **George H. W. Bush** during the war and helped persuade him to implement no-fly-zones in **Iraq** to help protect the Kurds in southern Iraq from the regime of Saddam Hussein. One minor disagreement with the Bush administration came over British plans to forcibly repatriate Vietnamese refugees being held in detention centers in **Hong Kong**. A more major problem came over the ethnic warfare in the Balkans following the disintegration of Yugoslavia that began in 1991. The Bush administration viewed it as a European affair and looked to the European nations to deal with the problem. When Bush was defeated in the 1992 presidential election,

Major found the new administration of **William Clinton** was also reluctant to get involved. However, President Clinton became increasingly more activist with regard to **Bosnia** and played a key role in the Dayton Peace Accords of 1995. The Clinton administration's relationship with Major's Conservative government was nevertheless strained after it appeared that the latter had supported Clinton's Republican opponents during the presidential election campaign, including providing details of Clinton's time at Oxford University as a **Rhodes scholar**. Major was annoyed by Clinton's decision to grant a visa to Sinn Fein leader **Gerry Adams** to visit the United States in 1994 and his subsequent invitation to the **White House** for St. Patrick's Day in March 1995. John Major lost the 1997 general election to Labour candidate **Tony Blair**.

MAKINS, ROGER (1904–1996). Roger Makins, later Lord Sherfield, was minister at the British Embassy in Washington between 1945 and 1947 and ambassador to the United States between 1952 and 1956. Makins's relationship with U.S. Secretary of State **John Foster Dulles** was considered less close than that of his immediate predecessor, **Sir Oliver Franks**, whose relationship with **Dean Acheson** was considered particularly cordial. However, Makins did play an important role in securing continued Anglo–American cooperation in the decade after the end of **World War II**. Most obviously, Makins was intimately involved in negotiating the atomic energy agreements in the late 1940s and mid-1950s. He has been held largely responsible for the modus vivendi of January 1948 and the atomic agreement of 15 June 1955. Makins was also in Washington at the time of the **Suez crisis** and forewarned the British government of the U.S. decision to withdraw the offer to finance the Aswan dam that came on 19 July 1956.

MALAYAN EMERGENCY. In July 1948, Great Britain declared a state of emergency in Malaya after communist guerrillas began attacking rubber plantations and their owners and workers. In an attempt to defeat the communist forces, the British authorities organized military resistance, which included their forces along with troops from Australia, New Zealand, Fiji, and East Africa. The emergency lasted until 1960, although the communist forces were defeated by 1958. Despite relentless pressure from British Foreign Secretary **Ernest Bevin**, the United States refused to provide military assistance in Malaya. Although Washington supported British action in Malaya and understood the importance of the dollar-earning capacity of Malaya's rubber and tin to Britain's economy, it was felt Southeast Asia was the sphere of influence of France and Britain. Fearing the Malayan Communist Party was Soviet inspired and thus part of a **Cold War** advance in Asia, Britain committed to an expensive, military intervention in Malaya, sending almost 50,000 troops there. *See also* MALAYSIA.

MALAYSIA. Just as Washington put pressure on Great Britain to step up its involvement in Vietnam, Britain was faced with its own crisis in the same region of the world. Although the Foreign Office had expected a reduced overseas military burden due to having fewer colonies to defend, in the short term the opposite happened as the British government felt forced to commit large numbers of troops in Malaysia. The Malaysian Federation had been established in September 1963 and comprised Malaya, Sabah, Sarawak (former British colonies), and Singapore (which seceded from the federation in August 1965). It was hoped that Malaysia would be aligned with Britain and, in exchange for offering base facilities, Britain would provide Malaysia with protection if needed. Britain was soon called on to honor its commitment. The Republic of Indonesia, under the leadership of Achmed Sukarno and backed by the communist bloc, opposed the union and announced a "state of confrontation" with Malaysia aimed at ending British influence in the area. Britain, Australia, and New Zealand gave military support to Malaysia in its attempts to defend itself against Indonesia, whose guerrillas fought intermittently between 1963 and the end of the confrontation in August 1966.

The British took a firm stance on Malaysia, refusing to make concessions to Jakarta and, after the United States made it clear that it would not help out militarily, committed large numbers of troops to the effort. There were 30,000 British servicemen stationed in Malaysia at the peak of the conflict (out of a total of 54,000 on duty in Southeast Asia)—the largest commitment of British troops to any one area since **World War II**. The Americans gave Britain verbal support in its campaign in Malaysia but did not offer any military assistance. Instead, the United States tried to mediate between the parties involved, hoping a diplomatic solution could be found before Indonesia turned to communism. Britain's defense of Western interests in Malaysia—Singapore was a key base in the effort to contain Chinese communism—meant that the governments of **Harold Macmillan**, **Alec Douglas-Home**, and **Harold Wilson** could emphasize their own efforts in the **Cold War** battle and thus avoid a commitment to the **Vietnam War**. However, the British lack of military restraint in Malaysia meant that it would appear hypocritical to Washington's ears to receive criticism of their own actions in Vietnam. American and South Vietnamese soldiers were trained in guerrilla tactics at the British-sponsored Jungle Warfare Training School in Jahore, Malaysia. *See also* MALAYAN EMERGENCY.

MANNING, SIR DAVID (1949–). A career diplomat, Sir David Manning acted as foreign policy adviser to Prime Minister **Tony Blair** from 2001 to 2003. In this role, he developed a close working relationship with President **George W. Bush**'s national security adviser, **Condoleezza Rice**. Manning was in New York when the terrorist attacks on the Twin Towers took place on **September 11, 2001**, having met with Deputy Secretary of State Richard Armitage in Washington, D.C., on the previous day. Manning also spoke with Rice most days during the **Iraq** crisis. He was influential in the development of Blair's Iraq policy and was sent to Washington in 2002 to try to persuade the Bush administration to go to the **United Nations** over Iraq. In 2003, he was appointed as British ambassador to the United States to replace Sir **Christopher Meyer**. The Iraq Study Group spoke with Manning during its investigations into the situation in Iraq before publishing its final report in December 2006. *See also* BAKER–HAMILTON COMMISSION.

MARSHALL, GEORGE C. (1891–1967). General George Marshall was an American general and chief of staff of the army during **World War II** and also served as secretary of state between 1947 and 1949 and secretary of defense between 1950 and 1951. During the **Arcadia Conference** of December 1941, as U.S. Army chief of staff, General Marshall proposed a unified command structure for the British and American forces fighting in the war. Despite overall cooperation between the two militaries, General Marshall clashed with his British counterparts over the timing of a cross-channel invasion. Marshall is best known, however, for being the architect of the European Recovery Program. *See also* MARSHALL PLAN.

MARSHALL PLAN (1947). The European Recovery Program (ERP) was outlined in a speech at Harvard University on 5 June 1947 by its architect, U.S. Secretary of State **George C. Marshall**. The Marshall Plan, as it became known, was a program to provide significant financial aid to help with the recovery and reconstruction of war-torn Europe. Marshall invited the European nations to present the United States with their own requests for aid and plans for recovery. The plan was approved by Congress 10 months later and by July 1947 the first aid shipments were arriving into Europe. The ERP lasted for five years, from 1947–1952, and invested $13.3 billion in 17 countries, with Britain receiving the largest share at just over £3 billion. The British government, led by Prime Minister **Clement Attlee**, was extremely grateful for the Marshall aid and the Foreign Secretary **Ernest Bevin** called the plan "a lifeline to sinking men." While there is some argument over the motives behind the Marshall Plan, it is clear that Washington was acting from a mixture of humanitarian concerns for the suffering of the European peoples and a desire to create strong economic foundations in Europe to prevent the spread of communism and provide sustained markets for American goods. *See also* COLD WAR.

MASON, GEORGE (1725–1792). George Mason was an American statesman who was so appalled by the brutalities committed by the British during the American **War of Independence** that he argued that hostility between the United States and Great Britain would endure.

MASSIVE RETALIATION. Building on the **New Look defense strategy** and the concept of mutually assured destruction (MAD), Secretary of State **John Foster Dulles** spelled out the doctrine of massive retaliation in a speech in January 1954. Dulles made it clear that the United States would respond to a Soviet attack by conventional or nuclear forces, with "massive retaliatory power," implying a disproportionate U.S. attack. *See also* COLD WAR.

MAYFLOWER. In 1620, the ship *Mayflower* carried 102 English settlers to Plymouth, Massachusetts, to form a successful colony in New England. Leaving Southampton, England, on 16 September 1620, the voyage to Massachusetts lasted 65 days and many of the passengers were Pilgrims. On landing at Cape Cod on 11 November 1620, the 41 free adult males pledged the Mayflower Compact, agreeing to a provisional form of government, the Civil Body Politic, and to abide by its laws. The ship finally landed at Plymouth on 21 December 1620. The ship returned to England on 15 April 1621. A replica model of the ship, *Mayflower II*, was built in 1957 and given as a gift to the United States by the British government, sailing across the Atlantic to be housed in the dock at Plymouth Rock.

MCMAHON ACT (1946). Passed by the U.S. Congress in August 1946, the McMahon Act made it illegal for the United States to share nuclear research with other nations. Having worked with the U.S. government on the development of nuclear weapons during **World War II** and coming after President **Harry S. Truman** and Prime Minister **Clement Attlee** had agreed at a meeting in Washington on 9 November 1945 that there should be "full and effective co-operation in the field of atomic energy" between the two countries, the British were annoyed by the subsequent act and began developing their own nuclear technology the following year. The act was repealed in 1958. *See also* ATOMIC BOMB.

MCNAMARA, ROBERT S. (1916–). Robert McNamara was appointed secretary of defense by President **John F. Kennedy** in 1961. He stayed in that position in the administration of **Lyndon B. Johnson** until he resigned in 1968. Before becoming secretary of defense, McNamara had been the president of Ford and had a reputation as an intelligent computer specialist who made cold, statistical analyses. In terms of Anglo–American relations, McNamara created a crisis when, in late 1962, he proposed the cancellation of **Skybolt** as a cost-cutting exercise, also believing nuclear deterrence was a matter best left to the United States. The government of **Harold Macmillan** was dismayed and humiliated by this prospect as Skybolt had been promised to the British government by President **Dwight D. Eisenhower**. Also, coming shortly after the **Cuban missile crisis**, when Great

Britain had been somewhat sidelined by the Kennedy administration, the plan to scrap **Skybolt** left the Macmillan government feeling marginalized and dependent on the United States. Macmillan then approached Kennedy, who reversed the decision. McNamara also introduced "**flexible response**" to the Kennedy foreign policy, causing some concern in Britain and encouraging Macmillan to push for nuclear arms talks. His central role in the escalation of the **Vietnam War** also meant that he was disappointed in his search for allies when the Labour government led by **Harold Wilson** refused to commit troops to the war. *See also* NUCLEAR (LIMITED) TEST BAN TREATY.

MEYER, SIR CHRISTOPHER (1944–). Sir Christopher Meyer served as British ambassador to the United States between 1997 and 2003. Meyer was in Washington at the time of the **September 11** attacks and the **Iraq War**; after ending his post, he published his memoirs. The memoirs were an insider's account of the decision-making process surrounding the decision to go to war in **Iraq** and criticized Prime Minister **Tony Blair** in his discussions with President **George W. Bush** for not being in command of the policy detail. Instead, Meyer described Blair as a man of moral certitude but a prime minister who allowed the Foreign Office, and its concerns about the wisdom of the war, to be marginalized.

MILIBAND, DAVID (1965–). Appointed British foreign secretary by Prime Minister **Gordon Brown** in June 2007, David Miliband is the second-youngest person to have occupied that office and the son of the late Marxist professor Ralph Miliband. Although Miliband studied in the United States at the Massachusetts Institute of Technology (MIT), he has urged Washington to take a stronger position on climate change and has also criticized Israeli attacks on Hezbollah.

MITCHELL, GEORGE J. (1933–). Former Democratic senator George Mitchell was appointed U.S. special envoy to Northern Ireland by President **Bill Clinton** in 1995 and was crucial to the establishment of all-party peace talks that culminated in the Good Friday peace agreement in 1998. Mitchell worked closely with Prime Minister **Tony Blair** and Northern Ireland secretary Marjorie (Mo) Mowlam. *See also* IRELAND.

MONROE DOCTRINE (1823). The Monroe Doctrine is a fundamental tenet of American foreign policy that has been in place since 1823. Since the 1810s, Spain had gradually lost control of its colonies in the Americas and fearing that Spain might try to regain these colonies with the help of Russia and France, the United States considered a suggestion from British Foreign Secretary George Canning that the two should issue a joint declaration to prevent this. Britain had established healthy trading relations with the newly independent nations and was keen for this to continue. After much discussion with U.S. Secretary of State John Quincy Adams and former presidents **Thomas Jefferson** and James Madison, President James Monroe decided to maintain U.S. independence. In December 1823, in his State of the Union address before Congress, Monroe warned Spain and its allies that the United States would "consider any attempt on their part to extend their system to any portion of this hemisphere as dangerous to our peace and safety" and that any attempt at recolonization would be viewed as "the manifestation of an unfriendly disposition toward the United States."

The Monroe Doctrine, as it became known, was perceived as a warning to Great Britain and the rest of Europe to keep out of the affairs of the Western hemisphere and in exchange the United States would not interfere in the internal concerns of Europe. At the time the United States would have had difficulty in enforcing the doctrine, and in 1833 when Great Britain seized the Falkland Islands from Argentina no action was taken. With the growth of American naval power in the late 19th century, the doctrine took on greater significance, and in 1904 President **Theodore Roosevelt** added the Roosevelt Corollary that asserted the United States' right to intervene in Latin America. The doctrine was reasserted during the **Cold War** when the United States used it to justify its military, intelligence, and aid operations in Latin America to prevent the extension of communist regimes in the region, most notably in its support of anticommunist forces in Nicaragua and El Salvador. *See also* VENEZUELAN BOUNDARY CRISIS.

MORGAN, J. P. (1837–1913). In 1895, J. Pierpont Morgan established an American investment and banking company, J. P. Morgan & Co., commonly known as the House of Morgan. The firm had its origins in Victorian Britain and thus Morgan had links to British financial houses. Morgan had been a successful financier since the American Civil War, and in the 1880s and 1890s organized the mergers of several steel and electric companies. At the beginning of the 20th century, the House of Morgan was one of the world's most prestigious and influential banking firms. Morgan began to arrange cash and credit for the British government, notably helping to finance the **Anglo–Boer War** (1899–1902). On the death of his father, J. P. Morgan Jr. (1867–1943) headed the firm. A natural Anglophile, Morgan Jr. spent much of his time in London, working with the London partner firm, Morgan Grenfell. Although the United States was neutral when **World War I** broke out, the House of Morgan aided the Allied cause by arranging the supply of military supplies from the United States on credit.

MORGENTHAU, HENRY (1891–1967). American secretary of the treasury between 1934 and 1945, Henry Morgenthau is best known for the Morgenthau Plan of 1944. The plan envisaged dealing with postwar Germany by disempowering it through harsh measures, such as deindustrialization and partitioning. On 16 September 1944, at the Second Quebec Conference, President **Franklin D. Roosevelt** managed to convince British Prime Minister **Winston Churchill** to accept the Morgenthau Plan, although both leaders backed away from it shortly afterward. As treasury secretary, Morgenthau also participated in the **Bretton Woods** Conference.

MULTILATERAL FORCE (MLF). In the early 1960s, in an effort to dissuade the British from continuing with its unilateral nuclear deterrent, and in order to deal with the issue of German rearmament, the administration of **John F. Kennedy** proposed a mixed-manned multilateral force. As a naval force, MLF would be crewed by **North Atlantic Treaty Organization** member forces and would carry nuclear weapons that would be under United States' control. The MLF proved unpopular with the British, who preferred to retain their independent nuclear capacity, not least because this provided a backup in the case of a U.S. withdrawal from the European theater. In 1964, Prime Minister **Harold Wilson** proposed an alternative **Atlantic Nuclear Force** (ANF) to President **Lyndon Johnson** and plans for the MLF were shelved.

MUNICH AGREEMENT (1938). In an attempt to prevent war with Germany, in September 1938, Prime Minister **Neville Chamberlain** flew to Munich to meet with Adolf Hitler of Germany, Benito Mussolini of Italy, and Edouard Daladier of France, over the Sudetenland crisis. Seen as the last and most significant attempt at **appeasement** by Great Britain, the agreement gave Germany half of Czechoslovakia, including the Sudetenland, in exchange for Hitler's agreement that he would make no more imperial demands. In addition, Britain and Germany pledged that they would never fight each other again. Chamberlain returned to England waving the paper containing the agreement and calling it a "peace for our time." President **Franklin D. Roosevelt** was relieved that war was averted and cabled Chamberlain to express his support but increasingly suspected Hitler would not stick to the agreement and began to argue for American rearmament. **Winston Churchill** denounced the agreement. Hitler reneged on the agreement by invading Poland on 1 September 1939 and Britain declared war on Germany on 3 September 1939. A generation of foreign-policy makers in Britain and America perceived the lesson to be learned from Munich is that aggressors should not be appeased. *See also* APPEASEMENT.

MURROW, EDWARD R. (1908–1965). One of America's most respected broadcast journalists, Edward Murrow played a crucial role in portraying the terrors of "the Blitz" on London to the American public and thereby encouraging them to reconsider the United States' neutrality in **World War I**. A novice journalist at the time, Murrow traveled to Britain in 1937 to become CBS's chief radio correspondent in Europe. He was able to draw on contacts he had made when he first visited London in 1935 as a representative of the International Institute of Education and made great efforts to understand British society. Murrow became a familiar voice in American living rooms when he reported on the Munich crisis for radio news; before the outbreak of World War II in 1939, Murrow negotiated with British government officials over the extent of censorship his reports would face. When World War II broke out, he became famous for his rooftop reports that began "This is London" and reported on the German bombing campaign that devastated London.

MUTUAL DEFENSE ASSISTANCE PROGRAM (MDAP). On 6 October 1949, President **Harry S. Truman** signed the Mutual Defense Assistance Act, which was designed to strengthen the North Atlantic Treaty (signed on 4 April 1949) by providing military assistance to free nations around the world. Great Britain was one of seven nations to receive initial assistance under the agreements, including Super Fortresses (B-29 bombers) in the early 1950s. *See also* BERLIN CRISIS; NORTH ATLANTIC TREATY ORGANIZATION.

– N –

NAPOLEONIC WARS (1803–1815). When the Napoleonic Wars began in Europe, the United States intended to remain neutral. This proved exceedingly difficult to achieve as neither Great Britain nor France respected its neutrality. Much to British annoyance, it soon became clear that America was prospering from its ability to transport goods from French and Spanish colonies in the Caribbean to Europe. Moreover, Britain felt this **trade** was aiding the French leader Emperor Napoleon by ensuring he received sufficient supplies. Conflict between Britain and America grew closer when in 1803 President **Thomas Jefferson** agreed to the Louisiana Purchase with Napoleon. Prompted by the Royal Navy's policy of impressment, in June 1807 tensions increased due to the *Chesapeake* **affair**. A direct war between Britain and America was avoided as Congress passed the **Embargo Act** in 1807 prohibiting American ships from trading with other nations. The act was repealed two years later when Congress acknowledged the damage being done to its own economy and it failed to force France and Britain to respect U.S. neutrality. When U.S. trade began again, it remained a risky business. British trade decrees, known as Orders in Council, were still in force and in 1807 Britain implemented a blockade around continental Europe to try to strangle the French war effort. As France implemented a similar blockade around Great Britain, U.S. ships continued to be seized by both belligerents. In 1812, President James Madison persuaded Congress to declare war on Great Britain in order to gain respect for America's rights as a neutral nation. *See also* WAR OF 1812.

NASSAU AGREEMENT (1962). The Nassau Agreement was negotiated between President **John F. Kennedy** and Prime Minister **Harold Macmillan** at Nassau in the Bahamas between 18 and 21 December 1962. The United States agreed to provide Britain with **Polaris** missiles as a substitute for **Skybolt**. The agreement was viewed as advantageous to Great Britain in financial terms as Britain was only required to pay 5 percent of the development costs plus the manufacturing. Kennedy envisaged that these missiles would be used in a multilateral **North Atlantic Treaty Organization** force. The agreement was seen as evidence of the recovery of Anglo–American relations after the **Suez crisis** and was partly attributed to the close relationship between Kennedy and Macmillan. The Nassau deal confirmed General Charles de Gaulle's view that Britain would be a Trojan horse in Europe if Britain were allowed to enter the **European Economic Community**. *See also* MULTILATERAL FORCE.

NATIONAL MISSILE DEFENSE (NMD). Known as the "Son of Star Wars," National Missile Defense (NMD) was a successor to President **Ronald Reagan**'s Strategic Defense Initiative (SDI) of the 1980s and became a political issue in Anglo–American relations during the first administration of **George W. Bush** when it was unclear what form it would take. While SDI's ambitious plan was to develop a shield in space against nuclear attack, NMD eventually evolved into a system of ground-based interceptors to prevent strategic ballistic missile attacks by so-called rogue states, such as North Korea, **Iran**, and **Iraq**. For the government of **Tony Blair**, NMD was politically sensitive as most of Europe opposed it because they feared U.S. commitment to it would spark off an arms race, and possibly revive the **Cold War** with Russia and **China**. Moreover, at that stage Britain was concerned about its cost, the likelihood of its effectiveness, and was not convinced of the nature of the threat from the named states. More pressingly, it would have a direct impact on Britain because it entailed the upgrading of RAF **Fylingdales radar installation** in North Yorkshire.

British Foreign Secretary **Robin Cook** expressed British concerns to U.S. Defense Secretary **Donald Rumsfeld**, U.S. Secretary of State **Colin Powell**, and National Security Adviser **Condoleezza Rice** on 6 February 2001. Washington pressed on with NMD and on 17

December 2002 made a formal request to the British government to use Fylingdales for this purpose, which was agreed to the following year. As a result, the radar station was the subject of increased protests by members of the **Campaign for Nuclear Disarmament** (CND).

NAVIGATION ACTS. In the 1650s and 1660s, the British Parliament passed a series of navigation acts aimed at protecting British **trade** from overseas competition and ensuring that trade with the colonies was carried out in British vessels, trade between colonies and other nations passed through Britain first, and certain goods could only be traded within the British Empire, including sugar and tobacco. In 1765, Prime Minister **George Grenville** insisted on enforcing the navigation acts and passed the **Stamp Act**. Restrictions on American trade were one of the major causes of the revolutionary war. *See also* WAR OF INDEPENDENCE.

NEUSTADT, RICHARD E. (1919–2003). An American political historian specializing in the U.S. presidency, Richard Neustadt served as an advisor to Democratic presidents **Harry S. Truman**, **John F. Kennedy**, **Lyndon B. Johnson**, and **William J. Clinton**. Neustadt wrote many notable books on the presidency and was one of the founding fathers of the Kennedy School of Government at Harvard University in 1966. Based on his insider knowledge of Anglo–American relations over three decades, in 1970 he published a book, *Alliance Politics*, drawing in particular on his knowledge of the **Skybolt crisis**. Following the death of his first wife, Neustadt later married the former British politician Baroness (Shirley) Williams of Crosby. In 2002, he lectured in Edinburgh on President **George W. Bush**'s response to the **September 11** attacks and was supportive of Prime Minister **Tony Blair**'s decision to try to influence Washington by acting as a close ally.

NEUTRALITY ACTS (U.S.). After World War I, the United States was determined not to be dragged into another European war, and in the 1930s (1935, 1937, and 1939) the U.S. Congress passed a series of neutrality acts to ensure this did not happen. The acts prohibited Americans from selling arms and other war materials to belligerents.

Amendments to the acts were made to accommodate the changing situation in Europe, particularly in relation to the situation in Great Britain and France after 1939. *See also* CASH AND CARRY; LEND-LEASE.

NEW LOOK DEFENSE STRATEGY. In May 1953, President **Dwight D. Eisenhower** established Operation Solarium to investigate U.S. military strategy in the **Cold War** and its related costs. Prompted by the high costs involved in the ground war in **Korea**, Eisenhower wanted a more cost-effective foreign policy. As a result of the Solarium findings, Eisenhower developed the **New Look defense strategy**. Eisenhower agreed to a containment strategy that combined nuclear and conventional forces but increased markedly the number of U.S. nuclear weapons, particularly bomber technology. The New Look strategy led Eisenhower to outline a policy of "massive retaliation" in the event of a Soviet military attack. The "more bang for the buck" policy impacted Anglo–American relations because it placed increased emphasis on alliances in order to encourage more burden sharing and avoid overlap. This led to British involvement in the U.S.-organized **South-East Asia Treaty Organization (SEATO)** in 1954. Anglo–American nuclear cooperation, which had been prohibited by the **McMahon Act** of 1946, was reestablished after the revision of the act in 1954. By 1955, an agreement had been reached to allow the exchange of information on limited aspects of civil and military atomic energy. More crucially for Anglo–American relations, in June 1956 an agreement was signed that provided sufficient information on nuclear submarine technology to allow Britain to develop its own submarine fleet that would be able to take advantage of the U.S. **Polaris missile** offered to Britain at the **Nassau** meeting in 1962. *See also* ATOMIC BOMB.

NEW TRANSATLANTIC AGENDA (1995). Building on the **Transatlantic Declaration** of November 1990, the New Transatlantic Agenda (NTA) was signed at a **European Union**–United States summit meeting in Madrid on 3 December 1995 by President **Bill Clinton**, European Commission President Jacques Santer, and Spanish Prime Minister Felipe González, then president of the European Council. Through joint action, the NTA set out to achieve global political and economic aims, including promoting peace and stability; fighting international crime, terrorism, and drug trafficking; and reducing **trade** barriers.

NIXON, RICHARD M. (1913–1994). Becoming Republican president in 1969 after having served as vice president under President **Dwight D. Eisenhower** between 1953 and 1961, Richard Nixon's time in the **White House** witnessed a cooling of the Anglo–American relationship. Nixon became president hoping to maintain a good working relationship with Great Britain. He paid an informal visit to Britain in February 1969, when he was received by **Queen Elizabeth II** and had friendly talks with Prime Minister **Harold Wilson**. His relations with Wilson's Conservative successor, **Edward Heath**, were not as cordial, despite visiting him in London in October 1970 and meeting with him in Bermuda in December 1970. Although Nixon was keen to establish a healthy Anglo–American relationship, Heath was determined to take Britain into the **European Economic Community** (EEC) and develop an Atlantic relationship based on an equal partnership between Europe and the United States. Consequently, although Nixon attempted to maintain the friendship between Britain and America by regular public references to the "**special relationship**," Heath remained unsentimental about Anglo–American relations. Kissinger later described Nixon as feeling like a "jilted lover" in relation to Heath.

By 1971 Nixon was speaking of a "natural relationship" between Britain and America. U.S. Ambassador **Walter Annenberg** believed the deterioration in relations was also due to the decision by the Nixon administration to engage in triangular diplomacy and exclude Britain from talks between the United States and **China** and the **Soviet Union**. With the Nixon administration facing a weakening U.S. economy—notably in comparison to European economies—the president and his advisers began to ask whether it was time for the European nations to take a greater share of the defense burden. The Nixon administration's announcement that 1973 would be the "**Year of Europe**" was not well received by the British government, not least because of its linkage between American military involvement in Europe and possible European **trade** concessions to the United States. Heath informed Kissinger that the United States should deal with the EEC as a group and not in bilateral relationships.

The two countries disagreed over policy in relation to the **Arab–Israeli War** of October 1973. Nixon was annoyed by Britain's refusal to allow American aircraft to use British bases to refuel on route to resupply the Israelis, and Britain was alarmed at the United States putting its forces on nuclear alert without consulting London. On 11 October 1973, at the height of the Arab–Israeli War, **Henry Kissinger** stopped Nixon from speaking to Heath believing the president was too drunk to talk. Nixon was discouraged from making a visit to Britain scheduled for July 1974 by the Wilson government as it was feared he would embarrass the queen because of the ongoing Watergate scandal.

NORTH ATLANTIC TREATY ORGANIZATION (NATO).
Founded on 4 April 1949, the North Atlantic Treaty Organization is the world's largest collective defense organization. The guiding principle remains one of mutual assistance should any member be attacked. As the **Cold War** emerged in the years after the end of World War II, Great Britain and the United States were instrumental in the formation of NATO as a bulwark against a perceived threat from the **Soviet Union**. Britain and the other Western European powers pushed for the U.S. military protection that had been suggested in the **Truman Doctrine**. Thus the formation of NATO would ensure the stationing of U.S. troops in Western Europe and financial investment in bases and equipment. The involvement of the United States in a formal military alliance was of major significance as it went against one of the cornerstones of American foreign policy, which was to avoid "entangling alliances." The **Berlin blockade** of 1948 encouraged the rapid formation of NATO, and the Soviet Union responded by forming the Warsaw Pact military alliance. U.S. Secretary of State **Dean Acheson** worked closely with British Foreign Secretary **Ernest Bevin** in creating the military alliance. The North Atlantic Treaty was signed in Washington, D.C., by the foreign ministers of Belgium, **Canada**, Denmark, France, Great Britain, Iceland, Italy, the Netherlands, Norway, Portugal, and the United States. In 1952, **Greece** and Turkey joined NATO, the Federal Republic of Germany joined in 1955, Spain in 1982, the Czech Republic, Hungary, and Poland in 1999, and Bulgaria, Estonia, Latvia, Lithuania, Romania, Slovakia, and Slovenia in 2004.

From its beginning, NATO's military leadership has been American, with the first Supreme Allied Commander in Europe (SACEUR) being General **Dwight D. Eisenhower**. The secretary-general of the North Atlantic Council—the policymaking body—has always been European. With the end of the Cold War, NATO had to rethink its *raison d'être* and during the crisis in **Kosovo** in March 1999, NATO moved from its defensive posture to an offensive one by launching an air assault against Serbia. By 1999, NATO had developed a new strategic concept that based its members' security on conflict prevention and crisis management, and began to reach out to non-NATO members through its Partnership for Peace program. In August 2003, NATO took control of the international forces in Kabul, **Afghanistan**.

NORTH, LORD (1713–1792). British prime minister from 1770 to 1782, Frederick North (Lord North) was unable to deal with the unrest in the American colonies that emerged with the **Boston Tea Party** in 1773. Lord North was considered to have an expertise in public finance, having worked in the treasury from 1759 to 1765 and serving as chancellor of the exchequer beginning in 1767. North's confidence in his financial abilities led him to make a fateful decision in relation to the Tea Act of 1773. Designed to rescue the ailing East India Tea Company, Lord North ensured the Tea Act retained the duty on tea, although reducing it from 6 pence to 3 pence. When the colonists responded angrily, culminating in the Boston Tea Party, North drafted legislation that became known collectively as the **Coercive Acts**, all aiming to punish Massachusetts for its actions. This led to the other colonies rallying to support Massachusetts and calling the First Continental Congress. The difficulties surrounding enforcement of the Coercive Acts led Lord North to realize that Britain was on the brink of war with the American colonies, and in an attempt to avoid this he proposed abolishing the Tea Act if the colonists agreed to pay for their own civil service. This change in attitude could not forestall the momentum toward the **War of Independence**, which began after the **battles of Lexington Green** and **Concord** on 19 April 1775, followed by the **battle of Bunker Hill** on 17 June. Despite offering his resignation to **King George III** on several occasions during the war, it was only after the British army suffered defeat at **Yorktown** in 1781 that Lord North was forced from the office of prime minister through a vote of no confidence in Parliament.

NOTT, SIR JOHN (1932–). John Nott was British secretary of defense during the **Falklands crisis** of 1982. Unlike the offer of resignation from the British foreign secretary, Lord **Peter Carrington**, Nott's offer after the Argentine invasion was not accepted by Prime Minister **Margaret Thatcher**. Nott consequently played a high-profile role in the ensuing undeclared war to recapture the islands, although later admitting he had had to look up the Falkland Islands on a globe when intelligence reports suggested a possible Argentine invasion. Nott's position during the war was much closer to that of Margaret Thatcher than the new foreign secretary, **Francis Pym**, who favored negotiation rather than armed conflict.

NUCLEAR NONPROLIFERATION TREATY (1968). Great Britain and the United States played a significant part in the negotiations that led to the signing of the Nuclear Nonproliferation Treaty on 1 July 1968. First signed in Washington, London, and Moscow by the United States, Great Britain, and the Soviet Union, the treaty has since been signed by over 180 countries. Designed to prevent the spread of nuclear weapons, existing nuclear powers agreed not to pass on nuclear weapons technology to nonnuclear states, and nonnuclear states agreed not to acquire nuclear weapons. All signatories committed to undertake negotiations on nuclear disarmament.

NUCLEAR (LIMITED) TEST BAN TREATY (1963). On 5 August 1963, the United States, Great Britain, and the **Soviet Union** signed a Limited Nonproliferation Treaty in Moscow. The treaty outlawed nuclear weapons testing in the atmosphere, outer space, and under water. Prime Minister **Harold Macmillan** had spent two years trying to persuade President **John F. Kennedy** to secure a nuclear test-ban treaty but it was the **Cuban missile crisis** of October 1962 that provided the final impetus for one.

– O –

OPEN DOOR POLICY. In late 1899 and early 1900, the U.S. secretary of state, **John Hay**, articulated an Open Door policy toward **China** in a series of "notes." Hay first proposed an international policy that would give all nations equal trading and commercial rights throughout China, and after the Boxer Rebellion, suggested that China's territorial and administrative integrity be maintained. The concept of an "open door," although not articulated, had been Great Britain's approach to China throughout the 19th century as Britain's sphere of influence in the country was challenged by other European nations and Japan. U.S. interest in China had increased in 1898 after they acquired the Philippines Islands after the **Spanish-American War** and became concerned about their trading interests with China. All the major powers agreed to respect the principles of the Open Door policy.

ORMSBY-GORE, DAVID. *See* HARLECH, LORD.

OWEN, DAVID (1938–). As British foreign secretary (1977–1979) in the Labour government of **James Callaghan**, David (later Lord) Owen worked closely with U.S. Secretary of State **Cyrus Vance** in attempting to find a solution to the problem of white rule in **Rhodesia**. Owen valued joint Anglo–American ventures and between 1992 and 1995, while he was European Union cochair of the Conference for the Former Yugoslavia, he worked with Vance again when they tried to broker peace in **Bosnia**. As a pro-European politician and one of the leading advocates for British entry into the **European Economic Community** (EEC), Lord Owen was critical of Britain sharing intelligence on European allies with the United States.

OWEN, ROBERT (1771–1858). Born in Newtown, Wales, in 1771, Robert Owen became one of Britain's most famous industrialists and reformers. He is often credited with being the founder of the cooperative movement and a pioneer of British socialism. By the age of 19, Owen was the successful owner of a Manchester cotton mill. From his knowledge as a successful entrepreneur, Owen began to argue that workers were more productive if they were treated better. He began to experiment with model communities, building one around his New Lanark mills, near Glasgow. New Lanark included an infant school, quality housing for the mill workers, and an early cooperative store. In 1826, Owen transplanted his ideas to the United States when he bought a settlement in Harmony, Indiana, and established another model community, New Harmony. Owen was aided in his American endeavor by his son Robert Dale Owen (1801–1877), who later became a U.S. congressmen and American ambassador to India. Although Owen's ideas influenced other progressive intellectuals and activists, none of his model communities proved long-lasting, with New Harmony lasting only three years. Four of Owen's sons became U.S. citizens.

– P –

PAGE, WALTER HINES (1855–1918). Walter Hines Page served as U.S. ambassador to Great Britain during **World War I** (1913–1918). A journalist, editor, and publisher before being appointed ambassador to London, Page encouraged the foundation of the **English-Speaking Union** (ESU) as a way of improving Anglo–American relations through educational and cultural exchange. As ambassador he was viewed by the administration of **Woodrow Wilson** as extremely pro-British and long urged the president to join the British cause. Page proved important in maintaining good relations between Britain and the United States during the period of American neutrality. Despite being an **Anglophile**, Page expressed his disgust at the British trench warfare that had resulted in carnage at the battle of the Somme on 1 July 1916 with 20,000 British killed within two hours of going over the top.

PAINE, THOMAS (1737–1809). Originally from Thetford in Norfolk, England, Thomas Paine was a political philosopher who wrote a series of pamphlets that were influential during the Revolutionary period. Paine immigrated to Philadelphia in 1774, became a minor government official, and quickly came into contact with advocates of American resistance to British rule, including John Adams. *Common Sense*, published in 1776, was Paine's most influential work and in it he denounced hereditary rule and advocated American independence. Unlike most pamphlet writers, Paine did not appeal only to the educated elite, instead writing in direct, readable style that meant his work was read widely, selling approximately 150,000 copies. *See also* WAR OF INDEPENDENCE.

PALESTINE. Part of the Ottoman Empire since 1517, during **World War I** British General Edmund Allenby was appointed commander in Palestine and drove the Turks out. On 2 November 1917, the British foreign secretary, Arthur Balfour, declared British support for a Jewish state in Palestine. In 1920, the **League of Nations** at the San Remo Conference assigned Palestine to be a British-mandated territory and they began their rule there in 1923. After **World War II**, with the revelations about the holocaust, President **Harry S. Truman** expressed his belief that the Jews were oppressed and deserved their own homeland. At the time approximately 250,000 Jewish displaced persons, who had escaped Nazi concentration camps, were living in refugee camps around Europe. Truman sent Earl G. Harrison to investigate the situation in Europe as the U.S. representative on the Intergovernmental Commission on Refugees. Harrison recommended that some of the Jewish refugees be admitted into the United States. Believing that existing immigration quotes would not allow such an effort, Truman began to put pressure on the British government to admit at least some of these refugees into Palestine.

Keen to maintain healthy relations with Arab states in the Middle East and aware that British soldiers in Palestine had been victims of Zionist terrorist attacks, Britain suggested that an Anglo–American Committee of Inquiry be set up to investigate the problem and in April 1946 it reported that 100,000 Jewish immigrants should be allowed to go to Palestine. Zionist activity continued in Palestine and by late 1946 Prime Minister **Clement Attlee** began to suggest a British withdrawal from the Middle East. On 15 February 1947, the British cabinet agreed to let the **United Nations** recommend a solution to the problem of Palestine. Truman's seemingly inconsistent approach on Palestine and the creation of Israel led to angry exchanges between London and Washington, with the British government suspecting that electoral politics in the United States was behind much of Truman's foreign policy. The British mandate ended on 14 May

1948, Israel became an independent state, and until March 1949 fought against Arab invasions. On 25 May 1950, Britain, the United States, and France signed the Tripartite Declaration, guaranteeing the territorial integrity of Israel's frontiers after the 1949 armistice. *See also* ARAB–ISRAELI WAR (1967); ARAB–ISRAELI WAR (1973).

PANAMA CANAL ACT. The United States began work on the Panama Canal in 1908 and opened it to shipping on 15 August 1914. The construction of the canal saved vessels a 6,000-mile voyage around South America by linking the Atlantic and Pacific oceans. In 1912, with the project nearing completion, the U.S. Congress passed legislation that President William H. Taft signed that exempted American ships using the canals from the tolls levied for its use. The British government protested immediately that the exemption violated the 1901 **Hay–Pauncefote Treaty**, which stated the canal should be open on equal terms to vessels from all nations. Despite the 1912 Democratic platform's approval of the act, when **Woodrow Wilson** became president he asked Congress to repeal the exemption clause of the Panama Canal Act, which they did on 11 June 1914. Wilson's success on this issue was seen as a victory over **Anglophobes** within Congress.

PANKHURST, CHRISTABEL (1880–1958). The daughter of suffragette Emmeline Pankhurst and Dr. Richard Pankhurst, Christabel Pankhurst also became a well-known British suffragette. In 1903, she founded, with her mother, the Women's Social and Political Union (WSPU). She became known as a militant feminist after she spat in a policeman's face when she was being restrained while being arrested for interrupting a Liberal Party meeting. As a radical suffragist who believed in "deeds not words," she continued to engage in direct action as well as speaking tours. She influenced many other women, including Alice Paul, who later became a leader of the U.S. suffragist movement, the National Woman's Party (NWP). Paul worked with the Pankhursts on their campaign for women's suffrage, personally smashing windows and facing imprisonment for her activities. After women gained the vote in Britain in 1918, Pankhurst failed to succeed in a political career, twice failing to be elected as a member of Parliament. She then turned her energies to Christian fundamentalism.

While visiting her mother in the United States in 1921, she became a member of the Second Adventist religious movement. A charismatic leader and impressive orator, Pankhurst embarked on speaking tours throughout America and when World War II started, she moved there, living in Los Angeles until her death in 1958.

PARIS PEACE CONFERENCE (1919). After the end of **World War I**, representatives of the former belligerent nations met at Versailles, Paris, to discuss a formal peace treaty. At the conference, which began on 18 January 1919 and lasted just over a year, the British and American positions diverged. President **Woodrow Wilson** wanted to make World War I "the war to end all wars" and arrived at the conference hoping to persuade the delegates to sign up to his **Fourteen Points** for a lasting peace. Much to Wilson's annoyance, European nations were preoccupied with ensuring Germany was punished and that reparations were paid, and were driven primarily by empirical concerns. As a result, Wilson was forced to accept a compromise peace. The **Versailles Treaty** was signed on 28 June 1919 but the conference continued in order to agree on several other treaties that dealt with territorial issues.

PARIS, TREATY OF. *See* VERSAILLES, TREATY OF.

PAX AMERICANA. As the United States developed its own empire in the late 19th century and early 20th, the term *Pax Britannica* was gradually replaced by the term *Pax Americana* (Latin meaning "American peace"). Its use became more predominant in the period after **World War II** when the United States emerged as the world's leading military and economic superpower and used its power and influence to attempt to ensure world peace and prosperity in its own image. *See also PAX BRITANNICA.*

PAX BRITANNICA. Critics and admirers of British imperialism have used the term *Pax Britannica* (Latin meaning "British peace") to describe the 19th- and early 20th-century period when British leaders believed that the British Empire would bring peace, progress, and civilization to the world. *See also PAX AMERICANA.*

PEARL HARBOR. The surprise attack by the Japanese on the U.S. naval fleet based in Pearl Harbor, Hawaii, on 7 December 1941, killed almost 2,400 Americans, destroyed five battleships and wrecked several others, and brought the United States in to **World War II**. For British Prime Minister **Winston Churchill**, who had been urging President **Franklin D. Roosevelt** to enter the war, the attack on Pearl Harbor and the United States' subsequent declarations of war against Japan on 8 December and Germany and Italy on 11 December, came as welcome news as he feared Great Britain would lose the war on its own. After the attack, rumors circulated that Roosevelt had allowed the attacks to take place despite having intelligence of the Japanese plan but these were not supported by evidence. Similarly, in recent years, it has been argued that Churchill was so desperate for U.S. military help in Europe that he deliberately withheld British intelligence, gathered through code-breaking,

PERSHING, JOHN J. (1860–1948). John "Black Jack" Pershing was commander of the American Expeditionary Forces (AEF) in **World War I**. Pershing refused to give in to British demands that U.S. troops be rushed to the Western Front to supplement depleted Allied forces. Ignoring pleas from British Field Marshal Sir **Douglas Haig**, Pershing took time to train and supply a separate American army in Europe, to be used in action when and where America saw fit, including successful offensives at Meuse–Argonne and St. Mihiel in France.

PILGRIM FATHERS. The Pilgrim Fathers were the second settlers of the future United States, landing at New Plymouth, Massachusetts, in December 1620, but the first to establish a permanent colony. Contrary to popular wisdom, the Pilgrim Fathers were not strictly Puritans but a group of separatist exiles from England who had fled to the Netherlands. Rather than wishing to reform the Anglican Church like most Puritans, the Separatists believed that a separate church was necessary. *See* PLYMOUTH ROCK.

PILGRIMS SOCIETY. The Pilgrims Society was established in 1902 as a British–American society to promote peace and goodwill between Great Britain and the United States. Its patron is the British monarch and its members have been, and remain, wealthy British and American bankers, businessman, and leading politicians. Known mainly as a dining club, the Pilgrim Society hosts large banquets of invited guests and holds a welcoming dinner for the incumbent American ambassador to Great Britain.

PINKERTON, ALLAN (1819–1884). A famous Anglo–American, Pinkerton was a member of the British Chartist movement from Glasgow, Scotland, before immigrating to the United States in 1842. Settling in Chicago, Pinkerton became a detective and later established the Pinkerton National Detective Agency, America's first detective agency. He pioneered techniques such as the surveillance of suspects and was involved in solving many of the train robberies of the mid-19th century. He also uncovered a plot to assassinate President Abraham Lincoln. His firm was also involved in strikebreaking and was deeply unpopular with the American labor movement.

PLYMOUTH ROCK. Arriving on the British ship *Mayflower* in 1620, 102 English colonists established the first permanent English settlement in New England at Plymouth Colony in Massachusetts. Many of the settlers were **Pilgrims** and, after landing, established a form of government, the Civil Body Politic, and elected John Carver as their first governor. Arriving on 26 December, the New England winter weather took its toll and half of the first settlers died from disease. However, within a generation there were almost 70,000 American colonists of British origin.

POLARIS MISSILE. During discussions in March 1960 with President **Dwight D. Eisenhower** on **Skybolt**, Prime Minister **Harold Macmillan** agreed to allow the United States to use the British naval base at **Holy Loch** for its submarine-launched Polaris missiles. Unlike the **Thor missile**, which had been under dual control, the Polaris missiles were under the sole control of the United States. Macmillan received much criticism in the House of Commons for this decision.

POTSDAM CONFERENCE (1945). Building on the **Yalta** Agreement of February 1945, the last of the wartime conferences involving the Big Three Allied powers—the United States, the **Soviet Union**, and Great Britain—was held in Potsdam, Germany, between 17 July and 2 August 1945. The three nations were represented by President **Harry S. Truman**, General Secretary Joseph Stalin, and Prime Minister **Winston Churchill**, although Churchill was replaced by **Clement Attlee** during the conference after the Labour Party won the 1945 general election. The conference met to deal with the surrender and control of Germany and finalized plans for the defeat of Japan. Prior to the conference, Churchill and British Foreign Secretary **Anthony Eden** had tried to encourage an Anglo–American collaboration against the Soviet Union. Churchill believed Roosevelt, and then Truman, was not fully aware of the dangers of a Russian advance through Europe. The United States, however, placed more emphasis on creating a **United Nations** that included the Soviet Union and was successful in drawing up its charter on 26 June. By the time the Potsdam Conference began, Washington had drawn closer to London's thinking, although still agreeing to Russian intervention in the war against Japan and generally searching for accommodation with the Soviets in the postwar world. The agreement reached at Potsdam divided Germany in four zones of occupation to be administered by American, British, Russian, and French military commanders. During the conference, Truman was informed of the successful explosion of an **atomic bomb** in the New Mexico desert and told Stalin of the United States' "powerful new weapon." On 26 July, the Potsdam declaration issued an ultimatum to the Japanese, threatening "prompt and utter destruction" should they fail to surrender unconditionally.

POWELL, COLIN (1937–). When Colin Powell became secretary of state in 2001, he was the highest ranking African American to serve in the U.S. government and, after a distinguished career, became the highest ranking African American in the military when he became a four-star general and became the chairman of the Joint Chiefs of Staff (1989–1993) under President **George H. W. Bush**. He also served as a national security adviser to President **Ronald Reagan** (1987–1989). During his period as chair of the Joint Chiefs of Staff, Powell oversaw Operation Desert Storm in the Persian **Gulf War**. As secretary of state under Bush, Powell agreed with Prime Minister **Tony Blair** that it was important to have international backing from the **United Nations** before intervening militarily in **Iraq**. He worked closely with British foreign secretary **Jack Straw** to build up a multi-national coalition in the **United Nations**. During this period, he is alleged to have described neoconservatives within the Bush administration as "fucking crazies" during a telephone conversation with Straw. Powell's pressure on Bush proved less decisive than the influence of **Donald Rumsfeld** and **Dick Cheney** and in January 2005 he resigned as secretary of state. *See also* IRAQ WAR.

PRESLEY, ELVIS (1935–1977). In the 1950s, American popular music dominated the British music scene. Although **Bill Haley and the Comets** made rock 'n' roll popular in Great Britain, selling more than one million copies of "Rock Around the Clock," it was Elvis Presley who became the most important American musical export to Britain and proved an enormous influence on British youth culture. Presley's singing talents, his good looks, youth, and gyratory movements on stage meant he attracted Britain's youth at the same time as he shocked the older generation. Presley had a massive impact on the British music scene, inspiring the **Beatles**, the Rolling Stones, and the Who, among many other groups. In May 1956, Elvis entered the American musical charts for the first time with "Heartbreak Hotel," reaching the number two position. In June 1957, he achieved his first British number one with the single "All Shook Up." In August 1957, the British Elvis Presley Fan Club was established. In January 1958, Elvis became the first artist to have a single go straight into the British charts at the number-one position, with "Jailhouse Rock," selling over 500,000 copies in its first three days. He reached a record-breaking five British number ones in November 1960 with "It's Now or Never." He went on to have an additional 16 singles reach the number-one slot in Britain, four of them posthumously. His music continues to be popular in Great Britain, with a re-release of the 1958 song "Jailhouse Rock" reaching number one for a second time in 2005. His feature films of the early 1960s also proved popular in Britain. Presley only visited Britain on one occasion, when he stopped over at Prestwick Airport in Scotland on 3 March 1960 on his way back to the United States after his military service in Germany.

PYM, SIR FRANCIS (1922–2008). Sir Frances Pym became British foreign secretary after the resignation of Lord **Peter Carrington** for his failure to predict or prevent the Argentine invasion of the British Falkland Islands. Pym's tenure in office was no less controversial as his position during the **Falklands War** conflicted with Prime Minister **Margaret Thatcher**'s. Pym believed the conflict could be resolved through negotiation, while Thatcher preferred an armed removal of the Argentines. After negotiating with **Alexander Haig**, who was engaged in shuttle diplomacy between London and Buenos Aires, Pym presented a proposal to end the conflict to the prime minister and the British cabinet. The proposal moved away from Thatcher's bottom line of self-determination for the islanders. Instead, it suggested the Argentine troops withdraw from the island before the British task force arrived but allowed for Argentine representation on the islands' councils, the possibility of an increased Argentine population on the island, and longer-term negotiations that would not return the status quo ante. Thatcher later wrote that she would have resigned had the War Cabinet accepted Pym's proposals. Shortly after the Thatcher government's reelection in the 1983 general election, Francis Pym was sacked from his position as foreign secretary.

– Q –

QUAKERS. The Religious Society of Friends, known as the Quakers, was founded in England in the 1650s as a nonconformist religious group that separated from the Puritans. Led by George Fox, Quakers emphasized the inner experience with God as the way to religious truth, rather than ritual and ceremony led by priests, and stressed the equality of all persons. Facing persecution and oppression in England, Quakers migrated to America. Considered a radical sect, Anglicans and Puritans in Massachusetts dealt harshly with Quakers who settled there; many of them were whipped and banished by colonial authorities. In 1659 and 1660, four Quakers returning to Boston from exile were hanged, including Quaker missionary Mary Dyer, who refused to stop preaching. Sailing from London in 1677, 230 Quakers set sail for New Jersey on board the ship *Kent*. A member of the Society of Friends, William Penn founded Pennsylvania in 1681 partly as a place of refuge for the Quakers and others facing religious persecution in Europe. The transatlantic ties between the Quakers were especially strong from the late 17th century to the mid-19th century. Not only were there family ties but the exchange of ideas was facilitated by regular speaking tours. *See also* ABOLITIONISTS.

QUEBEC AGREEMENT (1943). Signed by **Winston Churchill** and **Franklin D. Roosevelt** on 19 August 1943 during a conference in Quebec City, **Canada**, this agreement dealt with the issue of nuclear cooperation between the United States and Great Britain. Prior to the Quebec Agreement, the British government considered embarking on its own **atomic bomb** project that would rival the American's atomic research. The agreement prevented nuclear proliferation by subsuming British research into the U.S. Manhattan Project in exchange for full progress reports and an agreement not to use atomic research against one another, against third parties without each other's consent, and not to pass on nuclear secrets to third parties unless by mutual consent. British scientists and materials were shipped to the United States until after the end of the **World War II**.

– R –

REAGAN, RONALD (1911–2004). During his period in the White House (1981–1989), President Ronald Reagan developed a close personal and working relationship with Prime Minister **Margaret Thatcher** that led to a revitalization of the Anglo–American relationship. Great Britain's first female prime minister was the first foreign head of government to visit the Reagan White House in 1981 and the last foreign visitor in 1988. In all, the two leaders had 15 meetings during Reagan's two terms. The two leaders were ideologically compatible, both believing in market-led economies and minimal state government and respecting each other's anticommunist politics. The two politicians had their first face-to-face meeting in 1975 when Reagan was governor of California and Thatcher was the new Conservative leader of the Opposition. Despite their differing personalities, the two leaders developed a deep and obvious respect for one another. Reagan was glad to have a strong ally in the renewed **Cold War** that had emerged after the Soviet invasion of Afghanistan in 1979 and Thatcher was happy to play that role in order to boost Britain's position on the world stage and ensure the United States stayed committed to the defense of Europe.

When Reagan first entered the White House, he caused alarm in Britain and Europe by his hostile rhetoric toward the **Soviet Union**—calling it an "evil" in the world—and his suggestion that it might be possible under the nuclear "**flexible response**" strategy to confine a tactical nuclear exchange to Europe. This ratcheting up of world tension caused deep concern among the British public and even Thatcher tried to play down the president's rhetoric. In Britain, anti-American forces and antinuclear campaigners began to reemerge as news of the stationing of American cruise missiles was announced and Reagan's strident language added to a British sense of American dominance in the Anglo–American relationship. Thatcher agreed with Reagan's hard-line stance toward the Soviets, even if she was wary of the rhetoric. In March 1983, Reagan put pressure on the Soviet Union in the arms race by announcing the Strategic Defense Initiative (SDI), otherwise known as "**Star Wars**," and received British backing for it. Thatcher also agreed to a small British contribution to a "rapid deployment force" to be used in areas outside of **North Atlantic Treaty Organization** coverage suffering unexpected Soviet-backed attacks.

Despite their many points of agreement, Reagan and Thatcher did not always see eye-to-eye, with notable exceptions to their harmonious relationship being the **Falklands War** of 1982 when Reagan encouraged Thatcher to implement a cease-fire, and the U.S. invasion of **Grenada** in 1983, which Thatcher did not support. Reagan was able to count on British support in 1986 when U.S. planes were allowed to refuel at British air force bases on route to bombing **Libya**. Thatcher was surprised to find that, despite her friendship with Reagan, the president was happy to act independently at the Reykjavik summit with Soviet Premier Mikhail Gorbachev in 1986.

Despite being frail, Margaret Thatcher traveled to Ronald Reagan's state funeral in Washington, D.C., in June 2004. Her prerecorded eulogy at the funeral paid tribute to Reagan as a great president and a dear friend and argued that he won the **Cold War**. *See also* AFGHANISTAN, INVASION OF; CAMPAIGN FOR NUCLEAR DISARMAMENT; GREENHAM COMMON.

RENDITION FLIGHTS. In 2006 and 2007, the British governments of **Tony Blair** and **Gordon Brown** came under pressure from members of Parliament and human rights groups to criticize and introduce controls on the alleged U.S. practice of "extraordinary rendition," which is an extrajudicial covert transportation of suspected terrorists to third-party countries that engage in torture as an interrogation method. These third-party countries include Jordan, **Egypt**, Morocco, and **Afghanistan**. Rendition of detainees and suspected terrorists began in the 1990s under the administration of **William Clinton**. It is alleged that the number and types of renditions grew after the **September 11** attacks and President **George W. Bush**'s declaration of a "war on terror." Most of these renditions were so-called military renditions, involving the transfer of suspected terrorists or "unlawful combatants" from Afghanistan to the **Guantanamo Bay** detention center. In 2002 and 2003, the United States began to engage in "renditions to detention" that involved suspects outside of the Afghanistan area and, on occasion, ignored a British caveat in its telegrams that intelligence passed to the United States about these individuals should not be used as a basis for action.

In 2005, the British press began to report that Central Intelligence Agency (CIA) planes conducting rendition operations were using British airports and airspace, including Prestwick Airport in Scotland. News of these "rendition flights" or "ghost flights" led to questions being raised in Parliament about the British government's knowledge of this activity. British domestic concern was heightened in April 2006 when the U.S. director of national intelligence admitted to the existence of so-called black facilities that were secret CIA-run detention centers overseas, and housing dozens of "high-value" terrorist suspects. In July 2007, Britain's Intelligence and Security Committee found that British intelligence services were not complicit in any extraordinary rendition operations, and the British government denied any knowledge of CIA extraordinary rendition flights passing through British civilian airports, military airfields, or British airspace. It is clear that the issue of "rendition to detention" has caused some tension between British and American security and intelligence agencies operating under differing legal frameworks.

RHODES SCHOLARS. Rhodes scholarships are the oldest, most well known, and prestigious international fellowships in the world. When he died in 1902, British colonialist Cecil Rhodes left provision in his will for the establishment of a fellowship scheme that would bring young, intelligent scholars from the English-speaking world with leadership potential to Oxford University, where he had gained his degree. Rhodes hoped not only to attract the most able young people to what he considered the best university in the world but also those with character traits that would aid international peace and understanding. In addition to using their time in Oxford for intellectual and personal development, the fellows would also leave with a deeper knowledge, understanding, and affection for Great Britain. Since its inception at the beginning of the 20th century, hundreds of the best minds in America have spent at least one year studying at Oxford, including future secretary of state **Dean Rusk** in the 1930s and future U.S. president **William J. Clinton** in the 1960s.

RHODESIA. A self-governing British colony since 1922, southern Rhodesia became an issue in Anglo–American relations during the 1960s. As a precondition of full independence, Great Britain insisted that the country should have black majority rule. On 11 November 1965, Ian Smith, the Rhodesian prime minister, made a Unilateral Declaration of Independence (UDI) with the intent of preserving the white minority rule over the predominantly black population. UDI received international condemnation, and although some sections of the Conservative Party supported Smith, most in Britain denounced his actions and events prompted demonstrations around Britain, many of them demanding the use of force to resolve the issue. British Prime Minister **Harold Wilson** reacted by asking the **United Nations** to implement economic sanctions against the Smith government, and for first time the UN voted in favor of such action in 1966. The United States adopted a generally supportive stance toward Britain over Rhodesia. Although U.S. policy was predicated on the need to maintain good relations with black Africa during the **Cold War** struggle, this proved a difficult position for the United States to take because, as President **Lyndon Johnson** was reminded by many of his advisers, the sanctions affected U.S. oil exports. Despite numerous attempts at compromise deals with Smith to allow a gradual shift to black majority rule, there was little significant movement until the late 1970s.

Much to the unease of many within British diplomatic circles but with the British government's agreement, the United States intervened more overtly in 1976 when U.S. Secretary of State **Henry Kissinger** formulated a six-step plan toward black majority rule. After Smith reluctantly agreed to the principle of transferring power, further Anglo–American cooperation on the matter came during the presidency of **James Carter**, when Secretary of State **Cyrus Vance** worked with British Foreign Secretary **David Owen** on the details of a settlement plan in September 1977. In September 1979, much to U.S. satisfaction, an agreement on Rhodesia was finally reached at the Lancaster House conference in London after Foreign Secretary Lord **Peter Carrington** persuaded Prime Minister **Margaret Thatcher** to support an all-party solution. Rhodesia held its first multiracial elections and gained independence from Britain in April 1980, becoming known as Zimbabwe with Robert Mugabe as president.

RICE, CONDOLEEZZA (1954–). The first female and African American national security adviser, serving in the administration of President **George W. Bush** between 2001 and 2005, Condoleezza Rice was made secretary of state in 2005. As national security adviser, one of her first tasks was to reassure Britain about Bush's plans for a U.S. **National Missile Defense** (NMD) system, the successor to President **Ronald Reagan**'s **Strategic Defense Initiative** (SDI). On 7 February 2001, Rice met with British Foreign Secretary **Robin Cook** in Washington, D.C., in advance of Prime Minister **Tony Blair**'s visit to meet the new president. During that meeting, Rice explained U.S. plans for NMD and reassured Cook that Russia need not feel threatened by the antimissile shield as it was aimed at protecting the United States and its allies from so-called rogue states.

Rice played an important liaison role between Britain and America during the crisis surrounding **September 11** and the subsequent war in **Afghanistan**. She was a key supporter of the U.S. decision to take military action against **Iraq** in 2003 to remove Saddam Hussein from power, although she later acknowledged that there had been problems with U.S. intelligence related to Iraq. As secretary of state she established an effective working relationship with her British counterpart, **Jack Straw**. In October 2005, the British foreign secretary visited

Rice in her hometown of Birmingham, Alabama. When she visited England in 2006 and went to Blackburn, Lancashire, constituency home of Foreign Secretary Straw, Rice was the subject of anti–**Iraq War** protests. In February 2008, Rice met with British Foreign Secretary **David Miliband** and urged Britain and other European **North Atlantic Treaty Organization** powers to increase their commitment to operations in Afghanistan.

RIFKIND, MALCOLM. Malcolm Rifkind served as British defense secretary (1992–1995) and later foreign secretary (1995–1997) under the Conservative premiership of **John Major**. Rifkind fanned the flames of disagreement between Washington and London over **Bosnia** by responding to the proposal from Senator Bob Dole to lift the arms embargo with the words, "You Americans don't know the horrors of war," not realizing or remembering that Dole had fought in **World War II** and had been left permanently disabled.

ROANOKE ISLAND. The first failed attempt by the English to settle in North America and form a colony came at Roanoke Island in the 1580s, off the coast of what became North Carolina. Initiated by Sir Walter Raleigh, the effort to establish a permanent English settlement came in two separate endeavors. The first group of 108 Elizabethan settlers transported to Roanoke in 1585 by Sir Richard Grenville experienced problems in securing adequate supplies of food and increasingly difficult relations with the Native Americans, and were eventually picked up by Sir Francis Drake and returned to England the following year. The second colonial expedition to Roanoke came in 1587 when Raleigh sent 150 people to the island. Unlike the previous settlers, these new colonists included women and children and an English child, Virginia Dare, was subsequently born on American shores. Within months, the governor of the island, John White, returned to England for supplies and when he got back to Roanoke in 1590 he was unable to find any of the colonists. The disappearance of the settlers with no obvious explanation led to Roanoke becoming known as "The Lost Colony."

ROBESON, PAUL (1898–1976). An African American actor and singer, Paul Robeson was also known for his association with the civil rights movement and for his left-wing sympathies. Born in Princeton, New Jersey, the son of an escaped slave, and originally a successful athlete, Robeson went on to become a high-profile and respected black performer between the 1920s and 1950s. As a bass vocalist, his most famous role was as Joe in "Showboat," with his definitive version of "Ol' Man River." He played this role on Broadway and in 1928 in London. As an actor he traveled to Britain on a regular basis, touring the country with several plays. During a visit to England between 1948 and 1949, Robeson was under the scrutiny of the British intelligence services, and the Foreign Office supplied details of his activities to the Federal Bureau of Investigation (FBI). During the period of McCarthyism in the United States, Robeson was investigated by the House Un-American Activities Committee (HUAC) because of his association with the American Communist Party, his pro-Soviet comments, and his civil rights activities. Although Robeson denied he had ever been a member of the Communist Party, he was subpoenaed to testify before the House Committee in June 1956, where he refused to sign an affidavit declaring he was not a communist and under questioning attacked HUAC's activities. In 1950, the U.S. State Department revoked his passport, arguing that his comments about American racism were an embarrassment to the U.S. government. At the same time as he was unable to advance his career abroad, he was also blacklisted at home. When his passport was reinstated after eight years, he arrived in England in July 1958 to reprise his most famous theatrical role in England as William Shakespeare's *Othello*. He first played the role at the Savoy Theatre in 1930 and performed the role again at the Royal Shakespeare Theatre in Stratford-upon-Avon, Warwickshire, in 1959. During this period, Robeson spoke at a mass peace rally in Trafalgar Square, London.

ROLLING STONES, THE. Formed in 1962, the Rolling Stones became a successful British pop group that formed part of the so-called Second British Invasion of the United States in the mid-1960s. By the mid-1960s, the Stones' lineup was Mick Jagger, Keith Richards, Bill Wyman, Charlie Watts, and Brian Jones. Influenced by American rhythm and blues music and considered overtly sexual in style, the Stones had chart success in Great Britain before launching their American career. Their first British chart entry came in mid-1964 when their blues version of "It's All Over Now" reached number three. Jagger and Richards, as songwriters, achieved their first American chart success with "That Girl Belongs to Yesterday," although it was sung by American singer Gene Pitney. They first performed in the United States on 1 June 1964 and appeared on the *Ed Sullivan Show* on 25 October 1964. When they appeared on the show three years later, they were asked to change the lyrics of "Let's Spend the Night Together" to "let's spend some time together." They achieved their first number-one chart position in the United States with "(I Can't Get No) Satisfaction" in June 1965 and went on to have success with "Paint It Black" (1966), "Ruby Tuesday" (1967), and "Honky Tonk Woman" (1969). They ended the '60s by headlining the Altamont Speedway Free Festival in California on 6 December 1969, which ended in violence with a member of the crowd being stabbed to death by a Hell's Angel. The band became the most popular British act in the United States after the **Beatles** disbanded, and toured regularly, breaking records for attendance and gross receipts. They are now the longest active band in rock 'n' roll history.

ROOSEVELT, FRANKLIN D. (1882–1945). Democratic president Franklin D. Roosevelt served an unprecedented four terms in the White House (1933–1945); after a period of poor relations in the 1920s, Anglo–American relations improved markedly during his time in office. Roosevelt was elected believing the United States should be more interventionist in world affairs, and a visit to the Western Front during the First World War had instilled in him a horror of modern warfare. He had supported the Allied cause during **World War I**, when he served as assistant secretary of the navy, and opposed the move toward isolation in the war's aftermath. This belief was founded on a sense that the United States had a moral obligation to help ensure world peace but also through his understanding that U.S. economic interests needed protecting and developing in order to rescue the nation from the Depression.

Prior to **World War II** Roosevelt was not always able to work closely with the British due to differences and rivalries over **trade** and due to a strained relationship with Prime Minister **Neville Chamberlain**. Anglo–American cooperation in confronting Germany, Italy, and Japan was therefore limited. Roosevelt signaled that should war break out in Europe the United States would maintain its neutrality, but when war broke out in September 1939 he was persuaded to amend the **Neutrality Acts** to provide support to the Allies in the form of **Cash and Carry**, which allowed Britain to purchase war goods for cash. Roosevelt's sentiments were undoubtedly pro-British but Congress and the people were still isolationist and wanted to avoid entry into the war. When **Winston Churchill** became prime minister of Great Britain in May1940, Roosevelt came under increasing pressure to provide more material help and to enter the war as soon as possible. The two leaders began a working relationship that developed into a close friendship based on a unity of purpose—to defeat totalitarianism—and helped by regular wartime meetings and intimate correspondence. Soon after Winston Churchill became the British leader—and with the nations of Europe falling under the German blitzkrieg—Roosevelt agreed to the **destroyers-for-bases deal**.

In the 1940 presidential election, Roosevelt had to play a balancing act between looking prepared for war and insisting he was not about to intervene in Europe. Under pressure from his Republican opponent, Wendell Wilkie, Roosevelt was forced to pledge that he would not send "American boys into any foreign wars" but also provided more military aid to Britain and the Allies through the introduction of the **Lend-Lease** bill. In his State of the Union address in January 1941, Roosevelt outlined the **Four Freedoms** required for the world to be secure. This speech, intended to persuade Congress to pass Lend-Lease, signaled that the United States would become the "arsenal of democracy." The bond between Roosevelt and Churchill increased when the two had their first face-to-face meeting at Argentia Bay, off Newfoundland, when they agreed on the purposes of the war and issued the **Atlantic Charter**.

Despite agreeing on common principles, Roosevelt was determined to only take a united country to war. The surprise attack on **Pearl Harbor** by the Japanese proved an act of aggression that provided the prerequisite of national unity. Roosevelt asked Congress to declare war, speaking of 7 December 1941 as a "day of infamy." Once the United States had entered the war against Germany, Italy, and Japan, Roosevelt was determined to create a cooperative working relationship with the British government. Toward the end of the war, Roosevelt's anticolonialist views meant that he clashed with Churchill at the **Tehran** and **Yalta conferences** over Allied war strategy and also over the shape of the postwar world. Roosevelt was determined that the European powers should agree to wind down their empires; he proposed an internationally supervised trusteeship scheme for the French colonies in Indochina to smooth the transition toward full independence, and encouraged Churchill to liberate the peoples of India and Burma and allow them to be part of a British Commonwealth. Churchill was much more agreeable to Roosevelt's concept of a **United Nations** controlled by the four great powers — **China**, Great Britain, the Soviet Union, and the United States — commonly known as the **Four Policemen**.

When Roosevelt died on 12 April 1945 from a sudden cerebral hemorrhage, Churchill cabled Eleanor Roosevelt expressing his distress at losing a cherished friendship and spoke in the House of Commons about the country's greatest friend.

ROOSEVELT, THEODORE "TEDDY" (1858–1919). As U.S. Republican president between 1901 and 1909, Theodore Roosevelt helped cement the "rapprochement" in Anglo–American relations. Roosevelt recognized that an Anglo–American alliance would free his country to pursue its other external interests and would provide a counterweight to growing militarism in Germany. Influenced by **Anglo–Saxonist** ideas, and understanding that Great Britain and America were tied by a common language, extensive **trade** links, and a belief in democratic government, Roosevelt was determined as part of his foreign policy to cultivate an alliance with Britain. One of the ways this was achieved was through personal relationships between the Anglo–American elite, not least of which was Roosevelt's own close friendship with British diplomat Sir Cecil Spring-Rice.

In 1904 Roosevelt issued the Roosevelt Corollary to the **Monroe Doctrine**. With many Latin American nations in debt to European banks, Roosevelt feared intervention by the European powers. In order to prevent this, the amendment to the Monroe Doctrine asserted the right of the United States to intervene in Latin America and the Caribbean, acting as an international police power, to stabilize their economies. Great Britain did not challenge this assertion and, recognizing their decreasing influence in the region, also allowed the

United States to have sole control of the **Panama Canal** in 1901. Britain and America also reached agreement over the **Alaskan boundary dispute**. Despite the Anglo–American "**great rapprochement**," Roosevelt's views on British imperialism remained largely critical, regardless of the United States' emerging "sphere of influence" in Latin America and the Caribbean. *See also* HAY–PAUNCEFOTE TREATY; SPANISH–AMERICAN WAR.

RUMSFELD, DONALD (1932–). An experienced businessman and Republican politician, Donald Rumsfeld served as secretary of defense on two occasions. At 43 years old, he was the youngest ever secretary of defense when he was appointed on 20 November 1975 by President **Gerald Ford**. When he took the role again in November 2001 he was the oldest person to be appointed to the office at 74 years old. His experience and blunt-talking manner meant that he threatened to cause rifts in the Anglo–American relationship at critical junctures. In the lead-up to the war in **Iraq**, as Prime Minister **Tony Blair** attempted to get a second resolution in the **United Nations**, Rumsfeld announced in public that if necessary the United States would go it alone. Rumsfeld had been told by the British defense secretary, **Geoff Hoon**, that Blair might not be able to get support from the House of Commons for the involvement of British troops in Iraq without a second resolution authorizing war. Rumsfeld's public statement embarrassed Blair. Like **Dick Cheney**, Rumsfeld lost patience with Blair's attempts at maintaining an international coalition on Iraq. Rumsfeld also grew impatient with British criticism of the use of **Guantanamo Bay**. Rumsfeld resigned from his position on 18 December 2006 after receiving criticism from several U.S. military generals over his strategy in the **Iraq War**.

RUSK, DEAN (1909–1994). Former president of the Rockefeller Foundation, Dean Rusk served under Democratic presidents **John F. Kennedy** and **Lyndon Baines Johnson** as secretary of state for over eight years (1961–1969). As a **Rhodes scholar** in the 1930s, Rusk studied at Oxford University in Britain and was involved in debates over how to deal with the threat from Adolf Hitler's Germany. He observed the isolationist sentiment in Great Britain and the subsequent war with Germany, and learned the lesson that aggression had to be met with firm action. Rusk was considered a "hawk" in foreign policy terms, believing in taking firm military action to contain communism. Despite his personal links to Britain, he often took a hard line in dealing with the British governments. During his time in the State Department, the United States became embroiled in the **Vietnam War**, and Britain's lack of military involvement in the conflict was a disappointment to Rusk, who believed the British flag in Vietnam would have been of great symbolic significance in the propaganda battle. He told journalist **Louis Heren**, "All we needed was a regiment. The Black Watch would have done." He was also dismayed at the British announcement in January 1968 to withdraw its troops from **East of Suez**.

RUSSIA. Great Britain and the United States reacted with similar outrage at the news of the Bolshevik Revolution in October 1917. Both countries were alarmed at Vladimir Lenin's call for the destruction of the capitalist system and were angered by his pronouncement that **World War I** had been caused by rivalries between imperialist and capitalist nations. Lenin's decision to withdraw Russia from the war and make an alternative peace, in the Brest-Litovsk Treaty, fueled Anglo–American alarm. Washington and London broke off diplomatic relations with Russia and sent troops to help the Whites (opponents of the communists who favored a return to monarchical government) defeat the communists. Despite this intervention, the communists survived the civil war and British and American troops left Russia in 1920.

Despite America's nonrecognition of the Soviet government, humanitarian aid was provided to the victims of the 1921–1923 famine in Russia. In Britain, when the Labour Party formed its first government in 1924, it established diplomatic relations with the Soviet Union. In 1919, the United States experienced extreme anticommunism in the form of the so-called Red Scare, and it took until 16 November 1933 before President **Franklin D. Roosevelt** was willing to recognize the Soviet Union. During the interwar period, Roosevelt, like the British, hoped to establish peaceful accommodation with the Soviet Union, not least because of its increasing military power; despite several missions to Moscow, relations failed to improve and reached their lowest point in August 1939 when the Soviets signed the Molotov–Ribbentrop Pact (a nonaggression treaty) with Nazi Germany after the British refused an alliance with Moscow against Germany. Not until the German invasion of Soviet Union in June 1941 did the United States and Great Britain find common cause with Moscow, and President Roosevelt and Prime Minister **Winston Churchill** offered support and assistance to the Soviet leader, Joseph Stalin.

With the entry of the United States into **World War II** in December 1941, the Anglo–American allies joined the Soviet Union in the "Grand Alliance" against Germany, Italy, and Japan. Stalin disagreed with Churchill and Roosevelt on the timing of a second front that would help relieve his country from German attack and the issue was raised at the first meeting of allies in November 1943 at the **Tehran Conference**. By the time of the next conference at **Yalta** in February 1945, the second front had been opened with the **D-Day landings**, and all of the Big Three leaders were looking forward to the postwar world. By this stage, President Roosevelt was keeping some distance between himself and Churchill, in an attempt to create a close relationship with the Soviet Union. By the time of the final wartime conference at **Potsdam**, the U.S. attitude toward Russia had veered toward Britain's, which had grown increasingly suspicious of Soviet intentions in Europe and the Far East. With the **Harry S. Truman** administration's decision to use the **atomic bomb** to end the war with Japan, relations between the wartime allies began to deteriorate.

By the end of World War II, the Soviet Union had suffered an estimated 20 million dead and incalculable damage to its towns, cities, and infrastructure. The Red Army occupied much of Eastern and Central Europe and was determined that these areas provide a buffer zone from any future attack and a sphere of influence it could control. The British government pressed Washington to take a harder line with the Russians, and out of office, Churchill publicly declared this sentiment in his famous iron curtain speech in March 1946 in which he urged an Anglo–American alliance to resist the threat from Soviet expansionism and the spread of communism. By 1947, with the British withdrawal from **Greece** and Turkey, and the public announcement of the **Truman Doctrine**, the United States declared its intention to fight a battle to contain communism. Britain and America led the alliance against global communism and the formation of the **North Atlantic Treaty Organization** (NATO) in 1949, which was responded to by the Soviet Union with its military alliance, the Warsaw Pact, formed in 1955.

Despite the **Cold War**, and unlike the United States, Britain maintained some **trading** links with the Soviet Union. However, successive British governments remained committed to the Cold War battle, although not experiencing the same degree of anticommunism that flourished in the Americas in the early 1950s, peaking during the years of McCarthyism (1950–1954). When Stalin died in 1953, Prime Minister Churchill wanted to test the new Soviet leadership and called for a summit of the major world powers. He had begun to believe that some form of peaceful coexistence with the Russians might be possible. Washington did not respond to Churchill's proposal, fearing that the British might be drifting into appeasement. Britain continued to attempt to play the role of mediator between the two superpowers, not least of which during the **Berlin crisis** of 1958.

Despite having shared goals in relation to the Soviet Union, London and Washington disagreed over strategy on occasion. Notably, in the mid-1980s as the new détente between the Soviet Union and the West appeared to be leading President **Ronald Reagan** to consider a nonnuclear future, Prime Minister **Margaret Thatcher** became alarmed and reminded him of Britain and NATO's stance on maintaining a nuclear deterrent.

After the collapse of the Soviet Union in 1991, Anglo–American relations followed similar trajectories in relation to the new Russian Federation. Economic ties increased with Russia, and both London and Washington approved of the admittance of former Soviet allies and satellites into NATO in 1999 and 2004. In the aftermath of **September 11**, Britain and America hoped for closer cooperation with Russia on security issues such as international terrorism and organized crime. *See also* FULTON, MISSOURI, SPEECH.

– S –

SAN FRANCISCO CONFERENCE. Held between 15 April and 26 June 1945, the San Francisco conference was attended by representatives of 50 nations, all of which had been at war with Germany. The conference was assembled to determine the final structure and form of the **United Nations** organization, and the UN Charter was drafted and signed on 26 June. On 24 October, the charter was formally ratified at the first session of the General Assembly of the United Nations in London.

SANDYS, DUNCAN (1908–1987). Duncan Sandys was a British Conservative politician and **Winston Churchill**'s son-in-law, having married the prime minister's daughter, Diana, in 1935. Sandys was chairman of the **European Movement**'s international executive, minister of defense between 1957 and 1959, and minister for aviation between 1959 and 1960. In April 1957, Duncan Sandys issued a defense white paper to Parliament that was the culmination of strategizing on Britain's long-term defense planning by the military chiefs of staff. The white paper switched the emphasis from conventional arms to nuclear deterrent, led to the end of national conscription, and resulted in the closure of aircraft manufacturers in Britain. The Sandys defense paper served notice on the United States that Britain's financial situation would lead to hard decisions having to be taken due to the ongoing difficulties faced by the British economy. Most notably, Washington was faced with the possibility that Britain might end its global role, especially **East of Suez**.

SARATOGA, BATTLE OF (1777). Famous for its decisive role in the American Revolution, American success at the battle of Saratoga prompted the involvement of France in the **War of Independence** against Great Britain. In an attempt to isolate New England, British troops led by General John Burgoyne moved south from **Canada** in the summer of 1777, planning to join forces led by General William Howe who had gained control of New York City, with the aim of controlling New York state. Unaware of General Burgoyne's plans, Howe took his forces to attack Philadelphia and unwittingly left Burgoyne to fight alone against American militias that had assembled throughout New England to block his way, and fighting took place in Saratoga County in September and October 1777. British forces struggled against the sharpshooters of the militias and were forced to surrender to American General Horatio Gates on 17 October 1777. Victory at Saratoga finally persuaded the French that America could achieve victory over the British, and in 1778 France agreed to provide military assistance to the United States in a Treaty of Amity and Commerce.

SCHWARZKOPF, NORMAN (1934–). Known as "Stormin' Norman," U.S. Army General Norman Schwarzkopf is best known for being commander of the coalition forces during the Persian **Gulf War** of 1991. During the conflict, which was heavily televised, Schwarzkopf was a high-profile figure. He developed a good working relationship with the leader of the British forces, Sir **Peter de la Billière**.

SEITZ, RAYMOND (1940–). A career diplomat, Raymond Seitz served as **American** ambassador to Great Britain between 1990 and 1994 during the presidencies of **William J. Clinton** and **George W. Bush**. Seitz later published his account of the transatlantic relationship, *Over Here*, and revealed that Clinton had laughed at having to be reminded to use the term "**special relationship**" during his meeting with Prime Minister **John Major** in 1993. Seitz opposed the granting of a visa to Sinn Fein leader **Gerry Adams**. He chose to remain in Great Britain after his time at the Court of St. James.

SEPTEMBER 11, 2001. On Thursday, 11 September 2001, al-Qaeda terrorists flew hijacked aircraft into the World Trade Center Twin Towers in New York and the Pentagon building in Washington, D.C. An American Airlines plane, also hijacked as part of the same plot, crashed in fields in Pennsylvania. These surprise attacks had a major impact on international politics and Anglo–American relations. The attack on the World Trade Center resulted in nearly 3,000 victims, 67 of whom were British. Prime Minister **Tony Blair** immediately pledged support for the United States in the face of the attack. He flew to Washington and New York to express sympathy and solidarity with the United States and also engaged in a diplomatic mission to ensure a coalition of nations united against al-Qaeda leader Osama bin Laden and his followers, primarily among European and Middle Eastern nations. Blair met with President **George W. Bush** nine days after the attacks and spoke at St. Thomas Church in Manhattan during a memorial service for British victims. On 20 September 2001, with Tony Blair in attendance, President Bush declared to the U.S. Congress that "America has no truer friend than Great Britain" in recognition of the reaction by Blair's pledge to work "shoulder to shoulder" with the United States in the war against terrorism. On 13 September, at the Changing of the Guard at Buckingham Palace, the band of the Coldstream Guards played the "**Star-Spangled Banner**" as a symbolic gesture of British support for the United States. As Washington began to take more security measures, notably in the Patriot Act, two months after the attack the British House of Commons passed the Anti-Terrorism, Crime and Security Act. Blair's unswerving support for the United States after the attacks meant that Britain was a key ally in Bush's war on terror, noticeably in **Afghanistan** and later in **Iraq**.

SHENANDOAH. Along with the *Alabama*, the Confederate ship the CSS *Shenandoah* was built in a British dockyard as a merchant vessel, and once in Confederate hands they were fitted out as fighting ships and engaged in commerce raids. These commerce raiders played havoc with Union shipping with the *Shenandoah* attacking the U.S. whaling fleet in the North Pacific. Its activities featured in the *Alabama* **claims** against Britain after the end of the **American Civil War**.

SHULTZ, GEORGE P. (1920–). A former academic and businessman, George Shultz served as American secretary of state under President **Ronald Reagan** during the period 1982 to 1989. Shultz approved of the U.S. bombing of **Libya** in April 1986, although he did not believe Muammar al-Qaddafi's residence should be attacked, and was appreciative of Great Britain's support of its actions. In relation to the U.S. invasion of **Grenada** in 1983, Shultz expected Britain to support the Americans and was disappointed when Prime Minister **Margaret Thatcher** condemned American actions, feeling she was embarrassed by criticism in Britain that she was "Reagan's poodle." After leaving office, Shultz continued to serve as an informal adviser, noticeably to President **George W. Bush**, and **Tony Blair** visited him at his home in San Francisco in July 2006.

SIMPSON, WALLIS (1895–1986). In 1933, Wallis Simpson, a married American woman and Edward, Prince of Wales, began a romantic relationship. It is alleged that their relationship continued, largely without public scrutiny, until King George V died on 20 January 1936 and the prince of Wales ascended to the throne as **Edward VIII**. Due to a fascination with the British monarchy, and also because Edward was seen as a handsome, young, and fashionable prince who had visited New York in 1934, American newspapers were riveted by the affair. Britain was plunged into a constitutional crisis when it became clear that Mrs. Simpson was to divorce her husband and Edward intended to marry her. As the king, Edward was supreme governor of the Church of England, and the church did not permit divorced people to remarry. Moreover, as a divorcée, Wallis was not viewed in a positive light by the British establishment, including the Conservative government, led by Prime Minister Stanley Baldwin. Although it was rumored in the press that Edward VIII believed his marriage to Wallis might help cement an Anglo–American alliance, he was forced to choose between his throne and the woman he loved. He chose Wallis and on 10 December his abdication notice was witnessed. Edward was made the Duke of Windsor by the new king, George VI, and Wallis became Duchess of Windsor after their marriage on 3 June 1937; they spent the rest of their lives in France.

SKYBOLT CRISIS (1962). The Skybolt crisis of late 1962 was the most serious rift in Anglo–American relations since **Suez**. In March 1960, President **Dwight D. Eisenhower** promised to supply Skybolt missiles to the British once developed. In the negotiated agreement, signed in June, the United States agreed to bear the full costs of development and the British would pay for just the missiles themselves when they became available. At that time, the British nuclear deterrent was free-falling hydrogen bombs delivered by V-bombers, and the Royal Air Force was experiencing great difficulties in the development of its own medium-range ballistic missile, **Blue Streak**. Skybolt was an air-to-surface missile under development in the United States, and British acquisition would have extended the life of the V-bomber. With the cancellation of Blue Streak, the British placed all its missile plans in Skybolt. In November 1962, U.S. Secretary of Defense **Robert McNamara** decided to cancel Skybolt as a cost-effectiveness measure. An Anglo–American crisis ensued as the British claimed the United States had not given them advance warning of the decision. Moreover, the British felt Washington did not appear to understand the political repercussions of the cancellation for the government of **Harold Macmillan**, which was already facing numerous domestic crises, and suspected the administration of **John F. Kennedy** was using the cancellation as a means to encourage the British to commit more conventional forces to **North Atlantic Treaty Organization** (NATO). At a meeting in London between McNamara and British Secretary of Defence Peter Thorneycroft on 11 December, McNamara informed the British of his decision and the technical and financial reasons behind it (in its five tests the missile had experienced failure to fire and ignite) and tensions heightened, despite an offer by the United States to allow the British to continue to develop Skybolt if they so wished.

Prime Minister Macmillan met President Kennedy at **Nassau** in the Bahamas between 19 and 21 December determined to persuade the Americans to live up to the promise made in March 1960 that the British be allowed to buy **Polaris missiles** in the future and that these would be "independent" of the United States. To many in the U.S. State Department and the Pentagon, this was the opposite of what they wished for from the meeting, instead hoping that Britain would divest itself of an independent nuclear force and instead consider engaging in a mixed-manned **multilateral force** (MLF) including France and Germany. The British delegation achieved most of its objectives at the meeting at Nassau between 18 and 21 December; most importantly, the United States agreed to provide Polaris missiles as a substitute for Skybolt. Kennedy was perplexed at how the British had managed to get all they required at Nassau and subsequently asked **Richard Neustadt** to carry out a private postmortem.

SOUTH-EAST ASIA TREATY ORGANIZATION (SEATO). This collective security agreement was signed in Manila in September 1954. Its signatories were Australia, Great Britain, France, New Zealand, Pakistan, the Philippines, Thailand, and the United States. When the United States first mooted the idea in March 1954, Britain had been reluctant to agree to such an alliance because it did not want to jeopardize negotiations at the forthcoming **Geneva Conference** (April–July) and did not want to intensify East–West tensions in Southeast Asia. In a separate protocol, protection was extended to Cambodia, **Laos**, and **Vietnam**, although Britain and France never believed the Manila Treaty covered these countries. Consequently, although the United States considered its participation in SEATO a partial justification for its involvement in Vietnam, Britain did not. SEATO was phased out of existence in 1975.

SOVIET UNION. *See* RUSSIA.

SPANISH–AMERICAN WAR (1898). U.S. Secretary of State **John Hay** described the Spanish–American War (April–August 1898) as a "splendid little war." British reaction to it was largely supportive of the United States and indicative of a period of rapprochement between the United States and Great Britain at the end of the 19th century. In April 1898, the administration of William McKinley went to war with Spain over that country's treatment of the colony of **Cuba**. Many Cuban nationalists wanted independence from Spain, and in 1896 Spain sent 150,000 troops to Cuba to try to quell guerrilla warfare on the island. Not only did the United States consider the Spanish to be brutal and oppressive in their handling of the Cubans, but they were also concerned about American investments on the island. Although most of Europe supported the Spanish cause, Great Britain declared its neutrality and made pro-American statements. This was a friendlier response than might have been expected as only a few years earlier the British government had indicated that it would support Spain in its attempt to remain in control of Cuba. The British had feared that their trading interests in the Caribbean might be threatened if the United States gained influence there. Pro-American sympathy was rife in British newspapers and on hearing the news of the American declaration of war on 29 April 1898, the British public decked buildings in London in red, white, and blue streamers. The United States defeated the Spanish and granted formal independence to Cuba, although with significant restrictions placed on it under the Platt agreement. It also took control of Puerto Rico, Guam, and the Philippines. *See also* GREAT RAPPROCHEMENT.

SPECIAL RELATIONSHIP. The term "special relationship" is often used to describe Anglo–American relations since **World War II**. The origins of the term remain disputed, but it was used in public for the first time by **Winston Churchill** during his "Sinews of Peace" speech in **Fulton, Missouri**, in 1946. Churchill hoped to maintain the close relationship established by Great Britain and the United States during World War II. The British prime minister believed that shared values and language and similar worldwide responsibilities would ensure Anglo–American unity in the postwar world. Although the term has continued to be used to describe the ties between Britain and the United States, including intelligence and nuclear cooperation, it has more resonance in Great Britain than the United States and is used by critics and supporters.

STAMP ACT (1765). In an attempt to raise money to pay for British troops in America, including the building of an army garrison, the British Parliament passed the Stamp Act, introduced by **George Grenville**, on 22 March 1765. The Stamp Act raised revenue by taxing all legal and commercial documents, newspapers, playing cards, and other printed papers. Violators of the act were to be tried in the Vice-Admiralty Courts. The British felt they had little choice but to introduce this fund-raising tax as the colonial governments had not worked together to provide funds to support the expenses of the British troops. This act marked a shift in British policy toward America as it challenged colonial authority by imposing a direct, internal tax. Believing this was another example of taxation without representation, opposition to the act was immediate and the level of resistance surprised the British. Crowds in the cities, notably in Boston, began rioting. Known as the Sons of Liberty, the rioters attacked the tax collectors and their homes and offices. A more formal response came in the form of the Stamp Act Congress, convened in October 1765 to plan an official opposition to the British act. The congress attempted to find a compromise between acquiescence and rebellion, and focused on the issue of taxation only by consent and the right of colonists to trial by jury.

Despite the congress's petition for the repeal of the stamp tax, violent rebellion and public demonstrations continued to grow as the British prepared to enforce the act after November 1, 1765. Between 7 October and 24 October 1765, nine of the British colonies sent 27 delegates to the Stamp Act Congress in New York City and issued the Declaration of Rights and Grievances, which announced that the colonies were united in their opposition to the British. Opposition also extended to a boycott of British goods—nonimportation agreements—among merchants. The organization and involvement in the various forms of political rebellion against the introduction of the Stamp Act encouraged a sense of American identity and as such was a major step toward the American Revolution. After much debate in the British Parliament, the act was repealed on 17 March 1966. The debate indicated, however, that the British did not accept the validity of the Stamp Act Congress's claims but instead repealed the act as a matter of economic expediency as British merchants began to protest against the nonimportation agreements. Attempting to reassert its authority in the American colonies, the British Parliament passed the Declaratory Act asserting British power to pass and enforce laws in America. *See also* WAR OF INDEPENDENCE.

"STAR-SPANGLED BANNER." In September 1814, during the **War of 1812**, after burning much of Washington, D.C., the British attacked Baltimore; their successful repulsion by Americans provided the inspiration for Francis Scott Key's "Star-Spangled Banner," which became the national anthem of the United States in March 1931.

STAR WARS. The Strategic Defense Initiative (SDI), popularly known as "Star Wars," was a controversial research project announced by President **Ronald Reagan** on 23 March 1983. Hoping to utilize the latest laser technology in space, scientists had persuaded the president that it might be possible to shield the United States from a nuclear missile attack by using satellites to detect the launch of enemy missiles and then destroy them. In Great Britain and most of the rest of Europe, SDI sparked fears that Reagan might consider a limited nuclear war on the European continent and the nuclear balance of power—mutually assured destruction (MAD)—would be disturbed. Nevertheless, British Prime Minister **Margaret Thatcher** publicly endorsed SDI research on the grounds that it might prevent a Soviet missile attack. Behind the scenes, she expressed concern that if tested SDI would break existing arms control treaties, including the 1968 **Nuclear Nonproliferation Treaty**. Visiting Reagan in December 1984, Thatcher persuaded Reagan to issue a joint statement acknowledging SDI would be included in any discussions on arms control, and in 1985 Britain joined in the SDI project. After the dismantling of the **Soviet Union** and the end of the **Cold War**, the U.S. Congress cancelled the SDI program in 1993 after billions of dollars had been spent on its research, although research into similar but differently named space-based defense projects continued. Reagan and Thatcher both believed SDI had made the Russians realize that they could not afford to continue to compete with the United States in the arms race and thus contributed to the defeat of the Soviet Union in the Cold War. *See also* NATIONAL MISSILE DEFENSE.

STERLING AREA. By the late 19th century, sterling was the most acceptable currency in the world, based largely on Great Britain's dominance in international **trade**. Countries with trading and cultural ties to Britain—often members of the British Empire or later the British Commonwealth—using sterling or pegging their currencies to the pound sterling were part of the sterling area or sterling zone. These countries often held a high proportion of their foreign reserves in sterling. The sterling area and **imperial preference** were viewed by the United States as a form of protectionism. In 1941, the United States demanded that, in return for **Lend-Lease**, Britain pledge itself to abandon its imperial preference and sterling area systems.

STEWART, MICHAEL (1906–1990). During his first period as British foreign secretary (1965–1966), Michael Stewart was involved in attempts by the government of **Harold Wilson** to influence the administration of **Lyndon B. Johnson** on **Vietnam**. Stewart was in Washington when news of the American use of gas in Vietnam became headline news around the world in March 1965. Responding to the wishes of Prime Minister Wilson, in a prearranged meeting with President Johnson, Stewart berated the Americans for losing the moral high ground by using gas. Despite Johnson's defense of the use of gas, Stewart repeated British concern at the use of such methods in a speech to the National Press Club in Washington. This incident soured Johnson's view of Stewart and the Wilson government. Stewart served as foreign secretary under Wilson for a second time from 1968 to 1970 during the transition from the Johnson to the Nixon administration. Stewart apparently offended President **Richard Nixon** during talks. Nixon thought Stewart had adopted a patronizing tone and British Ambassador John Freeman was told of this complaint by **Henry Kissinger**.

STIMSON, HENRY (1867–1950). A Republican lawyer and statesman, Henry Stimson was American secretary of war prior to **World War I** (1911–1913) and served in the same position during **World War II** (1940–1945). In the interwar years, he served as secretary of state (1929–1933) and in that position was head of the U.S. delegation to the London Naval Conference in 1930 and 1931. He is most famous, however, for his proclamation of the so-called Stimson Doctrine in January 1932. In September 1931, Japanese forces invaded Manchuria and when fighting spread to the Chinese port of Shanghai, Great Britain and the United States had the option of intervening to preserve Chinese integrity under the Nine-Power Treaty that had been signed in Washington in 1922. Neither President Herbert Hoover nor Prime Minister **Ramsay MacDonald** was willing to intervene militarily or implement strong economic sanctions against Japan. This led Stimson to issue a note on 7 January to **China** and Japan outlining the principle of nonrecognition of situations brought about by violations of the **Kellogg–Briand Pact** of 1928. In other words, the United States refused to accept territorial changes brought about by force. Although the British were consulted, they viewed the Stimson Doctrine as a moral protest that carried no weight. Two days later the British government issued a statement that did not endorse the Stimson Doctrine, instead referring to the commitment to the Open Door policy for Manchuria and preferring to support a **League of Nations** resolution. As secretary of war under President **Franklin D. Roosevelt**'s leadership, Stimson worked closely with the British on Allied war strategy. Stimson challenged Roosevelt and Prime Minister **Winston Churchill** by insisting on a legal war trial for Nazi leaders at the end of the war.

STRAW, JACK (1946–). British Labour MP for Blackburn, Jack Straw's most important political office was foreign secretary between 2001 and 2006. Serving under Prime Minister **Tony Blair**, Jack Straw was head of the Foreign Office during the **September 11** attacks and coordinated the British response to the event and the subsequent Anglo–American military interventions in **Afghanistan** and **Iraq**, including helping to draft related **United Nations** Security Council resolutions. Straw developed a close working relationship with **Colin Powell** and his successor, **Condoleezza Rice**. In public, Straw backed the U.S.-led invasion of Iraq in March 2003, although press speculation suggested he had expressed doubts about the wisdom of British involvement to Prime Minister **Tony Blair**. Straw developed a close working relationship with Rice, visiting her in her home town of Birmingham, Alabama, in October 2005. The following year Rice visited Straw in his constituency of Blackburn, Lancashire, where the secretary of state faced protests against the Bush administration's Iraq policy. It was rumored in the press that Straw was removed from the Foreign Office on the request of the administration of **George W. Bush** because he made public comments ruling out military action against **Iran**.

SUEZ CRISIS. The Suez crisis (October 1956–March 1957) caused a major breach in postwar Anglo–American relations, contributed to the resignation of British Prime Minister **Anthony Eden**, and signified the end of Great Britain's role as one of the world's major powers. The crisis began when Egyptian leader President Gamal Abdel Nasser nationalized the Suez Canal on 26 July 1956. The canal's shares were owned mainly by Britain and France but Nasser felt forced to nationalize it after the United States and Britain pulled out of a deal to help finance the building of the Aswan dam on the Nile. Britain's response to the nationalization was predicated on two major concerns, neither of which the administration of **Dwight D. Eisenhower** fully appreciated. Firstly, the British government felt that Egyptian control of the Suez Canal threatened to damage its **trading** and supply routes, especially the security of its oil supplies. Secondly, the Suez Canal had great symbolic significance for the British as the gateway to the Indian Ocean. Eden therefore viewed Nasser's actions as damaging to the British economy but also felt the Egyptian was a dictator who should not appeased.

Between August and October, London attempted to find a diplomatic solution to the crisis including an offer to Nasser, which he declined, of Egyptian representation on the Suez Canal Company board and a percentage of its profits. Eden and his foreign secretary, **Selwyn Lloyd**, discussed the situation with U.S. Secretary of State **John Foster Dulles**. Initially, it appeared that the United States understood that Britain and Israel might resort to force. With no negotiated agreement in sight, on 14 October 1956 Eden held secret talks with French officials to discuss a military incursion to recover use of the canal. The result of this meeting was a plan that allowed Israel to invade Egypt as an excuse for British and French forces to intervene between two warring nations and thus seize the canal. On 29 October Israeli forces invaded Egypt and took the Sinai Peninsula. British and French airborne forces landed around Port Said on 5 November. By acting without the United States, Britain was attempting to show that it could act independently of Washington in defense of its own interests.

Coming close to the 1956 U.S. presidential election, President Eisenhower was furious that two of his major allies had not consulted with him prior to taking action and jeopardizing his stand as a peace candidate. In addition, Suez coincided with the Soviet invasion of Hungary, and Eisenhower thought British and Israeli action in the Middle East might damage the West's reputation at a time when communism should have been tarnished. Eisenhower demanded Britain and France withdraw their forces and, using financial pressures, secured this quickly; on 6 November Britain accepted a cease-fire. America's ability to end the British military incursion, and Eden's consequent humiliation, meant that Suez proved a watershed for British power and influence throughout the world.

SUGAR ACT (1764). Officially known as the American Revenue Act, the Sugar Act as it became known was passed by the British Parliament on 5 April 1764. The act modified the 1733 Sugar and Molasses Act, reducing the level of taxation on the import of non-British sugar into the American colonies from six pence per gallon to three pence. However, Lord Grenville, First Lord of the Treasury, was convinced that the new act should raise revenue to help offset the cost of the Seven Years' War and thus was clear that the act would be strictly enforced to deal with the rich **trade** in smuggling, and also ruled that the import of other goods should also be taxed, including wine, coffee, silk, and cloth. When the provisions of the act were enforced, the economy of New England suffered, and rebellion began. Cries of "no taxation without representation" began to be heard as the colonists protested against taxation by a distant parliament in Great Britain aimed at raising revenue. The act was passed at the same time as the Currency Act, which prohibited the American colonies from printing their own paper currency, and the colonists' unease at the passage of these two acts was part of the backdrop to the revolt against the Stamp Act passed in 1765. *See also* WAR OF INDEPENDENCE.

– T –

TEA ACT (1773). *See* BOSTON TEA PARTY.

TEHRAN CONFERENCE (1943). The first wartime meeting of the "Big Three" leaders—**Winston Churchill**, Joseph Stalin, and **Franklin D. Roosevelt**, representing the three Allied powers of Great Britain, the **Soviet Union**, and United States—took place in November 1943 in **Iran**. The major purpose of the Tehran Conference was to discuss the opening of a second front in Western Europe, something Stalin had requested since June 1941. The conference was a turning point in Anglo–American relations because prior to this time Britain had been considered the dominant partner in the relationship. By this stage, however, the United States' superior military and economic strength had begun to tell. Although Great Britain still had more troops at war in Europe than the Americans, these forces were increasingly dependent on the flow of U.S. war supplies under the terms of **Lend-Lease**.

Consequently, Washington was determined to hold Churchill to a commitment made in August 1943 to invade France during the following summer. In addition, having witnessed Russia's abilities in standing up to Germany's invasion of the Soviet Union, and recognizing that he would have to deal with Stalin in the postwar world, Roosevelt was keen to establish a closer relationship with the Soviet leader by demonstrating his independence from the British. Consequently Roosevelt refused to meet Churchill in private before and during the conference and sided with Stalin during disagreements, principally by outvoting Churchill on the invasion of France, which became the overriding military priority. At the conference it was agreed that British and American troops would be sent over to Western Europe in the spring of 1944 and the Normandy invasion, "Operation Overlord," would begin during May 1944; it was also agreed that an American supreme Allied commander be appointed. Roosevelt and Churchill also made other concessions to Stalin, including allowing him to establish puppet governments in East Europe. *See* D-DAY LANDINGS.

THATCHER, MARGARET (1925–). On 4 May 1979, Margaret Thatcher was elected the first woman British prime minister with a parliamentary majority of 44. She stayed in office until 1990. As a right-wing Conservative politician, Thatcher's political philosophy had long been to reverse socialism. She wanted less state intervention, a reduction in taxation levels, less public ownership and expenditure, more individual power, more competition, and more private ownership. She was keen to revitalize Anglo–American relations as she believed strongly that Europe needed the United States to maintain its security in the face of Soviet communism. Thatcher was able to establish a good working relationship with President **Jimmy Carter**, having a successful visit to Washington in December 1979 when she secured agreement on a U.S. deal to supply a new **Trident** system, the C-4 missile, for the British submarine fleet. Although supporting U.S. condemnation of the Soviet invasion of **Afghanistan**, Thatcher would not agree to a British boycott of the Moscow Olympics in 1980.

Her plans for a stronger Anglo–American partnership were boosted enormously by the election of **Ronald Reagan** in November 1980. Thatcher developed a close working relationship with the new Republican president over the course of his two terms in office (1981–1989). Sharing similar ideologies—both believed in the benefits of a free-market economy—the two struck up a transatlantic friendship unparalleled since the Churchill–Roosevelt years. The prime minister was the first foreign head of state to visit the Reagan **White House** in 1981 and the last one in 1988. The two politicians already knew one another and from the first official visit it was clear that the two leaders were compatible socially and in agreement over a number of key international issues, not least of which was their hard-line attitude to Soviet communism. When the **Falklands War** broke out in April 1982, Thatcher was to find, however, that Reagan still operated from a position of U.S. national interest. Although Reagan did eventually side with the British, there was a tense period of indecision. The limits of British influence were also demonstrated the following year when in October 1983 Thatcher objected to the U.S.

invasion of **Grenada**, a former British colony, but the invasion went ahead anyway.

Thatcher's support of the Americans often led to controversy in Britain, notably during the **Westland affair** when her government's decision to purchase American helicopters rather than consider the prospect of buying European ones led to the resignation of her defense secretary, Michael Heseltine, and in 1986 when she decided to allow U.S. aircraft to refuel in Britain en route to the bombing of **Libya**.

Reagan's determination to defeat Soviet communism and his provocative rhetoric in the early 1980s, including references to the possibility of a tactical nuclear war confined to Europe, worried many in Europe. In Britain, as the decision to station cruise missiles on British soil and buy Trident missiles was announced, the **Campaign for Nuclear Disarmament** (CND) was revived and British public opinion polls showed concern about the closeness of the Anglo–American defense relationship. Reagan's announcement of the Strategic Defense Initiative (SDI) in March 1983 was a sensitive domestic matter for Thatcher. In public, she greeted the news of "**Star Wars**" positively, arguing it was necessary in case of Soviet attack, but in private she was able to persuade Reagan to allow British interests to be taken into account and in December 1984 issued a joint statement on SDI that recognized it must fall within discussions about arms control. The following year Britain became an official partner in the SDI project.

In the final months of her premiership, Thatcher backed the administration of **George H. W. Bush** in its response to the Iraqi invasion of Kuwait. Her appreciation of, and friendship with, Ronald Reagan continued after she was forced from office in November 1990 and she flew to Washington to attend his funeral in 2004, despite being frail after suffering a stroke. *See also* GREENHAM COMMON; GULF WAR.

THOMPSON, SIR ROBERT (1916–1992). An experienced military adviser, having been in charge of Malayan defense during the **Malayan emergency**, Sir Robert Thompson led the British Advisory Mission (BRIAM) to Vietnam. At the request of the United States, the British government agreed to send a five-man police advisory force to South Vietnam (BRIAM) to help with the counterinsurgency battle. President **John F. Kennedy** and President **Lyndon Johnson** were interested in the lessons Thompson had learned in Malaya and how the rural village programs might be adapted to Vietnam. Thompson's ideas influenced the establishment of the "strategic hamlets" program but he soon became frustrated with the lack of unified leadership in Vietnam and came to believe the United States had made a crucial mistake in beginning the bombing campaign Rolling Thunder. *See also* VIETNAM WAR.

THOR MISSILE. During a meeting with Prime Minister **Harold Macmillan** in **Bermuda** on 22 March 1957, President **Dwight D. Eisenhower** agreed to station 60 intermediate-range Thor missiles in Great Britain under dual control as a stopgap until the British developed their own medium-range missile, the **Blue Streak**. The Thor rocket could be fitted with nuclear warheads and was capable of traveling 1,500 miles. By stationing the Thor missiles on British soil, the United States could reach the **Soviet Union** with its nuclear warheads. Launching of the missiles would be a joint decision, but control of the nuclear weapons resided with the United States. *See also* AMERICAN BASES IN BRITAIN.

THORNEYCROFT, PETER (1909–1994). Conservative Party MP and British defense secretary (1962–1964) during the **Skybolt crisis**, Thorneycroft had a strained relationship with his American opposite number, Secretary of Defense **Robert McNamara**, and was outraged when McNamara flew to London on 11 December to inform him of the cancellation of the missile.

TOWNSHEND ACTS (1767). After the intense opposition to the direct taxation introduced by the British in the **Stamp Act** of 1765, and following the subsequent repeal of the act in 1767, Charles Townshend, British chancellor of the exchequer, introduced the revenue bill that was passed by the British Parliament on 2 July 1867 that placed indirect (external) import taxes on items such as glass, paint, paper, and tea entering the American colonies. The taxes were aimed at raising revenue to pay for British troops in the American colonies, and more specifically, to pay the salaries of colonial officials. These custom duties proved extremely unpopular among the American colonists with repeated charges of "no taxation without representation" being heard. As with the Stamp Act, rebellion against the Townshend Duties included a nonimportation movement, violence against customs officials, and a move toward illegal smuggling of goods to avoid the taxation. The boycott of British goods placed sufficient economic pressure on the British that on 5 March 1770 Parliament repealed the duties on all goods except tea. The tax on the import of tea remained in place as a symbolic demonstration of Parliament's right to tax the American colonies and became the focus of political rebellion during the **Boston Tea Party** of 1773. *See* WAR OF INDEPENDENCE.

TRADE. Facilitated by a common language, as early as the 18th century, transatlantic trade proved vital to the economies of Great Britain and America and became a key component of Anglo–American relations. In the 18th century, trade across the Atlantic represented a form of proto-globalization, with prices of key commodities, such as wheat, in both countries influencing each other. After the American Revolution, the economic relationship between Great Britain and its former colony proved increasingly important to both nations. The United States needed continuing British direct investment to facilitate its growth, including the purchase of land, but it also benefited from financial support in the form of the purchase of bonds and stocks, particularly needed for the development of its infrastructure, including the railroads. In the aftermath of the **War of 1812**, Anglo–American trade continued to grow steadily, reaching a boom period in the 1830s, with Britain receiving large amounts of American cotton and tobacco, and exporting manufactured goods to the United States. By the mid-19th century, Britain was also importing huge quantities of foodstuffs from America, particularly grain for bread and alcohol, with the repeal of British Corn Laws in 1846 allowing for further expansion of trade. Merchant banking facilitated this growing trade, notably the House of Brown, and later through **Barings Bank**. Between 1820 and 1860, the United States was exporting nearly half of its goods to Britain. After 1895, U.S. engineering products also began to flood the British domestic market as American manufacturing developed. By 1914, American overseas investment in Britain had also increased markedly, with over 140 American companies operating in Britain.

Despite the growth in transatlantic trade throughout the 19th century and into the 20th century, Anglo–American trading agreements were difficult to reach, not least because of related maritime and territorial disputes. Although London encouraged Washington to adopt free trade, political parties in the United States were suspicious of the "British system"; out of a desire to protect growing American industries, they remained committed to protectionist policies, such as tariffs, although President Woodrow Wilson's **Fourteen Points** called for equality of trade and the removal of economic barriers, where possible. By the 1930s, when Britain and America witnessed severe economic depressions, Anglo–American relations witnessed increased rivalry over trade as both sides erected trade barriers to protect their own industries. Britain abandoned its traditional free-trade policy and imposed a general tariff, and Washington was particularly critical of Britain's implementation of its system of **imperial preference**. A growing trend toward the liberalization of trade was signaled, however, by the **Anglo–American Trade Agreement** of 1938 that allowed for a reduction in tariff levels. As the United States emerged from World War II as the world's economic superpower, Washington joined Britain in committing to reducing barriers to trade by signing the **General Agreement on Tariffs and Trade** (GATT). Despite the Europeanization of British trade after its entry into the **European Economic Community** in 1973 (later the European Union), the United States remained Britain's largest export market. In 2006, the United States still received £53.4 billion of British goods, while the United States exported $45.4 billion of goods to Britain. *See also* BROWN BROTHERS.

TRANSATLANTIC DECLARATION (1990). Issued on 22 November 1990, and negotiated by Secretary of State **James Baker**, the Transatlantic Declaration was an attempt to formalize relations between the United States and the European Union (EU) by establishing common goals and agreeing to hold regular summit meetings. In the lead-up to the declaration, British Prime Minster **Margaret Thatcher** was concerned by President **George H. W. Bush**'s enthusiasm for European integration, including monetary union. The formalization of regular meetings between the U.S. president and EU leaders was eventually built upon in 1995 when President **Bill Clinton** signed the **New Transatlantic Agenda**. *See also* EUROPEAN ECONOMIC COMMUNITY.

TRENT **AFFAIR.** In November 1861, the *Trent* affair was the first major diplomatic incident during the **American Civil War** and almost resulted in war between the United States and Great Britain. The doctrine of the freedom of the seas was brought into question when on 8 November the Union frigate USS *San Jacinto*, under the command of Captain Charles Wilkes, stopped and seized the neutral British mail steamer *Trent* on the high seas near the Bahamas. Wilkes had heard that the *Trent* was carrying two Confederate commissioners, James Murray Mason and John Slidell, on their way to Britain and France on diplomatic missions to persuade those countries to support the South in the war. The arrest and imprisonment of the two Southerners in Boston made Wilkes a hero in the North, but the incident led to a serious breach in relations between the United States and Britain and even threatened to break out into war. The incident occurred as Britain was on the verge of diplomatically recognizing the Confederacy, and the British asked for the surrender of the prisoners and an immediate apology. Both demands were acceded to after several weeks of tension.

TRIDENT MISSILE. By the late 1970s, the submarine-launched **Polaris missile** was up for renewal in Great Britain. In July 1980, President **Jimmy Carter** agreed with Prime Minister **Margaret Thatcher** that Britain would purchase 100 Trident I (C-4) missiles at a cost of just over £1 billion. As with the Polaris deal, Britain would pay only 5 percent of the total research and development costs. These favorable financial terms to Britain reflected the ongoing strong Anglo–American defense ties. When **Ronald Reagan** became president, Thatcher asked the United States if Britain could purchase the more powerful Trident II (D-5). This was agreed and Britain was privileged to gain access to American technology at a low cost, although Britain had to agree that the Trident missiles be assigned to **North Atlantic Treaty Organization** (NATO) (unless Britain's national interests were threatened). In March 2003, the government of **Tony Blair** gained the support of the House of Commons for its plans to renew its nuclear-submarine technology to carry the Trident missiles until the middle of the 21st century.

TRIPARTITE DECLARATION (1950). Great Britain, France, and the United States signed the Tripartite Declaration on 25 May 1950 in an attempt to deal with the issue of arms sales to Israel and the Arab states in the Middle East. In 1948 and 1949, sections of the U.S. Congress—notably the Jewish lobby—were alarmed at British sales of arms to Egypt. Britain was honoring commitments to Egypt made under the Anglo–Egyptian Treaty of 1936 and in response to the first **Arab–Israeli War**, during which Israeli forces shot down five Royal Air Force planes. In order to avoid an arms race in the Middle East, the U.S. State Department developed a plan under which Britain, France, and the United States acknowledged that Israel and the Arab states required a certain level of arms for self-defense purposes. All requests for arms would be considered under the principle of the Tripartite Declaration as it became known.

TROLLOPE, FRANCES (1780–1863). Frances Trollope was a British writer and mother of British author Anthony Trollope. She became an unpopular figure in the United States after she commented critically on Americans and their way of life. In 1827, she had gone to live in America to improve the family's fortunes but proved unsuccessful in her attempt to do so as the department store she set up in Cincinnati failed. She returned to England after almost four years and published a chronological account of her travels entitled *Domestic Manners of the Americans* (1832). In the book, Trollope portrayed Americans in a poor light, condemning their hypocrisy in rejoicing in liberty but maintaining a slave system and abusing the native population. She also condemned the lack of social classes, the evangelical revivals of the time, and the crude manners of Americans. Her views caused outrage in elite circles on both sides of the Atlantic but the book became a best seller.

TRUMAN DOCTRINE (1947). On 21 February 1947, the British Foreign Office sent a note to Washington giving notice to the administration of **Harry S. Truman** that it could no longer afford to provide British aid to **Greece** and Turkey and would end it on 31 March 1947. The importance of preventing **Soviet** influence in these countries was also stressed and a request was made that the United States take over supporting the anticommunist forces there. The timing of this decision came as a surprise to the U.S. State Department but it was understood that, in the aftermath of **World War II**, the government of **Clement Attlee** was faced with massive reconstruction costs and an ailing economy. On 12 March 1947, President Truman addressed Congress to persuade its members to appropriate funds to take over from the British in Greece. The wording of his speech indicated that this decision was far more significant as it announced to the world that the United States would fight the battle to contain communism around the globe. Congress agreed to provide $400 million in immediate aid to Turkey and Greece. *See also* COLD WAR.

TRUMAN, HARRY S. (1894–1972). On 12 April 1945, Vice President Harry S. Truman was thrust into highest office on the sudden death of **Franklin D. Roosevelt**. In 1948, he was elected president in his own right and stayed in office until early 1953. Coming to power as the war in Europe was coming to end, Truman inherited a close but increasingly difficult Anglo–American relationship as Roosevelt had begun to distance himself from **Winston Churchill** as he prepared for the postwar world. The British prime minister was pleased that Truman did not implement all of Roosevelt's plans, noticeably his anticolonialist ones, choosing not to follow FDR's trusteeship scheme. Before losing the general election in May 1945, Churchill had begun to warn Truman about the dangers posed by the **Soviet Union**. By the time of the **Potsdam Conference**, the president was more inclined to agree with his assessment. President Truman was not entirely sympathetic to the British and on some issues was much more hard line than this predecessor. He presided over the abrupt ending of **Lend-Lease** and did not prevent Congress from passing the **McMahon Act**, which effectively ended Anglo–American nuclear cooperation. As the **Cold War** developed, Britain put pressure on Truman not to return the United States to its prewar position of isolation. Although the United States had committed itself to the **United Nations** in 1945 and supported European reconstruction through the **Marshall Plan** in 1947, the government of **Clement Atlee** believed it was essential to European security to guarantee U.S. military support in the form of a collective alliance. In the aftermath of the **Berlin blockade**, the United States agreed to abandon isolationism by joining the **North Atlantic Treaty Organization** (NATO).

Truman's views on **Palestine** led to some disagreement with the Attlee government in the years leading up to the end of the British mandate in 1948, as the president made clear his sympathies lay with the

Jews. Truman came to value Anglo–American cooperation during the **Korean War**. *See also* TRUMAN DOCTRINE; WORLD WAR II.

TWAIN, MARK (1835–1910). Famous around the world, American author and humorist Mark Twain (real name Samuel Langhorne Clemens) was important in encouraging the rapprochement in Anglo–American relations that emerged at the end of the 19th century. Famous on both sides of the Atlantic for novels such *Tom Sawyer* (1876) and *The Adventures of Huckleberry Finn* (1884), he visited England on three separate occasions, first in 1872, then between 1873 and 1874, and finally in 1899. In 1872, he arrived in England determined to gain British copyright for his travel book *Roughing It* (1872) and to gather material for a satire on the English. His positive impressions of the English—acknowledging his enjoyment of English company and English dining to his wife and expressing the view that he would rather live in England than America—meant that the satire was never written, although he did base his novel *A Connecticut Yankee in King Arthur's Court* (1889) in England. When Twain visited Great Britain in 1899 he was fêted as a great author and was proud to acknowledge British support for the United States during the **Spanish–American War**. However, Twain became critical of the U.S. occupation of the Philippines that followed the war; he became an anti-imperialist campaigner and the vice president of the American Anti-Imperialist League between 1901 and 1910, and criticized British imperialist activity in Africa. In December 1900, he met a young **Winston Churchill** at the Waldorf-Astoria in New York and exchanged views on the recent **Anglo–Boer War**. In 1907, Twain received an honorary doctorate from Oxford University.

– U –

UK–USA MUTUAL DEFENSE AGREEMENT (1958). On 3 July 1958, after Great Britain had exploded its first hydrogen bomb, the United Kingdom and United States signed a secret bilateral treaty in Washington allowing for nuclear cooperation and the sharing of classified nuclear information with the aim of improving each party's "atomic weapon design, development, and fabrication capability."

Under the 1958 Agreement for Cooperation on the Uses of Atomic Energy for Mutual Defense Purposes, the United States and United Kingdom have shared nuclear technology and transferred materials and missiles between one another. Under the agreement, military personnel have been stationed and visited research laboratories on both sides of the Atlantic. The agreement has been regarded as a cornerstone of the "**special relationship**," as it has allowed Britain to maintain its nuclear status, and despite criticism about its legality (in the light of the 1968 **Nuclear Nonproliferation Treaty**) remains in place, although it was amended in June 2004 without debate in the British Parliament. It is currently under scrutiny in Britain due to the need to replace the **Trident missile**. *See also* ATOMIC BOMB.

UKUSA AGREEMENT. In 1947 or 1948, a secret agreement was made that tied together the signals intelligence organizations of Australia, **Canada**, Great Britain, New Zealand, and the United States. Although this agreement remains classified, it is argued that unlike the earlier **BRUSA Agreement** (1943), the commitment to share signals intelligence contained within it is not a reciprocal one. Great Britain, along with the other Commonwealth parties to the agreement, is committed to providing the United States with intelligence; the United States is not under a similar obligation. It is alleged that the English-speaking members of the UKUSA intelligence community—the National Security Agency (NSA) in the United States and the Government Communications Headquarters (GCHQ) in the United Kingdom—are assigned particular parts of the globe to monitor. In addition to intelligence sharing, the agreement also provides for the sharing of personnel, cooperation on code words, and the development of compatible intelligence systems.

UNITED NATIONS. During **World War II**, the Allied leaders— **Franklin D. Roosevelt**, **Winston Churchill**, and Joseph Stalin— acknowledged that after the conflict was over the world would need a more effective international organization to replace the discredited **League of Nations**. Prior to U.S. entry into the war, President Roosevelt had begun to plan for the postwar world, most notably with the **Atlantic Charter** of 1941. The term "United Nations" was used by Roosevelt to describe the Allied countries fighting the Axis powers

(Japan, Germany, and Italy) and appeared in the United Nations Declaration, which was signed on 1 January 1942 by 26 nations. The United States continued to take the lead in establishing the aims, structure, and organization of the United Nations (UN), although discussions with its other wartime allies—Britain, **China**, and the **Soviet Union**—ultimately shaped its final form. Major progress was made at the **Dumbarton Oaks Conference** in 1944 and at the **Yalta Conference** in February 1945 when it was agreed that the UN would be dominated by the five major allied powers, which would become permanent members of the Security Council: China, France, Great Britain, the Soviet Union, and the United States.

Prime Minister Churchill had serious concerns about President Roosevelt's views on colonialism and refused any suggestion that a special conference be convened to discuss territorial trusteeship and dependent areas. Roosevelt's successor, President **Harry S. Truman**, did not pursue the issue and the final UN Charter, which was agreed at the **San Francisco Conference** on 26 June 1945, did not address independence from colonial rule. The United Nations officially came into existence on 24 October 1945, when the charter had been ratified by the major powers and a majority of the signatories.

In the years since then, Britain and America have had varying degrees of commitment to the principles of the UN. In general, although the United States had consistently been the leading financial contributor to the UN (although reneging on its payments for many years), it has often been wary of multilateral action as a solution to international problems. Britain, on the other hand, has been more devoted to working through the UN where possible. The two nations have, however, often worked together within the UN but not always. One of the first major issues at the UN followed an Anglo–American Committee of Inquiry into the problem of Jewish immigration and settlement in the aftermath of World War II. Washington and London disagreed on the issue and on 2 April 1947 Britain referred the ethnic and political differences over **Palestine** to the UN. Britain and America continued to take separate positions on Palestine and when the UN General Assembly voted on a resolution recommending the partition of Palestine into the Jewish state of Israel and Arab Palestine, the United States voted for it while London abstained, making it clear that it was unwilling to police a partitioned Palestine and would withdraw its forces when its mandate ended in May 1948. Two years later, in June 1950, Britain and America worked together closely when the UN faced its most serious test since its formation, when North Korea invaded South Korea. On the day of the attack, the UN Security Council voted unanimously to condemn the invasion and called for an immediate cessation of hostilities. When this did not happen, the Security Council authorized military action, under its flag, to repel North Korean forces. While the **Korean War** proved the UN could provide a legal pretext for collective armed action, the dominant foreign policy issue of the 1960s—the **Vietnam War**—was much more contentious in the UN and, as it was largely viewed as a civil war, this was not the key forum for debate on the issue. Washington did appreciate British diplomacy at the UN during the 1960s, notably during the **Arab–Israeli War of 1967**, when its representative, Lord Caradon, was able to steer Resolution 242 through the UN on 22 November 1967 that called for "the withdrawal of Israel's armed forces from territories occupied in the recent conflict." Washington had earlier put forward a draft resolution that Britain did not support, as Britain felt the Arabs would see it as pro-Israeli and consequently found a choice of words that proved acceptable to all parties. This level of cooperation at the UN was not repeated during the **Arab–Israeli War of 1973**, when Britain refused to back a proposed American resolution calling for a cease-fire and a withdrawal by Arab forces from territory they had held previously. During the Persian Gulf crisis of 1990, Britain and America again worked together in the UN to ensure international action to dispel Iraqi forces from Kuwait. On the day of the invasion, 2 August 1990, the UN Security Council condemned Iraqi action and demanded an immediate withdrawal (Resolution 660). On 6 August 1990, Britain and America supported UN Resolution 661 on implementing **trade** sanctions against **Iraq** and Kuwait. Thatcher and Bush disagreed over the necessity of seeking additional resolutions to enforce Iraqi withdrawal from Kuwait. On this occasion, Britain was not convinced that a specific resolution was required to take action, arguing that Kuwait could organize a military response to its invasion under the self-defense principle of Article 51 of the UN Charter. Nevertheless, Britain supported Resolution 678 on 29 November 1990 authorizing member states to take "all necessary means" to implement Resolution 660. Anglo–American cooperation in the UN proved crucial in the lead-up to the **Iraq War**. The British ambassador at the UN, **Jeremy Greenstock**, worked with the U.S. ambassador to the UN, John D. Negroponte, to draft Resolution 1441 after intense negotiations with France and Russia. The resolution, which was passed unanimously by the UN Security Council, demanded that weapons inspectors be readmitted into Iraq and compliance with previous resolutions on weapons of mass destruction (WMDs). As this resolution did not contain a "a trigger for war" should Iraq not cooperate (referring instead to "serious consequences"), the British, along with other members of the Security Council, felt a second resolution explicitly authorizing the use of force against Iraq was necessary. Although the United States was less convinced of the need for such a resolution, it worked with London to try to secure its passage. Only when it became clear that the proposed resolution would not gain the required votes in the Security Council did Britain and American withdraw it, instead opting for a coalition force organized by the United States. *See also* GULF WAR.

– V –

VANCE, CYRUS. (1917–). Having worked together previously on **Rhodesia**, beginning in August 1992 former U.S. secretary of state Cyrus Vance and former British foreign secretary **Lord Owen** collaborated over a peace initiative on **Bosnia**. It was hoped that Vance's experience and reputation might engender greater U.S. interest in events in the Balkans. The resulting Vance–Owen plan did not receive the response in Washington that was hoped for, largely due to the forthcoming presidential election. Vance and Owen continued in their attempts to negotiate peace in Bosnia in 1993.

VENEZUELAN BOUNDARY CRISIS (1895–1896). In 1895, a 50-year boundary dispute between the colony of British Guiana and Venezuela erupted into a diplomatic crisis that threatened to deteriorate into war between Great Britain and the United States. The boundary in question lay in dense jungle and only became of importance with the discovery of gold and other mineral deposits in the late 1850s and the subsequent movement of British settlers into the area.

After many failed attempts to negotiate the boundary and having broken diplomatic relations with the British in 1887, the Venezuelan government in Caracas asked Washington to intervene, using an American lobbyist, William L. Scruggs, to make its case. Scruggs tapped into American fears that the British had imperial ambitions in Latin America. In 1895, the administration of **Grover Cleveland** agreed to get involved, asking the British to submit the boundary dispute to arbitration. Initially, the British ignored the U.S. request, believing it was none of their business. This prompted the United States to invoke the **Monroe Doctrine** more aggressively in a note from Secretary of State Richard Olney. Olney asserted American hegemony over the Western hemisphere and its right to intervene in the Venezuelan affair. When the premise of Olney's note was again rebuffed by British Prime Minister Lord Salisbury, the Cleveland administration sent a message to Congress on 17 December 1895 denouncing the British refusal to accept arbitration and making it clear that the United States would "resist by any means within its power" Britain's seizure of Venezuelan territory. The president's firm stance was applauded by the American press and public. Within weeks Lord Salisbury had agreed to international arbitration to settle the boundary dispute, partly because Britain was becoming more concerned about serious threats to its empire coming from France and Germany and the emergent crisis with the Boers in Africa. By November 1896, the crisis was over when an international commission agreed with most of Britain's claims. The Venezuelan crisis was a significant turning point in Anglo–American relations, as Britain was forced to acknowledge American power in the Western hemisphere. *See* ANGLO–BOER WAR.

VERSAILLES, TREATY OF (1783). Signed on 3 September 1783, the Treaty of Versailles (also known as the Treaty of Paris) ended the **War of Independence** (1775–1783). Great Britain acknowledged the independence of the United States (the 13 colonies were recognized as free and sovereign states) and fixed the boundaries of the United States up to the Great Lakes in the north and the Mississippi in the south. The treaty was considered favorable to the United States and a major achievement for the American negotiators, John Adams, Benjamin Franklin, and John Jay. The British, represented by David

Harley, secured access to the Mississippi River and the treaty recommended that the states return confiscated Loyalist property. The treaty was ratified by the American Continental Congress on 14 January 1784 and by the British Parliament on 9 April 1784.

VERSAILLES, TREATY OF (1919). Signed on 28 June 1919, the Treaty of Versailles was the peace settlement after the end of **World War I**. The **Paris Peace Conference** opened on 18 January 1919 with all the major powers in attendance. Signing the treaty under protest, Germany was forced to acknowledge its war guilt and agree to pay reparations, its colonies were placed under **League of Nation** mandates, and severe limitations were placed on the size of the German army and navy. There were also several provisions that dealt with territories, including the return of Alsace–Lorraine to the French. The treaty also contained the covenant of the League of Nations, which President **Woodrow Wilson** had pushed for and Prime Minister **David Lloyd-George** had supported. The U.S. Congress refused to ratify the Versailles Treaty.

VIETNAM WAR. From 1954 onward, Great Britain and the United States were at odds over Vietnam. At the end of **World War II**, British troops had helped to retake Indochina for the French and with American **trade** and colonial interests in the region, continued to take an active interest in events there. Prime Minister **Winston Churchill** refused President **Dwight D. Eisenhower**'s proposal to provide joint Anglo–American military support for the beleaguered French at Dien Bien Phu in 1954. Seeking allied participation in the war, the administration of **John F. Kennedy** approached Great Britain but was only provided with diplomatic support and a small police advisory mission, headed by **Sir Robert Thompson**. As U.S. involvement increased, Britain came under increasing pressure to consider a troop involvement. During his first summit meeting with President **Lyndon Johnson** at the White House in December 1964, Prime Minister **Harold Wilson** refused a request to provide a token British troop deployment to Vietnam, on the grounds that Britain was already overstretched militarily (having over 50,000 troops in **Malaysia**) and, as cochair of the 1954 **Geneva Conference**, wanted to remain as impartial as possible in order to help broker peace. Additionally, as a

Labour prime minister, Wilson was aware of the unpopularity of the U.S. war in Vietnam within the country and his own party. Wilson backed the Americans in public, although dissociating Britain from the U.S. bombing of Hanoi and Haiphong on 28 June 1966. In private, British diplomats and members of the Wilson government had serious doubts that the United States could win the war and found U.S. military tactics immoral, particularly the use of gas and napalm. Wilson made several attempts to negotiate peace in Vietnam.

– W –

WANAMAKER, SAM (1919–1993). In the era of McCarthyism many Americans became political emigrants and left the United States. The movie industry saw actors, directors, and producers leave the country. Sam Wanamaker decided to remain in England in 1952, where he was filming *Mr. Denning Moves North*, when he heard he had been blacklisted by the House Un-American Activities Committee (HUAC) because of his left-wing beliefs. Born in Chicago, Wanamaker became an actor, director, and producer after serving in the U.S. Army during **World War II**, working in theater and film. Settling in England and continuing a successful career in film and theater, he was the visionary force behind the New Globe Theatre, raising millions of dollars to build an exact replica of William Shakespeare's Globe Theatre. Wanamaker died in 1993, four years before the official opening of the New Globe.

WAR BRIDES. One of the unintended consequences of American entry into **World War II** was the GI war bride. By June 1944, there were 1,650,000 American servicemen stationed in the United Kingdom. In Britain, because of the higher pay, access to consumer goods, and their sexual encounters with British women, the GIs were accused of being "overpaid, oversexed, and over here." Although the U.S. government was unconcerned at their troops' sexual liaisons with the locals, they were worried that serious relationships might distract the GIs and even affect their willingness to fight. In 1942, the American War Department issued a circular preventing military personnel overseas from marrying without the approval of their commanding officer and requiring at least two months' notice. Moreover, GI wives did not have an automatic right to become American citizens. Despite these provisions, in the final year of the war, as the **D-Day landings** approached and German defeat seemed to be increasingly likely, the number of GI marriages in Britain increased noticeably.

At the end of war the British and American authorities discussed how to deal with the GI brides. The British Foreign Office felt that the matter was an American one and in December 1945 Congress passed the War Brides Act, allowing the spouses and children of U.S. citizens serving in World War II to enter the United States without undergoing many of the usual immigration procedures. Consequently, the first "war bride ship," SS *Argentina*, left Southampton on 26 January 1946 and arrived in New York on 4 February carrying 452 war brides, 173 children, and one war groom. It was followed by several others over the next five months, bringing approximately 70,000 British war brides, most of them young women, to join their husbands in America. Many of the war brides experienced difficulties in settling into their new home country and a significant percentage ended in divorce, but most endured and proved another Anglo–American link.

WAR OF 1812 (1812–1815). The War of 1812 was a by-product of the **Napoleonic Wars** and was fought between the United States and Great Britain beginning on 18 June 1812 with a U.S. declaration of war and ending in February 1815, although a peace treaty (the Treaty of Ghent) was signed in late 1814. The United States went to war over Britain's repeated violation of its sovereignty (including the seizure of U.S. ships on the high seas and the impressment of American sailors) and a desire to drive the British out of **Canada** and thus expand its own territory. U.S. troops expected to march into Canada while Britain was preoccupied fighting Napoleon in Europe. Instead, the war resulted in a military stalemate and, despite a numerical superiority, American troops failed to drive the British out of Canada, partly as a result of Native Americans fighting on Britain's side. The war is remembered partly because British troops reached Washington, D.C., and set fire to the **White House**.

WAR OF INDEPENDENCE (1775–1783). The American War of Independence resulted in the separation of the 13 British colonies from the mother country, Great Britain, and the formation of the United States of America. The origins of the war lay in the grievances held by the American colonists over the way in which they were governed. There were, however, a number of events that triggered war between the colonists and British that came under the rule of **George III**. Following the costly French and Indian wars, Prime Minister **George Grenville** attempted to help repay the British national debt by enforcing the **Navigation Acts** and introducing the **Sugar Act** in 1764 and the **Stamp Act** in 1765. Although used to the British Parliament regulating **trade**, colonists in America distinguished between that and attempts to raise revenue through the Grenville Act, and protests emerged based on cries of "no taxation without representation." Moreover, the implementation of direct taxation on the colonists threatened their sense of self-governance. The faraway Parliament in Britain was faced with growing rebellion by colonists, noticeably by merchants, who began to institute nonimportation bans on British goods. The Stamp Act was repealed but the British Parliament introduced external taxation through the **Townshend Acts** in 1767, only to find these also enraged the colonists and was forced to repeal these in 1770, except for the duty on tea.

Opposition to British rule grew as Committees of Correspondence were established throughout the colonies to coordinate action against the British, with information largely exchanged through letters. Resentment against the stationing of British troops in the American colonies was fueled by the **Boston Massacre** of 1770 and the continuing anger against British taxes resulted in the **Boston Tea Party** of 1773. Despite harsh action in the form of the **Coercive Acts** of 1774, the British government found that the American colonists were increasingly inspired toward revolution by the works of **Thomas Paine**.

War between Britain and America broke out in 1775 when fighting between them began at the **battles of Lexington Green** and **Concord** in April 1775. On 10 May 1775, the Second Continental Congress convened in Philadelphia and on 15 June **George Washington** was named commander in chief of the Continental Army. George III refused to acknowledge the colonies were in revolt until August 1775. On 4 July 1776, the **Declaration of Independence** was adopted and was signed four days later. The war became an international war in 1778 when France signed the Treaty of Alliance with the United States and in the following year Spain joined France as an ally. The involvement of France and Spain, along with the Dutch by 1781, ensured British defeat. British forces surrendered at **Yorktown** on 19 October 1781 and the British prime minister, **Lord North**, resigned on 20 March 1782. The War of Independence ended with the **Treaty of Versailles** signed on 3 September 1783 when Great Britain recognized American independence. On 17 September 1787, the U.S. Constitution was ratified.

WASHINGTON, GEORGE (1732–1799). George Washington was one of the Founding Fathers of the United States and became its first president in 1789, serving in that capacity until 1797. An English American (tracing his ancestors to Washington in the northeast of England), George Washington had a distinguished military record, including fighting for king and country during the Seven Years' War, and had been commander in chief of Virginian forces before resigning and becoming a member of the plantation elite and a local politician. During his time as a member of the Virginia colonial assembly and as a justice, Washington became an advocate of the patriot cause and supported the nonimportation of British goods. Washington was sent as a delegate from Virginia to the First Continental Congress; on 15 June 1775 at the Second Continental Congress in Philadelphia he was appointed general and commander in chief of the new Continental Army. Despite struggling with poorly trained troops and inadequate supplies, Washington managed to secure important victories over the British, most notably at **Saratoga** and **Yorktown** in 1781. Despite his republican ideology and his role in the **War of Independence**, Washington remained well respected in Britain and, as president, Washington presided over attempts to improve relations with the British, including sending John Jay to England in 1795 to negotiate over British interference with American ships and trade. The resulting **Jay Treaty** was successful in preventing a further war but was criticized for not securing neutrality for American shipping.

WASHINGTON NAVAL CONFERENCE (1921–1922). In response to fears of an expensive naval arms race and the role this might play in encouraging a second world war, representatives from Great Britain, France, Japan, Italy, and the United States met in Washington, D.C., to discuss limiting the size of each country's navy. Leading the American delegation was Secretary of State Charles Evans who proposed massive naval cuts, including a 10-year moratorium on the building of warships over 10,000 tons and the scrapping of commissioned ships, in order to leave the principal powers (the United States, Britain, and Japan) at a ratio of 5–5–3. British Foreign Secretary **Arthur Balfour**'s main consideration at the conference was whether to accept naval parity in terms of tonnage with the United States. Ultimately the British recognized that a naval arms race would be crippling economically and that they would lose the race to the United States. Consequently the Washington Naval Treaty was signed on 6 February 1922.

WASHINGTON, TREATY OF (1871). In the aftermath of the **American Civil War**, the United States and Great Britain had two outstanding matters to deal with in order to improve relations between the two and avoid war: the *Alabama* claims and **Canada**. The United States harbored grievances against the British as they had appeared to favor the South during the Civil War by building warships, including the *Alabama*, which were allowed to leave British ports and were used by Confederate forces to destroy Northern merchant ships. Canada felt a similar resentment toward the United States due to the activities of the **Fenian Brotherhood** following the Civil War. The Fenians, largely composed of Irish American veterans of the 1848 uprising in Ireland, launched armed raids into Canada between 1866 and 1871 in the hope of encouraging the British government to grant independence to Ireland. The raids were unsuccessful but because successive American administrations had turned a blind eye to Fenian activity, Canada claimed compensation should be paid by the United States for the damage they caused. Under the **Treaty of Washington** signed in Washington, D.C., on 8 May 1871, the British government expressed regret and agreed to arbitration in Geneva, Switzerland, to settle the so-called *Alabama* claims. The following year Britain paid the U.S. $15.5 million in compensation for the *Alabama* depredations. The treaty also dealt with cross-border issues between the United States and the newly formed dominion of

Canada. Although the prime minister of Canada, Sir John Macdonald, was one of five British commissioners during the discussions in Washington, the administration of Ulysses S. Grant refused to have the Fenian raids on the agenda. An agreement was reached, however, that allowed the United States access to Canadian fisheries for 12 years, and the United States was permitted to navigate the St. Lawrence in exchange for Canadian access to Lake Michigan. *See also* BRITISH NORTH AMERICA ACT.

WEBSTER–ASHBURTON TREATY (1842). Treaty signed on 9 August 1842 between the United States, represented by Secretary of State Daniel Webster, and Great Britain, represented by Baron Ashburton. The treaty resolved the Northeast boundary dispute (Maine and New Brunswick) over the location of the border between the United States and **Canada** that had led to the **Aroostock War**. Other clauses in the treaty provided for the extradition of criminals and cooperation in ending the slave **trade** from Africa.

WEINBERGER, CASPAR (1917–2006). American secretary of defense between 1981 and 1987, Casper Weinberger was a staunch **Anglophile**. A lifelong admirer of **Winston Churchill**, Weinberger citied him as a significant influence from the time he entered the U.S. Army as a private in 1941. As secretary of defense he arranged for Great Britain to obtain the **Trident** II (D-5) missile system on very good terms. He, along with President **Ronald Reagan**, believed it important that Britain retain its independent nuclear deterrent, and the missile deal signaled the continuance of the Anglo–American nuclear partnership. During the **Falklands War** of 1982, Weinberger immediately sided with the British. After the United States abandoned its public neutrality, Weinberger provided the British forces with weapons, most notably over 200 Sidewinder air-to-air missiles, 12 million gallons of aircraft fuel, military equipment, and the redirection of U.S. spy satellites to provide crucial intelligence. He also offered to send an American aircraft carrier, USS *Eisenhower*, if needed. Weinberger's unequivocal and instant support for the British during the Falklands War was not forgotten. In 1988, Caspar Weinberger was given an honorary knighthood for his assistance to Britain during the Falklands War and, despite having suffered two strokes,

80-year old **Margaret Thatcher** attended his funeral in Washington, D.C. *See also* TRIDENT MISSILE.

WESTERN EUROPEAN UNION (WEU). The Western European Union (WEU) was created after the modification of the 1948 **Brussels Treaty** on 23 October 1954 and signed in Paris. The WEU allowed for the involvement of the Federal Republic of Germany (FRG) and Italy in the collective defense pact that had been formed in 1948. The Paris agreement also granted the FRG full sovereignty with its accession to the WEU and **North Atlantic Treaty Organization.** The United States had proposed since 1950 that Germany be allowed to rearm and, after the failure of the **European Defence Community** (EDC), the Western European nations were able to agree that Germany's involvement in the WEU had appropriate safeguards on rearmament, limiting their maximum defense contribution to 12 divisions. The Paris agreements were welcomed by Washington as a move toward greater Western European unity.

WESTLAND AFFAIR. In 1985, Britain's only helicopter company, Westland, was on the verge of financial collapse. This led to a debate over the company's future and when an American competitor, the multinational United Technologies (the owner of Sikorsky helicopters) bid to buy Westland, a European consortium (France, Italy, and Great Britain) also put forward a bid to challenge it. In 1986, Prime Minister **Margaret Thatcher** showed support for the American company in preference to the European consortium, and the Westland board agreed to accept the Sikorsky offer. The European option had been favored by some within the British cabinet, including Defence Secretary Michael Heseltine, who campaigned publicly for the European consortium and was forced to resign shortly after Thatcher announced the decision. Thatcher's decision further polarized the Europe versus America debate in Britain and showed that the prime minister still favored the Anglo–American relationship.

WHEELER, CHARLES (1923–2008). British journalist and broadcaster, Charles Wheeler became the BBC's longest serving foreign correspondent, and one of its most respected; he was particularly well known in Great Britain for his coverage of American affairs. After much of his early journalistic career was spent covering events in Eastern Europe, he arrived in the United States as the BBC's Washington correspondent in 1965 when he reported on the race riots and the assassination of Martin Luther King Jr., opposition to the **Vietnam War**, and the Watergate scandal. He left Washington in 1973 but maintained an interest in American affairs that led him to produce a documentary series, *Wheeler on America* (1996), in which he surveyed social and political changes in the United States during the post war period.

WHITE HOUSE. Symbol of the American presidency and the U.S. government, building of the White House began in 1792 and was occupied by its first residents, President John Adams and his wife, Abigail Adams, in 1800. It remains the private residence of the president as well as a working public building. In August 1814, the White House survived a fire started by the British during the **War of 1812**. Having insufficient numbers to occupy Washington, D.C., under the instruction of British General Robert Ross, British troops attempted to destroy as much of the city as possible by burning its public buildings. Hoping to achieve a psychological victory by burning the nation's capitol, the British army systematically set fire to the U.S. Treasury Building, the House of Representatives and the Senate (including the Library of Congress), and the White House. President Madison and his cabinet had already fled the capital but the First Lady, Dolly Madison, only left the White House at the last minute, in the process rescuing many valuable artifacts, including a portrait of **George Washington**. It was reported that on entering the White House, the British troops found the dining hall ready for dinner and promptly helped themselves to food and wine before attempting to destroy the building. Contrary to popular belief, the White House did not receive its name after attempts to mask smoke damage, as evidence shows the name had already been used before the War of 1812.

"WHITE MAN'S BURDEN." In response to the U.S. success in the **Spanish–American War**, British imperialist Rudyard Kipling wrote the poem "The White Man's Burden" in 1899. Imperialists on both sides of the Atlantic took the poem as encouragement to colonize and to take on the "burden" of ruling for the benefits of the mother nation and those under paternalistic rule. The poem fit in with the vision of Anglo–Saxon civilization that was prevalent at the turn of the century. *See* ANGLO–SAXONISM.

WHITEFIELD, GEORGE (1714–1770). George Whitefield was an English evangelical preacher and one of the founders of Methodism, who traveled to America in 1738 and began to visit the colonies regularly to deliver sermons to large crowds. Whitefield became a good friend of Benjamin Franklin. In September 1740, he arrived in Newport, Rhode Island, and began what historians have labeled "the first **great awakening**."

WILSON, CHARLES E. (1890–1961). Serving as American secretary of defense between 1953 and 1957, Charles Wilson was heavily involved in implementing President **Dwight D. Eisenhower's New Look defense strategy**. In 1954, he defended the British from criticism after the government of **Winston Churchill** refused to join the United States in a plan to become militarily involved in the war in Indochina. *See also* VIETNAM WAR.

WILSON, HAROLD (1916–1995). Labour Prime Minister Harold Wilson came into 10 **Downing Street** in October 1964 speaking of a "close" rather than "**special relationship**" with the United States. Part of the reason for this redefinition of Anglo–American relations was Wilson's recognition that President Charles de Gaulle of France could veto Britain's application for entry to the **European Economic Community**. Despite placing the Anglo–American alliance at the center of British foreign policy, Wilson's first government (1964–1970) saw a cooling of relations between London and Washington because of three major problems: the **Vietnam War**, the pound sterling, and the withdrawal of British troops from **East of Suez** in 1968. Wilson's working relationship with President **Lyndon Johnson** was tested by his refusal to send British forces to the war in Vietnam. Although agreeing to support the war diplomatically, Wilson argued he could not commit troops to the war in Southeast Asia because Britain was overstretched military, particularly because of its commitment to **Malaysia**. He also recognized that his slim majority in the House of Commons and the unpopularity of the Vietnam War in Britain meant that a troop commitment could lead to the end of the Labour government. Moreover, Wilson believed Britain, as a **Geneva Conference** cochair, would jeopardize its ability to broker peace if it became a belligerent. Wilson engaged in several Vietnam peace initiatives, attempting to play the "honest broker," including a Commonwealth peace initiative in June 1965 and an attempt to establish a phased peace by working with Soviet Premier Alexei Kosygin in February 1967. Although Wilson was unable to establish a warm relationship with Johnson, largely because of Vietnam, he was able to gain U.S. support in a number of key areas, notably support for the struggling pound sterling and a willingness to consider an **Atlantic Nuclear Force** (ANF) rather than a **multilateral force** (MLF). Recognizing Britain's economic difficulties, and much to the Johnson administration's disappointment, Wilson was forced to announce on 16 January 1968 the withdrawal of British troop from East of Suez and acknowledge that Britain could no longer afford a worldwide military presence.

When **Richard Nixon** became president in January 1969, Wilson and his government had concerns that U.S. foreign policy might favor France over Britain. Wilson was pleased to find that he was able to get on well with the new president and was able to discuss his recent talks with Russian Prime Minister Alexei Kosygin. However, by 1974 with the Watergate scandal at its height, Wilson determined to keep his distance from Nixon and in private asked the Foreign Office to put Nixon off visiting London in July 1974. Wilson was reelected prime minister in 1974 and resigned the office two years later on health grounds.

WILSON, WOODROW (1856–1924). Noted for his independent and moral approach to foreign affairs, Woodrow Wilson was the Democratic U.S. president from 1912 to 1920. Having kept the United States out of **World War I** since 1914, even after the sinking of the *Lusitania*, Wilson took the United States to war in April 1917 on the basis that U.S. naval vessels had been attacked by Germany but also on moral grounds: that the United States must make the world "safe for democracy" and the Great War must be a "war to end all war." A liberal internationalist, Wilson did not agree with Britain's war aims—which he suspected included expanding the British Empire— and did not join the Allies, instead keeping the United States as an associate power. Wilson disagreed with British Prime Minister **David Lloyd-George** on military strategy during the conflict and on the nature of the peace that should follow it. Prior to the war's end, Wilson announced his **Fourteen Points** that should secure a lasting peace, including provisions for open diplomacy, free **trade**, national self-determination, and an international security organization, the **League of Nations**, to prevent future wars. Wilson was devastated by the reception of the Fourteen Points received at the **Paris Peace Conference** in 1919, when Lloyd-George and French leader Georges Clemenceau outmaneuvered him in the peace negotiations. The **Versailles Treaty**, signed on 28 June 1919, bore little resemblance to Wilson's peace plan, apart from a commitment to the League of Nations. Instead, it assigned war guilt to Germany and extracted a commitment by Germany to pay heavy war reparation. Wilson's disillusionment with the peace treaty was compounded by the U.S. Senate's refusal to ratify U.S. entry into the League of Nations. A regular visitor to Great Britain, Wilson enjoyed cycling holidays in the Lake District.

WINFIELD HOUSE. Winfield House in Regent's Park, London, is the official residence of the U.S. ambassador to the Court of St. James. Set in 12 acres, Winfield House is a stately mansion that is close to the center of London and has been owned by the U.S. government since 1955. The home of American ambassadors in London has often been the site of diplomatic transactions and discussions, often involving visiting U.S. presidents.

WINTHROP, JOHN (1588–1649). Born in Groton, Suffolk, in England, John Winthrop was a **Puritan** lawyer, persecuted for his religious beliefs, who led a migration on the ship *Arbella* in 1630. In London, Winthrop had been elected the first governor of the Massachusetts Bay Colony and embarked on the journey with the company charter in hand. The fleet of 11 ships—containing approximately 350 colonists—led by the *Arbella*, arrived in Salem, Massachusetts, in June 1630 and the migrants later settled in Boston. Winthrop is most famous for a sermon he wrote onboard the *Arbella*. In "A Model of Christian Charity," Winthrop called for the new community to be a model of Protestant Christianity, "as a city upon a hill" and acknowledged that "the eyes of all people are upon us."

WOOLWORTHS. In 1879, Frank W. Woolworth established his first five-and-dime discount store in the United States. Becoming a major retail chain by the early 20th century, the main features of Woolworths stores were the fixed prices and off-the-shelf availability of a range of goods from food to toys. Woolworths opened its first British store on 5 November 1909 in Liverpool, with an upper price limit of six pence. "Woolies," as the store became known, was one of the first American chain stores to be successful in Great Britain, opening hundreds of stores and becoming a feature of most city high streets and shopping centers.

WORLD WAR I (1914–1918). When war broke out in Europe in July 1914 after Austria–Hungary declared war on Serbia, triggering the alliance system that led Great Britain to declare war against Germany on 4 August, the United States proclaimed its neutrality. The Triple Alliance (Central powers) of Germany, Austria–Hungary, and Italy faced the Triple Entente (Allied powers) of Britain, France, and Russia. For almost three years the administration of Woodrow Wilson kept the United States out of the war despite pressure from Britain to get involved. Over that period, however, several factors impeded strict neutrality on America's part. Not only did ethnic groups in the United States take sides, but Anglo–American rapprochement at the turn of the century also meant that key members of the Wilson administration—including the president, his adviser **Edward House**, his secretary of state Robert Lansing, and U.S. Ambassador to Britain **Walter Hines Page**—were anti-German in sentiment and consequently veered toward supporting the Allied nations. Despite feeling moral outrage at British trench warfare and being critical of all empires, the president was well aware of the economic ties the United States had with Britain and felt that his own internationalist principles of democracy, self-determination, and free **trade** stood more chance of acceptance if the British and Allied nations were not defeated. By 1915, American neutrality favored the Allies, not least because, although the United States continued to trade with all belligerent nations, Britain benefited the most from this due to its dominance on the high seas. Britain was also tied to the United States financially, as the country began to receive American loans in October 1915 from the House of Morgan and by the end of the war had borrowed $3.7 billion.

Determined not to enter the war, Wilson attempted to mediate the war and on 22 February 1916 the House–Grey memorandum was presented to the British government of Prime Minister Herbert Asquith. It argued that in the president's opinion it was time to hold a conference to put an end to the war and suggested that the United States would probably enter the war against Germany should the Allies agree to the proposal but Germany refused. Troubled by the inclusion of the word "probably" and feeling more could be gained by a military victory, the British did not respond.

Although the United States argued that its neutrality ensured the freedom of seas, this was not accepted by either Germany or Britain, as both wished to strangle the other's economy. U.S. vessels were soon subjected to search and seizure of war goods. Germany's decision to use U-boat submarine warfare against enemy and neutral ships (British merchant vessels flew neutral flags) resulted in the attack on the British liner *Lusitania* in May 1915, which killed 124 Americans, and a later attack in March 1916 on a French steamer, the *Sussex*, killing 4 Americans and injuring 21 others. Both of these international incidents increased anti-German opinion in the United States but President Wilson took action to ensure German agreement not to attack merchant vessels without warning. At the same, Britain's brutal crushing of the Easter Rising in **Ireland** damaged its moral reputation in the United States and Anglo–American relations soured still further when the impact of Britain's blockade of Germany began to damage American commercial interests, not least because Britain began blacklisting companies suspected of trading with Germany.

With the danger of the United States drifting into war with Britain, Wilson became more determined to find peace and pledged to treat all belligerents equally. This led to a Federal Reserve Board warning to American banks of the danger of trading in short-term bonds from belligerent nations. Great Britain's increasing dependence on American loans to help finance the war, including the selling of British Treasury bonds, meant that the British felt they were cornered into accepting American mediation to end the war. On 18 December 1916, Wilson sent identical notes to the warring nations asking them to state their peace terms fully and clearly in order to find common ground. Britain did not appreciate being treated in the same manner as the

Germans and did not take Wilson's note, or his proposals for a new world order that included plans for a **League of Nations**, seriously and did not respond.

Fortunately for Britain, whose financial situation became even more perilous, the discovery of the **Zimmerman telegram** in January 1917 and Germany's launching of unrestricted submarine warfare in early February 1917 led Washington to break off diplomatic relations with the country. At Wilson's request, the U.S. Congress declared war on the German empire on 6 April 1917, joining the Allied nations as an "associate power" rather than signing a treaty of alliance. This meant that the United States was willing to cooperate with Britain but would retain the right to sign a peace treaty on its own terms. This decision reflected Wilson's internationalist principles and his understanding that the United States had differing aims from the Allies, based largely on making the world "safe for democracy" and reforming world politics rather than securing an empire.

As far as the British were concerned, American forces were slow to mobilize for war. Between April and December 1917, only 175,000 troops had reached Britain. The American "doughboys" as they became known, stopped briefly in Britain, before traveling to France. U.S. military involvement in **World War I** contributed greatly to the Allied victory, which was reached when Germany agreed to an armistice on 11 November 1918. The influx of American men and materiél tipped the balance, not least because they boosted the morale of the Allies. During the fight at sea, Britain and the United States cooperated closely with a joint command under the control of a British admiral. There was less cohesion on land as the commander of the American Expeditionary Force (AEF), General **John J. Pershing**, determined he would not split U.S. units to be sent to the front line. By the time the final German offensive began in July 1918, there were 1.2 million American troops in France but few saw action until they launched the St. Mihiel offensive of 12 September and took the lead role in Meuse–Argonne campaign that started on 26 September.

America's involvement in World War I marked the growing importance of the United States in world affairs, particularly in relation to Great Britain. Notably, the United States became a creditor nation for the first time. Moreover, Wilson had negotiated the armistice with

Germany and was determined to play a leading role in the subsequent peace talks. *See also* VERSAILLES, TREATY OF (1919).

WORLD WAR II (1939–1945). World War II witnessed the flowering of the so-called **special relationship** between Great Britain and the United States. Britain declared war on Germany on 3 September 1939 after Hitler ignored an ultimatum to withdraw its troops from Poland. The administration of Franklin D. Roosevelt had watched as British and French attempts at **appeasement** had failed to check the territorial ambitions of Nazi Germany. Early in 1938, responding to the suggestion of Undersecretary of State Sumner Welles, President Roosevelt forwarded to Prime Minister **Neville Chamberlain** a proposal for a U.S. organized peace conference. Chamberlain preferred direct negotiations with Hitler and Benito Mussolini and did not respond positively enough or quickly enough for Roosevelt to develop the plan. Reflecting a desire not to be dragged into another war, an isolationist Congress passed a series of **Neutrality Acts** in 1935, 1936, and 1937. The acts prohibited the shipments of arms to belligerents, forbade loans to belligerents, and introduced the principle of **Cash and Carry** on purchase and shipment of all nonmilitary goods.

When war broke out, the United States declared its official neutrality though another Neutrality Act passed on 4 November 1939, although President Roosevelt acknowledged in a fireside chat the impossibility of being neutral in thought. Opinion polls indicated that the public favored the Allies and agreed that the United States should aid Britain and France but still felt the president should keep the country out of war. This isolationist sentiment began to change when the "Phoney War" between Britain and Germany turned to actual fighting when Hitler invaded Finland, Belgium, and the Netherlands between March and May 1940. Roosevelt was pressured by the new British Prime Minister **Winston Churchill** to aid the Allies, and the president began to argue that the best way to keep the United States out of the war was to become the "arsenal of democracy" and enable Britain to win by providing it with sufficient aid and weaponry. Roosevelt agreed to the **destroyers-for-bases** deal in August 1940 and in March 1941 Congress approved the **Lend-Lease** Act that allowed the United States to lend weapons to the Allies rather than selling them.

Indicating Roosevelt's growing interest in shaping the postwar world, in January 1941 Roosevelt outlined the **Four Freedoms** he felt every human being was entitled to as the basis for world peace. Determined to influence any peace settlement, the president met with Prime Minister Churchill for the first time at Placentia Bay in Newfoundland in August 1941 to discuss the war and plans for the postwar world. The **Atlantic Charter** that emerged as a result of the meeting signaled a growing Anglo–American unity in the war against Germany and served to establish a personal relationship between the two leaders. It was events in Asia that finally forced the United States to enter the Second World War. The Japanese attack on **Pearl Harbor** on 7 December 1941 led President Roosevelt to ask Congress to declare war on Japan and four days later Germany and Italy declared war on the United States.

As Allies in the war against totalitarianism, Churchill was determined that Britain and America should focus on defeating Germany first and sailed to the United States on 12 December to ensure that Washington agreed. Despite Pearl Harbor, Roosevelt agreed that Germany represented the greater threat and the two leaders agreed to a unified military command under the Combined Chiefs of Staff with its headquarters in Washington, D.C., with a supreme commander in each theater of war. In Europe, General **Dwight D. Eisenhower** acted as supreme commander and oversaw the Normandy landings. Military cooperation was matched by intelligence cooperation, with Britain taking the lead in breaking the German Enigma code at Bletchley Park. Ultimately, intelligence sharing during World War II resulted in the **UKUSA Agreement**.

American entry into World War II also led to an influx of U.S. military personnel into Britain. Anglo–American cooperation was made much easier by the personal relationships and contacts between the governments. Not only did Churchill and Roosevelt have a friendly relationship but U.S. Army Chief of Staff General **George C. Marshall** and Field Marshal Sir John Dill, head of the British military mission, were also close friends. In addition, the number of British diplomats and ministry officials in Washington rose from a 1939 level of fewer than 20 to over 9,000 by the end of the war. Between 1942 and 1945, around two million U.S. servicemen were stationed in Great Britain, and U.S. bases were established throughout Britain.

The arrival of GIs in Britain took place as British servicemen went overseas and there was some friction with the locals, particularly as British women had relationships with Americans and many went on to marry. On the whole, facing common enemies the two nations worked in a spirit of cooperation and unity.

The "Big Three" Allies—Britain, the **Soviet Union**, and United States—cooperated on many levels and proved successful in defeating Germany and Japan, but there were disagreements along the way. The most serious strategic difference came over the timing of a cross-channel invasion. Britain favored delaying an invasion of France as it was being successful in the Mediterranean campaign; America favored a direct confrontation with Germany much sooner, supported by the Russians who were desperate for a second front to be opened up. Churchill was able to persuade his allies to invade North Africa in November 1942 and postpone an invasion of France. The Roosevelt administration suspected Churchill might have been concerned more with preserving the British Empire—noticeably in India and the Middle East—than in defeating Germany quickly. Disagreements between Roosevelt, Stalin, and Churchill over this issue came to the fore at the summit meeting in **Tehran** in November 1943 and the invasion was postponed until June 1944.

With the success of the invasion of France, renewed attention was given to the war against Japan. Again, there were tensions between the British and U.S. military leadership over strategy. U.S. General "Vinegar Joe" Stilwell believed his British superior, Lord Louis Mountbatten, commander of the South-East Asia Command (SEAC) was motivated by imperial concerns, particularly the decision that British and Commonwealth ground forces retake Burma from the Japanese. SEAC was nicknamed "Save England's Asiatic Colonies" by Americans. Meanwhile U.S. forces faced the Japanese on the Pacific islands, incurring great losses in the process. As America faced the prospect of an invasion of Japan, news of the successful explosion of an **atomic bomb** reached Truman. Britain and the United States worked together during the war on the development of the atomic bomb, which was dropped on Hiroshima and Nagasaki to end the war. Victory in Europe (VE-Day) came on 8 May 1945, followed by Victory in Japan (VJ-Day) on 15 August 1945.

Despite the fact that there had been disagreements over strategy and some distance between Washington and London during the Tehran, **Yalta**, and **Potsdam conferences** over the plans for the postwar world, World War II had witnessed an enormous leap forward in Anglo–American defense and intelligence cooperation and deeper cultural and political ties between the two transatlantic powers. The war had left a legacy of U.S. worldwide commitments and a military foothold in the United Kingdom. By the end of World War II, it was clear that the United States had risen to economic and military superpower status, and Great Britain's position as a junior partner in the Anglo–American alliance had been confirmed. *See also* AMERICAN BASES IN BRITAIN; ARCADIA CONFERENCE; D-DAY LANDINGS; WAR BRIDES.

– Y –

YALTA CONFERENCE (1945). Yalta on the Black Sea coast of the Crimea was the setting for the second wartime meeting of the so-called "Big Three"—Premier Joseph Stalin of the **Soviet Union**, Prime Minister **Winston Churchill** of Great Britain, and President **Franklin D. Roosevelt** of the United States. The weeklong meeting (4–11 February 1945) allowed for the continuation of planning to end **World War II** that had progressed during the **Tehran Conference**, and to consider the shape of the postwar world. As with the Tehran Conference, Roosevelt maintained a distance from Churchill at Yalta and by this stage in the war the British prime minister had begun to suspect Soviet intentions in Europe. Despite Roosevelt being more trusting of the Soviets, nevertheless there was continued Anglo–American agreement on prioritizing the end of war in Europe and securing the Big Three alliance as the best means to end the entire war. The meeting resulted in Stalin's agreement to enter the war against Japan 90 days after the end of the war in Europe and endorsement of the plans to form an international peacekeeping organization, the **United Nations**.

Much discussion focused on Poland and the Soviet desire for security in Eastern Europe through the creation of friendly states on its borders. The states that the Soviet Union had already annexed, including the Baltic states of Lithuania, Latvia, and Estonia, would remain under Soviet control, and it was agreed that Poland's eastern border would be changed to allow the Soviet Union an additional security buffer and that Poland would be compensated by additional territory on its western borders gained from Germany at the end of the war. The Soviet Union also agreed to free elections in Poland. Although Churchill and Roosevelt were later criticized for conceding too much territory and influence to the Soviet Union, especially in Eastern Europe, at the time the two leaders felt they had little choice but to acknowledge the presence of the Red Army on European soil and recognized the Soviet Union would be needed to end the war in the Pacific.

YEAR OF EUROPE. At the behest of President **Richard Nixon**, Secretary of State **Henry Kissinger** announced that 1973 would be the "Year of Europe." The Nixon administration envisaged that this diplomatic initiative would refocus U.S. foreign policy after a decade of focusing on Vietnam. During a speech delivered on 23 April 1973, Kissinger spoke of a "new **Atlantic Charter**" between the United States and its European allies "setting the goals for the future." The Nixon administration hoped to reduce economic rivalry and reopen the issue of burden-sharing in defense. The initiative was not received well in European circles as it came as the **Vietnam War** ended and the Watergate scandal was being investigated. In addition, in Great Britain the government of **Edward Heath** had not been informed of Kissinger's ideas before the announcement and refused to speak with the Nixon administration alone. Instead, talks between the United States and the nine **European Economic Community** member-governments began half-heartedly and were scuppered by the outbreak of the Yom Kippur War in 1973. *See also* ARAB–ISRAELI WAR (1973).

YOM KIPPUR WAR (1973). *See* ARAB–ISRAELI WAR (1973).

YORKTOWN, SURRENDER AT (1781). After five years of fighting in the American **War for Independence** beginning in 1776, British General Charles Cornwallis's troops surrendered at Yorktown in

1781, leading the British to seek peace. Britain's surrender in the war had been secured by the entry of its old enemies, France and Spain, on the side of the United States' revolution. In 1783, the **Versailles Peace Treaty** acknowledged America's independence and established its borders south of the Great Lakes and as far west as the Mississippi.

– Z –

ZIMMERMAN TELEGRAM. On 17 January 1917, British intelligence intercepted a telegram from the German foreign minister, Arthur Zimmerman, to the German envoy in Mexico (via the German ambassador in the United States) suggesting a German–Mexican alliance in the event of the United States entering the war. Mexico would invade northward and regain New Mexico, Arizona, and Texas in a peace settlement. As the British did not want to reveal that they were reading U.S. cables as well as German ones, they obtained a second copy of the cable from a Mexican agent, and on 24 February, **Arthur Balfour**, the British foreign secretary, informed the Americans of the so-called Zimmerman telegram. The United States published details of the telegram on 1 March, further encouraging anti-German feeling and leading the nation closer to entry into **World War I**.

Appendix A
List of U.S. Presidents and Secretaries of State

President	Term in Office
George Washington	1789–1797
John Adams (F)	1797–1801
Thomas Jefferson (R)	1801–1809
James Madison (R)	1809–1817
James Monroe (R)	1817–1825
John Quincy Adams (Ind)	1825–1829
Andrew Jackson (D)	1829–1837
Martin Van Buren (D)	1837–1841
William H. Harrison (W)	Mar–Apr 1840
John Tyler (W)	1841–1845
James K. Polk (D)	1845–1849
Zachary Taylor (W)	1849–1850
Millard Fillmore (W)	1850–1853

Secretaries of State	Term in Office
Thomas Jefferson	1789–1793
Edmund Randolph	1794–1795
Timothy Pickering	1795–1797
Timothy Pickering	1797–1800
John Marshall	1800–1801
James Madison	1801–1809
Robert Smith	1809–1811
James Monroe	1811–1817
John Quincy Adams	1817–1825
Henry Clay	1825–1829
Martin Van Buren	1829–1831
Edward Livingston	1831–1833
Louis McLane	1833–1834
John Forsyth	1834–1837
John Forsyth	1837–1841
Daniel Webster	Mar–Apr 1840
Daniel Webster	1841–1843
Abel P. Upshur	1843–1844
John C. Calhoun	1844–1845
James Buchanan	1845–1849
John M. Clayton	1849–1850
John M. Clayton	1849–1850
Daniel Webster	1850–1852
Edward Everett	1852–1853

President		Secretary of State	
Franklin Pierce (D)	1853–1857	William L. Marcy	1853–1857
James Buchanan (D)	1857–1861	Lewis Cass	1857–1860
		Jeremiah S. Black	1860–1861
Abraham Lincoln (R)	1861–1865	William H. Seward	1861–1865
Andrew Johnson	1865–1869	William H. Seward	1865–1869
Ulysses S. Grant (R)	1869–1877	Elihu B. Washburne	March 1869
		Hamilton Fish	1869–1877
Rutherford B. Hayes (R)	1877–1881	William M. Evarts	1877–1881
James A. Garfield (R)	Mar–Sep 1881	James G. Blame	Mar–Sep 1881
Chester Arthur (R)	1881–1885	James G. Blaine	Sep–Dec 1881
		Frederick T. Frelinghuysen	1881–1885
Grover Cleveland (D)	1885–1889	Thomas F. Bayard Sr.	1885–1889
Benjamin Harrison (R)	1889–1893	James G. Blaine	1889–1892
		John W. Foster	1892–1893
Grover Cleveland (D)	1893–1897	Walter Q. Gresham	1893–1895
		Richard Olney	1895–1897
William McKinley (R)	1897–1901	John Sherman	1897–1898
		William R. Day	Apr–Sep 1898
		John Hay	1898–1901
Theodore Roosevelt (R)	1901–1909	John Hay	1901–1905
		Elihu Root	1905–1909
		Robert Bacon	Jan–Mar 1909
William H. Taft (R)	1909–1913	Philander C. Knox	1909–1913
Woodrow Wilson (D)	1913–1921	William Jennings Bryan	1913–1915

President	Term in Office	Secretaries of State	Term in Office
		Robert Lansing	1915–1920
		Bainbridge Colby	1920–1921
Warren Harding (R)	1921–1925	Charles Evans Hughes	1921–1925
Calvin Coolidge (R)	1925–1929	Frank B. Kellogg	1925–1929
Herbert Hoover (R)	1929–1933	Henry L. Stimson	1929–1933
Franklin D. Roosevelt (D)	1933–1945	Cordell Hull	1933–1944
		Edward Stettinius Jr.	1944–1945
Harry S. Truman (D)	1945–1953	James F. Byrnes	1945–1947
		George Marshall	1947–1949
		Dean Acheson	1949–1953
Dwight D. Eisenhower (R)	1953–1961	John Foster Dulles	1953–1959
		Christian Herter	1959–1961
John F. Kennedy (D)	1961–1963	Dean Rusk	1961–1963
Lyndon B. Johnson (D)	1963–1969	Dean Rusk	1963–1969
Richard Nixon (R)	1969–1974	William P. Roger	1969–1973

Gerald Ford (R)	1974–1977	Henry Kissinger	1973–1974
Jimmy Carter (D)	1977–1981	Henry Kissinger	1974–1977
		Cyrus Vance	1977–1980
		Edmund Muskie	1980–1981
Ronald Reagan (R)	1981–1989	Alexander Haig	1981–1982
		George P. Shultz	1982–1989
George H. W. Bush (R)	1989–1993	James Baker	1989–1992
		Lawrence Eagleburger	1992–1993
William Clinton (D)	1993–2001	Warren Christopher	1993–1997
		Madeleine Albright	1997–2001
George W. Bush (R)	2001–2009	Colin Powell	2001–2005

(F) = Federalist; (W)= Whig; (Ind) = Independent; (D) = Democratic; (R) = Republican

Appendix B
List of British Prime
Ministers and Foreign Secretaries

Prime Minister	Term in Office	Foreign Secretary	Term in Office
George Grenville (W)	1763–1765		
The Marquess of Rockingham (W)	1765–1766		
William Pitt the Elder (W)	1766–1768		
The Duke of Grafton (W)	1768–1770		
Lord North (T)	1770–1782		
The Marquess of Rockingham (W)	Mar–Jul 1782	Charles James Fox	Mar–Jul 1782
The Earl of Shelburne (W)	1782–1783	The Lord Grantham	1782–1783
The Duke of Portland (W)	Apr–Dec 1783	Charles James Fox	Apr–Dec 1783
William Pitt the Younger (T)	1783–1801	The Earl Temple	Dec–Dec 1783
		The Duke of Leeds	1783–1791
		The Lord Grenville	1791–1801
Henry Addington (T)	1801–1804	The Lord Hawkesbury	1801–1804
William Pitt the Younger (T)	1804–1806	The Lord Harrowby	1804–1805
		The Lord Mulgrave	1805–1806
		Charles James Fox	Feb–Sep 1806
The Lord Grenville (W)	1806–1807	Viscount Howick	1806–1807
The Duke of Portland (T)	1807–1809	George Canning	1807–1809
		The Earl Bathurst	Oct–Dec 1809
Spencer Percival (T)	1809–1812	The Marquess Wellesley	1809–1812
The Earl of Liverpool (T)	1812–1827	The Viscount Castlereagh	1812–1822
		George Canning	1822–1827
George Canning (T)	Apr–Aug 1827	The Earl of Dudley	Apr–Aug 1827
Viscount Goderich (T)	1827–1828	The Earl of Dudley	1827–1828

Prime Minister		Foreign Secretary	
The Duke of Wellington (T)	1828–1830	The Earl of Aberdeen	1828–1830
The Earl Grey (W)	1830–1834	The Viscount Palmerston	1830–1834
Viscount Melbourne (W)	Jul–Nov 1834	The Viscount Palmerston	Jul–Nov 1834
The Duke of Wellington (T)	Nov–Dec 1834	The Viscount Palmerston	Nov–Dec 1834
Sir Robert Peel (C)	1834–1835	The Duke of Wellington	1834–1835
Viscount Melbourne (W)	1835–1841	The Viscount Palmerston	1836–1841
Sir Robert Peel (C)	1841–1846	The Earl of Aberdeen	1841–1846
Lord John Russell (W)	1846–1852	The Earl Granville	1851–1852
The Earl of Derby (C)	Feb–Dec 1852	The Earl of Malmesbury	Feb–Dec 1852
The Earl of Aberdeen (W)	1852–1855	Lord John Russell	1852–1853
		The Earl of Clarendon	1853–1855
Viscount Palmerston (Lib)	1855–1858	The Earl of Clarendon	1855–1858
The Earl of Derby (C)	1858–1859	The Earl of Malmesbury	1858–1859
Viscount Palmerston (Lib)	1859–1865	The Earl Russell	1859–1865
The Earl Russell (Lib)	1865–1866	The Earl of Clarendon	1865–1866
The Earl of Derby (C)	1866–1868	The Lord Stanley	1866–1868
Benjamin Disraeli (C)	Feb–Dec 1868	The Lord Stanley	Feb–Dec 1868
William E. Gladstone (Lib)	1868–1874	The Earl of Clarendon	1868–1870
		The Earl Granville	1870–1874
Benjamin Disraeli (C)	1874–1880	The Earl of Derby	1874–1878
		The Marquess of Salisbury	1878–1880
William E. Gladstone (Lib)	1880–1885	The Earl Granville	1880–1885
The Marquess of Salisbury (C)	1885–1886	The Marquess of Salisbury	1885–1886
William E. Gladstone (Lib)	Feb–Jul 1886	The Earl of Rosebery	Feb–Aug 1986

Prime Minister	Term in Office	Foreign Secretary	Term in Office
The Marquess of Salisbury (C)	1886–1992	The Earl of Iddesleigh	1886–1887
		The Marquess of Salisbury	1887–1892
William E. Gladstone (Lib)	1892–1894	The Earl of Rosebery	1892–1894
The Earl of Rosebery (Lib)	1894–1895	The Earl of Kimberley	1894–1895
Marquess of Salisbury (C)	1895–1902	The Marquess of Salisbury	1895–1900
		The Marquess of Lansdowne	1900–1902
Arthur Balfour (C)	1902–1905	The Marquess of Lansdowne	1902–1905
Sir Henry Campbell Bannerman (Lib)	1905–1908	Sir Edward Grey	1905–1908
Herbert H. Asquith (Lib)	1908–1916	Sir Edward Grey	1908–1916
David Lloyd George (Lib)	1916–1922	Arthur Balfour	1916–1919
		The Marquess Curzon of Kedleston	1919–1922
Andrew Bonar Law (C) of Kedleston	1922–1923	The Marquess Curzon	
Stanley Baldwin (C)	1922–1923		
	1923–1924	The Marquess Curzon of Kedleston	1923–1924
Ramsay Macdonald (L)	Jan–Nov 1924	Ramsay Macdonald	Jan–Nov 1924
Stanley Baldwin (C)	1924–1929	Sir Austen Chamberlain	1924–1929
		Ramsay Macdonald (L/National Government)	1929–1935
		Arthur Henderson	1929–1931
		The Marquis of Reading	Aug–Nov 1931
		Sir John Simon	1931–1935

Prime Minister	Dates	Foreign Secretary	Dates
Stanley Baldwin (C)	1935–1937	Anthony Eden	1935–1937
Neville Chamberlain (Conservative/ National Government)	1937–1940	Anthony Eden	1937–1938
		Viscount Halifax	1938–1940
Winston Churchill (Conservative Coalition)	1940–1945	Anthony Eden	1940–1945
Clement Attlee (L)	1945–1951	Ernest Bevin	1945–1951
		Herbert Morrison	Mar–Oct 1951
Winston Churchill (C)	1951–1955	Sir Anthony Eden	1951–1955
		Harold Macmillan	Apr–Dec 1955
Anthony Eden (C)	1955–1957	Selwyn Lloyd	1955–1957
Harold Macmillan (C)	1957–1963	Selwyn Lloyd	1957–1960
		The Earl of Home	1960–1963
Alec Douglas-Home (C)	1963–1964	R.A. Butler	1963–1964
Harold Wilson (L)	1964–1970	Patrick Gordon-Walker	1964–1965
		Michael Stewart	1965–1966
		George Brown	1966–1968
		Michael Stewart	1968–1970
Edward Heath (C)	1970–1974	Sir Alec Douglas-Home	1970–1974
Harold Wilson (L)	1974–1976	James Callaghan	1974–1976
James Callaghan (L)	1976–1979	Anthony Crosland	1976–1977
		David Owen	1977–1979

Prime Minister	Term in office	Foreign Secretary	Term in office
Margaret Thatcher (C)	1979–1990	Lord Carrington	1979–1982
		Francis Pym	1982–1983
		Sir Geoffrey Howe	1983–1989
		John Major	1989–1989
		Douglas Hurd	1989–1990
John Major (C)	1990–1997	Douglas Hurd	1990–1995
		Malcolm Rifkind	1995–1997
Tony Blair (L)	1997–2007	Robin Cook	1997–2001
		Jack Straw	2001–2006
		Margaret Beckett	2006–2007
Gordon Brown (L)	2007–	David Miliband	2007–

(W) = Whig; (T) = Tory; (C) = Conservative; (Lib) = Liberal; (L) = Labour

Appendix C
List of U.S. Ambassadors to Great Britain

Name	Title	Dates of Appointment
John Adams	Minister Plenipotentiary	1785–1788
Thomas Pinkney	Minister Plenipotentiary	1792–1796
Rufus King	Minister Plenipotentiary	1796–1803
James Monroe	Minister Plenipotentiary	1803–1807
William Pinkney	Minister Plenipotentiary	1808–1811
Jonathan Russell	Chargé d'Affaires	1811–1812
John Quincy Adams	Envoy Extraordinary and Minister Plenipotentiary	1815–1817
Richard Rush	Envoy Extraordinary and Minister Plenipotentiary	1817–1825
Rufus King	Envoy Extraordinary and Minister Plenipotentiary	1825–1826
Albert Gallatin	Envoy Extraordinary and Minister Plenipotentiary	1826–1827
James Barbour	Envoy Extraordinary and Minister Plenipotentiary	1828–1829
Louis McLane	Envoy Extraordinary and Minister Plenipotentiary	1829–1831
Martin Van Buren	Envoy Extraordinary and Minister Plenipotentiary	1831–1832
Aaron Vail	Chargé d'Affaires	1832–1836
Andrew Stevenson	Envoy Extraordinary and Minister Plenipotentiary	1836–1841
Edward Everett	Envoy Extraordinary and Minister Plenipotentiary	1841–1845
Louis McLane	Envoy Extraordinary and Minister Plenipotentiary	1845–1846
George Bancroft	Envoy Extraordinary and Minister Plenipotentiary	1846–1849
Abbott Lawrence	Envoy Extraordinary and Minister Plenipotentiary	1849–1852
James R. Ingersoll	Envoy Extraordinary and Minister Plenipotentiary	1852–1853
James Buchanan	Envoy Extraordinary and Minister Plenipotentiary	1853–1856
George M. Dallas	Envoy Extraordinary and Minister Plenipotentiary	1856–1861
Charles Francis Adams	Envoy Extraordinary and Minister Plenipotentiary	1861–1868

Reverdy Johnson	Envoy Extraordinary and Minister Plenipotentiary	1868–1869
J. Lothrop Motley	Envoy Extraordinary and Minister Plenipotentiary	1869–1870
Robert C. Schenck	Envoy Extraordinary and Minister Plenipotentiary	1870–1876
Edwards Pierrepont	Envoy Extraordinary and Minister Plenipotentiary	1876–1877
John Welsh	Envoy Extraordinary and Minister Plenipotentiary	1877–1879
James Russell Lowell	Envoy Extraordinary and Minister Plenipotentiary	1880–1885
Edward J. Phelps	Envoy Extraordinary and Minister Plenipotentiary	1885–1889
Robert T. Lincoln	Envoy Extraordinary and Minister Plenipotentiary	1889–1893
Thomas F. Bayard	Ambassador Extraordinary and Plenipotentiary	1893–1897
John Hay	Ambassador Extraordinary and Plenipotentiary	1897–1898
Joseph Choate	Ambassador Extraordinary and Plenipotentiary	1899–1905
Whitelaw Reid	Ambassador Extraordinary and Plenipotentiary	1905–1912
Walter Hines Page	Ambassador Extraordinary and Plenipotentiary	1913–1918
John W. Davis	Ambassador Extraordinary and Plenipotentiary	1918–1921
George Harvey	Ambassador Extraordinary and Plenipotentiary	1921–1923
Frank B. Kellogg	Ambassador Extraordinary and Plenipotentiary	1923–1925
Alanson B. Houghton	Ambassador Extraordinary and Plenipotentiary	1925–1929
Charles G. Hawes	Ambassador Extraordinary and Plenipotentiary	1929–1931
Andrew W. Mellon	Ambassador Extraordinary and Plenipotentiary	1932–1933
Robert Worth Bingham	Ambassador Extraordinary and Plenipotentiary	1933–1937
Joseph P. Kennedy	Ambassador Extraordinary and Plenipotentiary	1938–1940
John G. Winnant	Ambassador Extraordinary and Plenipotentiary	1941–1945
W. Averell Harriman	Ambassador Extraordinary and Plenipotentiary	Apr–Oct 1946

Name	Title	Dates of Appointment
O. Max Gardner	Ambassador Extraordinary and Plenipotentiary	1946–Died before taking office
Lewis W. Douglas	Ambassador Extraordinary and Plenipotentiary	1947–1950
Walter S. Gifford	Ambassador Extraordinary and Plenipotentiary	1950–1953
Winthrop W. Aldrich	Ambassador Extraordinary and Plenipotentiary	1953–1957
John Hay Whitney	Ambassador Extraordinary and Plenipotentiary	1957–1961
David K. E. Bruce	Ambassador Extraordinary and Plenipotentiary	1961–1969
Walter H. Annenberg	Ambassador Extraordinary and Plenipotentiary	1969–1974
Elliot L. Richardson	Ambassador Extraordinary and Plenipotentiary	1975–1976
Anne Legendre Armstrong	Ambassador Extraordinary and Plenipotentiary	1976–1977
Kingman Brewster Jr	Ambassador Extraordinary and Plenipotentiary	1977–1981
John J. Louis Jr.	Ambassador Extraordinary and Plenipotentiary	1981–1983
Charles H. Price II	Ambassador Extraordinary and Plenipotentiary	1983–1989
Henry E. Catto Jr.	Ambassador Extraordinary and Plenipotentiary	1989–1991
Raymond G. H. Seitz	Ambassador Extraordinary and Plenipotentiary	1991–1994
William J. Crowe Jr.	Ambassador Extraordinary and Plenipotentiary	1994–1997
Philip Lader	Ambassador Extraordinary and Plenipotentiary	1997–2001
William S. Farish	Ambassador Extraordinary and Plenipotentiary	2001–2004
Robert H. Tuttle	Ambassador Extraordinary and Plenipotentiary	2005–

Appendix D
List of British Ambassadors to the United States

Name	Titles	Dates of Appointment
George Hammand	Minister to the United States of America	1791–1795
Robert Liston	Envoy Extraordinary and Minister Plenipotentiary	1796–1800
Anthony Merry	Envoy Extraordinary and Minister Plenipotentiary	1803–1806
Hon. David Montague Erskine	Envoy Extraordinary and Minister Plenipotentiary	1807–1809
Francis James Jackson	Envoy Extraordinary and Minister Plenipotentiary	1809–1811
Augustus John Foster	Envoy Extraordinary and Minister Plenipotentiary	1811–1812
Sir Charles Bagot	Envoy Extraordinary and Minister Plenipotentiary	1815–1820
Stratford Canning	Envoy Extraordinary and Minister Plenipotentiary	1820–1824
Sir Charles Richard Vaughan	Envoy Extraordinary and Minister Plenipotentiary	1825–1835
Henry Stephen Fox	Envoy Extraordinary and Minister Plenipotentiary	1835–1843
Sir Richard Pakenham	Envoy Extraordinary and Minister Plenipotentiary	1843–1847
Sir Henry Bulwer	Envoy Extraordinary and Minister Plenipotentiary	1849–1852
Sir John Fiennes Twistleton Crampton	Envoy Extraordinary and Minister Plenipotentiary	1852–1856
Francis Napier, 10th Lord Napier	Envoy Extraordinary and Minister Plenipotentiary	1857–1858
Richard Bickerton Pernell Lyons, 2nd Baron Lyons of Christchurch	Envoy Extraordinary and Minister Plenipotentiary	1858–1865
Sir Frederick Bruce	Envoy Extraordinary and Minister Plenipotentiary	1865–1867
Sir Edward Thornton	Envoy Extraordinary and Minister Plenipotentiary	1867–1881
Sir Lionel Sackville-West	Envoy Extraordinary and Minister Plenipotentiary	1881–1888
Sir Julian Pauncefote	Envoy Extraordinary and Minister Plenipotentiary	1889–1893
Sir Julian Pauncefote	Ambassador to the United States of America	1893–1902
Sir Michael Henry Herbert	Ambassador to the United States of America	1902–1903

Sir Henry Mortimer Durand	Ambassador to the United States of America	1903–1906
James Bryce	Ambassador to the United States of America	1907–1913
Sir Cecil Spring-Rice	Ambassador to the United States of America	1913–1918
Rufus Isaacs, 1st Earl of Reading	Ambassador to the United States of America	1918–1919
Edward Grey, 1st Viscount Grey of Fallodon	Ambassador to the United States of America	1919–1920
Sir Auckland Geddes	Ambassador to the United States of America	1920–1924
Sir Esme Howard	Ambassador to the United States of America	1924–1930
Sir Ronald Lindsay	Ambassador to the United States of America	1930–1939
Philip Kerr, 1st Marquess of Lothian	Ambassador to the United States of America	1939–1940
Edward Wood, 3rd Viscount Halifax	Ambassador to the United States of America	1940–1946
Archibald Clark-Kerr, 1st Baron Inverchapel	Ambassador to the United States of America	1946–1948
Sir Oliver Franks	Ambassador to the United States of America	1948–1952
Sir Roger Makins	Ambassador to the United States of America	1953–1956
Sir Harold Caccia	Ambassador to the United States of America	1956–1961
Sir David Ormsby-Gore, later 5th Baron Harlech	Ambassador to the United States of America	1961–1965
Sir Patrick Dean	Ambassador to the United States of America	1965–1969
John Freeman	Ambassador to the United States of America	1969–1971
George Baring, 3rd Earl of Cromer	Ambassador to the United States of America	1971–1974
Sir Peter Ramsbottom	Ambassador to the United States of America	1974–1977
Peter Jay	Ambassador to the United States of America	1977–1979
Sir Nicholas Henderson	Ambassador to the United States of America	1979–1982
Sir Oliver Wright	Ambassador to the United States of America	1982–1986
Sir Antony Acland	Ambassador to the United States of America	1986–1991

Name	Titles	Dates of Appointment
Sir Robin Renwick	Ambassador to the United States of America	1991–1995
Sir John Kerr	Ambassador to the United States of America	1996–1997
Sir Christopher Meyer	Ambassador to the United States of America	1997–2003
Sir David Manning	Ambassador to the United States of America	2003–2007
Sir Nigel Sheinwald	Ambassador to the United States of America	2007–

Bibliography

CONTENTS

Scholars and commentators on Anglo–American relations are numerous, particularly in Great Britain. Indeed, most of the major academic authorities on the "special relationship" are British, perhaps reflecting how much more important it is to the junior partner in the current alliance. Consequently, there is no shortage of published works on the topic. Those providing overviews of the relationship, particularly in the post-1945 period, vary in their interpretations of how "special" it is. Those following a realist or "functional" perspective, currently the orthodox position, tend to argue that Washington and London have always operated their foreign policies on the basis of national interest, with the relationship being at its strongest during times when these interests have converged.

The first section contains general works that provide overviews of the Anglo–American relationship. The debate about the nature of the "special relationship" appeared in the classic works by H. C. Allen, *Conflict and Concord: The Anglo–American Relationship since 1783* and *Great Britain and the United States: A History of Anglo–American Relations, 1783–1952*. For a broad overview, including an analysis of the cultural links between Britain and America, see David Dimbleby and David Reynolds, *An Ocean*

Apart: The Relationship between Britain and America in the Twentieth Century, and Kathleen Burk, *Old World, New World: The Story of Britain and America*. For a more recent focused study of the "special relationship" since the early 1960s, see John Dumbrell, *A Special Relationship: Anglo–American Relations in the Cold War and After*.

Not included in this bibliography, but obviously of considerable use to readers and researchers, are the other volumes in this series of Historical Dictionaries of U.S. Diplomacy that deal with specific periods. Further information on the general background, including foreign policy, can be found in the volumes in the series of Historical Dictionaries of U.S. Historical Eras. Finally, for more about the major wars, see the volumes, among others, on the Civil War, the Spanish-American War, the War of 1812, World War I, World War II, the Korean War and Vietnam War, and the Cold War in the series of Historical Dictionaries of War, Revolution, and Civil Unrest. These books are all published by Scarecrow Press of Lanham, Maryland, and can be looked up on the website www.scarecrow press.com

The second section of the bibliography provides a selection of works on the Revolutionary era. For a survey of the vast literature on the American War of Independence, see Gwenda Morgan, *The Debate on the American Revolution*. The classic and still popular study is the four-volume work by Sir George Otto Trevelyan, *The American Revolution*. For an examination of ideas driving the leaders of the American Revolution, see Bernard Bailyn, *The Ideological Origins of the American Revolution*. A comprehensive survey of the breakdown in relations between Britain and the American colonies is provided in Pauline Maier, *From Resistance to Revolution: Colonial Radicals and the Development of American Opposition to Britain, 1765–1776*. Another classic study from a British perspective is Piers Mackesy, *The War for America, 1775–1783*. A good overview for beginners is Gordon S. Wood, *The American Revolution: A History*.

In the aftermath of the War of Independence, and for most of the 19th century, Britain and the United States struggled to establish a harmonious relationship. Much of the literature in the third section focuses on the border conflicts and economic rivalry that characterized Anglo–American relations during this period. For an up-to-date analysis of the War of 1812, see Jon Latimer, *1812: War with America*.

Section III of the bibliography also provides a selection of works that examine the tense relationship between Britain and America during the American Civil War. The classic, pioneering work examining Anglo–American relations during the American Civil War is E. D. Adams, *Great Britain and the American Civil War*, first published in 1925. For more emphasis on economic relations during this period, see Frank L. Owlsley, *King Cotton Diplomacy: Foreign Relations of the Confederate States of America*. For a more balanced study of the importance of diplomacy in the Union's success, see Howard Jones, *Union in Peril: The Crisis over British Intervention in the Civil War*. Stuart Anderson's *Race and Rapprochement: Anglo–Saxonism and Anglo–American Relations* offers the best discussion of the importance of racial and cultural kinship in the rapprochement between Britain and America that emerged between 1895 and 1904. For an examination of Britain's response to the growing strategic power of the United States in the late 19th century—particularly its growing navy—see Anne Orde, *Eclipse of Great Britain: The United States and British Imperial Decline, 1895–1956*.

The fourth section contains a selection of works that cover key events and issues in 20th-century Anglo–American relations. For works that fall outside of World War I, World War II, and the Cold War, see Lestyn Adams's study based on an examination of official and private papers, *Brothers across the Ocean: British Foreign Policy and the Origins of the Anglo–American "Special Relationship" 1900–1905*, which offers a history of the early special relationship between Britain and America, outlining Britain's period of adjustment as the United States threatened its position of global hegemony. The best overview of Anglo–American relations during World War I is Kathleen Burk, *Britain, America and the Sinews of War, 1914–1918*. A useful study of the tense interwar period, see John E. Moser, *Twisting the Lion's Tail: American Anglophobia between the World War*, alongside B. J. C. McKercher, *Anglo–American Relations in the 1920s: The Struggle for Supremacy*.

Not surprisingly, the literature on the development of Anglo–American alliances formed during World War II is voluminous. See Randall B. Woods, *A Changing of the Guard: Anglo–American Relations, 1941–1946*. For an accessible overview of the personal and working relationship that developed between President Franklin D. Roosevelt and Prime Minister Winston Churchill, see Warren F. Kimball, *Forged in War: Roosevelt, Churchill, and the Second World War*. For a more controversial analysis of Winston Churchill's role in the formation of the wartime alliance, see John Charmley, *Churchill's Grand Alliance: The Anglo–American Special Relationship 1940–1957*.

Section IV also contains a variety of works that address Anglo–American relations during the Cold War, featuring all aspects of the burgeoning links between Britain and the United States. For a rich analysis of the role of the British in the origins of the Cold War, see Terry Anderson, *The United States, Great Britain and the Cold War, 1941–1947*. The best volume on the development of the intelligence relationship during the Cold War is Richard Aldrich, *The Hidden Hand: Britain, America and Cold War Secret Intelligence*. For a serious study of Anglo–American military cooperation, see John Baylis, *Anglo–American Defence Relations, 1939–1980*; and for an overview of the economic relationship during the Cold War, see Alan Dobson, *The Politics of the Anglo–American Economic Special Relationship, 1940–1984*.

Despite being Cold War allies, Britain and America had several disagreements during this period. For a scholarly treatment of the Suez crisis, see Scott Lucas, *Divided We Stand: Britain, the United States and the Suez Crisis*; for an examination of British unease during the Cuban missile crisis, see Len Scott, *Macmillan, Kennedy, and the Cuban Missile Crisis*; and for an assessment of the impact of the Vietnam War on Anglo–American relations, see Sylvia Ellis, *Britain, America, and the Vietnam War*.

The fifth section in the bibliography deals with events and debates that occupied Anglo–American relations in the aftermath of the Cold War. For a masterly examination of the "special relationship" during the Clinton-Blair and Bush-Blair years, see Peter Riddell, *Hug Them Close*. On the Iraq War, see the important account by journalist William Shawcross, *Allies*.

The National Archives (formerly the Public Record Office) in Kew hold British official records on Anglo–American relations. Corresponding American government documents are contained at the Library of Congress in Washington, D.C., and for presidents from Franklin D. Roosevelt onwards, the presidential libraries.

Another source of information, primary documents, and latest news on Anglo–Americans is the growing number of reliable websites. The websites of the U.S. Embassy, London (http://www.usembassy.org.uk/) provide a history of the building at Grosvenor Square, key speeches by the current ambassador, and embassy press releases. Likewise, the website of the British Embassy, Washington (http://www.britain-info.org/) contains similar information. The Library of Congress hosts a website (http://www.loc.gov/exhibits/british/) based on a joint project and exhibition it held with the British Library. The site features overviews of different periods in British–American relations, images, and primary documents on a range of topics from the early English settlements in America to British war brides in World War II. The British Broadcasting Company (BBC; http://news.bbc.co.uk/1/hi/world/americas/ 1913522.stm) provides regular updates and commentaries on the Anglo–American "special relationship."

I. GENERAL WORKS AND REFERENCE WORKS

Allen, H. C. *Conflict and Concord: The Anglo–American Relationship since 1783.* New York: St. Martin's Press, 1960.

———. *Great Britain and the United States: A History of Anglo–American Relations 1783–1952.* London: Odhams Press, 1954.

Allen, H. C., and Roger Thompson, eds. *Contrast and Connection: Bicentennial Essays in Anglo–American History.* Athens: Ohio University Press, 1976.

Bartlett, C. J. *"The Special Relationship": A Political History of Anglo–American Relations since 1945.* London: Longman, 1992.

Baylis, John. *Anglo–American Defence Relations, 1939–80: The Special Relationship.* Basingstoke, England: Macmillan, 1981.

———, ed. *Documents in Contemporary History: Anglo–American Relations since 1939: The Enduring Alliance.* Manchester, England: Manchester University Press, 1997.

———. "The 'Special Relationship': A Diverting British Myth?" In *Haunted by History: Myths in International Relations*, ed. Cyril Buffet and Beatrice Heuser. Oxford: Berghahn Books, 1998.

Beer, Janet, and Bridget Bennett, ed. *Special Relationships: Anglo–American Affinities and Antagonisms 1854–1936.* Manchester, England: Manchester University Press, 2002.

Bell, Coral. *The Debatable Alliance: An Essay in Anglo–American Relations.* Oxford: Oxford University Press, 1964.

Beloff, Max. "The Special Relationship: An Anglo–American Myth." In *A Century of Conflict (1850–1950): Essays for APJ Taylor*, ed. Martin Gilbert. London: H. Hamilton, 1966.

Bolsover, Philip. *America over Britain.* London: Lawrence & Wishart, 1953.

Brandon, Henry. *Special Relationship: A Foreign Correspondent's Memoirs from Roosevelt to Reagan.* Basingstoke, England: Macmillan, 1988.

Buchan, Alastair. "Mothers and Daughters (or Greeks and Romans)." *Foreign Affairs* 54, no. 4 (July 1976): 645–66.

Burk, Kathleen. *Old World, New World: The Story of Britain and America.* Boston: Little, Brown, 2007.

Commager, Henry Steel, ed. *Britain through American Eyes.* New York: McGraw-Hill, 1974.

Curtis, Mark. *The Great Deception: Anglo–American Power and World Order.* London: Pluto, 1998.

Danchev, Alex. *On Specialness: Essays in Anglo–American Relations*. Basingstoke, England: Macmillan, 1998.

Dawson, Raymond, and Richard Rosencrance. "Theory and Reality in the Anglo–American Alliance." *World Politics* 19 (October 1966): 21–51.

Dickie, John. *"Special" No More. Anglo–American Relations: Rhetoric and Reality*. London: Weidenfeld & Nicolson, 1994.

Dimbleby, David, and David Reynolds. *An Ocean Apart: The Relationship between Britain and America in the Twentieth Century*. London: Guild, 1988.

Dobson, Alan. *Anglo–American Relations in the Twentieth Century: Of Friendship, Conflict and the Rise and Decline of the Superpowers*. London: Routledge, 1995.

——. "Labour or Conservative: Does It Matter in Anglo–American Relations?" *Journal of Contemporary History* 25, no. 4 (October 1990): 387–407.

Duckenfield, Mark, ed. *Battles over Free Trade: Anglo–American Experiences with International Trade, 1776–2006*. London: Pickering & Chatto, 2008.

Dumbrell, John. *A Special Relationship: Anglo–American Relations in the Cold War and After*. Basingstoke, England: Macmillan, 2001.

Engdahl, F. William. *A Century of War: Anglo–American Oil Politics and the New World Order*. London: Pluto Press, 2004.

Englander, David, ed. *Britain and America: Studies in Comparative History, 1760–1970*. New Haven, Conn.: Yale University Press, 1997.

Epstein, L. *Britain—Uneasy Ally*. Chicago: University of Chicago Press, 1954.

Gelber, L. *America in Britain's Place: The Leadership of the West and Anglo–American Unity*. New York: Frederick I. Praeger, 1961.

Grayling, Christopher, and Christopher Langoon. *Just Another Star: Anglo–American Relations since 1945*. London: Harrap, 1988.

Hathaway, Robert M. *Great Britain and the United States: Special Relations since World War II*. Boston: Twayne, 1990.

Hitchens, Christopher. *Blood, Class and Nostalgia*: *Anglo–American Ironies*. London: Chatto & Windus, 1990.

Hollowell, Jonathan, ed. *Twentieth-Century Anglo–American Relations*. Basingstoke, England: Palgrave, 2001.

Jones, Peter. *America and the British Labour Party: The Special Relationship at Work*. London: I. B. Tauris, 1995.

Kandiah, Michael David, and Gillian Staerck. "'Reliable Allies': Anglo–American Relations." In *British Foreign Policy, 1955–64: Con-*

tracting Options, ed. W. Kaiser and G. Staerck. Basingstoke, England: Macmillan, 2000.

Kaufman, Will, and Heidi Slettedahl Macpherson. *Britain and the Americas: Culture, Politics, and History*. Santa Barbara, Calif.: ABC Clio, 2005.

Lehmkuhl, Ursula, and Gustav Schmidt, eds. *From Enmity to Friendship: Anglo–American Relations in the Nineteenth and Twentieth Century*. Augsburg, Germany: Wibner, 2005.

Leuchtenburg, W. E., et al. *Britain and the United States: Views to Mark the Silver Jubilee*. London: Hutchinson, 1979.

Leventhal, Fred M., and Roland Quinault, eds. *Anglo–American Attitudes: From Revolution to Partnership*. Aldershot, England: Ashgate, 2000.

Louis, William Roger, and Hedley Bull, eds. *The Special Relationship: Anglo–American Relations since 1945*. Oxford: Oxford University Press, 1986.

Marsh, S., and J. Baylis. "The Anglo–American 'Special Relationship': The Lazarus of International Relations." *Diplomacy and Statecraft* 17, no. 1 (March 2006): 173–211.

McDonald, Ian S. *Anglo–American Relations since the Second World War*. New York: St. Martin's Press, 1974.

McFarlane, Anthony. *The British in the Americas, 1480–1815*. London: Longman, 1994.

Neustadt, Richard E. *Alliance Politics*. New York: Columbia University Press, 1970.

———. *Report for JFK: The Skybolt Crisis in Perspective*. Ithaca, N.Y.: Cornell University Press, 1992.

Nicholas, Herbert G. *Britain and the United States*. Baltimore, Md.: Johns Hopkins University Press.

———. *The United States and Britain*. Chicago: University of Chicago Press, 1975.

Ovendale, Ritchie. *Anglo–American Relations in the Twentieth Century*. Basingstoke, England: Macmillan, 1998.

Patten, Christopher. *Cousins and Strangers: America, Britain, and Europe in a New Century*. New York: Times Books, 2006.

Pelling, Henry. *America and the British Left: From Bright to Bevan*. London: Adam & Charles Black, 1956.

Pells, Richard. *Not Like Us: How Europeans Have Loved, Hated and Transformed America*. New York: Basic Books, 1997.

Rasmussen, Jorgen, and James M. McCormick. "British Mass Perceptions of the Anglo–American Relationship." *Political Science Quarterly* 108, no. 3 (Autumn 1993): 515–41.

Renwick, Robin. *Fighting with Allies: America and Britain in Peace and War.* Basingstoke, England: Macmillan, 1996.

Reynolds, David. "Rethinking Anglo–American Relations." *International Affairs* 65, no. 1 (Winter 1989): 89–111.

———. "A 'Special Relationship'? America, Britain and the International Order since the Second World War." *International Affairs* 62, no. 1 (Winter 1985): 1–20.

Russell Mead, Walter. *God and Gold: Britain, America and the Making of the Modern World.* London: Atlantic Books, 2007.

Russett, Bruce M. *Community and Contention: Britain and America in the Twentieth Century.* Cambridge: Massachusetts Institute of Technology Press, 1963.

Sarson, Steven. *British America 1500–1800: Creating Colonies, Imagining an Empire.* London: Hodder Arnold, 2005.

Staerck, Gillian. "The Role of the British Embassy in Washington." *Contemporary British History* 12, no. 3 (Autumn 1998): 115–38.

Temperley, Howard. *Britain and America since Independence.* Basingstoke, England: Palgrave Macmillan, 2002.

Turner, Arthur Campbell. *The Unique Partnership: Britain and the United States.* New York: Bobbs-Merrill, 1971.

Ward, Joseph P., ed. *Britain and the American South: From Colonialism to Rock and Roll.* Jackson: University Press of Mississippi, 2003.

Warner, Geoffrey. "The Anglo–American Special Relationship." *Diplomatic History* 13, no. 4 (Winter 1989): 479–500.

Watt, D. C. *Succeeding John Bull: America in Britain's Place.* Cambridge: Cambridge University Press, 1984.

Wheeler-Bennett, John. *Special Relationships: America in Peace and War.* London: Macmillan, 1975.

Wiener, Joel, and Mark Hampton, ed. *Anglo–American Media Interactions, 1850–2000.* Basingstoke, England: Palgrave Macmillan, 2007.

Williams, Andrew. *Failed Imagination? The Anglo–American New World Order from Wilson to Bush.* Manchester, England: Manchester University Press, 2007.

Wright, Esmond. "The Special Relationship." *History Today* 41, no. 4 (April 1991): 53–57.

Ziegler, John. *In Search of the "Special Relationship" with Britain.* Raleigh, N.C.: Pentland Press, 2000.

II. AMERICAN REVOLUTION

Bailyn, Bernard. "The Central Themes of the American Revolution: An Interpretation." In *Essays on the American Revolution*, ed. S. Kurtz and J. Hutson. Chapel Hill: University of North Carolina Press, 1973.

——. *The Ideological Origins of the American Revolution*. Cambridge, Mass: Belknap Press, 1982.

Bemis, Samuel Flagg. *The Diplomacy of the American Revolution*. New York: American Historical Association, 1935.

——. *Jay's Treaty: A Study in Commerce and Diplomacy*. New Haven, Conn.: Yale University Press, 1923.

Bicheno, Hugh. *Rebels and Redcoats: The American Revolutionary War*. London: HarperCollins, 2003.

Bickham, Troy O. "Sympathizing with Sedition? George Washington, the British Press, and British Attitudes during the American War of Independence." *William and Mary Quarterly* 59, no. 1 (January 2002): 101–22.

Black, Jeremy. *George III: America's Last King*. New Haven, Conn.: Yale University Press, 2006.

Bonwick, Colin. *English Radicals and the American Revolution*. Chapel Hill: University of North Carolina Press, 1977.

Boorstin, Daniel J. *The Americans: The Colonial Experience*. New York: Random House, 1958.

Bridenbaugh, Carl. *Mitre and Sceptre: Transatlantic Faiths, Ideas, Personalities, and Politics, 1689–1775*. New York: Oxford University Press, 1962.

Conway, Stephen. *The British Isles and the War of American Independence*. New York: Oxford University Press, 1992.

Dickerson, Oliver M. *The Navigation Acts and the American Revolution*. Philadelphia: University of Pennsylvania Press, 1951.

Dickinson, H. T., ed. *Britain and the American Revolution*. London: Longman, 1998.

Douglas, Edward Leach. *Roots of Conflict: British Armed Forces and Colonial Americans, 1677–1763*. Chapel Hill: University of North Carolina Press, 1986.

Duberman, Martin B. *Charles Francis Adams, 1807–1886*. Boston: Houghton Mifflin, 1961.

Dull, Jonathan R. *A Diplomatic History of the American Revolution*. New Haven, Conn.: Yale University Press, 1985.

Foner, Eric. *Tom Paine and Revolutionary America*. New York: Oxford University Press, 1976.

Freeman, Douglas Southall. *George Washington: A Biography* (7 vols.) New York: Scribner's, 1948–1957.

Geiter, Mary K., and W. A. Speck. *Colonial America: From Jamestown to Yorktown*. London: Palgrave, 2002.

Greene, Jack. *Colonies to Nation, 1763–1789: A Documentary History of the American Revolution*. New York: W. W. Norton, 1975.

——. *Understanding the American Revolution: Issues and Actors*. Charlottesville: University of Virginia Press, 1995.

Higginbotham, Don. *Daniel Morgan: Revolutionary Rifleman*. Chapel Hill: University of North Carolina Press, 1961.

——. *The War of American Independence: Military Attitudes, Policies, and Practice, 1763–1789*. New York: Macmillan, 1971.

Kammen, Michael G. *A Rope of Sand: The Colonial Agents, British Policies, and the American Revolution*. Ithaca, N.Y.: Cornell University Press, 1969.

Knollenberg, Bernhard. *Growth of the American Revolution, 1766–1775*. New York: Free Press, 1975.

——. *Origins of the American Revolution: 1759–1765*. New York: Macmillan, 1960.

Labaree, Benjamin W. *The Boston Tea Party*. New York: Oxford University Press, 1964.

Lutnick, Solomon. *The American Revolution and the British Press, 1775–1783*. Columbia: University of Missouri Press, 1967.

McCullough, David. *1776: America and Britain at War*. London: Allen Lane, 2005

Mackesy, Piers. *The War for America, 1775–1783*. Cambridge, Mass.: Harvard University Press, 1964.

Maier, Pauline. *From Resistance to Revolution: Colonial Radicals and the Development of American Opposition to Britain, 1765–1776*. New York: W. W. Norton, 1992.

——. "John Wilkes and American Disillusionment with Britain." *William and Mary Quarterly* 20 (1963): 373–95.

Marshall, P. J. *The Making and Unmaking of Empires: Britain, India, and America, c. 1750–1783*. Oxford: Oxford University Press, 2007.

Mason, Bernard. *The Road to Independence: The Revolutionary Movement in New York, 1773–1777*. Lexington: University of Kentucky Press, 1966.

Middlekauff, Robert. *The Glorious Cause: The American Revolution, 1763–1789*. Oxford: Oxford University Press, 2007.

Miller, John C. *Origins of the American Revolution*. Boston: Little, Brown, 1943.

Morgan, Edmund S., ed. *Prologue to Revolution: Sources and Documents on the Stamp Act Crisis, 1764–1766*. Chapel Hill: University of North Carolina Press, 1959.

Morgan, Edmund S., and Helen Morgan. *The Stamp Act Crisis: Prologue to Revolution*. New York: Collier Books, 1963.

Morgan, Gwenda. *The Debate on the American Revolution*. Manchester, England: Manchester University Press, 2007.

Morris, Richard B. *The American Revolution Reconsidered*. New York: Harper & Row, 1967.

Nettels, Curtis P. *George Washington and American Independence*. Boston: Little, Brown, 1951.

Norton, Mary Beth. *The British-Americans: The Loyalist Exiles in England, 1774–1789*. Boston: Little, Brown, 1972.

Perry, Keith. *British Politics and the American Revolution*. Basingstoke, England: Palgrave Macmillan, 1990.

Reich, Jerome R. *British Friends of the American Revolution*. Armonk, N.Y.: M. E. Sharpe, 1998.

Ritcheson, Charles R. *British Politics and the American Revolution*. Norman: University of Oklahoma Press, 1954.

Rudé, George. *Wilkes and Liberty: A Social Study of 1763 to 1774*. Oxford: Clarendon Press, 1962.

Schlesinger, Arthur M., Sr. *The Colonial Merchants and the American Revolution, 1763–1776*. New York: Columbia University Press, 1918.

———. *Prelude to Independence: The Newspaper War on Britain, 1764–1776*. New York: Alfred A. Knopf, 1958.

———. *Toward Lexington: The Role of the British Army in the Coming of the American Revolution*. Princeton, N.J.: Princeton University Press, 1965.

Shy, John, ed. *The American Revolution*. Northbrook, Ill.: AHM, 1973.

Smith, Paul H. *Loyalists and Redcoats: A Study in British Revolutionary Policy*. Chapel Hill: University of North Carolina Press, 1964.

Sosin, Jack M. *Agents and Merchants: British Colonial Policy and the Origins of the American Revolution, 1763–1875*. Lincoln: University of Nebraska Press, 1965.

Thomas, Peter D. G. "George III and the American Revolution." *History* 70, no. 228 (February 1985): 16–31.

———. *Revolution in America: Britain and the Colonies, 1763–1776.* Cardiff: University of Wales Press, 2002.

Trevelyan, George Otto. *The American Revolution*, Vols. 1–4. London: Longmans, Green, 1899–1905.

Tucker, Robert. *The Fall of the First British Empire: Origins of the War of Independence.* Baltimore, Md.: Johns Hopkins University Press, 1982.

Weintraub, Stanley. *Iron Tears: America's Battle for Freedom, Britain's Quagmire, 1775–1783.* New York: Simon & Schuster, 2005.

Whiteley, Peter. *Lord North: The Prime Minister Who Lost America.* London: Hambledon Press, 1996.

Wood, Gordon S. *The American Revolution: A History.* New York: Modern Library, 2002.

Wright, Esmond. A *Tug of Loyalties: Anglo–American Relations, 1765–85.* London: University of London, 1975.

III. RELATIONS IN THE 19TH CENTURY

Adler, Dorothy R. *British Investment in American Railways, 1834–1898.* Charlottesville: University Press of Virginia, 1970.

Anderson, Stuart. *Race and Rapprochement: Anglo–Saxonism and Anglo–American Relations, 1895–1904.* Rutherford, N.J.: Fairleigh Dickinson University Press, 1981.

———. "Racial Anglo–Saxonism and the American Response to the Boer War." *Diplomatic History* 2, no. 3 (July 1978): 219–36.

Barker, Anthony J. *Captain Charles Stuart: Anglo–American Abolitionist.* Baton Rouge: Louisiana State University Press, 1986.

Benn, Carl. *The War of 1812.* Oxford: Osprey, 1992.

Bolt, Christine. *The Anti-Slavery Movement and Reconstruction: A Study in Anglo–American Co-operation, 1833–1877.* Oxford: Oxford University Press, 1969.

———. *Feminist Ferment: "The Woman Question" in the USA and England, 1870–1940.* London: UCL Press, 1995.

Bourne, Kenneth. *Britain and the Balance of Power in North America, 1815–1908.* Berkeley: University of California Press, 1967.

Brandon, Ruth. *The Dollar Princesses: The American Invasion of the European Aristocracy 1870–1914.* London: Weidenfeld & Nicolson, 1980.

Campbell, Charles S., Jr. "The Anglo–American Crisis in the Bering Sea, 1890–1891." *Mississippi Valley Historical Review* 48, no. 3 (December 1961): 393–414.

Carwardine, Richard. *Transatlantic Revivalism: Popular Evangelicalism in Britain and America, 1790–1865.* Westport, Conn.: Greenwood Press, 1978.

Cook, Adrian. *The Alabama Claims: American Politics and Anglo–American Relations, 1865–1872.* Ithaca, N.Y.: Cornell University Press, 1975.

Crawford, Martin. *The Anglo–American Crisis of the Mid-Nineteenth Century: "The Times" and America, 1850–1862.* Athens: University of Georgia Press, 1987.

DeConde, Alexander. "Entangling Alliance: Politics and Diplomacy under George Washington." *Political Science Quarterly* 73, no. 4 (December 1958): 624–25.

Fladeland, Betty. *Men and Brothers: Anglo–American Anti-Slavery Cooperation.* Urbana: University of Illinois Press, 1972.

Flavell, Julie, and Stephen Conway. *Britain and America Go to War: The Impact of War and Welfare in Anglo–America, 1754–1815.* Gainesville: University Press of Florida, 2004.

Frankel, Jeffrey A. "The 1807–1809 Embargo against Great Britain." *Journal of Economic History* 42, no. 2 (June 1982): 291–308.

Gantt, Jonathan W. "Irish–American Terrorism and Anglo–American Relations, 1881–1885." *Journal of the Gilded Age and Progressive Era* 5 (October 2006): 325–57.

Gelber, Lionel. *The Rise of Anglo–American Friendship: A Study in World Politics, 1898–1906.* London: Oxford University Press, 1938.

Hammett, Hugh B. "The Cleveland Administration and Anglo–American Naval Friction in Hawaii, 1893–1894." *Military Affairs* 40, no. 1 (February 1976): 27–32.

James, William. *Naval Occurrences of the War of 1812: A Full and Correct Account of the Naval War between Great Britain and the United States of America, 1812–1815.* Dulles, Va.: Brassey's, 2004.

Jenkins, Brian. *Fenians and Anglo–American Relations during Reconstruction.* Ithaca, N.Y.: Cornell University Press, 1969.

Jones, Howard. "The Caroline Affair." *Historian* 38, no. 3 (May 1976): 485–502.

———. *To the Webster-Ashburton Treaty: Study in Anglo–American Relations, 1783–1843.* Chapel Hill: University of North Carolina Press, 1977.

———. *Union in Peril: The Crisis over British Intervention in the Civil War.* Chapel Hill: University of North Carolina Press, 1992.

Jones, Howard, and Donald A. Rakestraw. *Prologue to Manifest Destiny: Anglo–American Relations in the 1840s.* Wilmington, Del.: Scholarly Resources, 1997.

Kaufman, Scott. *The Pig War: The United States, Britain, and the Balance of Power in the Pacific Northwest, 1846–1872*. Lanham, Md.: Lexington Books, 2003.

Latimer, Jon. *1812: War with America*. Cambridge, Mass.: Harvard University Press, 2007.

Magnus, Philip. *Gladstone: A Biography*. London: John Murray, 1954.

Mahon, John K. *The War of 1812*. Gainesville: University Press of Florida. 1972.

Matthews, Joseph J. "Information Diplomacy in the Venezuelan Crisis of 1896." *Mississippi Valley Historical Review* 50 (September 1963): 66–77.

Merk, Frederick. *The Oregon Question: Essays in Anglo–American Diplomacy and Politics*. Cambridge, Mass.: Harvard University Press, 1967.

Montgomery, Maureen E. *Gilded Prostitution: Status, Money, and Transatlantic Marriages, 1870–1914*. London: Routledge, 1989.

Neale, R. G. *Great Britain and United States Expansion: 1898–1900*. Lansing: Michigan State University Press, 1966.

Orde, Anne. *The Eclipse of Great Britain: The United States and British Imperial Decline, 1895–1956*. New York: St. Martin's Press, 1996.

Perkins, Bradford. *The Cambridge History of American Foreign Relations*, Vol. 1: *The Creation of a Republican Empire, 1776–1865*. Cambridge: Cambridge University Press, 1993.

———. *Castlereagh and Adams: England and the United States, 1812–1823*. Berkeley: University of California Press, 1964.

———. *The Causes of the War of 1812: National Honor or National Interest*. Malabar, Fla.: Robert E. Krieger, 1983.

———. *The First Rapprochement: England and the United States, 1795–1805*. Philadelphia: University of Pennsylvania Press, 1955.

———. *The Great Rapprochement: England and the United States, 1895–1914*. New York: Atheneum, 1968.

———. *Prologue to War: England and the United States 1805–1812*. Berkeley: University of California Press, 1964.

Perkins, Edwin J. *Financing Anglo–American Trade: The House of Brown, 1800–1880*. Cambridge, Mass.: Harvard University Press, 1975.

Ritcheson, Charles R. *Aftermath of Revolution: British Policy toward the United States, 1783–1795*. Dallas, Tex.: Southern Methodist University Press, 1969.

Sexton, Jay. *Debtor Diplomacy: Finance and American Foreign Relations in the Civil War Era 1837–1873*. Oxford: Clarendon Press, 2005.

Simmons, James C. *Star-Spangled Eden: 19th Century America through the Eyes of Dickens, Wilde, Frances Trollope, Frank Harris and Other British Travelers.* New York: Carroll & Graf, 2000.

Stevens, Kenneth R. *Border Diplomacy: The Caroline and McLeod Affairs in Anglo–American–Canadian Relations, 1837–1842.* Tuscaloosa: University of Alabama Press, 1989.

Taylor, Claire. *British and American Abolitionists: An Episode in Transatlantic Understanding.* Edinburgh: Edinburgh University Press, 1974.

Temperley, H. W. V. *The Foreign Policy of Canning, 1822–1827: England, the Neo-Holy Alliance, and the New World.* London: Frank Cass, 1966.

Thistlethwaite, Frank. *The Anglo–American Connection in the Early Nineteenth Century.* Philadelphia: University of Pennsylvania Press, 1959.

Tulloch, H. A. "Changing British Attitudes towards the United States in the 1880s." *Historical Journal*, 20, no. 4 (December 1977): 824–40.

Weinberg, Adelaide. *John Elliot Cairnes and the American Civil War: A Study in Anglo–American Relations.* London: Kingswood Press, 1970.

American Civil War, 1861–1865

Adams, E. D. *Great Britain and the American Civil War.* London: Longmans, Green, 1925.

Allen Salisbury, W. *The Civil War and the American System: America's Battle with Britain, 1860–1876.* New York: Campaigner, 1978.

Baldelli, Pia B. Celozzi. *Power Politics, Diplomacy, and the Avoidance of Hostilities between England and the United States in the Wake of Civil War.* Lewiston, N.Y.: Edwin Mellen Press, 1998.

Barnes, James J., and Patience P. Barnes. *The American Civil War through British Eyes*, Vol. 1: *Dispatches from British Diplomats, November 1860–April 1862.* Lawrence: University Press of Kentucky, 2003.

——. *The American Civil War through British Eyes*, Vol. 2: *Dispatches from British Diplomats, April 1862–February 1863.* Kent, Ohio: Kent State University Press, 2005.

——. *The American Civil War through British Eyes*, Vol. 3: *Dispatches from British Diplomats, February 1863–December 1865.* Kent, Ohio: Kent State University Press, 2005.

Beloff, Max. "Great Britain and the American Civil War." *History* 37 (February 1952): 40–48.

Bellows, Donald. "A Study of British Conservative Reaction to the American Civil War." *Journal of Southern History* 51, no. 4 (November 1985): 505–26.

Berwanger, Eugene H. *The British Foreign Service and the American Civil War*. Lawrence: University Press of Kentucky, 2006.

Blackett, R. J. M. *Divided Hearts: Britain and the American Civil War.* Baton Rouge: Louisiana State University Press, 2001.

Brady, E. A. "A Reconsideration of the Lancashire Cotton Famine." *Agricultural History* (July 1963): 156–62.

Campbell, Duncan Andrew. *English Public Opinion and American Civil War*. London: Boydell Press, 2003.

Ellison, Mary. *Support for Secession: Lancashire and the American Civil War*. Chicago: University of Chicago Press, 1971.

Farnie, D. A. "The Cotton Famine in Great Britain." In *Great Britain and Her World, 1750–1914: Essays in Honour of W. O. Henderson*, ed. B. M. Radcliffe. Manchester, England: Manchester University Press, 1975.

Ferris, Norman B. *The Trent Affair: A Diplomatic Crisis*. Knoxville: University of Tennessee Press, 1977.

Foner, Philip S. *British Labor and the American Civil War*. New York: Holmes & Meier, 1981.

Fuller, Howard J. *Clad in Iron: The American Civil War and the Challenge of British Naval Power*. Westport, Conn.: Praeger, 2007.

Grant, Alfred. *The American Civil War and the British Press*. Lanham, Md.: Scarecrow Press, 1999.

Hernon, Joseph. "British Sympathies in the American Civil War: A Reconsideration." *Journal of Southern History* 33, no. 3 (1967): 357–67.

Hollett, David. *The Alabama Affair: Great Britain and the American Civil War*. Wilmslow, England: Sigma Leisure, 1993.

Jenkins, Brian. *Britain and the War for the Union*, Vol. 1. Montreal: McGill-Queens University Press, 1974.

———. *Britain and the War for the Union*, Vol. 2. Montreal: McGill-Queens University Press, 1980.

Jones, Howard. *The Union in Peril: The Crisis of British Intervention in the Civil War.* Chapel Hill: University of North Carolina Press, 1977.

Jones, Wilbur D. "The British Conservatives and the American Civil War." *American Historical Review* 58 (1953): 527–43.

Kramer, Paul. A. "Empires, Exceptions, and Anglo–Saxons: Race and the Rule between the British and United States Empires, 1880–1910." *Journal of American History* 88, no. 4 (March 2002): 1315–53.

Landry, Harral E. "Slavery and the Slave Trade in Atlantic Diplomacy, 1850–1861." *Journal of Southern History* 47, no. 2 (May 1961): 187–207.

Larsen, Peter. "Sir Mortimer Durand in Washington: A Study in Anglo–American Relations in the Era of Theodore Roosevelt." *Mid-America* 66, no. 2 (April–July 1984): 65–78.

Mathieson, William L. *Great Britain and the Slave Trade, 1839–1865.* London: Longmans, Green, 1929.

Merli, Frank J. *The Alabama, British Neutrality, and the American Civil War.* Bloomington: Indiana University Press, 2004.

———. *Great Britain and the Confederate Navy, 1861–1865.* Bloomington: Indiana University Press, 2004.

Merli, Frank J., and Theodore A. Wilson. "The British Cabinet and the Confederacy: Autumn 1962." *Maryland Historical Magazine* 65 (1970): 239–62.

Myers, Phillip E. *Caution and Cooperation: The American Civil War in British-American Relations.* Kent, Ohio: Kent State University Press, 2008.

Owlsley, Frank Lawrence. *King Cotton Diplomacy: Foreign Relations of the Confederate States of America.* Chicago: University of Chicago Press, 1931.

Rothstein, Morton. "America in the International Rivalry for the British Wheat Market, 1860–1914." *Mississippi Valley Historical Review* 47, no. 3 (December 1960): 401–18.

Salisbury, Allen. *The Civil War and the American System: America's Battle with Britain, 1860–1876.* Washington, D.C.: Executive Intelligence Review, 1992.

Spencer, Warren F. *The Confederate Navy in Europe.* Tuscaloosa: University of Alabama Press, 1983.

Tertius deKay, James. *The Rebel Raiders: The Warship "Alabama," British Treachery and the American Civil War.* London: Pimlico, 2004.

Villiers, Brougham, and H. W. Chesson. *Anglo–American Relations, 1861–1865.* Whitefish, Mont.: Kessinger, 2007.

Whitridge, "British Liberals and the American Civil War." *History Today* 12 (1962): 688–94.

Wright. D. G. "Bradford and the American Civil War." *Journal of British Studies* 8, no. 2 (May 1969): 69–85.

IV. 20TH CENTURY

Adams, Lestyn. *Brothers across the Ocean: British Foreign Policy and the Origins of the Anglo–American "Special Relationship" 1900–1905.* London: I. B. Tauris, 2005.

Bennett, Edward M. *Separated by a Common Language: Franklin Delano Roosevelt and Anglo–American Relations, 1933–1939: The Roosevelt–Chamberlain Rivalry*. Lincoln, Neb.: iUniverse, 2002.

Burk, Kathleen. "Finance, Foreign Policy and the Anglo–American Bank: The House of Morgan, 1900–1931." *Historical Research* 61, no. 145 (June 1988): 199–211.

———. "The Lineaments of Foreign Policy: The United States and a 'New World Order,' 1919–1939." *Journal of American Studies* 26, no. 3 (December 1992): 377–92.

Burton, David H. "Theodore Roosevelt and His English Correspondents: The Intellectual Roots of the Anglo–American Alliance." *Mid-America* 53, no. 1 (January 1971): 12–34.

———. "Theodore Roosevelt and the 'Special Relationship' with Britain." *History Today* 23 (1973): 527–35.

Campbell, A. E. "Great Britain and the United States in the Far East, 1895–1903." *Historical Journal* 1, no. 2 (1958): 154–75.

Campbell, C. S. *Anglo–American Understanding, 1898–1903*. Baltimore, Md.: Johns Hopkins University Press, 1957.

Carleton, David. "Great Britain and the Coolidge Naval Disarmament Conference of 1927." *Political Science Quarterly* 83, no. 4 (December 1968): 573–98.

Cohrs, Patrick O. *America, Britain, and the Stabilisation of Europe, 1919–1932*. Cambridge: Cambridge University Press, 2006.

———. *The Unfinished Peace after World War I: America, Britain and the Stabilisation of Europe, 1919–1932*. Cambridge: Cambridge University Press, 2006.

Collier, Basil. *The Lion and the Eagle: British and Anglo–American Strategy, 1900–1950*. London: Macdonald, 1972.

Coogan, John W. *The End of Neutrality: The United States, Britain, and Maritime Rights, 1899–1915*. Ithaca, N.Y.: Cornell University Press, 1981.

Costigliola, Frank. "Anglo–American Financial Rivalry in the 1920s." *Journal of Economic History* 37, no. 4 (1977): 911–34.

———. *Awkward Dominion: American Political, Economic and Cultural Relations with Europe, 1919–1933*. Ithaca, N.Y.: Cornell University Press, 1984.

Cowman, I. *Dominion or Decline: Anglo–American Naval Relations on the Pacific 1937–1941*. Oxford: I. Berg, 1996.

Egerton, George. "Ideology, Diplomacy and International Organisation: Wilsonism and the League of Nation in Anglo–American Relations,

1918–1920." In *Anglo–American Relations in the 1920s: The Struggle for Supremacy*, ed. B. J. McKercher. Edmonton: University of Alberta Press, 1991.

Gardner, Lloyd. *Safe for Democracy: The Anglo–American Response to Revolution, 1913–1923*. Oxford: Oxford University Press, 1984.

Goldstein, Erik. "The Evolution of British Diplomatic Strategy for the Washington Conference." *Diplomacy & Statecraft* 4, no. 3 (November 1993): 35–39.

Gregory, Ross. *Walter Hines Page: Ambassador to the Court of St. James's*. Lexington: University Press of Kentucky, 1970.

Haron, Miriam Joyce. "Palestine and the Anglo–American Connection." *Modern Judaism* 2, no. 2 (May 1982): 199–211.

Harrison, Richard A. "A Presidential Demarche: Franklin D. Roosevelt's Personal Diplomacy and Great Britain, 1936–7." *Diplomatic History* 5, no. 3 (Summer 1981): 245–72.

Hogan, Michael J. *Informal Entente: The Private Structure of Cooperation in Anglo–American Diplomacy, 1918–1928*. Columbia: University of Missouri Press, 1977.

Jackson, Ian. *The Economic Cold War: America, Britain, and East-West Trade, 1948–63*. New York: Palgrave, 2001.

Kennedy, Greg. *Anglo–American Strategic Relations and the Far East, 1933–1939*. Portland, Ore.: Frank Cass, 2002.

———. "Depression and Security: Aspects Influencing the United States Navy during the Hoover Administration." *Diplomacy & Statecraft* 6, no. 2 (July 1995): 342–72.

———. "Neville Chamberlain and Strategic Relations with the U.S. during His Chancellorship." *Diplomacy & Statecraft* 13, no. 1 (March 2002): 95–120.

Keynes, John Maynard. *The Collected Writings of John Maynard Keynes*, Vol. 16: *Activities 1914–1919*. London: Macmillan, 1971.

Kreider, Carl. *The Anglo–American Trade Agreement: A Study of British and American Commercial Policies, 1934–1939*. Princeton, N.J.: Princeton University Press, 1943.

Lentin, Antony. *Lloyd George, Woodrow Wilson and the Guilt of Germany: An Essay in the Pre-History of Appeasement*. Baton Rouge: Louisiana State University Press, 1984.

Link, Arthur S. *Wilson the Diplomatist: A Look at His Major Foreign Policies*. Baltimore, Md.: Johns Hopkins Press, 1957.

MacDonald, Callum A. *The United States, Britain and Appeasement*. Basingstoke, England: Palgrave Macmillan, 1981.

MacMillan, Margaret. "Isosceles Triangle: Britain, the Dominions and the United States at the Paris Peace Conference of 1919." In *Twentieth Century Anglo–American Relations*, ed. Jonathan Hollowell. Basingstoke, England: Palgrave, 2001.

McKercher, B. J. C. *Anglo–American Relations in the 1920s: The Struggle for Supremacy.* Edmonton: University of Alberta Press, 1991.

———. *The Second Baldwin Government and the United States, 1924–1929.* Cambridge: Cambridge University Press, 1984.

———. *Transition of Power: Britain's Loss of Global Pre-eminence to the United States, 1930–1945.* Cambridge: Cambridge University Press, 1999.

———. "Wealth, Power and the New International Order: Britain and the American Challenge in the 1920s" *Diplomatic History* 12, no. 4 (Fall 1988): 411–42.

McKercher, B. J. C., and Lawrence Aronsen, eds. *The North Atlantic Triangle in a Changing World: Anglo–American-Canadian Relations, 1902–1956.* Toronto, Ont.: University of Toronto Press, 1996.

McKercher, B. J. C., and S. Enjamio. "Brighter Futures, Better Times: Britain, the Empire, and Anglo–American Economic Competition in Cuba, 1898–1920." *Diplomacy & Statecraft* 18, no. 4 (December 2007): 663–87.

Moser, John E. *Twisting the Lion's Tail: American Anglophobia between the World Wars.* Basingstoke, England: Macmillan, 1999.

Murfett, Malcolm H. *Fool-Proof Relations: The Search for Anglo–American Naval Cooperation during the Chamberlain Years, 1937–1940.* Kent Ridge: Singapore University Press, 1984.

Offner, Arnold A. "Appeasement Revisited: The United States, Great Britain, and Germany, 1933–1940." *Journal of American History* 62, no. 2 (September 1977): 384–93.

Ovendale, Ritchie. *"Appeasement" and the English-Speaking World: Britain, the United States, the Dominions and the Policy of "Appeasement,"1937–1939.* Cardiff: University of Wales Press, 1975.

Parker, R. A. C. "The Pound Sterling, the American Treasury and British Preparations for War, 1938–1939." *English Historical Review* 98, no. 387 (April 1983): 261–79.

Parsonage, Catherine. *The Evolution of Jazz in Britain, 1880–1935.* Aldershot, England: Ashgate, 2005.

Perkins, Bradford. *The Great Rapprochement: England and the United States, 1895–1914.* New York: Atheneum, 1968.

Price, Christopher. *Britain, America, and Rearmament in the 1930s: The Cost of Failure*. Basingstoke, England: Palgrave, 2001.

Reynolds, David. *The Creation of the Anglo–American Alliance, 1937–41: A Study in Competitive Co-operation*. London: Europa, 1981.

Roberts, Andrew. *"The Holy Fox": A Life of Lord Halifax*. London: Weidenfeld & Nicolson, 1991.

Rock, William R. *Chamberlain and Roosevelt: British Foreign Policy and the United States, 1937–1940*. Columbus: Ohio State University Press, 1988.

Rogers, Daniel T. *Atlantic Crossings: Social Politics in a Progressive Age*. Cambridge, Mass.: Harvard University Press, 1998.

Russett, Bruce. *Community and Contention: Britain and America in the Twentieth Century*. Cambridge, Mass.: MIT Press, 1963.

Sbardellati, John, and Tony Shaw. "Booting a Tramp: Charlie Chaplin, FBI, and the Construction of the Subversive Image in Red Scare America." *Pacific Historical Review* 72, no. 4 (November 2003): 495–530.

Schatz, Arthur W. "The Anglo–American Trade Agreement and Cordell Hull's Search for Peace, 1936–1938." *Journal of American History* 57, no. 1 (June 1970): 85–103.

Schuker, Stephen A. *The End of French Predominance in Europe: The Financial Crisis of 1924 and the Adoption of the Dawes Plan*. Chapel Hill: University of North Carolina Press, 1976.

Self, Robert. *Britain, America and the War Debt Controversy: The Economic Diplomacy of an Unspecial Relationship, 1917–1945*. London: Routledge, 2006.

Tilchin, William N. *Theodore Roosevelt and the British Empire: A Study in Presidential Statecraft*. New York: St. Martin's Press, 1997.

———. "Theodore Roosevelt, Anglo–American Relations, and the Jamaica Incident of 1907." *Diplomatic History* 19, no. 3 (Summer 1995): 385–406.

Vale, Vivian. *The American Peril: Challenge to Britain on the North Atlantic, 1901–1904*. Dover, N.H.: Manchester University Press, 1984.

Venn, Fiona. *The Anglo–American Oil War: International Politics and the Struggle for Foreign Petroleum, 1912–1945*. London: I. B. Tauris, 2007.

Watt, D. C. *Succeeding John Bull: America in Britain's Place 1900–1975*. Cambridge: Cambridge University Press, 1984.

Whitham, Charlie. "Seeing the Wood for the Trees: The British Foreign Office and the Anglo–American Trade Agreement of 1938." *Twentieth Century British History* 16, no. 1 (2005): 29–51.

Willert, Sir Arthur. *The Road to Safety: A Study in Anglo–American Relations*. New York: Frederick A. Praeger, 1953.

World War I, 1914–1918

Allard, Dean C. "Anglo–American Naval Differences during World War I." *Military Affairs* 44, no. 2 (April 1980): 75–81.

Beach, Jim. "Origins of the Special Intelligence Relationship? Anglo–American Intelligence Co-operation on the Western Front, 1917–1918." *Intelligence and National Security* 22, no. 2 (April 2007): 229–49.

Burk, Kathleen. *Britain, America and the Sinews of War, 1914–1918*. Boston: Allen & Unwin, 1985.

———. "The Diplomacy of Finance: British Financial Missions to the United States, 1914–1918." *Historical Journal* 22, no. 2 (1979): 351–72.

Fowler, W. B. *British-American Relations, 1917–1918: The Role of Sir William Wiseman*. Princeton, N.J.: Princeton University Press, 1969.

Roberts, Priscilla. "The Anglo–American Theme: American Visions of an Atlantic Alliance, 1914–1933." *Diplomatic History* 21, no. 3 (Summer 1997): 333–64.

———. "The First World War and the Emergence of American Atlanticism, 1914–20." *Diplomacy & Statecraft* 5, no. 3 (November 1994): 569–97.

———. "World War I and Anglo–American Relations: The Role of Philip Kerr and the Round Table." *Round Table: The Commonwealth Journal of International Affairs* 95, no. 383 (January 2006): 113–39.

Tillman, Seth. *Anglo–American Relations at the Paris Peace Conference of 1919*. Princeton, N.J.: Princeton University Press, 1961.

Trask, David. *Captains and Cabinets: Anglo–American Naval Relations, 1917–1918*. Columbia: University of Missouri Press, 1972.

Williams, Joyce C. *Colonel House and Edward Grey: A Study in Anglo–American Diplomacy*. Lanham, Md.: University Press of America, 1985.

Woodward, David R. *Trial by Friendship: Anglo–American Relations, 1917–1918*. Lexington: University Press of Kentucky, 1993.

World War II, 1939–1945

Aldrich, Richard J. *Intelligence and the War against Japan: Britain, America and the Politics of Secret Service*. New York: Cambridge University Press, 2000.

Aldritt, Keith. *The Greatest of Friends: Franklin D. Roosevelt and Winston Churchill, 1941–1945*. London: Robert Hale, 1995.

Andrews, Christopher. *Secret Service: The Making of the British Intelligence Community*. London: Heineman, 1985.

Bath, Alan Harris. *Tracking the Axis Enemy: The Triumph of Anglo–American Naval Intelligence*. Lawrence: University Press of Kansas, 1998.

Bercuson, David J., and Holger H. Herwig. *One Christmas in Washington: Churchill and Roosevelt Forge the Grand Alliance*. London: Weidenfeld & Nicolson, 2005.

Bernstein, Barton J. "The Uneasy Alliance: Roosevelt, Churchill, and the Atomic Bomb, 1940–1945." *Western Political Quarterly* 29, no. 2 (June 1976): 202–30.

Best, A. *Britain, Japan and Pearl Harbor: Avoiding the War in East Asia, 1936–1941*. London: Routledge, 1995.

Charmley, John. *Churchill's Grand Alliance: The Anglo–American Special Relationship, 1940–1957*. London: Hodder & Stoughton, 1995.

Clarke, Sir Richard. *Anglo–American Economic Collaboration in War and Peace, 1942–1949*. Oxford: Oxford University Press, 1982.

Dallek, Robert. *Franklin D. Roosevelt and American Foreign Policy, 1932–1945*. New York: Oxford University Press, 1979.

Danchev, Alex, ed. *Establishing the Anglo–American Alliance: The Second World War Diaries of Brigadier Vivian Dykes*. London: Brassey's, 1990.

———. *Very Special Relationship: Field-Marshal Sir John Dill and the Anglo–American Alliance, 1941–44*. London: Brassey's, 1986.

Dobson, Alan P. *U.S. Wartime Aid to Britain, 1940–1946*. London: Croom Helm, 1986.

Duke, Simon. *U.S. Defence Bases in the United Kingdom: A Matter for Joint Decision?* Basingstoke, England: Macmillan, 1987.

Edmonds, Robin. *The Big Three: Churchill, Roosevelt and Stalin in Peace and War*. New York: W. W. Norton, 1991.

Freeman, Lawrence K. "Roosevelt's 'Grand Strategy' to Rid the World of British Colonialism: 1941–1945." *American Almanac* (July 14, 1997). Available online at http://american_almanac.tripod.com/lkffdr.htm (accessed 12 November 2008).

Gilbert, Martin. *Churchill and America*. New York: Free Press, 2005.

Gill, Sadiq Ali. *Anglo–American Diplomacy and the Emergence of Pakistan, 1940–1947*. Lahore, Pakistan: University of the Punjab, 1990.

Hathaway, Robert. *Ambiguous Partnership: Britain and America, 1944–1947*. New York: Columbia University Press, 1981.

———. *Great Britain and the United States: Special Relations since World War II.* Boston: Twayne, 1990.

Hilton, Stanley. "The Welles Mission to Europe, February–March 1940: Illusion or Realism?" *Journal of American History* 58, no. 1 (June 1971): 93–120.

Hinsley, F. H., and Alan Stripp, eds. *Codebreakers: The Inside Story of Bletchley Park.* New York: Oxford University Press, 1993.

Holland, James. *Together We Stand: Britain, America, and the War in North Africa, May 1942–May 1943.* London: HarperCollins, 2005.

Jakub, Jay. *Spies and Saboteurs: Anglo–American Collaboration and Rivalry in Human Intelligence Collection and Special Operations, 1940–45.* New York: St. Martin's Press, 1999.

Jones, Matthew. *Britain, the United States, and the Mediterranean War, 1942–1944.* New York: St. Martin's Press, 1996.

Keynes, John Maynard. *The Collected Writings of John Maynard Keynes,* Vol. 23: *Activities 1940–1943: External War Finance.* London: Macmillan, 1979.

———. *The Collected Writings of John Maynard Keynes,* Vol. 26: *Activities 1941–1946: Shaping the Post-War World: Bretton Woods and Reparations.* London: Macmillan, 1980.

Kimball, Warren F. *Churchill and Roosevelt: The Complete Correspondence.* 3 vols. Princeton, N.J.: Princeton University Press, 1984.

———. *Forged in War: Roosevelt, Churchill, and the Second World War.* New York: Morrow, 1997.

———. *The Most Unsordid Act: Lend-Lease, 1939–1941.* Baltimore, Md.: Johns Hopkins University Press, 1969.

Kolko, Gabriel. *The Politics of War: Allied Diplomacy and the World Crisis of 1943–1945.* New York: Pantheon Books, 1990.

Kondapi, C. *Allied War Diplomacy and Strategy, 1940–45.* Madras, Ore.: Woodside Books, 1994.

LaFeber, Walter. "Roosevelt, Churchill, and Indochina: 1942–45." *American Historical Review* 80, no. 5 (December 1975): 1277–95.

Lane, Ann, and Howard Temperley, eds. *The Rise and Fall of the Grand Alliance, 1941–45.* London: Macmillan, 1995.

Lash, Joseph P. *Roosevelt and Churchill, 1939–1941: The Partnership That Saved the West.* London: Deutsch, 1977.

Leutze, James R. *Bargaining for Supremacy: Anglo–American Naval Collaboration, 1937–1941.* Chapel Hill: University of North Carolina, 1977.

Loewenheim, Francis L., Harold D. Langley, and Manfred Jonas, eds. *Roosevelt and Churchill: Their Secret Wartime Correspondence.* London: Barrie & Jenkins, 1975.

Louis, William R. *Ends of British Imperialism: The United States and the Decolonization of the British Empire, 1941–1945*. London: I. B. Tauris, 2006.

———. *Imperialism at Bay, 1941–1945: The United States and the Decolonization of the British Empire*. Oxford: Clarendon Press, 1986.

Mahl, Thomas E. *Desperate Deception: British Covert Operations in the United States, 1939–1944*. McLean, Va.: Brassey's, 1998.

McKercher, B. J. C. *Transition of Power: Britain's Loss of Global Pre-eminence to the United States, 1930–1945*. Cambridge: Cambridge University Press, 1999.

Millgate, Helen D. *Got Any Gum, Chum? GIs in Wartime Britain 1942–1945*. Stroud, England: Sutton, 2001.

Nadeau, Remi. *Stalin, Churchill and Roosevelt Divide Europe*. New York: Praeger, 1990.

Neumann, William L. *After Victory: Churchill, Roosevelt, Stalin and the Making of the Peace*. New York: Harper & Row, 1967.

Nicholas, H. G., ed. *Washington Despatches, 1941–45: Weekly Political Reports from the British Embassy*. Chicago: University of Chicago Press, 1981.

Ovendale, Ritchie. *Britain, the United States and the End of the Palestine Mandate, 1942–1948*. Woodbridge, England: Boydell Press, 1989.

Overy, Richard. *Why the Allies Won*. New York: W. W. Norton, 1997.

Parmar, Inderjeet. *Special Interests, the State and the Anglo–American Alliance, 1939–1945*. London: Frank Cass, 1995.

———. *Think Tanks and Power in Foreign Policy: A Comparative Study of the Role and Influence of the Council on Foreign Relations and the Royal Institute of International Affairs*. Basingstoke, England: Palgrave Macmillan, 2004.

Paul, Septimus H. *Nuclear Rivals: Anglo–American Atomic Relations, 1941–1952*. Columbus: Ohio State University Press, 2000.

Reynolds, David. *From World War to Cold War: Churchill, Roosevelt and the International History of the 1940s*. Oxford: Oxford University Press, 2006.

———. *Lord Lothian and Anglo–American Relations, 1939–1940*. Philadelphia: American Philosophical Society, 1983.

———. *Rich Relations: The American Occupation of Britain, 1942–1945*. London: HarperCollins, 1995.

Rusbridger, James, and Eric Nave. *Betrayal at Pearl Harbor: How Churchill Lured Roosevelt into World War II*. New York: Summit Books, 1991.

Ryan, Henry B. *The Vision of Anglo–America: The US–UK Alliance and the Emerging Cold War, 1943–1946*. Cambridge: Cambridge University Press, 1987.

Sainsbury, Keith. *Churchill and Roosevelt at War: The War They Fought and the Peace They Hoped to Make*. Basingstoke, England: Macmillan, 1994.

———. *The Turning Point: Roosevelt, Stalin, Churchill and Chiang Kai-shek, 1943: The Moscow, Cairo and Tehran Conferences*. New York: Oxford University Press, 1985.

Sbrega, John J. "Anglo–American Relations and the Selection of Mountbatten as Supreme Allied Commander, South East Asia." *Military Affairs* 46, no. 3 (October 1982): 139–145.

Schukert, Edfrieda Berthiaume, and Barbara Smith Scibetta. *War Brides of World War II*. Novato, Calif.: Presidio Press, 1988.

Skidelsky, Robert. *John Maynard Keynes*, Vol. 3: *Fighting for Britain, 1937–1946*. London: Macmillan, 2000.

Smith, Bradley F. *The Ultra-Magic Deals and the Most Secret Relationship, 1940–1946*. Novato: Calif.: Presidio Press, 1993.

Smith, Graham. *When Jim Crow Met John Bull: Black American Soldiers in World War II Britain*. New York: St. Martin's Press, 1988.

Shogan, Robert. *Hard Bargain: How FDR Twisted Churchill's Arm, Evaded the Law and Changed the Role of the American Presidency*. New York: Scribner, 1995.

Smith, Kevin. *Conflict over Convoys: Anglo–American Logistics Diplomacy in the Second World War*. New York: Cambridge University Press, 1996.

Stafford, David. *Roosevelt and Churchill: Men of Secrets*. London: Little, Brown, 1999.

Stettinius, Edward R. *The Diaries of Edward R. Stettinius, Jr., 1943–1946*, ed. Thomas M. Campbell and George C. Herring. New York: Franklin Watts, 1975.

Stoler, Mark A. *Allies in War: Britain and America against the Axis Powers, 1940–1945*. London: Hodder Arnold, 2005.

Thorne, Christopher. *Allies of a Kind: The United States, Britain, and the War against Japan, 1941–45*. New York: Oxford University Press, 1979.

Virden, Jenel. *Good-bye Piccadilly: British War Brides in America*. Urbana: University of Illinois Press, 1996.

Watts, F., ed. *Voices of History, 1943–44: Speeches and Papers of Roosevelt, Churchill, Stalin, Chiang, Hitler and Other Leaders Delivered during 1943*. New York: Gramercy, 1944.

Whitfield, Andrew. *Hong Kong, Empire, and the Anglo–American Alliance, 1941–1945.* New York: Palgrave, 2001.

Whitham, Charlie. "On Dealing with Gangsters: The Limits of British 'Generosity' in the Leasing of Bases to the United States, 1940–41." *Diplomacy & Statecraft* 7, no. 3 (November 1996): 589–630.

Wills, Matthew B. *Wartime Mission of Harry L. Hopkins.* Raleigh, N.C.: Pentland Press, 2005.

Woods, Randall B. *A Changing of the Guard: Anglo–American Relations, 1941–1946.* Chapel Hill: University of North Carolina Press, 1990.

The Cold War, 1945–1991

Acheson, Dean. *Present at the Creation: My Years at the State Department.* New York: W. W. Norton, 1969.

Aldous, Richard, and Sabine Lee, ed. *Harold Macmillan and Britain's World Role.* Basingstoke, England: Macmillan, 1995.

Aldrich, Richard J. "British Intelligence and the Anglo–American 'Special Relationship' during the Cold War." *Review of International Studies* 24, no. 1 (1998): 331–51.

———. *The Hidden Hand: Britain, America and Cold War Secret Intelligence.* New York: Penguin-Putnam, 2002.

———. *Intelligence and the War against Japan: Britain, America and the Politics of Secret Service.* Cambridge: Cambridge University Press, 2000.

Anglo–Allen, H. C. "The Anglo–American Relationship in the Sixties." *International Affairs* 39, no. 1 (January 1963): 37–48.

Almog, Orna. *Britain, Israel and the United States, 1955–1958.* London: Routledge, 2003.

Anderson, Duncan. *The Falklands Islands, 1982.* Oxford: Osprey, 2002.

Anderson, Terry H. *The United States, Great Britain and the Cold War, 1944–1947.* Columbia: University of Missouri Press, 1981.

Ashton, Nigel. *Eisenhower, Macmillan and the Problem of Nasser.* Basingstoke, England: Macmillan, 1996.

———. *Kennedy, Macmillan and the Cold War: The Irony of Interdependence.* Basingstoke, England: Palgrave, 2001.

Attlee, Clement. "Britain and America: Commons Aims, Different Opinions." *Foreign Affairs* 32, no. 2 (January 1954): 190–202.

Ball, S. J. "Military Nuclear Relations between the United States and Great Britain under the Terms of the McMahon Act, 1946–1958." *Historical Journal*, 38, no. 2 (1995): 439–54.

Bamford, J. *The Puzzle Palace: America's National Security Agency and Its Special Relationship with Britain's GCHQ*. Boston: Houghton Mifflin, 1982.

Barker, Elisabeth. *The British between the Superpowers, 1945–50*. London: Macmillan, 1983.

Bartlett, C. J. *"The Special Relationship": A Political History of Anglo–American Relations since 1945*. London: Longman, 1992.

Baylis, John. *Anglo–American Defence Relations, 1939–80: The Special Relationship*. Basingstoke, England: Macmillan, 1981.

———. *The Diplomacy of Pragmatism: Britain and the Formation of NATO, 1942–1949*. Kent, Ohio: Kent State University Press, 1993.

Beckett, Ian F. W. "Robert Thompson and the British Advisory Mission to South Vietnam, 1961–1965." *Small Wars and Insurgencies* 8, no. 3 (October 1997): 43–44.

Belmonte, Laura. "Anglo–American Relations and the Dismissal of MacArthur." *Diplomatic History* 19, no. 4 (Fall 1995): 641–68.

Bluth, C. "Anglo–American Relations and the Falklands Conflict." In *International Perspectives on the Falklands Conflict*, ed. Alex Danchev. Basingstoke, England: Macmillan, 1992.

Botti, Timothy J. *The Long Wait: The Forging of the Anglo–American Nuclear Alliance, 1945–1958*. New York: Greenwood, 1987.

Boyce, D. George. *The Falklands War*. London: Palgrave, 2005.

Boyle, Peter. "The British Government's View of the Cuban Missile Crisis." *Contemporary British History* 10, no. 3 (Autumn 1996): 22–38.

Brinkley, Douglas. "Dean Acheson and the 'Special Relationship': The West Point Speech of December 1962." *Historical Journal* 33, no. 3 (September 1990): 599–608.

Bullock, Alan. *Ernest Bevin: Foreign Secretary, 1945–51*. New York: W. W. Norton, 1983.

Burk, Kathleen. "The Americans, the Germans, and the British: The 1976 IMF Crisis." *Twentieth Century British History* 5, no. 3 (1994): 351–69.

Burk, Kathleen, and Alec Cairncross. *"Goodbye Great Britain": The 1976 IMF Crisis*. New Haven, Conn.: Yale University Press, 1992.

Busch, Peter. *All the Way with JFK? Britain, the US, and the Vietnam War*. Oxford: Oxford University Press, 2003.

Campbell, Duncan. *The Unsinkable Aircraft Carrier: American Military Power in Britain*. London: Michael Joseph, 1984.

Chi-Kwan, Mark. *Hong Kong and the Cold War: Anglo–American Relations, 1949–1957*. Oxford: Oxford University Press, 2004.

Clark, Ian. *Nuclear Diplomacy and the Special Relationship: Britain's Deterrent and America, 1957–1962*. Oxford: Clarendon Press, 1994.

Clark, Ian, and David Angell. "Britain, the United States and the Control of Nuclear Weapons: The Diplomacy of the Thor Deployment, 1956–58." *Diplomacy and Statecraft* 2, no. 3 (November 1991): 153–77.

Clark, Ian, and Nicholas J. Wheeler. *The British Origins of Nuclear Strategy, 1945–1955*. New York: Clarendon Press, 1989.

Colman, Jonathan. *A "Special Relationship"? Harold Wilson, Lyndon B. Johnson, and Anglo–American Relations at the Summit*. Manchester, England: Manchester University Press, 2004.

Combs, Arthur. "The Path Not Taken: The British Alternative to U.S. Policy in Vietnam, 1954–1956." *Diplomatic History* 19, no. 1 (Winter 1995): 33–57.

Croft, Stuart. *The End of Superpower: British Foreign Office Conceptions of a Changing World, 1945–51*. Aldershot, England: Dartmouth, 1994.

Danchev, Alex. "The Cold War 'Special Relationship' Revisited." *Diplomacy & Statecraft* 17, no. 3 (September 2006): 579–95.

———. *Oliver Franks: Founding Father*. New York: Clarendon Press, 1993.

Defty, Andrew. *Britain, America, and Anti-communist Propaganda, 1945–53: The Information Research Department*. London: Routledge, 2004.

Deighton, Anne, ed. *Britain and the First Cold War*. London: Macmillan, 1990.

———. *The Impossible Peace: Britain, the Division of Germany and the Origins of the Cold War*. Oxford: Clarendon Press, 1990.

Dobson, Alan P. "Informally Special? The Churchill–Truman Talks of January 1952 and the State of Anglo–American Relations." *Review of International Studies*, 23, (1997): 27–47.

———. *Peaceful Air Warfare: The United States, Britain and the Politics of International Aviation*. Oxford: Clarendon Press, 1991.

———. *The Politics of the Anglo–American Economic Special Relationship 1940–1984*. New York: St. Martin's Press, 1988.

———. "The Special Relationship and European Integration." *Diplomacy and Statecraft* 2, no. 1 (March 1991): 79–102.

———. "The Years of Transition: Anglo–American Relations 1961–1967." *Review of International Studies* 16, no. 3 (July 1990): 239–58.

Dockrill, Michael. "Anglo–American Relations and the Korean War, June 1950–June 1951." *International Affairs* 62, no. 3 (Summer 1986): 459–76.

Dockrill, Saki. *Britain's Retreat from East of Suez: The Choice between Europe and the World?* Basingstoke, England: Palgrave, 2002.

———. "Forging the Anglo–American Global Defence Partnership: Harold Wilson, Lyndon Johnson and the Washington Summit, December 1964." *Journal of Strategic Studies* 23, no. 4 (December 2000): 107–29.

Dorril, Stephen, and Robin Ramsay. *Smear! Wilson and the Secret State.* London: Grafton, 1992.

Dumbrell, John. "The Johnson Administration and the British Labour Government: Vietnam, the Pound and East of Suez." *Journal of American Studies* 30, no. 2 (August 1996): 211–31.

Dumbrell, John, and Sylvia Ellis. "British Involvement in Vietnam Peace Initiatives, 1966–1867: Marigolds, Sunflowers, and 'Kosygin Week.'" *Diplomatic History* 27, no. 1 (January 2003): 113–49.

Eden, Anthony. *Memoirs*, Vol. 3: *The Reckoning.* London: Cassell 1965.

Edmonds, Robin. *Setting the Mould: The United States and Britain, 1945–1950.* New York: Norton, 1986.

Edwards, Jill. *Anglo–American Relations and the Franco Question, 1945–55.* Oxford: Clarendon Press, 1999.

Eisenhower, Dwight D. *The White House Years: Waging Peace, 1956–1961.* London: Heinemann, 1961.

Ellis, Sylvia. *Britain, America, and the Vietnam War.* Westport, Conn.: Praeger, 2004.

———. "Lyndon Johnson, Harold Wilson and the Vietnam War: A Not So Special Relationship?" In *Twentieth-Century Anglo–American Relations*, ed. Jonathan Hollowell. Basingstoke, England: Palgrave, 2001.

Ellison, James. "Defeating the General: Anglo–American Relations, Europe and the NATO Crisis of 1966." *Cold War History* 6, no. 1 (February 2006): 85–111.

———. *The United States, Britain and the Transatlantic Crisis: Rising to Gaulist Challenge, 1963–1968.* Basingstoke, England: Palgrave, 2008.

Engel, Jeffrey A. *Cold War at 30,000 Feet: The Anglo–American Fight for Aviation Supremacy.* Cambridge, Mass.: Harvard University Press, 2007.

Ferraro, Matthew F. *Tough Going: Anglo–American Relations and the Yom Kippur War of 1973.* Lincoln, Neb.: iUniverse.com, 2007.

Fielding, Jeremy. "Coping with Decline: U.S. Policy towards the British Defence Reviews of 1966." *Diplomatic History* 23, no. 4 (Fall 1999): 633–56.

———. "The Primacy of National Security? American Responses to the British Financial Crisis of 1949." *Diplomacy & Statecraft* 11, no. 1 (March 2000): 163–88.

Finer, Herbert. *Dulles over Suez: The Theory and Practice of His Diplomacy.* Chicago: Quadrangle Books, 1964.

Fish, M. Steven. "After Stalin's Death: The Anglo–American Debate over a New Cold War." *Diplomatic History* 10, no. 4 (Fall 1986): 333–56.

Folly, Martin H. "Breaking the Vicious Circle: Britain, the United States, and the Genesis of the North Atlantic Treaty." *Diplomatic History* 12, no. 1 (Winter 1988): 59–78.

Foot, Rosemary J. "Anglo–American Relations in the Korean Crisis: The British Effort to Avert an Expanded War, December 1950–January 1951." *Diplomatic History* 10, no. 1 (January 1986): 43–57.

Forrestal, James. *The Forrestal Diaries: The Inner History of the Cold War.* London: Cassell, 1952.

Franks, Oliver. "The Special Relationship 1947–1952." In *Adventures with Britannia: Personalities, Politics and Culture in Britain,* ed. William R. Louis. Austin: Texas University Press, 1995.

Frazier, Robert. *Anglo–American Relations with Greece: The Coming of the Cold War, 1942–47.* New York: St. Martin's Press, 1991.

Freedman, Lawrence, ed. *Britain and the Falklands War.* London: Blackwell, 1988.

———. *The Troubled Alliance: Atlantic Relations of the 1980s.* London: Heinemann, 1983.

Freeman, J. P. G. *Britain's Nuclear Arms Control Policy in the Context of Anglo–American Relations, 1957–68.* New York: St. Martin's Press, 1986.

Gardner, Richard. *Sterling-Dollar Diplomacy: Anglo–American Collaboration in the Reconstruction of Multilateral Trade.* New York: Oxford University Press, 1956.

Geelhoed, E. Bruce, and Anthony O. Edmonds. *Eisenhower, Macmillan and Allied Unity, 1957–1961.* Basingstoke, England: Palgrave Macmillan, 2003.

Gelb, Leslie H. *Anglo–American Relations, 1945–1949: Toward a Theory of Alliances.* New York: Garland, 1988.

Goodman, Michael. "With a Little Help from My Friends: The Anglo–American Atomic Intelligence Partnership." *Diplomacy & Statecraft* 18, no. 1 (January 2007): 155–83.

Gore-Booth, Paul. *With Great Truth and Respect.* London: Constable, 1974.

Gormly, James L. "The Washington Declaration and the 'Poor Relation': Anglo–American Atomic Diplomacy, 1945–1946." *Diplomatic History* 8, no. 2 (April 1984): 125–44.

Gowing, Margaret. *Independence and Deterrence: Britain and Atomic Energy, 1945–52*. 2 vols. London: Macmillan, 1974.

Grosser, Alfred. *The Western Alliance: European–American Relations since 1945*. New York: Random House, 1980.

Hahn, Peter L. *The United States, Great Britain and Egypt, 1945–1956: Strategy and Diplomacy in the Early Cold War*. Chapel Hill: University of North Carolina Press, 1991.

Hamilton, Keith. "Britain, France, and America's Year of Europe, 1973." *Diplomacy & Statecraft* 17, no. 4 (December 2006): 871–95.

Hammond, P. Y. "The 1976 UK–IMF Crisis: The Markets, the Americans and the IMF." *Contemporary British History* 11, no. 3 (Autumn 1997): 1–17.

Harbutt, F. R. *The Iron Curtain: Churchill, America, and the Origins of the Cold War*. Oxford: Oxford University Press, 1986.

Healey, Denis. *The Time of My Life*. London: Michael Joseph, 1989.

Henderson, Nicholas. *The Birth of NATO*. Boulder, Colo.: Westview Press, 1983.

———. *Mandarin: The Diaries of an Ambassador, 1969–1982*. London: Weidenfeld & Nicolson, 1994.

Hogan, Michael J. *The Marshall Plan: America, Britain and the Reconstruction of Western Europe, 1947–1952*. Cambridge: Cambridge University Press, 1989.

Hollander, Paul. *Anti-Americanism: Critiques at Home and Abroad 1964–1990*. New York: Oxford University Press, 1992.

Hopkins, Michael F. *Oliver Franks and the Truman Administration: Anglo–American Relations, 1948–1952*. London: Routledge, 2003.

Horne, Alistair. *Macmillan*, Vol. 2: *1957–1986*. London: Macmillan, 1989.

Hughes, Geraint. "Britain, the Transatlantic Alliance, and the Arab–Israeli War of 1973." *Journal of Cold War Studies* 10, no. 2 (Spring 2008): 3–40.

Inder Signh, Anita. *The Limits of British Influence: South Asia and the Anglo–American Relationship, 1947–1956*. London: Pinter, 1993.

Jackson, Robert. *United States Air Forces in Britain: Its Aircraft, Bases and Strategy since 1948*. Shrewsbury, England: Airlife, 2000.

Jakub, Jay. *Spies and Saboteurs: Anglo–American Collaboration and Rivalry in Human Intelligence Collection and Special Operations, 1940–45*. Basingstoke, England: Palgrave Macmillan, 1999.

Johnson, Lyndon B. *The Vantage Point: Perspectives of the Presidency, 1963–1969*. New York: Holt, Rinehart & Winston, 1971.

Jones, Martin. *Failure in Palestine: British and United States Policy after the Second World War*. London: Mansell, 1986.

Jones, Matthew. "Anglo–American Relations after Suez, the Rise and Decline of the Working Group Experiment, and the French Challenge to NATO, 1957–59." *Diplomacy & Statecraft* 14, no. 2 (March 2003): 49–79.

———. *Conflict and Confrontation in South East Asia, 1961–65: Britain, the United States, Indonesia and the Creation of Malaysia*. Cambridge: Cambridge University Press, 2002.

———. "'Maximum Disavowable Aid': Britain, the United States and the Indonesian Rebellion, 1957–58." *English Historical Review* 114, no. 459 (November 1999): 1179–1216.

Kaplan, Lawrence S., ed. *American Historians and the Atlantic Alliance*. Kent, Ohio: Kent State University Press, 1991.

Kaufman, Victor S. *Confronting Communism: U.S. and British Policies toward China*. Columbia: University of Missouri Press, 2001.

Kelly, Saul. *Cold War in the Desert: Britain, the United States and the Italian Colonies, 1945–52*. London: Palgrave, 2000.

Kennan, George. *Memoirs, 1925–1950*. Boston: Little, Brown, 1967.

Keynes, John Maynard. *The Collected Writings of John Maynard Keynes*, Vol. 26: *Activities, 1941–1946: Shaping the Post-War World: Bretton Woods and Reparations*. London: Macmillan, 1980.

Kissinger, Henry. *The White House Years*. Boston: Little, Brown, 1979.

———. *Years of Upheaval*. Boston: Little, Brown, 1982.

Krieger, Joel. *Reagan, Thatcher and the Politics of Decline*. New York: Oxford University Press, 1986.

Kunz, Diane. *Butter and Guns: America's Cold War Economic Diplomacy*. New York: Free Press, 1997.

———. *The Economic Diplomacy of the Suez Crisis*. Chapel Hill: University of North Carolina Press, 1991.

———. "'Somewhat Mixed Up Together': Anglo–American Defence and Financial Policy during the 1960s." *Journal of Imperial and Commonwealth History* 27, no 2 (1999): 213–32.

Knight, Wayne Stone. "Labourite Britain: America's 'Sure Friend'? The Anglo–Soviet Treaty Issue, 1947." *Diplomatic History* 7, no. 4 (1983): 267–82.

Kyle, Keith. *Suez: Britain's End of Empire in the Middle East*. London: I. B. Tauris, 2002.

Lankford, Nelson D. *The Last American Diplomat: The Biography of David K. E. Bruce, 1898–1977*. Boston: Little, Brown, 1996.

Leffler, Melvyn P. *A Preponderance of Power: National Security, the Truman Administration, and the Cold War*. Palo Alto, Calif.: Stanford University Press, 1992.

Leigh, David. *The Wilson Plot: How the Spycatchers and Their American Allies Tried to Overthrow the British Government*. New York: Pantheon, 1988.

Lerche, Charles O. "The United States, Great Britain, and SEATO: A Case Study in the Fait Accompli." *Journal of Politics* 18, no. 3 (August 1956): 459–78.

Louis, Wm. Roger. "The Dissolution of the British Empire in the Era of Vietnam." *American Historical Review* 107, no. 1 (February 2002): 1–25.

Lowe, Peter. "An Ally and a Recalcitrant General: Great Britain, General MacArthur and the Korean War, 1950–1." *English Historical Review* 105, no. 416 (July 1990): 624–53.

———. *The Origins of the Korean War*. New York: Addison Wesley Longman, 1997.

Lucas, Scott W. *Divided We Stand: Britain, the United States and the Suez Crisis*. London: Sceptre, 1996.

MacDonald, Callum. *Britain and the Korean War*. Oxford: Basil Blackwell, 1990.

Macmillan, Harold. *Pointing the Way: 1959–1961*. London: Macmillan, 1972.

———. *Riding the Storm: 1956–59*. London: Macmillan, 1971.

Maisch, Christian J. "The Falkland/Malvinas Islands Clash of 1831–32: U.S. and British Diplomacy in the South Atlantic." *Diplomatic History* 24, no. 2 (Spring 2000): 185–209.

Manderson-Jones, R. B. *The Special Relationship: Anglo–American Relations and Western European Unity 1947–1956*. London: London School of Economics, 1972.

Marsh, Steve. *Anglo–American Relations and Cold War Oil*. New York: Palgrave Macmillan, 2003.

Martin, Edwin W. *Divided Counsel: The Anglo–American Response to Communist Victory in China*. Lexington: University Press of Kentucky, 1986.

Mauer, V. "Harold Macmillan and the Deadline Crisis over Berlin." *Twentieth Century British History* 9, no. 1 (1998): 54–85.

McKenzie, Francine. "Renegotiating a Special Relationship: The Commonwealth and Anglo–American Economic Discussions, September–December 1945." *Journal of Imperial and Commonwealth History* 26, no. 3 (1998): 71–93.

McNeill, William H. *America, Britain and Russia: Their Conflict and Co-operation, 1941–46*. London: Oxford University Press, 1953.

Melissen, Jan. "Pre-Summit Diplomacy: Britain, the United States and the Nassau Conference, December 1962." *Diplomacy & Statecraft* 7, no. 3 (November 1996): 652–87.

———. "The Restoration of the Nuclear Alliance: Great Britain and Atomic Negotiations with the United States, 1957–1958." *Contemporary Record* 6, no. 1 (Summer 1992): 72–106.

———. *The Struggle for Nuclear Partnership: Britain, the United States and the Making of an Ambiguous Alliance, 1952–1959*. Groningen, Netherlands: Styx, 1993.

———. "The Thor Saga: Anglo–American Nuclear Relations, U.S. IRBM Development and Deployment in Britain, 1955–1959." *Journal of Strategic Studies* 15, no. 2 (June 1992): 172–205.

Murray, Donette. *Kennedy, Macmillan, and Nuclear Weapons*. New York: St. Martin's Press, 2000.

Nixon, Richard. *The Memoirs of Richard Nixon*. New York: Grosset & Dunlap, 1978.

Nunnerly, David. *President Kennedy and Britain*. London: Bodley Head, 1972.

Ovendale, Ritchie. *The English-Speaking Alliance: Britain, the United States, the Dominions and the Cold War, 1945–1951*. London: Allen & Unwin, 1985.

———. "Great Britain and the Anglo–American Invasion of Jordan and Lebanon in 1958." *International History Review* 16, no. 2 (1994): 284–304.

Pearson, Ivan. "The Syrian Crisis of 1957, the Anglo–American 'Special Relationship,' and the 1958 Landings in Jordan and Lebanon." *Middle Eastern Studies* 43, no. 1 (January 2007): 45–64.

Pelling, Henry. *Britain and the Marshall Plan*. Basingstoke, England: Palgrave Macmillan, 1988.

Petersen, Tore T. *The Middle East between the Two Great Powers: Anglo–American Co-operation, 1952–1957*. New York: St. Martin's Press, 2000.

Ponting, Clive. *Breach of Promise: Labour in Power, 1964–1970*. London: Penguin, 1990.

Priest, Andrew. "In American Hands: Britain, the United States and the Polaris Nuclear Project, 1962–1968." *Contemporary British History* 19, no. 3 (September 2005): 355–76

———. *Kennedy, Johnson and NATO: Britain, America and the Dynamics of Alliance, 1962–1968*. London: Routledge, 2006.

Rawnsley, G. D. "How Special Is Special? The Anglo–American Alliance during the Cuban Missile Crisis." *Contemporary Record* 9, no. 3 (Winter 1995): 586–601.

Reynolds, David. "A 'Special Relationship'?: America, Britain and the International Order since World War II." *International Affairs* 62, no. 1 (1985): 1–20.

Richardson, Louise. *When Allies Differ: Anglo–American Relations during the Suez and Falklands Crises*. New York: St. Martin's Press, 1996.

Richelson, Jeffrey T., and Desmond Ball. *The Ties That Bind: Intelligence Cooperation between the UKUSA Countries—The United Kingdom, the United States of America, Canada, Australia and New Zealand*. Hemel Hempstead, England: Allen & Unwin, 1985.

Roy, Raj. "The Battle for Bretton Woods: America, Britain and the International Financial Crisis of October 1967–March 1968." *Cold War History* 2, no. 2 (January 2002): 33–60.

———. "No Secrets between 'Special Friends': America's Involvement in British Economic Policy, October 1964–April 1965." *History* 89, no. 295 (2004): 399–423.

Ruane, Kevin. "Anthony Eden, British Diplomacy and the Origins of the Geneva Conference of 1954." *History Journal* 37, no. 1 (March 1994): 153–72.

———. "Containing America: Aspects of British Foreign Policy and the Cold War in South-East Asia, 1951–1954." *Diplomacy & Statecraft* 7, no. 1 (March 1996): 141–74.

———. "Refusing to Pay the Price: British Foreign Policy and the Pursuit of Victory in Vietnam, 1952–1954." *English Historical Review* 110, no. 435 (1995): 70–92.

———. *The Rise and Fall of the European Defence Community: Anglo–American Relations and the Crisis of European Defence, 1950–55*. Basingstoke, England: Macmillan, 2000.

Ruane, Kevin, and James Ellison. "Managing the Americans: Anthony Eden, Harold Macmillan and the Pursuit of 'Power-by-Proxy' in the 1950s." *Contemporary British History* 18, no. 3 (Autumn 2004): 147–67

Schrafstetter, S. "'Loquacious . . . and Pointless as Ever?' Britain, the United States and the United Nations Negotiations on International Control of Nuclear Energy, 1945–1948." *Contemporary British History* 16, no. 4 (Winter 2002): 87–108.

Scott, Leonard. *Macmillan, Kennedy and the Cuban Missile Crisis: Political, Military and Intelligence Aspects*. Basingstoke, England: Macmillan, 1999.

———. "On the Brink: Britain and the Cuban Missile Crisis." *Contemporary Record* 5, no. 3 (1991): 507–18.

Shlaim, Avi. "Britain, the Berlin Blockade and the Cold War." *International Affairs* 60, no. 1 (Winter 1983–1984): 1–14.

Shultz, George P. *Turmoil and Triumph: My Years as Secretary of State*. New York: Scribner's, 1993.

Smith, Geoffrey. *Reagan and Thatcher*. London: Bodley Head, 1990.

Smith, Joseph, ed. *The Origins of NATO*. Exeter, England: University of Exeter Press, 1990.

Stafford, David, and Rhodri Jeffreys-Jones. *American-British-Canadian Intelligence Relations 1939–2000*. London: Frank Cass, 2000.

Steininger, Rolf. "The Americans Are in a Hopeless Position: Great Britain and the War in Vietnam, 1964–65." *Diplomacy & Statecraft* 8, no. 3 (November 1997): 237–85.

Stueck, William. "The Limits of Influence: British Policy and American Expansion of the War in Korea." *Pacific Historical Review* 55, no. 1 (February 1986): 65–96.

Tarling, Nicholas. *Britain, Southeast Asia and the Onset of the Cold War, 1945–1950*. Cambridge: Cambridge University Press, 1998.

Taylor, Richard. *Against the Bomb: The British Peace Movement, 1958–1965*. Oxford: Oxford University Press, 1988.

Thatcher, Margaret. *Downing Street Years*. London: HarperCollins, 1993.

Thorne, Christopher. "Indochina and Anglo–American Relations." *Pacific Historical Review* 45, no. 1 (February 1976): 73–96.

Toschi, Simona. "Washington-London-Paris: An Untenable Triangle (1960–1963)." *Journal of European Integration History* 1, no. 2 (1995): 81–109.

Turnbull, C. Mary. "Britain and Vietnam, 1948–1955." *War and Society* 6, no. 2 (September 1988): 104–24.

Twigge, Stephen, and Len Scott. *Planning Armageddon: Britain, the United States, and the Command of Western Nuclear Forces, 1945–1964*. Amsterdam: Harwood Academic, 2000.

Wheeler, Nicholas. "British Nuclear Weapons and Anglo–American Relations, 1945–54." *International Affairs* 62, no. 1 (Winter 1985–1986): 71–86.

Wilford, Hugh. *The CIA, the British Left, and the Cold War: Calling the Tune?* London: Routledge, 2003.

Williamson, Daniel C. *Separate Agendas: Churchill, Eisenhower, and Anglo–American Relations, 1953–1961*. Lanham, Md.: Lexington Books, 2006.

Wilson, Craig. "Rhetoric, Reality and Dissent: The Vietnam Policy of the British Labour Government, 1964–1970." *Social Science Journal* 23, no. 1 (1986): 17–31.

Wilson, Harold. *The Labour Government, 1964–1970: A Personal Record*. London: Weidenfeld & Nicolson, 1971.

Wyn Rees, G. *Anglo–American Approaches to Alliance Security, 1955–60*. Basingstoke, England: Macmillan, 1996.

Young, Hugo. *One of Us: Life of Margaret Thatcher*. London: Pan Books, 1990.

Young, John. "Britain and LBJ's War." *Cold War History* 2, no. 3 (April 2002): 63–92.

———. "Killing the MLF? The Wilson Government and Nuclear Sharing in Europe, 1964–66." *Diplomacy and Statecraft* 14, no. 2 (June 2003): 295–324.

———. "The Wilson Government and the Davies Peace Mission to North Vietnam, July 1965." *Review of International Affairs* 24, no. 4 (October 1998): 545–62.

———. *Winston Churchill's Last Campaign: Britain and the Cold War, 1951–1955*. Oxford: Oxford University Press, 1996.

Young, Ken. "A Most Special Relationship: The Origins of the Anglo–American Nuclear Strike Planning." *Journal of Cold War Studies* 9, no. 2 (Spring 2007): 5–31.

———. "No Blank Cheque: Anglo–American (Mis)understanding and the Use of the English Airbases." *Journal of Military History* 71, no. 4 (October 2007): 1133–68.

V. POST–COLD WAR RELATIONS

Aldrich, Richard J. "Transatlantic Intelligence and Security Cooperation." *International Affairs* 80, no. 4 (July 2004): 731–53.

Andrews, David M. *The Atlantic Alliance under Stress: U.S.-European Relations after Iraq*. Cambridge: Cambridge University Press, 2005.

Azubuike, Samuel. "The 'Poodle Theory' and the Anglo–American 'Special Relationship.'" *International Studies* 42, no. 2 (2005): 123–39.

———. "Still Buying Insurance: The Realism behind Tony Blair's Post–September 11 Evangelization." *Review of International Affairs* 3, no. 1 (October 2003): 64–80.

Beeson, Mark. "The Declining Theoretical and Practical Utility of 'Bandwagoning': American Hegemony in the Age of Terror." *British Journal of Politics and International Relations* 9, no. 4 (November 2007): 618–35.

Bluth, Christopher. "The British Road to War: Bush, Blair and the Decision to Invade Iraq." *International Affairs* 80, no. 5 (2004): 871–92.

Campbell, Alistair. *The Blair Years: Extracts from the Alistair Campbell Diaries*. London: Hutchinson, 2007.

Cook, Robin. *The Point of Departure*. London: Simon & Schuster, 2003.

Coughlin, Con. *American Ally: Tony Blair and the War on Terror*. London: Politico's, 2006.

Curtis, Mark. *The Great Deception: Anglo–American Power and World Order*. London: Pluto Press, 1998.

Danchev, Alex. "Accomplicity: Britain, Torture and Terror." *British Journal of Politics and International Relations* 8, no. 4 (November 2006): 587–601.

———. "Greeks and Romans: Anglo–American Relations after 9/11." *RUSI Journal* 148, no. 2 (April 2003): 16–19.

———. "Tony Blair's Vietnam: The Iraq War and the 'Special Relationship' in Historical Perspective." *Review of International Studies* 33, no. 2 (1997): 189–203.

de la Billière, Peter. *Storm Command: Personal Account of the Gulf War*. London: HarperCollins, 1995.

Dumbrell, John. "The US–UK 'Special Relationship' in a World Twice Transformed." *Cambridge Review of International Affairs* 17, no. 3 (October 2004): 437–50.

———. "Winston Churchill and American Foreign Relations: John F. Kennedy to George W. Bush." *Journal of Transatlantic Studies* 3, no. 1 (2005): 31–42.

———. "Working with Allies: The United States, the United Kingdom, and the War on Terror." *Politics & Policy* 34, no. 2 (2006): 452–72.

Dunne, Tim. "'When the Shooting Starts': Atlanticism in British Security Strategy." *International Affairs* 80, no. 5 (2004): 893–909.

Dyson, Stephen B. "Personality and Foreign Policy: Tony Blair's Iraq Decisions." *Foreign Policy Analysis* 2, no. 2 (2006): 289–306.

Finlan, Alistair. *The Royal Navy in the Falklands Conflict and the Gulf War*. London: Routledge, 2004.

Freedman, Lawrence, and Efraim Karsh. *The Gulf War 1990–1991: Diplomacy and War in the New World Order*. London: Faber & Faber, 1994.

Gordon, Philip. *Allies at War: America, Europe and the Crisis over Iraq*. New York: McGraw-Hill, 2004.

Harris, Robin. "America, The Hague, and Ante Gotovina: The Railroading of a Former U.S. Ally." *American Spectator 39, no. 2* (March 2006): 14–17.

Hoggett, Paul. "Iraq: Blair's Mission Impossible." *British Journal of Politics and International Relations* 7, no. 3 (2005): 418–28.

Hyde-Price, Adrian. *European Security in the Twenty-first Century: The Challenge of Multipolarity.* London: Routledge, 2006.

Jakub, Jay. "The Anglo–American 'Special Relationship' in the Post Cold-War World: Much More Than Meets the Eye." *Defense & Security Analysis* 11, no. 3 (December 1995): 318–21.

Kampfner, John. *Blair's Wars.* London: Free Press, 2003.

Kennedy-Pipe, Caroline, and Rhiannon Vickers. "'Blowback' for Britain? Blair, Bush, and the War in Iraq." *Review of International Studies* 33, no. 2 (2007): 205–22.

Kimball, Warren. "Dangerously Contagious? The Anglo–American Special Relationship." *British Journal of Politics and International Relations* 7, no. 3 (2005): 437–41.

Lynch, Timothy J. "The Gerry Adams Visa in Anglo–American Relations." *Irish Studies in International Affairs* 14 (November 2003): 33–44.

——. *Turf War: The Clinton Administration and Northern Ireland.* Aldershot: Ashgate, 2004.

Maclean, Craig, and Alan Patterson. "A Precautionary Approach to Foreign Policy? A Preliminary Analysis of Tony Blair's Speeches on Iraq." *British Journal of Politics and International Relations* 8, no. 3 (August 2006): 331–446.

Marsh, S. "Crude Diplomacy: Anglo–American Relations and Multinational Oil." *Journal of Contemporary British History* 21, no. 1 (2007): 25–54.

——. "September 11 and Anglo–American Relations: Reaffirming the 'Special Relationship.'" *Journal of Transatlantic Studies* 1, Special Edition (2003): 56–75.

McCausland, Jeffrey, and Douglas Stuart, eds. *US–UK Relations at the Start of the 21st Century.* Carlisle, Pa.: Strategic Studies Institute, 2006.

Mervin, David. *George Bush and the Guardian Presidency.* New York: St. Martin's Press, 1996.

Naughtie, James. *The Accidental American: Tony Blair and the Presidency.* New York: Public Affairs, 2004.

Niblett, Robin. "Choosing between America and Europe: A New Context for British Foreign Policy." *International Affairs* 83, no. 4 (July 2007): 627–41.

O'Malley, Eoin. "Setting Choices, Controlling Outcomes: The Operation of Prime Ministerial Influence and the UK's Decision to Invade Iraq." *British Journal of Politics and International Relations* 9, no. 1 (2007): 1–9.

Parmar, Inderjeet. "Catalysing Events, Think Tanks, and American Foreign Policy Shifts: A Comparative Analysis of the Impacts of Pearl Harbor 1941 and 11 September 2001." *Government and Opposition* 40, no. 1 (Winter 2005): 1–25.

———. "'I'm Proud of the British Empire': Why Tony Blair Backs George W. Bush." *Political Quarterly* 76, no. 2 (April 2005): 218–31.

Rachman, Gideon. "Is the Anglo–American Relationship Still Special?" *Washington Quarterly* 24, no. 2 (Spring 2001): 7–120.

Riddell, Peter. *Hug Them Close: Blair, Clinton, Bush and the "Special Relationship."* London: Politico's, 2004.

Seitz, Raymond. *Over Here.* London: Weidenfeld & Nicolson, 1998.

Seldon, Anthony. *Blair.* London: Free Press, 2004.

Shawcross, William. *Allies: The US, Britain, and Europe, and the War in Iraq.* New York: Public Affairs, 2004.

Simms, Brendan. *Unfinest Hour: Britain and the Destruction of Bosnia.* London: Allen Lane, 2001.

Thatcher, Margaret. *Statecraft: Strategies for a Changing World.* London: HarperCollins, 2002.

Treverton, Gregory. "Britain's Role in the 1990s: An American View." *International Affairs* 66, no. 4 (1990): 703–10.

Walt, Stephen. *Taming American Power: The Global Response to US Primacy.* New York: W. W. Norton, 2005.

Wither, James. "British Bulldog or Bush's Poodle? Anglo–American Relations and the Iraq War." *Parameters* 33, no. 4 (Winter 2003–2004): 67–82.

———. "An Endangered Partnership: The Anglo–American Defence Relationship in the Early Twenty-first Century." *European Security* 15, no. 1 (March 2006): 47–65.

Woodward, Bob. *Plan of Attack.* New York: Simon & Schuster, 2004.

About the Author

Sylvia Ellis is principal lecturer in history at the University of Northumbria at Newcastle after having also lectured at the University of Sunderland. She received a master's degree from the University of Rhode Island and a doctorate from the University of Newcastle upon Tyne. She has published widely on Anglo–American relations, with an emphasis on the post–World War II relationship between Great Britain and the United States, and especially their relations during the Vietnam War. This includes journal articles, essay contributions, and book chapters, as well as the book *Britain, America, and the Vietnam War* (2004). Dr. Ellis is a Fellow of the Royal Historical Society, a member of the British Association of American Studies, and serves on the executive committee of the Transatlantic Studies Association.